# Crossroads of European histories

## Multiple outlooks on five key moments in the history of Europe

French version:

*Carrefours d'histoires européennes – Perspectives multiples sur cinq moments de l'histoire de l'Europe*


ISBN: 978-92-871-6077-5

Cover design: Graphic Design Worshop, Council of Europe
Layout: Desktop Publishing Unit, Council of Europe


Council of Europe Publishing
F-67075 Strasbourg Cedex
http://book.coe.int


ISBN: 978-92-871-6031-7

© Council of Europe, December 2006
Printed in Belgium

# Editor's introduction
*Robert Stradling*

When we began, in 2002, to plan the five conferences which led to the papers repro-
duced in this book we had two overarching objectives. First, we wanted to take as
our starting point the collapse of communism in the USSR and in central and eastern
Europe and the events which followed, not least the emergence of 15 separate countries as a result of the break-up of the Soviet Union, the velvet divorce between the
Czechs and the Slovaks in 1993 and the violent conflicts that led to the fragmentation
of Yugoslavia. Whilst historians continue to debate whether or not the transition which
began in 1989 marked the end of an era, it would certainly seem to be the case that the
changes in central and eastern Europe in the 1990s did not simply arise out of the end
of the Cold War but reflected longer-term developments and aspirations, which could
be traced back over the previous two centuries.

This extended period has been characterised by repeated attempts with varying
degrees of success to convert ideas and ideologies into social and political actions and
structures. At the same time it has also been characterised by an overlapping series
of contests, often violent and bloody, between these ideas and ideologies: absolute
monarchy versus the sovereignty of the people; autocracy and dictatorship versus
constitutional government; multi-ethnic empires versus the demand for national self-
determination; balance of power versus collective security; communism versus capitalism; totalitarianism versus liberal democracy.

Perhaps the most obvious starting point for this enterprise was the French Revolution
but the bicentennial celebrations in 1989 had generated many publications in various
languages and, after some discussions, we decided to take the revolutions of 1848
as our starting point and 1989 as our end point. At first sight 1848 may seem a surprising choice. After all, in less than two years the old orders had been restored and
the Habsburg empire, which had seemed in terminal decline in the spring of 1848,
had regained power in central Europe and northern Italy, and elsewhere the old orders
had also been restored thanks to the conservatism of the peasantry, the internal divisions within the ranks of the revolutionary forces, the growing concern amongst the
middle classes about social disorder and unrest and the widespread fear of the reign
of terror that had followed the French Revolution. Nevertheless, the return of the old
orders did not mean that nothing had changed. From this point on people increasingly
formed and joined political parties and social movements, which in turn began to align
themselves with particular social classes, while more and more women of all social
classes became politicised and mass circulation newspapers emerged with their own
political agendas.

At the same time the "genie of nationalism", set loose by the French Revolution and
then subsequently articulated by Romanticism in the early 19th century, became a
popular cause in 1848, and was never returned to the bottle but, instead, gradually

evolved from the preserve of educated elites into an ideology that could mobilise the masses.

Having established our parameters we then began to identify other key moments in the intervening 140 years for the focus of the project and the associated conferences. There was no shortage of possible candidates and no shortage of advocates for each of the proposed critical moments and turning points either. In the end the planning group selected three other events in recent European history which, we felt, helped to explain the momentous developments which took place in the last decade and a half of the twentieth century. These were the Balkan wars of 1912-13, the peace conferences and re-structuring of Europe in 1919, and the re-structuring of Europe and the emergence of the Cold War after 1945.

The developments at the end of the two world wars virtually selected themselves. The 'Wilsonian' idea of national self-determination raised expectations across central and eastern Europe, but while new nation-states emerged other minorities remained disappointed and became disillusioned. Within many of the new states there were internal divisions which re-emerged in the 1930s and 40s and again after 1989. In others democracy proved a fragile plant and soon succumbed to authoritarian forces. Yet, at the same time, developments in 1919 also set the international political and national agenda for the next seventy years: the emergence of the United States and Japan as global powers; the growing mutual distrust between Russia and the Western powers; the irredentist aspirations of the defeated nations; the attraction of socialism for many in the West matched by the fear that many others had of the spread of Bolshevism; the recurring demands for independence by national and religious minorities; the idealistic desire for a means of ensuring collective security and a lasting peace clashing with the political realities and the national interests of the more powerful nations.

Although it could be argued that the Second World War was the culmination of a conflict between the Great Powers that had been ongoing in various forms since the mid-19th century, and that the internal divisions that had been apparent in some states such as Yugoslavia since their inception in 1919 deteriorated into civil wars; it could also be argued that in spite of the tensions brought about by the division of Europe into two camps a kind of balance of power emerged, imposed by the two superpowers, which for the next forty years or so kept the lid on the cauldron of minority issues and border disputes which had plagued central and eastern Europe for much of the first half of the 20th century.

It is within this context that we decided that the fifth of our critical moments over the last 150 years should be the Balkan wars of 1912-13. The Balkan crisis of 1908-14 had emerged largely as a result of growing nationalism in the region and the declining power of the Ottoman Empire. The tensions re-emerged at the outbreak of the Second World War and determined to a large extent whether national groupings supported the Allies or the Axis Powers. Then, after a period of apparent calm and stability during the Cold War the same national and religious issues re-surfaced within the federal Yugoslavia and between Serbia and Albania in the 1990s.

At this point it should be stressed that these five key years – 1848, 1913, 1919, 1945 and 1989 – were always intended to be emblematic of wider changes that had taken place. For example, we anticipated that historians writing about the Balkan wars would not restrict themselves to the years 1912 and 1913 but would probably want to trace back the origins at least to 1878 if not earlier. Similarly, we assumed that those who were writing about the events of 1989 in central and eastern Europe would want to go back to the Brezhnev era and the coming to power of Gorbachev and then make observations about the developments in the initial post-communist era in the 1990s.

Our second main objective in planning the five conferences and the production of this book was to encourage "multiperspectivity". The Council of Europe had been using the term in its literature on the teaching of history since around 1990. Broadly speaking this represented a commitment to move away from a grand narrative approach to European history towards one that focused on a multiplicity of overlapping narratives. To encourage this we invited historians to present papers which reflected different national perspectives on the same events and developments and to engage with each other and with the other participants in round-table discussions about the variety of perspectives – national and historiographical – that were presented. It has not been possible to incorporate those discussions into this publication but they have greatly influenced the structure and content of the CD-Rom which is the other main component of this Council of Europe project.

Finally, I would like to express my gratitude to the authors who have contributed to this book not only for their texts but also for taking part so wholeheartedly in the other proceedings at the conferences. The memory of a group of eminent historians from all over Europe taking part in a simulation of the Bosnian crisis of 1908 will stay with me for a very long time: illuminating, stimulating and a great deal of fun. The background notes, role cards and rules of engagement for the simulation can be found on the CD-Rom. I would also like to express my heartfelt thanks to the ministries of foreign affairs and education in France, Germany (and the Georg Eckert Institute in Braunschweig), Greece, Hungary and Ukraine for helping with the organisation of the five conferences. The opportunity to discuss the Yalta Conference in the Livadia Palace itself or to convene in Sèvres to discuss the peace treaties of 1919-21 was a very special experience, which all who took part greatly appreciated.

# Contents

## PART ONE – 1848 in European history

## PART TWO – 1912-13 in European history

# PART THREE – 1919 in European history

# PART FOUR – 1945 in European history

# PART FIVE – 1989 in European history

# The authors

Professor Pierre Barral, Department of History, University Paul-Valéry, Montpellier, France

Professor Jean-Jacques Becker, Professor Emeritus, University Paris X-Nanterre and President, Centre de Recherche de l'Historial de Péronne sur La Grande Guerre, France

Professor Wolfgang Benz, Technological University, Berlin, Germany

Professor Halil Berktay, Department of History, Faculty of Arts and Social Sciences, Sabanci University, Istanbul, Turkey

Professor Lavinia Betea, Political Sciences Department, Bucharest University, Romania

Dr Peter Bihari, Historian, Budapest, Hungary

Professor Włodzimierz Borodziej, Institute of History, Warsaw University, Poland

Dr Carol Capita, Faculty of History, Bucharest University, Romania

Academician Professor Alexander Chubaryan, Institute of World History, Russian Academy of Science, Moscow, Russian Federation

Dr Alin Ciupala, Faculty of History, Bucharest University, Romania

Dr Zsolt Enyedi, Political Science Department, Central European University, Budapest, Hungary

Professor Alexei Filitov, Institute of Universal History, Russian Academy of Sciences, Moscow, Russian Federation

Dr Helen Gardikas-Katsiadakis, Research Centre for the Study of Modern Greek History, Academy of Athens, Greece

Professor Manfred Görtemaker, Department of History, Potsdam University, Germany

Professor Jussi Hanhimäki, Department of International History and Politics, Graduate Institute of Intenational Studies, Geneva, Switzerland

Professor Ivan Ilchev, Department of History, Sofia University, Bulgaria

Dr Tvrtko Jakovina, Department of History, Zagreb University, Croatia

Professor Karl Kaser, Department of History, Graz University, Austria

Professor Ioannis Koliopoulos, Department of Modern History, Aristotelian University, Thessaloniki, Greece

Professor Wolfgang Krieger, Department of History, Philipps-University, Marburg, Germany

Professor Gerd Krumeich, Department of History, Heinrich-Heine University, Düsseldorf, Germany

Professor Mikhailo Kyrsenko, Department of History, National University, Kiev, Ukraine

Professor Dieter Langewiesche, Department of History, Tübingen University, Germany

Dr Martin McCauley, School of Slavonic and East European Studies, University of London, United Kingdom

Ms Maria Ochescu, Ministry of Education, Valcea, Romania

Dr Janos Rainer, Director of the Institute for the History of the 1956 Hungarian Revolution, Budapest, Hungary

Dr Rainer Riemenschneider, Historian, Georg Eckert Institute for International Textbook Research, Braunschweig, Germany

Professor Jan Rychlik, Faculty of Arts, Institute of Czech Republic, Charles University, Prague, Czech Republic

Professor Alan Sharp, School of History and International Affairs, University of Ulster, United Kingdom

Professor Wolfram Siemann, Department of History, University of Munich, Germany

Dr Robert Stradling, Project adviser and editor, University of Edinburgh, United Kingdom

Dr Ruth Tudor, Historian, Wales, United Kingdom

Professor Arutyun Ulunyan, Institute of World History, Russian Academy of Sciences, Russian Federation

Professor Dimitri Vezyroglou, University of Paris I, France

Professor Odd Arne Westad, Department of International History, London School of Economics, London, United Kingdom

# Foreword

On 31 October 2001 the Committee of Ministers of the Council of Europe adopted Recommendation Rec(2001)15 on history teaching in twenty-first-century Europe.

This was the outcome of lengthy Council of Europe work and project activity on history teaching going back to the early 1950s. The recommendation then was, and still is, the only instrument of its kind in Europe.

It deals with various questions such as syllabus content, learning approach, teacher training and use of new technologies, but above all it offers a clear statement of the objectives which history teaching should have in the twenty-first century.

It highlights two important considerations:

– history teaching occupies a vital place in the training of responsible and active citizens and in developing respect for all kinds of differences within a democratic society;

– history teaching should develop pupils' intellectual ability to analyse and interpret information critically and responsibly through dialogue, through the search for historical evidence and through open debate based on multiperspectivity, especially through discussing controversial and sensitive issues.

In launching the European Dimension in History Teaching programme in 2002, the Education Committee saw the project as providing teacher trainers, teachers and pupils with a set of resources on a number of historic events, together with methodological suggestions and examples of multiperspectivity. In particular it was hoped that this would enable teachers to introduce the general principles of Recommendation Rec(2001)15 into their classrooms.

Putting the general principles into practice involves adoption and development of multiperspectivity in the presentation of historical events and historical fact: any historic event is open to different approaches, conceptual convergences or divergences or particular interpretations according to the standpoint, objectives and historical or political context of the person explaining, describing or presenting it.

This is not just a matter of national differences or nuances in presenting and interpreting the facts: the differences also stem from different philosophies or conceptions of history, constant research developments, changes in perceptions over time, and contexts or standpoints specific to particular social groups.

The concept of multiperspectivity is one that has been the subject of much study and reflection in the course of previous work. The findings are outlined in "Multiperspectivity in history teaching", a handbook by Robert Stradling, the project adviser.

The final project outcome is a set of materials with three closely linked components: the complete papers of the conferences on five key moments in recent European history, a DVD of original documents relating to the five key moments, and a teaching manual.

The present book, *Crossroads of European histories: multiple outlooks on five key moments in the history of Europe*, is the first of these components. Obviously the papers given at the five conferences do not exhaust possible viewpoints – they are only a few examples, to which the teacher is of course free to add.

Nor do the papers reflect any official position of the countries the authors are from, or of the Council of Europe. The views, which are diverse, are the authors' alone.

The book thus pushes no particular position and is fully meaningful only when used together with the other two components (the DVD and the teaching manual) in course design or lesson preparation. Depending on the syllabus, the teaching objectives and the resources available, the teacher will also need to supplement it with additional material and research.

This toolkit is made available to history teachers as an aid to meeting the objectives laid down in Recommendation Rec(2001)15. It does not challenge member states' right to set their own history syllabuses.

Nevertheless there is ongoing debate about history teaching in most member states, and the plural approach and methodology adopted here should suggest further new avenues for exploration.

The kit will also enable history teaching to be what the recommendation advocates: a force for reconciliation, recognition, understanding and mutual trust between peoples, and for consensually building an integrated Europe based on a common historical and cultural heritage whose diversity is enriching, even in areas able to create tension and occasional trauma.

# PART ONE

# 1848 in European history

# PART ONE

# 1848 in European history

# Introduction to 1848

The year 1848 was a momentous one. In February the Communist Manifesto had been published. A cholera epidemic, caused by drinking contaminated water, swept across Europe killing many adults and children who had already been weakened by two years of bad harvests. It was also the year in which serfdom and other manifestations of feudalism were brought to an abrupt end across most of central and eastern Europe. But 1848 is best known as "the year of revolutions" with people manning the barricades in France, the German and Italian states, Austria, Hungary and most of central and eastern Europe.

Uprisings were not unexpected. Indeed, during the previous thirty years there had been waves of political agitation, popular unrest and rebellion in different parts of Europe. There were military coups and civil wars in Portugal, Naples and Spain. In 1821 the Greeks had risen up against their Ottoman overlords; they gained their independence in 1829. In the same year the Ottoman Empire was forced to concede self-government to Serbia and the Danubian principalities. The 1830 Revolution in France sparked off demonstrations in Brussels, which led to Belgium declaring its independence. Meanwhile there was popular unrest in Poland, which was suppressed by Russian forces. In October 1847 Metternich reviewing the situation throughout Europe, observed "I am an old doctor; I can distinguish a passing illness from a mortal ailment … we are in the throes of the latter". Just four months later he was not alone in thinking that the death knell was ringing for the old European order.

And yet just a year later the old conservative forces were back in power. The British historian G.M. Trevelyan later described 1848 as a possible turning point "when Europe failed to turn". Nevertheless, the 1848 Revolutions still left a legacy that had a longer-term impact on much of Europe. The restoration of the authority of the Habsburg monarchy did not totally suppress the nationalist aspirations of the different peoples that made up that multi- national, multi- lingual state. In the Italian and German states the idea of unification would not go away. Even the most traditional monarchies began to recognise the need for constitutional reforms.

The revolutions also changed the political culture of each country. They had politicised many people and encouraged them to organise themselves into political parties, trades unions, and occupational and professional associations that would act on behalf of their interests. More women became active in public life. There was an increasing association between particular political parties and different social classes, and a rapid growth in newspapers that supported particular political positions. In some countries too the internal political map was transformed for the next one hundred years or more with certain areas remaining either radical or conservative, much as they had in 1848.

*Crossroads of European histories*

In short, the revolutions of 1848 helped to set the political and social agenda for much of Europe for the rest of the nineteenth century and beyond.

# Chapter 1
# The European dimension of 1848: from democracy to the nation-state

*Dieter Langewiesche*

When the 150th anniversary of the 1848 Revolution was celebrated five years ago, the commemoration often turned into a major spectacle. It was in Germany that the anniversary was probably celebrated most – and marketed with a vengeance, too. Felt hats of a type worn by the revolutionary leaders were offered as ideal attire for celebrating the revolution and for revolution hikes, along with "revolutionaries' wine" and revolution beer, brewed according to the original 1848 recipe.

This great wave of celebrations 150 years after the event contrasted sharply with the poor image the revolution tended to have in the nineteenth century. It was seen as the failed bourgeois revolution – a problematic description. Although the revolution failed to achieve its aims anywhere in Europe, it did have a major impact. We would be justified in calling it a turning point in European history. I will look at this turning point from the two angles of democracy and nationalism.

In order to understand what happened at that time, we must first consider how dramatically the range of information available to people in Europe had expanded.

## The Europeanisation of information

Both the revolution and the opposing forces of the counter-revolution brought Europe together as a unit in 1848. During the revolution, the continent grew into an area of communication and action with an unprecedented concentration of information – both geographically and socially, and also across the political boundaries that had traditionally kept women out of male-dominated public affairs. With the revolution, there was a sudden improvement in access to information for all classes, and the will to take advantage of this also grew dramatically. Never before had Europe been covered by such a tight-knit information network that basically no longer excluded anyone.

The Europeanisation of information paved the way for the spread of revolution throughout the continent. The signal for this went out from the revolution in Paris in February; the result was the emergence of a European public conscience. People all over Europe looked to Paris, "Europe's constantly beating heart", as the German author Fanny Lewald once called the city. She had travelled to Paris as soon as the news of the February revolution broke to witness developments at first hand (Lewald,

1969, p. 7). It was there in Europe's revolutionary capital that the revolutionaries and their opponents played out their hopes and their fears. In February, the political revolution triumphed in Paris, while only four months later, in June 1848, the social revolution was defeated there. Yet both events – victory and defeat – were of significance to the whole of Europe.

Although Europe's gaze was fixed on Paris, all over the continent the revolutions had their own causes and goals. They did follow the same basic pattern, however. In all cases, there were two main goals: firstly, democratising the political and social order, and secondly, insofar as the various societies were not organised in nation-states – and this applied to most of Europe – there were calls for national self-determination. The forces that were active in these two central areas of reform supported one another to some extent. However, they also came into conflict whenever several nations laid claim to particular territories. Democracy and nationalism, the two great hopes of 1848, therefore created a Europe whose peoples became aware of one another, regardless of national boundaries. A European public emerged, binding Europe together in a common information area. At the same time, however, this revolutionary Europe strove to become a Europe of nations and nation-states. Democracy and nationalism interacted, yet the two goals also quickly came into conflict with each other.

## 1848: A series of constitutional revolutions

What did democratisation mean to the people of Europe in 1848?

Democratisation and the introduction of parliamentary government were key demands of the revolutionary movements everywhere. However, the question of how far these reforms should go triggered bitter disputes about the constitutional order of the future. These came to a head in the argument about the form of government that should be adopted: republic or parliamentary monarchy? This divided the revolutionary movements into two camps that opposed each other vigorously.

In the first half of the nineteenth century, the constitutional monarchy had established itself as the predominant form of government in Europe. Many reformers in 1848 went a step further: they called for parliaments on the continent to be strengthened at the expense of the relevant monarchies. The supporters of parliamentary monarchies of that kind, which existed only in Great Britain at the time, had to fight on two fronts: against the monarchs themselves, who did not want to give up any powers, and against republicans, for whom loss of power on that scale did not go far enough.

Following the French Revolution in 1789, the republican form of government became the subject of highly emotional and bitter debate all over Europe. In a manner difficult for us to comprehend today, the republic was not seen as just a form of government. On the contrary, expectations of good fortune clashed with fears of destruction and ruin. The French author Gustave Flaubert brought the aura that surrounded the word republic in 1848 to life in his novel *Education sentimentale* with the words

"The republic has been proclaimed. We will be happy now! ... Poland and Italy are to be freed ... No more kings ...! Freedom for the whole world! Freedom for the whole world!"

This enthusiasm of a Parisian revolutionary was set against the fears about the republic that left not only conservatives and liberals shuddering. Many democrats also believed that the republic contained the seeds of revolutionary terror of the kind seen in 1793. In Flaubert's brilliant phrase, "the blade of the guillotine glistened in every syllable of the word 'republic'" (Flaubert, 1869).

Only in France did people realise in 1848 that the republic would not necessarily lead to terror of the kind that occurred after 1789. Other states had to wait longer to experience the tamed "bourgeois republic". The time was not ripe for it in 1848. Opponents of the republic demonised it as the "red republic" or "freedom with robbery and murder" (*Der Gränzbote*, 29 November 1851, quoted in Langewiesche, 1993, p. 38). But its supporters saddled it with excessively high expectations, too. These included dreams of salvation, set against no less unrealistic visions of doom.

In 1848, democratisation of the system of government primarily involved broadening the possibilities for public participation. To that end, the power of the ruling dynasties had to be reduced and the influence of the old political elites curtailed. The attempt to achieve this by constitutional means was one of the key features of the 1848 Revolution. The constitution – not the guillotine or barricades – was the key tool for moving closer to the ideal of equal citizens. I would therefore call 1848 a constitutional revolution – a revolution that aimed to bring about a new form of liberalised, democratic government.

All countries that were affected by the revolution, or the wave of reforms it brought with it, either introduced constitutions or began liberalising existing constitutions. In 1848-49, constitutions were no longer merely conceded by the state authorities. The constitutions of the revolutionary years embodied the principle of the sovereignty of the people. They were drawn up by elected parliaments, which themselves became the focus of political affairs. Never before had the public shown such active interest in politics, never before had they had such close ties at European level, never before had they come together so strongly to formulate their goals and never before had so many newspapers been published in European countries as was the case in 1848. The press reached into all areas of public life and helped people to organise. Those who wanted to build organisations extending beyond regional boundaries depended on newspapers as means of communication. The varied range of newspapers and the dense network of associations – both of which simultaneously resulted from and contributed to the revolution – were closely linked with one another. Like the public, the electorate also changed fundamentally during the revolutionary years. It assumed a democratic form, taking in a broader range of voters than ever before.

However, the society that began to emerge remained a male society. And this was true throughout Europe, too. Only men were allowed to vote and stand for election, and only they could hold office in central and local government. At a lower level, however, the revolution changed the political relationship between the sexes fundamentally.

Women read newspapers in 1848 and also published newspapers themselves. They took part in political gatherings, listened to parliamentary debates and expressed their views on the political issues of the time – in letters, at political meetings and on the barricades. They were active there, too. Above all, however, they used what were then the key tools for shaping opinions and objectives: associations. The number of women's associations grew sharply, and the first such associations were founded in countries where there had been none before.

Although women therefore took up the increased opportunities for political partici-pation, they did not enjoy equal rights anywhere. Only very few men, even including those on the left, were prepared to recognise women as citizens with equal rights. There are many examples of how men disliked the way women moved out of their traditional roles during the revolution.

It was in 1848 that what I regard as one of the key aspects of women's emancipation in the nineteenth century really became clear for the first time. The more politics took place within institutions, the fewer opportunities women had to take part – both ini-tially and for a long time. That did not change until the twentieth century. Regardless of all political differences, the 1848 reformers were united by a shared objective: they demanded structural reforms, guaranteed by constitutional standards and the transfor-mation of state institutions. These were to provide a permanent home for the demo-cratic civil society of the future. However, state institutions were a male monopoly. That did not change when the electorate was extended massively in social terms in 1848. Politics in institutions remained closed to women.

Yet the revolution increased political freedoms for everybody and therefore drove on the politicisation of society. It was possible to found modern political parties in places where they had previously been banned. Political activists set up long-term organisa-tions, adopted programmes for which they tried to lobby public support, put forward candidates for elections and attempted to establish ties between the political associa-tions outside parliament and parliamentary groups. The associations became centres for political education. Although they were concentrated in urban areas, they also began to move into the country. The high proportion of the rural population involved in the final phase of the revolution reflected a political learning process that would not have been possible without the many political associations. Although government repression following the revolution did rein in this grassroots politicisation of society by political organisations, it did so only temporarily. The far-reaching politicisation and organisation of society in political associations was one of the lasting results of the 1848 Revolution.

Although this does not mean that all sections of society were affected to the same extent by the revolution, none remained completely unaffected. Women, the rural population and workers were all politicised by the events of 1848. The same was also true of Jews, the clergy, university lecturers, schoolteachers, students and school pupils. As a general rule for the degree of involvement in the revolution and political affairs during the revolution, it can be said that men took a greater part than women in the political gatherings, petitions, organisations and debates of the revolutionary period, town dwellers were more active than country dwellers, craftsmen more active than farmers and peasants, and the middle classes more active than aristocrats. Yet the revolution meant much greater politicisation for the whole of society. People who wanted to make a mark in political affairs or in government institutions had to become politically active. That was also a lasting result of the 1848 Revolution.

The traditional elites also found themselves having to play a public role if they wanted to have an impact in political terms, as they were no longer able to rely on well-established methods for holding on to power. New centres of power and new types of politics emerged. For the first time ever representative democracy seemed to be gaining hold in Europe. Liberals and democrats lobbied hard for it, but conservatives also took a more public stance, founded associations and newspapers, called meetings and organised petitions so as to avoid being squeezed out of the political arena. Those who wanted to fight the revolution had to use its means. That also included the use of force – and not only on the side of the counter-revolution. Although the revolution was ultimately put down everywhere with the aid of regular troops, before then the revolutionary governments themselves had also had no qualms about using the armed forces and citizens' militias whenever they felt that they and their policies were threatened by other parts of the revolutionary movement.

Let us now turn to the national revolution – the second main component of the revolution, alongside the constitutional revolution or revolution in the system of government.

## 1848: A series of national revolutions

For many people, the revolution began in 1848 with a wonderful dream. They expected a springtime of Europe's peoples. However, the dream of a peaceful Europe of equal nations faded within a few months in 1848. The idea of the nation did indeed become the strongest bond in Europe's revolutionary movements. While it united people who pursued different objectives, under the influence of this powerful ideal, the interests of the various nations also clashed and led them to enter into alliances that ran contrary to their democratic objectives. When the straitjacket of political reaction was shattered by the revolutionary movements in 1848, the hoped-for springtime of Europe's peoples failed to materialise. Wherever the various nations competed with one another for territory, the nation as a community of freedom became a fighting community.

The revolution was faced with a huge task. In order to carry out the revolutionary programmes of Europe's peoples, states had to be united while federations made up of various nationalities had to be divided. The problems differed from case to case but wars loomed everywhere. All the countries directly affected by the revolution waged national revolutionary wars of unification and secession in 1848. Only the revolutionaries' fatherland was an exception to this warlike pattern. France's existence as a nation–state was already established; no one challenged it. The French revolutionaries' programme did not therefore include any nationalist claims. Yet even the French republic took up arms and intervened in Italy against the Roman Republic in 1849.

In order to assess what happened when the democratisation of Europe was accompanied by the rise of nationalism and European nation-states, I would now like to take a brief look at the contexts in which the various national movements emerged.

Let us begin with the Habsburg monarchy. Almost all of the lines of conflict between nations that opened up in 1848 intersected in the multi-ethnic Habsburg Empire. As a multi-ethnic state, the Habsburg Empire opposed the reorganisation of Europe in new nation-states. It was therefore automatically a focal point of the conflicts between different nations in 1848. None of the many nations had a majority within the multi-ethnic monarchy and in many areas they lived cheek by jowl. Competing territorial claims were bound to arise. The Habsburg monarchy therefore became a laboratory for national experiments for which there could be no easy solutions.

A young student in Vienna, who was both a revolutionary activist and also a monarchist – to whom we owe many informative insights into the progress of the revolution and the problems of nationalism – and who was a German from Bukovina who saw himself as a citizen of Greater Austria, recognised the dilemma facing the revolution very clearly and described it very powerfully:

> "Is it not often the case … [he wrote to his father in Chernovtsy] that one man's freedom can mean lack of freedom for another man; for instance, the movement in Italy means freedom for the Italians, but also a threat to our German Tyrol. Such problems of politics and philosophy really can bring you to despair. The harsh reality of politics can totally deform what philosophy has well-meaningly constructed." (Langewiesche, 1993, p. 104ff)

The Viennese student from the multi-ethnic Habsburg province of Galicia saw the conflicts between the various nationalities with the eyes of a Habsburger who hoped for a democratised monarchy and, although he recognised the revolutionary awakening of the other nationalities, did not wish the unity of the Habsburg Empire to be undermined. And naturally he had no doubts at all about wanting it to remain under German leadership.

Even at the beginning of the revolution, anyone who observed the non-German peoples in Vienna closely could have guessed that the dream of a "springtime of peoples" might end in a nightmare of nationalities. That became evident earlier and more clearly in the Habsburg capital than anywhere else. At the end of March 1848, delegations of all the Slav peoples arrived to make their wishes known to the public and the authorities. Slovaks, Serbs, Croats, Czechs and Poles came to Vienna and fraternised in celebrations of unity. Yet they were only united against the Hungarian nation's claim to power and against the German national revolutionary movement's calls for a nation-states within the boundaries of the German Confederation *(Deutscher Bund)*, in other words, including Bohemia, Moravia and Austrian Silesia. This joint opposition was the only unifying factor of "Austro-Slavism", which aimed to bring about areas of national autonomy in between the all-powerful German and Hungarian nations, while also having to reconcile the competing territorial claims of the Slav peoples.

The Prague Slav Congress in June 1848, at which the key issues concerning the nationalities in the Habsburg monarchy were debated, is not usually treated kindly in history books. However, a fair observer would have to say that peaceful solutions were proposed, whereas later generations turned to military options and attempted to "nationalise" ethnically mixed areas by force, either by oppressing national minorities or by forcing them to leave – a process for which our era has come up with the euphemism "ethnic cleansing".

The resolutions adopted by the Slav Congress aimed at a federal Habsburg monarchy in which all nationalities would enjoy the same rights. The *Manifesto to the Nations of Europe* said that the nationalities issue was crucial to Austria and that equality of rights for all nationalities must be the fundamental principle of any sound constitution for Austria, failing which the inevitable result would be ethnic conflict within the monarchy, leading to devastation if not total destruction of the state (*Manifesto*, quoted after Josef Kolejka).

The Prague Slav Congress was like a condensed version of all the ethnic problems that confronted Europe in 1848. It called for a federal Habsburg monarchy. Yet what that would actually involve and what "equality of all nationalities" should mean remained highly controversial. Many Czechs aimed primarily for the autonomy of the three Bohemian crown lands (Bohemia, Moravia and Austrian Silesia) within the Habsburg monarchy, while decisively rejecting integration in a German nation-states. The Croatian national revolutionaries aimed for a similar autonomous status for their "Triune Kingdom" (Croatia, Slavonia and Dalmatia) within the overall Habsburg monarchy, while calling for the historic link with the Hungarian crown to be weakened – and, following the outbreak of the Hungarian war of independence, during which the Croats sided with the Austrian Emperor, openly challenging it.

Like the Habsburg Empire of which it was part, the Kingdom of Hungary was a multi-ethnic state, whose various peoples no longer wished to accept Magyar domination. It was not only the Croats who called for more rights or total separation from Hungary, for the Serbs in southern Hungary also called for their own political institutions, especially a Serbian assembly. A national movement also developed among the Slovaks, again calling for more rights for their own people. The Hungarian national revolutionaries were not prepared to accept these demands. Only towards the end of the revolution, when the defeat of all the revolutionary movements was already on the cards, did they begin to change their position.

In view of the ethnic rivalries, the calls to preserve the Habsburg monarchy as a state unit were the only real chance of preventing an ethnic conflict that would set all the various peoples against one another. However, the monarchy as a whole would have had to be federalised. Both the Prague Slav Congress and the draft constitution prepared by the Austrian Reichstag recognised this. But both were thwarted by the counter-revolution and the lack of agreement among the various peoples. The old elites around the Habsburg court were just as opposed to a genuinely federal solution as were the national movements. For a federation would by no means only have led to greater autonomy for the respective majority peoples. It would also have involved their losing power to the other peoples. Perhaps it might have been possible to find suitable federal arrangements. But a learning process of that kind, which at least some sections of the national movements seemed willing to accept and which the Austrian Reichstag also tried to promote in its Kremsier constitution, was prevented by the victory of the counter-revolution.

However, it would be much too simplistic only to blame the counter-revolution for the competition between European nations that went hand in hand with the move towards greater democracy in 1848. The extent to which democrats and liberals were also involved in the conflict can be seen if we look at the Polish revolution. As a nation divided into three, the Poles hoped to take a first step towards national rebirth in the Prussian province of Poznan (Posen) in 1848. Although most people in Poznan were Poles, Germans were in the majority in the western districts. It was therefore inevitable that a "national reorganisation", which the new Prussian government and also the Prussian parliament initially supported in 1848, would cause great difficulties. European freedom movements had failed to take this into account when they emphatically took up the cause of the restoration of Poland in the decades leading up to the revolution. Following the failure of the Polish rising in 1831, many Polish associations were set up in the German Confederation and offered Polish exiles both moral and also financial support. However, this solidarity between peoples soon turned into national rivalry when matters came to a head in 1848. The representatives of the old Prussian regime and the German nation ultimately joined forces against the restoration of a Polish state and the Prussian military pushed this policy through. The result was total defeat of the Polish movement, from which German-Polish relations in Poznan (Posen) did not recover. Nationalism gained an ever-stronger hold there, too.

Italy also saw major conflicts and war in 1848 and 1849. At the time, an Italian nation-states could only have been achieved against the will of the Habsburg monarchy and the German national revolution, as Lombardy and Venetia belonged to the Habsburgs, and parts of Upper Italy belonged to the German Confederation. National conflicts were therefore inevitable. They led to a war between the Habsburg monarchy and the Italian national movement, which resulted in the Italian revolution taking shape around the Italian armies. A central state authority in which the national movement could have been represented did not emerge. This meant that the conditions under which the Italian national movement operated were very different from the developments in neighbouring countries. The focus of the movement for Italian unity was not a national parliament but the battlefields of the struggle against Austrian forces.

I will not go into any further details here, nor look in depth at the bitter national debates and conflicts between the German and Danish revolutionary movements. Was the long process leading from a Nordic kingdom to a Danish nation-states to be completed in 1848? Could the predominantly German duchies of Schleswig and Holstein be included in the Danish state? An angry dispute over the matter broke out in the Danish and German national revolutionary movements, ultimately leading to a war in which the Prussian king attempted to impose the German claims over the Danish ones by military force. Only because Europe's Great Powers intervened was the bloody decision delayed until the German-Danish war of 1864.

By comparison, the dispute between the German national movement and the Netherlands about the status of the Duchy of Limburg, which was part of the German Confederation, was settled without much harm being done. Even there, however, the explosiveness of the situation triggered by the nation-state policies of the nineteenth century whenever competing territorial claims arose was obvious. Even in Norway, increasing calls were made in 1848 for independence from Sweden, with which the country shared a king. There and only there did the peaceful division of a confederation during the century of national movements and nation-statess succeed: in 1905, Sweden and Norway went their separate ways without a war of secession being waged. That had never been achieved anywhere before and, thereafter, the Scandinavian states were to remain a shining example that nobody else followed.

Democrats may be somewhat depressed by this assessment of the 1848 Revolutions in Europe. For wherever nations laid competing claims to particular territories, the moves towards greater democracy and the hoped-for "springtime of Europe's peoples" ended on the battlefield of national rivalries. Nevertheless, there were also some more hopeful developments.

The Hungarian national movement attempted to make concessions to the demands of the other nationalities in 1849. It is impossible to tell whether this could have proved successful, as the victory of the counter-revolution put an end to the moves. The efforts by the Austrian Reichstag to reorganise the Habsburg monarchy on a federal basis in order to satisfy the various nationalities' calls for self-determination without undermining the unity of the state were also swept aside by the victorious counter-revolution.

The German national movement showed moderation, too. It is true that imperialist dreams on a terrifying scale were articulated in the Frankfurt National Assembly, with calls being made in some quarters for German hegemony from the North Sea and the Baltic to the Adriatic and the Black Sea. But the National Assembly was moderate in its policies. It was faced with a huge task for which no precedents existed: state integration and secession had to be combined in a single act, while government and society had to be democratised at the same time. The German national revolutionary movement ultimately settled for a solution excluding Austria, which would have been strategically acceptable to Germany's neighbours. The proposals failed because the most powerful German princes, who would have lost power, rejected them.

## Conclusion

It can be said that the revolutionary movements in 1848 brought Europe together in a vast area of communication. This Europeanisation would not have been possible without the nationalisation of politics. Europe grew closer together during the revolutionary period, but this had both positive and negative consequences for its peoples. It was not only the policy of democratic reforms that was Europeanised in 1848, but also the policy of counter-revolutionary reaction, accompanied by the national reconstruction of large parts of the continent. The idea of the nation as a guarantee or promise of democracy and progress was still at the heart of the national revolution in 1848, but its drawbacks – exclusion, stereotypical depiction of enemies and readiness for war – also began to become more obvious. Although the revolution did not create these two faces of nationalism, it probably made them more prominent and greatly increased their appeal in geographical and social terms. That was also one of the legacies of the 1848 Revolution.

## Bibliography

Flaubert, Gustave, *Education sentimentale*, Paris, 1869.

Kolejka, Josef, "Der Slawenkongress in Prag im Juni 1848. Die slawische Variante einer österreichischen Föderation" in Rudolf Jaworski and Robert Luft (eds.), *1848/49 – Revolutionen in Ostmitteleuropa*, Oldenbourg, Munich, 1996.

Langewiesche, Dieter, *Republik und Republikaner*, Von der historischen Entwertung eines politischen Begriffes, Stuttgart, 1993.

Lewald, Fanny, *Erinnerungen aus dem Jahr 1848*, Selected extracts published by Dietrich Schäfer, Frankfurt, 1969.

# Chapter 2
# The French view of Europe in 1848

*Pierre Barral*

Following the upheavals of the revolution and the armed expansion under the Empire, France was seen by its neighbours as Europe's *enfant terrible*. After 1815, the Restoration and July Monarchies brought stability at home and a more subdued foreign policy. The sudden uprising of 1848 triggered a desire throughout France to create a free society. This frenzied, precarious and short-lived adventure provokes a feeling of well-meaning if somewhat patronising sympathy in today's historians.

## The Second Republic

Over the course of a remarkably turbulent year, three great turning points stand out, times when opposing currents of opinion clashed, society's most deep-rooted forces were revealed and the nation's political course was set. February was majestic, June tragic and December ambiguous.

In February 1848, a rebellion in Paris brought down the July Monarchy, which was itself the product of a Paris rebellion 18 years earlier. This regime, which had set out to reconcile order with freedom had in fact become ossified in a maintenance of the status quo, ironically known as the *juste milieu*. For several months, the government led by the historian François Guizot had been under pressure from a campaign of banquets at which the opposition vainly demanded the expansion of the very restricted, tax-based suffrage ("electoral reform") and that members of the upper échelons of the civil service be excluded from membership of parliament ("parliamentary reform").

The enormous banquet planned in Paris for 22 February was banned, but the tide of unco-ordinated unrest could not be stemmed. The National Guard, a citizen militia which up to then had been faithful to the government, even started shouting *Vive la Réforme!* Panicking soldiers fired into the crowd, and the demonstration turned into a riot. Guizot's resignation failed to restore order, and the efforts of his rivals Molé and Thiers were equally unsuccessful. Barricades were set up all over Paris, and Marshal Bugeaud, named Commander of Troops, was no longer able to control the situation. The shocked King Louis-Philippe abdicated on the morning of 24 February, and plans to install a regency for his grandson were quickly abandoned. A provisional government was formed which, as in 1830, the rest of France accepted with docile obedience.

Thus, began the spring of "poetic illusions", a time when the French, with their customary liking for extremes, gave free rein to idealistic optimism and romantic sentiment. France was declared a republic, as it had been in 1792, but, to avoid the bloodletting of the Terror, abolished capital punishment for political dissidence. Universal suffrage, which only a handful of Utopians had dared dream of, was declared in a wave of fervour. Although extended only to men, as seemed natural at the time, the number of voters swelled at once from 250 000 (those paying the most in taxes) to nine million. This was a huge leap. In Britain the same reform took much longer, being carried out in four stages between 1832 and 1918.

In a famous passage, Alexis de Tocqueville describes the procession of citizens to the polling stations:

"taking care to follow alphabetical order, I wanted to join the line at the proper place for my name, as I knew that, in democracy and in all democratic countries, one must be chosen to lead and not simply assume leadership."

The Constituent Assembly was set up and an Executive Committee took over from the provisional government. In this new climate of freedom, the number of newspapers multiplied and impassioned debates flourished in Paris clubs. And slavery was abolished in the colonies (fifteen years after its prohibition by Britain).

The newly established Republic also espoused a social dimension, and Albert (a mechanic) was given a symbolic seat in the otherwise very bourgeois provisional government. Albert rejected the red flag as a sign of disorder but "pledged to guarantee the existence of the worker by guaranteeing work". It was, however, no easy task to implement this "organisation of work", to use a popular slogan of the time. The groups who talked of "socialism" had not yet formed a genuine party and their programme was tantamount to the construction of a utopia. Instead of a "Ministry of Progress" as some impatient radicals had demanded, a committee of workers' delegates moved into the Palais du Luxembourg, where the peers of France had previously sat, to study possible solutions. This was not enough to pacify the protestors. Isolated incidents occurred in rural and forest areas, whilst, in Paris, the demonstrations escalated amidst growing agitation: a non-violent demonstration on 17 March, a demonstration controlled by the National Guard on 16 April, and a temporary invasion of the Assembly on 15 May.

In June, this smouldering fire flared up in Paris when, under pressure from parliament, the Executive Committee took issue with the disorderly development of the National Workshops. For two years, France had been suffering an economic crisis that, as my mentor Ernest Labrousse would say, combined an old-fashioned farming crisis with a new-style industrial crisis. Unemployment was widespread, and the unemployed had no insurance. In an attempt to alleviate the problem, several public works schemes were started, but they attracted too many workers and their management was poor. Louis Girard rightly called them a "mixture of unemployment fund and charitable workshop". In an attempt to alleviate the situation, a ministerial decree dated 21 June called on the youngest of these workers to enlist in the army or leave Paris. This decision was seen as a provocation by the workers, unemployed or not, who rose in mass revolt. Lacking formal leadership and any plan of action, the rioters turned violent in their desperation. A well-meaning negotiator was told at the barricades: "Ah, Mr Arago, you have never gone hungry".

The Executive Committee assigned the task of restoring order to the War Minister, General Cavaignac. A leftist soldier (a more common breed in France than in Central Europe), whose father had been a member of the 1793 Convention and whose recently deceased brother had been an ardent republican, Cavaignac was also a career army officer with a distinguished record in the conquest of Algeria. He was given control of a reinforced garrison of troops, the National Guard protecting the bourgeois areas of Paris and some volunteers drawn from the provinces. In a four-day battle (23-26 June), the working-class quarters of eastern Paris were re-conquered by cannon. On each side between 40 000 and 50 000 combatants are estimated to have taken part, with the loss of 1 600 lives in the government camp and more on the protestors' side (whereas in February there were no more than a few dozen casualties).

This was the year's second great turning point, when the nation's moral unity was shattered in blood. Property owners, whether republicans or monarchists, saw, in the words of de Tocqueville, a liberal aristocrat, "a class struggle, a servile war", which "had not the aim of changing the form of the government, but of remodelling the social order". The workers, whether socialists or not, felt they had been brutally repressed and abandoned to their unhappy fate. An emotional George Sand, the famous woman writer, was to say, "I no longer believe in a republic that starts by killing its own proletariat".

The constitution, which had been debated over the summer, put into practice the principles of the moderate republican majority in the Constituent Assembly. The only republics then in existence were federal states, the Swiss Federation and the United States of America. In "one and indivisible" France, tentative proposals for decentralisation were swiftly rejected (Riemenschneider, 1985). A strict separation was laid down between the legislative power, exercised by a single chamber (the Assembly), and the executive power, conferred on the President of the Republic. The latter was to be elected by universal suffrage, after a famous dispute in which the ardent Lamartine overcame the moderate Grévy. The natural choice for this role seemed to be General Cavaignac, who had, since June, presided over a *de facto* dictatorship with a calm respect for legality.

The Right, which in spring had been somewhat subdued, had, since then, progressively recovered its poise. In France, it was currently unable to take power by force (as had happened in Austria and Prussia) as the army remained loyal to the Republic, as much by discipline as conviction. The Right was furthermore split between the Legitimists, faithful to the elder branch of the Bourbon dynasty, and the Orleanists, who had supported the July Monarchy. Although this schism ruled out the restoration of the monarchy, the Right's leaders played the parliamentary game and became the "Party of Order" or the "Union of the rue de Poitiers" with a conservative programme. But the question of whom to put forward as presidential candidate remained unresolved, as the few names that had been proposed were unacceptable to one or other of the diverse factions.

It was at this time, however, that a new figure came to prominence, Prince Louis Napoleon. Twice, this nephew of the great emperor had attempted to provoke a coup d'état, failing spectacularly on both occasions. This time, he had gathered around himself a Bonapartist core of a handful of retired army officers and a few opportunists. Despite adopting vaguely socialistic rhetoric, he made overtures to representatives of the Party of Order. Many of the latter, thinking they would be able to manipulate him, decided to support his candidature. On 10 December 1848 came the third and final turning point of the year: an ignominious defeat for Cavaignac with 1 500 000 votes, the radical republican Ledru-Rollin with 370 000, and barely 17 000 for the now exhausted Lamartine – but, for the prince, a landslide victory with 5 500 000 votes. It was an extraordinary triumph in the long history of French elections (the only equivalent is our recent second round in 2002!). The agreement sealed between the Party of Order leaders had been vindicated by the people's verdict, assuredly helped in no small part by the transfiguration of the Napoleonic legend.

## The fraternity of peoples

During these times of political upheaval at home, the French of 1848 were also keenly aware of the parallel stirrings of nationalist movements abroad, movements which, in Poland and Italy, had in fact started earlier than in France. In the monarchist camp, former minister Rémusat wrote, "we saw this sudden disturbance that affected all of Europe only as a guarantee of continuing peace". The republicans, however, wished to spread their exhilarating sense of freedom far beyond the confines of France's borders. They wanted to see other nations free themselves from the shackles of their reactionary governments.

The poet Victor Hugo, already famous at this time, waxed vibrantly lyrical when a tree of liberty was planted in front of his home in Paris on the Place des Vosges, "Let us all be men of good faith, let us spare neither our efforts nor our sweat. Let us spread sympathy, charity and fraternity to our neighbours and then to the whole world".

In the popular song *Le Chant des soldats*, composed by Pierre Dupont, the mood was more revolutionary and bellicose:

| | |
|---|---|
| *Les Républiques nos voisines* | Our neighbouring republics |
| *De la France invoquent le nom* | Invoke France's name |
| *Que les Alpes soient des collines* | Let the Alps become mere hills |
| *Pour les chevaux et les canons.* | For horses and cannons. |
| *Aux armes, courons aux frontières!* | To arms, let us run to the borders! |
| *Qu'on mette au bout de nos fusils* | Let us aim our guns |
| *Les oppresseurs de tous pays* | At the oppressors of all nations |
| *Les poitrines des Radetskys!* | And the chests of all Radetskys! |
| *Les peuples sont pour nous des frères* | All peoples are our brothers |
| *Et les tyrans des ennemis.* | And tyrants our enemies. |

As Maurice Agulhon has pointed out, these magnanimous outpourings did not pre-clude xenophobic acts against foreign workers, Belgians in Douai and Italians in

Marseilles. There were significant foreign populations in the larger towns and cities, which have always been centres of immigration in France.

In spring 1848, some immigrants, swept along by a political enthusiasm heightened by the economic crisis, sallied forth to their native countries. On 25 March, at the appropriately named hamlet of Risquons-tout, the local gendarmes arrested without much difficulty some groups of Belgians crossing the border into their home country. On 30 March, natives of Savoy backed by activists from Lyons briefly occupied the town of Chambéry, which then still belonged to the Kingdom of Piedmont. In April, a German division of Paris-based workers and Polish sympathisers entered the Grand Duchy of Baden, itself already in some turmoil, from Strasbourg. This rather disorganised and belated campaign, under the less than convincing leadership of the poet Georg Herwegh, was, however, doomed to failure. Indeed, the spark of revolution coming from France was never to ignite outside its borders. Even if Central European revolutionaries were encouraged by the example set in Paris, their wide-ranging actions were completely independent.

The French of 1848 reserved their strongest sympathies for the cause of "martyred Poland". The basis for this was threefold: memory of an ancestral alliance, indignation at seeing a nation divided up among three avid empires, and the participation of Polish volunteers in the Revolution and the Empire. More recently, French public opinion had supported the Warsaw uprising of November 1830. After this rebellion had been put down, thousands of patriotic Polish army officers had fled to France. Although these turbulent soldiers were kept away from the capital as a precautionary measure, Parisian high society had fêted several well-known Polish figures, Prince Czartoryski, the musician Chopin and the poet Mickiewicz. In April 1848, Poland was again in the news when Berlin refused to grant autonomy to the Grand Duchy of Poznan. A Parisian political club started a petition supporting this "heroic yet unfortunate nation" which was carried by a large crowd to the Assembly on 15 May. Although more a pretext than a demand for action, the choice of subject was nonetheless significant. As Pierre de la Gorce observed, "The ringing name of 'Poland' was enough to bring out onto the streets the inoffensive and rather foolish crowds which, in all riots, hide troublemakers and make any policing impossible".

Pro-unification liberal movements in the Italian states were followed with enthusiasm in France, as was the Czech emancipation campaign in Bohemia and, less unanimously, the struggle for Hungarian independence. Once more, it was Pierre Dupont who called for his countrymen to show solidarity against the rulers of the Old Order:

| | |
|---|---|
| *De Pesth à Rome les étapes* | From Pest to Rome on each stretch of road |
| *Seraient des bûchers de martyrs.* | Will be a martyr's stake |
| *Les cosaques, hideux satrapes,* | Cossacks, hideous satraps |
| *Assouviraient leurs désirs.[...]* | Sate their desires […] |
| *Soldats, arrêtons cette horde![...]* | Soldiers, arrest that horde! […] |
| *Canons, de vos gueules géantes* | Cannons, with your great mouths |
| *Refoulez la marche du Czar!* | Turn back the marching army of the tsar! |

Support for the German Revolution in principle was, however, tempered by feelings of perplexed apprehension. The French had not forgotten the heated debates of the international crisis of 1840 or the nationalistic songs written at the time on the Rhine as a German river – or was it French? As Rainer Riemenschneider has shown, declarations from the *Paulskirche* regarding Alsace's Germanic culture were a cause for concern. On 18 October, Charles Dupin, a prominent politician, claimed, "The men of Alsace would take up arms against the Diet of Frankfurt, if it claimed that, by their dialect, they should be Germans". On a more general level, Jules Dufaure, who would go on to have a successful career as a minister, called on the members of the Constituent Assembly to be fully aware that "a large country on our doorstep is trying to become a State of 50 million people".

Faced with these popular risings abroad, the new Paris government refused to over-react. Lamartine, the only man of European stature in the provisional government, was Minister for Foreign Affairs. In a memorandum to ambassadors dated 4 March, he wrote: "If Providence has decreed that the hour of reconstruction of some oppressed nations in Europe and beyond has arrived", if in the Italian States "the right of the people to come together to create a unified Italy was opposed by force, France would feel justified in itself taking up arms to defend these legitimate movements for national growth". This hyperbole was checked in the following sentences to counter any suspicion that he was trying to spread a revolutionary gospel. France would "refrain from spreading any blind or incendiary propaganda among its neighbours. She knows that the only lasting freedoms are those born naturally on their own soil". Rémusat, a man from the previous regime, observed mischievously that Lamartine "cloaked his careful, conciliatory policies in empty humanitarian rhetoric. His poetic style contrasted with Guizot's prose".

Behind this eloquent façade, little concrete action was taken. To the disappointment of radicals, the only support Lamartine gave to the Poles of Poznan was a restrained word with Berlin. To Frankfurt, he sent only an informal observer. His acolyte Jules Bastide, a rather colourless and overly serious Jacobin journalist, deplored "the formidable power" of the nascent Reich and the "palpable mood of expansion developing in Germany". As an opponent of the union of the Kingdom of Lombardy and Venice with Piedmont, he preferred "a confederation of sovereign states" in the Italian peninsula to "the formation of an Italian monarchy". Moreover, Prince Louis Napoleon had not forgotten his militant past in Modena as a member of the Carbonari, but, at the beginning of his mandate, was not yet strong enough to force his opinions on his conservative ministers.

Amongst them was the prudent de Tocqueville, briefly Minister for Foreign Affairs in summer 1849, who set the double maxim of "breaking unreservedly with revolutionary currents abroad" whilst "never resuscitating the passions of the old regimes". He remained unmoved by the failure of the attempts to bring democracy and unity to Germany and by the crushing of the supporters of Hungarian independence. In Italy, he tried in good faith to mediate peacefully in the conflict between the two opposing camps. To this end, an expeditionary force was sent to Rome, where republicans led by Mazzini had overthrown the temporal power of the Pope. However, under pressure from the Catholics and against the wishes of de Tocqueville, the expeditionary force eventually restored the Pope's power by force of arms, and the protests of an outraged Left in France were to no avail.

## The French vision of Europe

France came once again to the fore in the context of the international order that marked this era. It was a time of respite in its overseas expansion, falling between the imperialist surges of 1760 and 1880. The great powers kept their attention focused on Europe, and diplomatic relations functioned in the framework of a system commonly known as "the Concert of Europe". Following the fall of Napoleon, the rulers of Russia, Austria and Prussia had signed "the Holy Alliance", an essentially ideological proclamation, and most importantly, had accepted the solidarity pact put to them by Britain on 20 November 1815. Having originally been kept under surveillance, France was subsequently admitted into this inner circle. For three decades, rivalries fermented and disagreements emerged, notably on the subject of marriage alliances in the Spanish royal family. The will to keep the status quo intact nonetheless prevailed. The mainstay of this conservative outlook was the elderly Austrian chancellor Metternich, who remained in office until the Viennese uprising of 15 March 1848.

On taking office, Lamartine sought to rebuild the nation's self-esteem whilst reassuring foreign governments. In his instructions to ambassadors, he subtly tried to reconcile these opposites. Whereas, "in the eyes of the French Republic, the 1815 treaties no longer exist in law [...] the borders stipulated in these treaties are a fact it accepts as a starting point for its relations with other countries". Therefore, for France, "the 1815 treaties exist only as facts to be modified by common accord". Setting for itself "the goal of reaching these modifications peacefully and lawfully", France, insisted Lamartine, desired "to enter into the family of established governments as a lawful power and not as a destabilising influence on the European order". These were all credible declarations, because, as Rémusat noted, they emanated from a minister "largely indifferent to military glories, hostile to the Empire and whose methods and tone could not offend international diplomacy". It was true that "this suited the mood of an Assembly which was in no way warlike and where all members, even those sitting high on the Mountain [the Left], took little interest in foreign policy". This was because essentially "the spirit of belligerent propaganda that had so stirred the people of 1830 had very much cooled down in the people of 1848".

This approach remained unchanged in the period of Cavaignac's rule. Rémusat again: "externally, where neither necessity nor duty nor public opinion asked anything of him, he did nothing, or so little that it could be said he had no policy at all". And, at the Quai d'Orsay, de Tocqueville set himself the objective "not to aspire to a position which we may have held in other eras and which the current state of the world no longer allows us, but to occupy proudly the place that still remains for us".

Public opinion was much less circumspect. In its view, the hoped-for emancipation of Europe's nations would bring an end to war, which was rather simplistically held to be the fault of monarchs' greed alone. Democracy, it was claimed, would lead to international relations being carried out entirely differently. On 21 August 1849, Victor Hugo opened a Peace Congress with persuasive oratory:

> "Gentlemen, is this sacred notion of world peace, all nations bound by a common thread with the Gospel as supreme authority, mediation instead of war, is this sacred notion practical, is this hallowed idea possible? I join you in answering and I answer without hesitating, yes! And, whether we are French, English, Belgian, German, Russian, Slav, European or American, what do we have to do to reach this great day as soon as possible? To love one another."

Hugo went on to enthuse over technical advances made: "See how the causes of war disappear along with the causes of suffering! How once distant peoples come together! How distances are getting shorter. And coming together leads to fraternity!" The tragedies of the twentieth century would show this idealistic optimism to be nothing more than a naive illusion: the conflicts unleashed by popular nationalism would shed far more blood than the petty wars of *Ancien Régime* kings.

Carried along by his enthusiasm, Hugo presented a prescient vision of Europe's destiny. On 17 July 1851, in the Legislative Assembly, he declared prophetically,

> "The French people have chiselled out of indestructible granite and placed in the very heart of this monarchical continent the foundation stone of an immense structure to come, which one day will be known as the United States of Europe!"

This concept, owing much to the American model, belonged more to the realm of utopian dreams than that of political reality. According to the minutes of the debate, it was greeted with "murmurings" in the Chamber and "a long burst of laughter on the right".

Yet, at this time, it was still just an empty slogan. While in exile, he explained at a banquet in February 1855 the philosophy that inspired him:

> "The Continent would be a single people, the nationalities would live their own lives as part of a wider community: Italy would belong to Italy, Poland to Poland, Hungary to Hungary [note that the examples chosen reveal much about his sympathies], France would belong to Europe and Europe would belong to humanity."

From then on, "Europe being but a single nation, Germany would be to France and France to Italy as Normandy now is to Picardy and Picardy to Lorraine". The optimistic conclusion he drew was that there would be "no more wars and so no more armies" – it was still unimaginable that danger might yet come from outside Europe.

This broad-brush picture of a future Europe included a bold prediction, which we can now see being realised. A continent of "free rivers, straits and oceans". From an economic standpoint "free trade; no more borders, customs or octrois". Even "a continental currency, in the form of both coins and notes, backed by Europe in its entirety and driven by the free activity of 200 million men". Politically, "the Assembly of the United

States of Europe would be elected by the universal suffrage of all the peoples of the continent". It would, he continued, find answers for "all humanity's questions", because our prophet had in no way foreseen the future dominance of America and Russia. In contrast, as early as 1835, his contemporary, de Tocqueville, saw that these two nations seemed "secretly destined by Providence to sway the destinies of half the world […] the principal instrument of the former being freedom, of the latter servitude".

Victor Hugo's Europe, we should add, would make Paris its capital. On 2 March 1848, he unblushingly declared, "For three centuries, France has been first amongst nations. […] Friends, brothers, fellow citizens, let us create in the whole world, by the greatness of our example, the empire of our ideas. Let every nation be proud and content to resemble France". "The Great Nation", as it called itself in 1792, saw itself as a model. Even though it no longer dreamed of armed expansion, its arrogant belief in its superiority over other nations in language, culture and ideas was undiminished. As Maurice Agulhon, the greatest authority on this period, has pointed out, the truth is that, "in this respect, the spirit of 1848 shrouded in humanitarian discourse the perpetuation of the French nationalism provoked as a reaction to the 1815 treaties".

## Bibliography

Agulhon, Maurice, *1848 ou l'apprentissage de la République*, Seuil, 1972.

Agulhon, Maurice, *Les Quarante-huitards*, Julliard, 1975.

De La Gorce, Pierre, *Histoire de la Seconde République française*, Plon, 1886.

De Remusat, Charles, *Mémoires de ma vie*, Plon, Vol. IV, 1962.

De Tocqueville, Alexis, *Souvenirs (Œuvres complètes*, Vol. XII, 1964).

Girard, Louis, *La IIe République*, Calmann-Lévy, 1968.

Pena Ruiz, Henri, and Scot, Jean-Paul, *Un poète en politique. Les combats de Victor Hugo*, Flammarion, 2002.

Pouthas, Charles, *Démocratie, réaction, capitalisme*, PUF, 1983.

Renouvin, Pierre, *Histoire des relations internationales*, Hachette, Vol. V, 1954, pp. 193-218.

Riemenschneider, Rainer, *Dezentralisation und Regionalismus in Frankreich um die Mitte des 19. Jahrhunderts*, Bonn, 1985.

Vigier, Philippe, *La vie quotidienne en province et à Paris pendant les journées de 1848*, Hachette, 1982.

# Chapter 3
# Germany and the Habsburg monarchy, 1848-49

*Wolfram Siemann*

This chapter looks at its subject from four different angles. Firstly, it examines the extent to which Germany's relationship with the Habsburg monarchy at the time of the European revolution of 1848-49 was both special and difficult. Next, it shows how far the Habsburg monarchy played a part in the national revival in Germany and central Europe. Thirdly, it looks at the paralysis of the revolution, while the fourth and final aspect is the historical one, with particular reference to the role of the Habsburg monarchy.

## Germany's relationship with the Habsburg monarchy in 1848-9

Prague historian Jiří Kořalka, in his monumental work on the *Habsburg monarchy*, gave the volume that deals with the empire in the system of international relations the title *Germany and the Habsburg monarchy, 1848-1918* (Kořalka, 1993 edn). This wording is itself problematic, for it assumes that Germany and the Habsburg monarchy are separate, with a relationship between them developed in the context of international relations. This is surprising for, until 1866, the Habsburg monarchy and considerable parts of its territory belonged to the German Confederation, and it was represented among the 38 German states as the *Präsidialmacht* of the German Confederation in the National Assembly convened in Frankfurt. Viennese historian Heinrich Lutz expressed the dilemma differently, entitling his portrayal of a large part of the nineteenth century: *Between Habsburg and Prussia: Germany 1815-1866* (Lutz, 1985). Would it not have been more logical to opt for: "Between Austria and Prussia"? And what does "Germany" mean? Is Germany really "*between* Habsburg and Prussia"?

This is not a new dilemma, being one of which the contemporaries of the 1848 Revolution were especially aware. Franz Grillparzer wrote in his Viennese diary on 18 April 1848: "Such nice people the Austrians! They are now considering how they can unite with Germany without uniting with Germany! That will be difficult to achieve, rather like a couple trying to kiss while keeping their backs turned!" (quoted by Siemann, in Haider and Hye, 2003).

Kořalka described it as "Austria's existential dilemma vis-à-vis the German question", one which had emerged in the European revolution of 1848, when the merely theoretical treatises of the period before the March revolution gave way to political consideration, during the revolution of the bourgeoisie, of the question of whether, and, if so, to what extent, Austria was inherently a part of Germany. The key question was no less than whether the Habsburg empire should continue, be divided up or be destroyed (Kořalka, op. cit., p. 4).

A surviving caricature from the democratic periodical *Reichstags-Zeitung* shows a two-headed imperial eagle beneath an imperial crown, with "Prussia" inscribed on one wing and "Austria" on the other. The heads are those of Heinrich von Gagern, who presided over the Frankfurt National Assembly, and Anton Ritter von Schmerling, Imperial Prime Minister. Their backs are joined together as if they were Siamese twins. It is nice to imagine that Grillparzer may have had this lithograph in mind. The reference beneath it to Orestes and Pylades is only comprehensible to students of the classics: it is supposed to indicate that von Gagern, like Orestes killing his own mother with Pylades' help, stifled the hope of a democratic Germany, in collusion with von Schmerling.

The 1848/9 revolution ushered in the era of nation-states in central Europe. Those nationalities that were grouped together under supranational rule (in Prussia, under the Habsburg monarchy and in the Russia of the tsars) felt obliged to try to unite members of their own nationality within a sovereign state, set up under a modern west European-style constitution. As well as the Germans, this particularly affected the Poles, Hungarians and Italians. Initially, the Czechs, Slovaks, Slovenians, Croats and Ruthenians were still ready to regard autonomy under Habsburg sovereignty as adequate. The Czechs and the Italians of South Tirol should really have joined in with the formation of a nation-states in Frankfurt, on the grounds of their inherited membership of the German Confederation, but they resolutely rejected this.

Orest & Pylades.

In the context of international law, the dilemma between the transnational state and the national tendency had begun with the "Deutsche Bundesakte" adopted at the Congress of Vienna on 8 June 1815. In the preamble, the "sovereign princes and free cities of Germany" agreed on their joint intention of coming together "in a firm federation" for the sake of the "security and independence of Germany and the peace and balance of Europe" (Huber, 1978, p. 84ff).

The German Confederation and the Habsburg monarchy had something in common, both having stemmed, as pre-national creations, from what had been known as the Holy Roman Empire of the German Nation. This represented a group of sovereign lands led by princes or the cities' patricians, with scant account being taken of any national peculiarities. Anyone who compares a map of the pre-1806 Old Empire with the borders of the German Confederation founded in 1815 quickly sees that, with the exception of the Belgian Netherlands and some minor deviations, the borders of the German Confederation faithfully follow those of the Old Empire.

This is why the Confederation contained so many non-German nationalities, and also why the western part of the Habsburg monarchy – containing Italian, Czech, Slovenian and Croatian nationalities – was, constitutionally, part of the German Confederation. This legacy of the Old Empire is also why the Duchy of Schleswig and the Prussian provinces of Poznań and East and West Prussia were not part of the Confederation, though voices began to call for their inclusion in 1848, during the phase of national agitation, and the provisional central authority, with Prussia, went to war against Denmark over Schleswig. Thus the German Confederation by no means provided a suitable framework for a unified German nation-states, if the aim was ethnic homogeneity rather than a confederation modelled on that of Switzerland.

## The role of the Habsburg monarchy in the national revival in Germany and central Europe

In view of this confusion of tendencies in Germany in respect of states and nations, there is no obvious reason for the initial enthusiasm of the Habsburg monarchy for the national German upsurge – or, to be more precise, no obvious reason why the Germans envisaged centring their reconstituted state on Frankfurt rather than Vienna. From today's standpoint it is difficult to grasp how strongly, regardless of the pressure stemming from revolutionary events, the old-established structures, in particular the framework of the German Confederation, still left their mark.

The German Confederation standardised the constitutional process that had stemmed from the revolution, basing its new electoral constituencies on the boundaries that had already existed in the Confederation's territory, as if this were a matter of course. This situation did not change until the constitutional process was at an end, for the constituent National Assembly, despite all the experiences of the year of the revolution, laid down in the first paragraph of the "Constitution of the German Empire" of 28 March 1849, that "the German Empire consists of the territories of the previous German Confederation" (Huber, 1978, p. 375).

There are five weighty reasons why the German-speaking population of the Habsburg monarchy initially played a lively part in the German national upsurge and the ensuing constitution-building in Frankfurt.

### 1. A new freedom

The Austrian population, during the restoration and pre-March revolutionary period, had formed an image of a Metternich-style system, keeping living conditions as a whole at a low level, with differing social effects. Although recent historians describe the transition to the "modern" era as full of contradictions and much more complex, and also take different views of the Austrian chancellor, writers at the time had the

Wše dobra Konstituce __ žada trochu Komoce.

Jede gute Verfassung braucht einen kleinen Stoß (Kat. 118)

impression of an oppressive, immobile system, the collapse of which would usher in an era of freedom and well-being. Educated bourgeois and liberal members of the nobility, prominent among them publicists and authors, had shaped this image, as part of which the free press should function as a mouthpiece for the people.

This massive hope for the future, linked to the fall of Metternich, was by no means confined to the Germans of the monarchy. That is abundantly clear to anyone who looks at a Czech cartoon showing a fleeing Metternich, his head circled by croaking ravens and his feet borne along by miniature railway locomotives. In the distance, a flag bearing the word "Constitution" flies from a triumphal arch.

It was the hallmark of the pan-European revolution that it propagated a single core programme encompassing all regional and territorial peculiarities, spreading this with breathtaking speed and striving towards a common aim. It related not only to the states of the German Confederation stemming from Mannheim – the source of the "March demands" – but also to the furthest corners of the Habsburg monarchy, such as the remote Moldavian town of Kronstadt, and postulated the right to nationality, political representation in elected parliaments and a written constitution guaranteeing citizens' rights. It spread by no means one-dimensionally, but ranged from Paris to south-western Germany, from Milan and Vienna to Berlin, from the many royal seats to peripheral areas, reverberating from there back to the capital cities: thus the revolution for a time created a pan-European area of communication, on which it also rested (see, for instance, Dowe, Haupt and Langewiesche, 1998; Jaworsky and Luft, 1996; and Haider and Hye, 2003). The movement took on particular force because it reached beyond the bourgeoisie into the broad circles of the peasantry, for whom freedom meant first and foremost the removal of their superfluous burdens, duties and dependencies.

## 2. The "peoples' spring"

The feeling of being part of a united opposition front – and of playing a part in a huge process of obtaining freedom – spread as the "peoples" became more aware of their national identity and came to regard themselves as subjects of history. This culminated in the Utopia of the "peoples' spring", encompassing what are termed the "unliberated" nationalities of Poles, Czechs, Hungarians and Italians, in particular.

The best-known artistic representation came from French lithographer Frédéric Sorrieu, who depicted the Utopia of friendship between peoples in a series of lithographs in which the peoples were united in a peaceful world order, a "universal democratic and social republic". The best-known of them is the first, entitled *Le Pacte*. A never-ending stream of peoples wends its way towards the statue of Freedom, portrayed as a female allegory. In her left hand, she carries the flame of enlightenment, while her right rests upon the Declaration of the Rights of Man. The shattered symbols of the European monarchies lie in the foreground, while Christ as the embodiment of brotherliness hovers above. A "holy alliance" of peoples is to take over from the holy alliance of princes.

The Utopia of the "peoples' spring" was pan-European, and subsequent historians cannot fail to be amazed that the supporters of revolution initially took this belief in the future to be compatible, as if this were self-evident, with the existence of the

Habsburg monarchy. But the leading politicians and generals of the monarchy, in contrast, were aware from the outset of the fundamental threat posed by the revolution to the existence of a state composed of several peoples. Four pictorial examples, from various nations in the early days of the revolution, document the way in which the pathos of the freedom movement (against the Old System) seemed to include peaceful understanding between nations. The pictures originated in Pressburg, Milan, Prague and Berlin.

A stylised depiction glorifies the Hungarian folk hero and poet Sándor Petöfi as he recites his poem encouraging the Magyars to rebel on 15 March 1848 in Pest. This contemporary lithograph is regarded as having sparked the national Hungarian revolt.

There is no doubt that the colour lithograph printed in Milan and showing the *risorgimento d'Italia 1848* still reflects the belief that it will be possible for the resurrection of Italy to be achieved with the exponents of the *ancien régime*, for an allegory of Italy, raised to the heavenly spheres, is accompanied by those monarchs who had given their states constitutions: Pius IX, Charles Albert of Sardinia-Piedmont and Leopold of Tuscany, representing the Habsburgs, as Italy repels the Austrian troops and pushes them down into the underworld.

IL RISORGIMENTO D'ITALIA
1848

The same message goes out from the lithograph of "the Slav Whit Monday mass in Prague, 1848" produced under a title in both German and Czech, depicting the mass of 12 June 1848 attended by large numbers from every social group, reflecting the hopeful optimism expressed that day in the proclamation of the Congress of Slavs that had gathered in Prague. It was at this gathering that the delegates supporting the "peoples' spring" suggested "converting the imperial state into a confederation of nations with equal rights", accordingly convening for this purpose a "general European Congress of peoples to resolve all international issues", on the grounds that "free peoples understand each other better than paid diplomats".

The aim was to overcome the language barrier and enable people to understand one another, as illustrated in impressive fashion by the Berlin appeal of 3 April 1848, calling on people to join in the "great republican assembly" in honour of the "great European revolution". The appeal poster makes clear that speeches were to be given in German, English and French. Such notices have to be regarded as serious expressions of the proclaimed will to achieve a peaceful understanding between nations.

There is no need to emphasise particularly the fact that this Utopia of the peoples' spring did not do justice to the complexity of the conflicting motives for action which underlay the European revolution. The newly free press of the year of revolution revealed this political practice as an unrealistic Utopia and did not spare from biting sarcasm the motor of enforced party formation. The contradictions came to light when the members of parliaments tried to found nation-states and to draw their borders. Borders bring war with them, just as much as any kind of separation does. The Germans and Danes in Schleswig felt this, as did the Poles in Poznań, the Czechs in Bohemia and Moravia, and the Hungarians and Italians in their areas of the Habsburg monarchy.

Cartoons also revealed the severe consequences for the relationship between the Austrian empire and Germany. A Viennese cartoon focused on the explosive force of nationalities and the problematic position of Austria in the German Confederation. It was clear that German unity would be rent asunder because of this: "Take it steadily, gentlemen; if it tears, it might fall!".

### 3. Austria's chance to take a German road

A third reason for the temporary ray of national German hope in the Habsburg monarchy stems from a specific phase when the huge state seemed to be dissolving and an opportunity seemed to be opening up, just fleetingly, for Austria to take a "German road". This was the case when Metternich's closest confidant, Count Franz Hartig, called for the cession of Lombardy, something which Archduke Johann was for a while still willing to accept in October 1848. In addition, Hungary in any case seemed to be lost to the monarchy that summer. Prime Minister Wessenberg expected to lose Galicia, and Franz Stadion, the Austrian governor of Lemberg, said on 6 May 1848 that it would be impossible to keep Galicia (for further details, see Höbelt, 1998). During this phase of external collapse of the monarchy as a whole, it seemed plausible for its Germans to play a part in the Frankfurt effort to achieve national unification.

### 4. The barricade myth

There was also a "barricade myth" which encouraged an over-estimate of the forces of revolution. Almost all the illustrations of barricades in Berlin, Vienna, Paris and

Frankfurt that have come down to us suggest that a way had been found of standing up to the old military forces and vanquishing traditional armies in revolutionary times. This "barricade myth", coupled with the expectations of citizens' militias, was first highlighted by Langewiesche (in Bachofer and Fischer, 1983). It is clear from the only two surviving daguerreotypes of 1848 barricades that the reality was considerably worse than the lithographed coloured and stylised images of barricades. Without the usual heroics of the stylised pictures used for publicity purposes, the first image is one of streets blocked off by stones, pieces of furniture and household equipment, and the blockade has been cleared away in the second picture, following the "battle of June".

## 5. Elections

In the end, the first pan-German elections on the territory of the German Confederation and the election of Archduke Johann of Austria on 29 June 1848 as Imperial Administrator demonstrated to Austrians in a way that could hardly be overestimated the need to take part in a pan-German constitution process. It has to be borne in mind here as well that Archduke Johann had been appointed as the emperor's representative shortly before this, on 16 June 1848. It did seem, in a way, however strongly it was disputed in the *Paulskirche* (St Paul's Church in Frankfurt) by democrats and Prussians alike, that the future form of the German Empire, including Austria, had been pre-established.

An anonymous lithographer recorded this contemporary feeling of unity in the summer of 1848 in a way which is reminiscent of the Biedermeier period. With a medallion of the Imperial Administrator, Archduke Johann, in the centre, and with two women, allegorical representations of Germania and Libertas, standing to the rear, a bowing academic, an officer, a priest, a militiaman, a soldier, a peasant, a trader, a craftsman and a worker represent every social category (with the exception of any women). The motto beneath the picture reads "No more Prussia and no more Austria, Germany is unified, strong and noble, as solid as its mountains".

The idea was for the whole of Germany to be unified through a confederation of states, a German navy and a German army, all on the basis of freedom of the press, the arming of the people and the right of association. Appropriately, in an atmosphere of optimism about the future, the Imperial Administrator's entrance into Frankfurt on 11 July 1848 led to a celebration of national unity. His arrival was staged in exactly the same way as the traditional *Adventus* of the German Holy Roman Emperor in Frankfurt.

## The paralysis of the revolution

It is clear from the progress of the revolution throughout Europe and from the events in the royal seats of Berlin and Vienna, at the headquarters of the provisional central authority in Frankfurt, and in the parliamentary bodies, why success was not forthcoming in the attempt to create a new constitutional basis for relations between Germany and Austria in the conditions prevailing during the revolution.

Even leaving aside all the contradictions within society in the material, legal and psychological spheres, which were part of the transition from the system of estates to a system of classes defined in economic terms, the underestimate of the power of the standing armies underlay the failure of the European revolution and it can still be seen as a central factor (Langewiesche in Dowe, Haupt and Langewiesche, pp. 915-32). The military operations of 1848-9 look very much like a plan to consolidate power in the hands of the old aristocratic elites.

If we just confine ourselves to the Habsburg monarchy, the key events of 1848 were the bombardment of Cracow on 26 April, the bombardment of Prague by Windischgrätz on 13 June, Radetzky's entrance into Milan on 6 August, and the culmination and collapse of the revolution in Vienna under Windischgrätz's bombardment between 6 October and 1 November. A signal was sent out by the summary execution of Robert Blum on 9 November. His contemporaries immediately understood that it was not merely a revolutionary who had been shot, but that the whole Frankfurt effort to create unity had thus been cut short by the Austrian military, when it had ended the life of such a prominent member of the *Paulskirche* assembly. Blum's execution was a central symbol of the failure of the effort to forge a pan-German constitution including the Habsburg monarchy.

Schwarzenberg, the new Prime Minister, unambiguously stated in the programme presented to the Reichstag, which met in the Moravian town of Kremsier on 27 November 1848, that

> "It is not in the tearing apart of the monarchy that greatness lies, nor in its weakening that Germany will be strengthened. It is both a German and a European need for Austria to remain as a single state." (Huber, 1978, p. 360)

Providing a kind of counterpoint, the Frankfurt National Assembly, in its constitution of 28 March 1849, emphasised this tearing-apart of the monarchy, expressly stating in its second paragraph that a German country could not have the same head of state as a non-German country on the basis of a common constitution, government and administration. The Habsburg monarchy was reduced to a German area subject to the imperial constitution and imperial legislation, with the "non-German" parts to be treated as separate areas.

Schwarzenberg's conception of the "tearing-apart of the monarchy" was not all that new, for it corresponded to the position taken by the Habsburg monarchy in the German Confederation. It was subject to federal decisions only in respect of those parts that belonged to the Confederation; the imperial state put the 1849 Frankfurt model strictly into practice internally through what was known as the Austro-Hungarian Compromise of 1867. This brought the dual monarchy into existence. Decisive factors in the failure, looking beyond any individual actions, were doubtless the state and reliability of the nationally mixed Austrian army. If we look at the military-territorial authorities and the division of the army within the monarchy in February 1848, it is clear that, leaving aside the core country, Hungary, the army was stationed in peripheral areas of the monarchy, namely areas that were unstable on account of their non-German nationalities: Lombardo-Venetia, Bohemia, Moravia and Galicia (Kořalka, 1993, Vol. 5, p. 204).

The abdication of Emperor Ferdinand on 2 December and the enthronement of young Franz Joseph marked the final part of the move towards neo-absolutism with military support. The failure of the revolution as a result of military intervention was by no means purely an Austrian, but a pan-German matter, bearing in mind the intervention of what were known as the imperial troops, who, with the help of regiments from Prussia, Hesse, Baden, Württemberg and Bavaria, brought the revolution to an end, in south-western Germany last of all. It is clearly uncertain whether the Austrian army, with the support of the Croatian regiments in particular, would have been able to defeat the Hungarian uprising, had Russian troops not come to their assistance.

## The growing exclusion of Austria

In terms of history, we cannot confine our attention solely to the two most notable years of the German and Austrian revolution, 1848 and 1849. We should remember that not only did the process of exclusion of Austria culminate in 1866, but there was also a similar process of self-exclusion going on. Thus the two had been growing apart in a structural process, which had begun well before 1848. American historian Peter J. Katzenstein was among the first to draw attention to this development (Katzenstein, 1976). In the context of the revolution, Dieter Langewiesche in particular has high-lighted the tendencies that led towards separation.

Looking back at the process of separation after a period of many years, we can see that, whereas Emperor Joseph II's reforms soon ground to a halt, and Austria as a state went bankrupt in 1811, Prussia and the states of the Confederation of the Rhine carried out reforms with which the Habsburg monarchy was only able to catch up when the phase of neo-absolutism had begun. So the monarchy was left out, missing out during the pre-March revolution period on a chance to learn about the political culture of constitutionalism. It was long overlooked that this created a political catalyst which bound the individual German states together, in their dealing with conflicts between provincial assemblies (*Landtage*), through everyday parliamentary business and, last but not least, through shared rituals extending into the extra-parliamentary social realm. Of course, even Prussia did not yet have a constitution in the modern sense, but it did have lively provincial assemblies, especially in the Rhineland, Westphalia and East Prussia.

The Habsburg monarchy missed out during the July revolution of 1830, when another constitutionalisation process went on in the remaining federal German states. The creation of the customs union without Austria was already taken by Metternich to mean that Austria had been pushed out of "Germany". The social development of the monarchy was left out of the organised German nationalism of the 1830s and 1840s, a nationalism that found its binding force in the gymnastics associations, choirs and groups of German Catholics of the period. Similarly, the Austrian political elites of the opposition were, both before 1848, and, as Langewiesche has pointed out, in the year of revolution, excluded from liberal and democratic networks (Langewiesche, 1991, p. 763). On the whole, the national umbrella organisations of associations that based themselves in Frankfurt, Berlin or Leipzig no longer included the Austrians. Similarly, the monarchy remained unaffected by the campaign for an imperial constitution in the spring of 1849, and tendencies for separation also appeared during the constitution-building process of the Frankfurt National Assembly. The election of Friedrich Wilhelm IV as Emperor provided further unequivocal proof of the division, as is clear from the votes cast by the members from Austria. The cut became even clearer when the Frankfurt National Assembly collapsed. Only a tiny number of the constituencies represented by the members of the rump parliament in Stuttgart and the assembly in Gotha were Austrian (Best and Weege, 1996, pp. 484-93).

Overall, the situation is most aptly described by the term "unequal partners", if we look at the difficult "German question" in the conditions of 1848-49 (Gehler et al., 1996). It also has to be remembered that successful nation-building requires the formation of a historical folk memory: the generally accepted legend of a nation's origin, its "shared values" and its fund of symbols draw on its major events and traditions. The historical legacy that had bound Austria and Germany – the ancient tradition of the empire – was no longer appropriate to the modern nation-state. The new tradition, which grew out of the revolution of 1848-49, nevertheless – unlike the "glorious" French Revolution of 1789 – found in failure the dimension that could move the masses and get them involved: namely in the cult of respect for those who fell in the March revolution and for Robert Blum. When the creation of a legacy began, however, references to 1848-49 retained their duality, both in the lesser German empire of 1871 and in the post-1866 separated Austria (Siemann, 1999).

# Bibliography

Best, Heinrich, and Wilhelm Weege (eds.), *Biographisches Handbuch der Abgeordneten der Frankfurter Nationalversammlung 1848/49*, Düsseldorf, 1996.

Dowe, Dieter, Heinz-Gerhard Haupt and Dieter Langewiesche (eds.), *Europa 1848: Revolution und Reform*, Bonn, 1998.

Gehler, Michael, Rainer F. Schmidt, Harm-Hinrich Brandt and Rolf Steininger (eds.), *Ungleiche Partner? Österreich und Deutschland in ihrer gegenseitigen Wahrnehmung. Historische Analysen und Vergleiche aus dem 19. und 20. Jahrhundert*, Stuttgart, 1996.

Haider, Barbara, and Hans Peter Hye (eds.), *1848: Ereignis und Erinnerung in den politischen Kulturen Mitteleuropas*, Vienna, 2003.

Höbelt, Lothar, *1848. Österreich und die deutsche Revolution*, Vienna and Munich, 1998.

Huber, Ernst Rudolf (ed.), *Dokumente zur deutschen Verfassungsgeschichte*, Vol. 1, Stuttgart u.a., 1978, p. 84 ff.

Jaworsky, Rudolf, and Robert Luft (eds.), *1848/49. Revolutionen in Ostmitteleuropa*, Munich, 1996.

Katzenstein, Peter J., *Disjoined partners: Austria and Germany since 1815*, Berkeley, CA, 1976.

Kořalka, Jiří, *Deutschland und die Habsburgermonarchie, 1848-1918*, Vol. 6.2 of *Die Habsburgermonarchie, 1848-1918,* ed. Adam Wandruszka and Peter Urbanitsch, Vienna, 1993, pp. 1-158.

Langewiesche, Dieter, "Die Rolle des Militärs in den europäischen Revolutionen von 1848/49" in Wolfgang Bachofer and Holger Fischer (eds), *Ungarn – Deutschland: Studien zu Sprache, Kultur, Geographie und Geschichte*, Munich, 1983, pp. 273-88.

Langewiesche, Dieter, "Deutschland und Österreich: Nationswerdung und Staatsbildung in Mitteleuropa im 19. Jahrhundert" in *Geschichte in Wissenschaft und Unterricht*, No. 42, 1991, pp. 754-66.

Lutz, Heinrich, *Zwischen Habsburg und Preußen: Deutschland 1815-1866*, Berlin, 1985.

Siemann, Wolfram, "Der Streit der Erben – deutsche Revolutionserinnerungen" in Dieter Langewiesche (ed.), *Die Revolutionen von 1848 in der europäischen Geschichte: Ergebnisse und Nachwirkungen; Beiträge des Symposions in der Paulskirche vom 21. bis 23. Juni 1998*, Munich, 2000 (Supplement No. 29 of the *Historische Zeitschrift*), pp. 123-54.

Siemann, Wolfram, "Großdeutsch – kleindeutsch? Österreich in der deutschen Erinnerung zu 1848/49", p. 97 in Barbara Haider and Hans Peter Hye (eds.), *1848: Ereignis und Erinnerung in den politischen Kulturen Mitteleuropas*, Vienna, 2003, pp. 97-111.

## Illustrations

Nos. 1, 2, 5, 8, 9 taken from Germanisches Nationalmuseum (ed.), *1848: Das Europa der Bilder*. 2 vols., Nuremberg, 1998.

Nos. 3, 6, 7 taken from Lothar Gall (ed.), *1848, Aufbruch zur Freiheit*, Frankfurt, 1998.

No. 4 taken from "Freiheit, schöoner Götterfunken! Europa und die Revolution 1848/49", *Zeit-Punkte*, 1, Hamburg, 1998.

# Chapter 4
# The Hungarian Revolution of 1848 and its consequences

*Peter Bihari*

> "The Hungarians are the Frenchmen of the nineteenth century."
> (George Weerth, *Neue Rheinische Zeitung*, 19 May 1849)

## Traditions

Many people say there is too much history per square kilometre in our Eastern European region, or else – as the Italian Claudio Magris once wrote – the peoples of Eastern Europe do not know the art of how to forget. These very true remarks refer to the "burden of history" in this part of Europe: past injuries and prejudices too often prevent these peoples or countries from shaping their present and their future. It can also be felt strongly in Hungary: often, parties that agree on the future have sharply divergent views about the country's past and they tend to re-fight old battles in historical disguises. By contrast, in more fortunate countries, the opposite is normally true.

However, even if I think Magris is right, I will try to argue that history can also be a source of strength; it can even be a liberating force in shaping the present and the future. So this chapter is not about the events of 1848-49, but about the commemoration of that revolutionary year. My main concern is to demonstrate how and why 1848-49 became the most important part of the Hungarian historical inheritance, and what sort of historical consciousness it helped to found. I will not try to avoid the myths, legends and cults that surround the greatest revolution of the Hungarians.

Hungarian scholars unanimously say that the events of 1848-49 meant the most decisive transformation in the history of the country – one that can be measured against the formation of the Christian kingdom by Saint Stephen around the year 1000. The transformation may be characterised by two notions: modernisation and nationality. The two, as we shall see, went hand in hand; no wonder that recent public opinion polls unanimously show that most Hungarians choose 1848 as the period of which they are the most proud in their history.

Indeed, everyday experiences also confirm this picture. Of the three state holidays, 15 March, the day of the 1848 Revolution, is very definitely the most popular, as it also means the beginning of spring. (And it is easy to connect it to the "springtime of peoples".) If today people walk along the main street of a Hungarian village or small town, it usually bears the name of Lajos Kossuth or Sándor Petőfi, the two main heroes of 1848-49. The main square is generally called Széchenyi- or Deák-square after "the greatest Hungarian" and "the sage of the country", both of them members of the first Hungarian Government in 1848. I took a map of Budapest and found that at least 75 streets and squares are named after the nine members of Count Batthyány's government – probably the most outstanding government this country has ever had. Another 16 bear the name of the revolutionary poet, Sándor Petőfi; thus the total number of places and institutions named after participants in the revolution and the following war of independence could easily be several hundred in Budapest alone.

Let me give one more example. When listening to the public radio – Radio Kossuth or Radio Petőfi – on the national holiday of 15 March, the speaker gives an account of those eminent Hungarians decorated with the highest awards, the Kossuth- or the Széchenyi-award. One more statistic: more than 250 publications appeared on the 1848-49 revolution for the 150th anniversary in 1998 (of course, in Hungarian). Professional and public interest about the revolutionary year does not lessen.

The first anniversary of the revolution was already being celebrated on 15 March 1849, using the tricolour of the national banner (this was defined by the fundamental April Laws in 1848, as was the national coat of arms), and:

> "enthusiastic youngsters as well as soldiers pledged, with a solemn oath, that Habsburg tyrants will never enter this beloved country which they redeemed with their blood to found one of the most liberal states in Europe."

After the defeat of 1849, a great number of so-called Kossuth banknotes and tricolour banners were hidden – the former in such quantities that they are of not much value in antique shops. In cemeteries, old gravestones can often be seen with the inscription "*honvéd* [member of the revolutionary army] in 1848/49". This means that this was the only significant fact of which the deceased was proud, the only thing he wanted posterity to know.

Various cults and myths, of course, became intertwined with these forms of commemoration and mourning, for example, Petőfi reciting his *Song to the nation* – "Rise up, Hungarian!", a sort of Hungarian *Marseillaise* – on the steps of the National Museum on 15 March. The memorial tablet and the wreath are there, though it was certainly not the place where the revolutionary poet sang the song. Or, take the epithets given to Kossuth, which had already been created in his lifetime: "our father Kossuth", "the Moses of the Hungarians", "the great exile", "the Messiah of the nation", "the holy old man", "the new Washington". Soon after his death in 1894, a number of statues were erected in his honour – altogether 75 by 1914 (among them 32 full-length figures). His cult may be compared *(mutatis mutandis)* with that of Bismarck in Imperial Germany.

## Commemorations

Below, I have chosen some important turning points in order to show the patterns of commemoration associated with 1848. After the period of absolutism in the 1850s, the first public – but, of course, unofficial – celebration took place in 1860. The atmosphere was passionate and a young student was shot dead by the police. In that year, the tricolour cockade and the black ribbon were already firmly established as the national symbol of that day.

The 50th anniversary in 1898 proved to be a curious one, as it coincided with the 50th anniversary of Franz Joseph's accession to the Austrian throne. Consequently, a strange "parallel action" began to evolve. Ferenc Kossuth – son of Lajos Kossuth and leader of the 1848 Independent Party – declared that "the nation wants to live and remember together with its king", and proposed that a law should commemorate the events of 15 March. After stormy debates, the Members of Parliament agreed to a compromise – there would indeed be a law, but the new, official holiday would be 11 April – the sanctifying of the April Laws by the king. This corresponded to the nature of the "lawful revolution" in 1848.

Large sections of public opinion remained dissatisfied with this compromise. From now on, declared most of the newspapers, there would be an official holiday on 11 April and a real national one on 15 March. Mention must be made of the "proletariat" of Budapest, which, for the first time, made separate celebrations with radical demands under red banners. The non-parliamentary Social Democratic Party was the only significant force that turned down the national(ist) consensus in the interpretation of 1848 and made a separate commemoration of it.

During the First World War, the legacy of 1848 was reinterpreted in a sharply anti-Russian and anti-Slavic way, as a sort of revenge for the defeat of 1849. But, with the defeat of 1918, the old pattern of the "lawful Hungarian revolution" would be swept aside. The date of 15 March replaced 11 April, as "this day can not be exterminated from the heart of the Hungarian people". And with the short-lived triumph of the Hungarian Bolsheviks in 1919, the proletarian masses came to be identified with the revolutionaries of 1848. The socialist speaker declared that

> "there will be but two nations on earth confronting each other – so said Petőfi [!] – the good and the evil. And we trample down this evil, this evil capitalism. Let us swear that we will not be last in this great battle."

This was already the cry of the socialist world revolution.

A new turn came with the loss of Greater Hungary, the victory of the counter-revolution and the establishment of a right-wing regime between the two world wars. The year 1848 kept its place, but was deprived of its liberal-democratic features. The radically nationalist, anti-liberal interpretation is clear in the memorial speech of Endre Bajcsy-Zsilinszky – a racist politician who, in 1944, became one of the few martyrs of the anti-Nazi Hungarian resistance. In 1923, he said (characteristically to an audience of paramilitary unionists):

> "Do we possess and rule our economy and the stock exchange, our literature and the press? No, we have to regain the lost positions everywhere. We need a strong nation, a strong state – no more freedom, but more state intervention."

49

Curiously, during this period, with the approach of the 80th anniversary of the revolution, 15 March was made an official holiday by a parliamentary resolution (in 1927/28). But, in the inter-war years, the mood remained essentially the same: the catastrophe of the Peace Treaty of Trianon (1920) was identified with the catastrophe of Arad (1849); sorrow for the deaths, demand for inner consolidation and preparation for the resurrection of Hungary remained the main motives of the commemorations.

In the years of the Second World War, the official line remained anti-Russian and anti-Bolshevik, but, for the small leftist opposition, the legacy of 1848-49 was welcome in order to emphasise anti-German and anti-Nazi viewpoints. Significantly, this anti-German trend remained for the next twenty to thirty years, as nothing was easier than to identify the Habsburgs with the Germans, and put all the blame on them for the failures of Hungarian history. After 1945, it was not that difficult to build the new commemorations on the old nineteenth-century independent traditions.

The next turning point was 1945, when liberation from fascism proved to be a good start for a leftist reinterpretation of history. It was only now, according to the new canon, nearly 100 years after the glorious 1848, that the revolution had reached its true goals, an independent and democratic Hungary. It was pointless to question the true nature of the new democracy, or indeed to speak of independence. The anti-German and anti-Habsburg line became even more pronounced, while the Russian intervention could easily be explained by the nature of evil tsarism, destroyed for good by the great Bolshevik party.

This trend became much stronger by the 100th Anniversary in 1948, which coincided with the start of the Cold War and the completion of the one-party communist system in Hungary. The Communist Party took great pains to control the commemorations. They proclaimed themselves the true and only heirs of 1848. Petőfi was reinstated as the main hero of the revolution. Now, the poet would join the Communist Party or would have done so in 1848 – had there been one. With the hysteria of the Cold War, a few more shifts of emphasis became visible. Party leader, Mátyás Rákosi, appeared as an (even more perfect) reincarnation of Lajos Kossuth. Tito, the mean traitor, became equal to the Croatian leader, Ban Jelacic. It seemed that, in the totalitarian dictatorships, the memory of 1848 was totally taken over by the ruling party. However, this was not the whole story. From 1950, a new decree abolished 15 March as an official holiday. It remained a day off for schools, but a normal working day for working people. The memory of 1848 was still potentially dangerous.

The anti-Stalinist revolution in 1956 clearly followed the pattern of 1848. The restitution of the so-called "Kossuth coat of arms" as well as of 15 March as a national holiday and 6 October as the day of national mourning were included in all the lists of demands made by the demonstrators. Even the communist speaker could not deny this fact after the restoration of the regime. The ideas of 1848 have been falsified many times in the last 110 years – he said on 15 March 1958 – but the events of 1956 outdid all previous falsifications.

"The counter-revolution of 1956 started disguised, in the costumes of 1848 ... [But] we will wipe out the shame which the counter-revolution put on the banner of Kossuth, Petőfi and Táncsics." [The latter was a peasant politician in 1848]

After some hesitation, the status of 15 March remained as it was in the 1950s: an organised day off for children and a working day for adults. And after the suppressed revolution, the so-called Kádár-consolidation ("those who are not against us are with us") worked well for more than a decade. The first small cracks appeared at the beginning of the 1970s. The new generation was less frightened than their parents and some of them did not restrict themselves to the tacit consent of the "soft dictatorship". The first unofficial demonstration in 1972 went almost unnoticed; only Radio Free Europe gave an account of it. But, in the next year, a short communiqué was published on the back page of the party paper *Népszabadság*. "Hooligans taken into custody" said the title:

"After the normal commemorations held on our national holiday, 15 March, a few hundred irresponsible persons tried to make a nationalist demonstration in downtown Budapest. The gathering was dispersed. In the course of restoring order, identities were checked and, among the initiators of the gathering, 41 people were taken to police headquarters in Budapest."

Not many 15 March anniversaries passed without some demonstration after 1972. The choreography was usually the same: small gatherings at the statue of Petőfi, the march to the square of [the Polish general of 1848-49] József Bem – as in 1956 – though it was never actually reached because of police intervention. March remained a dangerous month even in the 1970s.

A (hopefully) final turn came with the collapse of state socialism. The ruling party tried to prevent radicalisation and, in December 1987, the Politburo recommended that 15 March should again be declared a national holiday. In 1988, March was free again, but by then it was no longer enough. One of the greatest signs of the changing times took place on 15 March 1989. The new demand was for the official recognition of the 1956 Revolution. One placard said: "[premier] Imre Nagy = [premier] Lajos Batthyány, Kádár = Haynau [the bloodthirsty Austrian general of 1849]". The two revolutions were once again inextricably linked, their legacies reinforced each other in order to achieve present-day political goals.

If we try to distinguish between the three main historical periods, it becomes clear that, between 1867 and 1918, the differences were mainly about emphasis: whether it was the revolutionary tradition attached to 15 March or the contractual tradition attached to 11 April that expressed the essence of 1848. Then, from 1920 to 1944, there was a complete split between right and left which also reflected the fundamental opposition of liberal-democratic and national(istic) values. Finally, after 1945-48, the legacy of March was expropriated and used for the exclusive political legitimation of a totalitarian regime (with less and less success or confidence after 1956). But, before I try to speak about the present situation, I would like to draw some more general conclusions.

# Conclusions

Even the great conservative and pro-Habsburg historian, Gyula Szekfű, had to admit that 1848 had become the focus of all revolutionary traditions of Hungarian history. In a way, it continued or united the anti-Habsburg struggles for independence of the seventeenth century, and became a pattern for all the later efforts for a free and independent Hungary as well. "The masses ceased to think about '48, they only felt about it, they grasped it with their hearts and feelings instead of their minds", he wrote. Accordingly, its symbols – the tricolour, the cockade, Petőfi's *Song to the nation* – played an important part at each turning point of history, from 1850 until the present day. Most important among these cults or symbols are the so-called Twelve Points, the summary of revolutionary demands in March 1848. Indeed, in the last 100 years, twelve points may be found with authentic or modernised contents, such as in 1918, 1945, 1956, 1988 and 1989. (To compare the later years with the two following years of change would be interesting.)

As it hopefully turned out from the brief account of the commemorations, 15 March has always been a holiday for the opposition. It is not surprising in a country that had rarely experienced freedom and independence. Spring, youth, liberty and independence have become inextricably linked in people's minds and hearts. Nor is it surprising that those in power did their utmost to use 1848 for their own purposes, to legitimise their government or political system – sometimes with remarkably poor results. As one historian aptly put it, the "power of March" was usually stronger than "March of the power".

However, one fundamental question still remains to be answered: how should we interpret the immense importance of 1848 in Hungarian history? Does the revolutionary year itself offer some explanation? Are we to attribute it to later developments, or – this is my suggestion – did both "internal" and "external" factors play an important part? Perhaps, it is not unhelpful to remember once more that myths and stereotypes play a crucial role here. They do not "distort" reality, they form reality.

As we have seen, 1848, summarised chiefly in the fundamental April Laws, meant a decisive transformation in Hungary. However, it was not an artificial break, as it came from the previous decades of the "reform era" marked by Széchenyi and Kossuth. Thus, it was both reformist and revolutionary. Some contemporaries mentioned that it proved to be one of the first such liberal-patriotic transformations in this part of Europe.

Secondly – and this is rare in the history of revolutions – the events of March took place without any bloodshed, without even any significant violence. The subsequent war of independence was fought with more than enough bloodshed, but the process itself contributed to the formation of three stereotypes: Hungarians are peaceful and respect the law; they are brave soldiers and fight only when necessary; finally (and this is perhaps the most important), both the peaceful revolution and the defensive war of independence underlined national unity, a condition and result of the revolutionary year. (No matter how much the Hungarian 1848 resembled the French Revolution of 1789, there was no guillotine and no real rupture among the Magyars in their revolution.) This national unity was not lessened but strengthened by the part played by Budapest. For the first time, the twin cities of Buda and Pest were officially called Budapest. 1848 was the period when it truly became the capital of the Hungarian nation.

Thirdly, and this was also a rare phenomenon in this part of Europe, 1848 was both national and liberal-democratic together. No matter how I tried to demonstrate that the two main factors or forces were often played off against each other, it is enough to glance at the Twelve Points or the April Laws to see that the two went hand in hand. It is perhaps a strange phenomenon to mention in happier parts of the continent, but it is far from normal in Central and Eastern Europe.

Fourthly, was the revolution a success? It is not so easy to answer either yes or no. It was put down by the strongest army in the world, but it successfully resisted everybody else. In this respect, not only the revolution but the war of independence was nearly a success. Even the triumphant Austrians did not dare undo all the achievements of '48 after the Hungarian defeat in 1849. In fact, it can be taken for granted that the famous Compromise *(Ausgleich)* of 1867 could not have been concluded without 1848, since the revolution gave immense self-confidence to the Hungarian political elite, backed also by public opinion.

All in all, 1848 was the fundamental moment of Hungarian nation-building and nationalism. This remains true, even if we now know that it unavoidably helped to develop the rival nationalisms in Eastern and Central Europe. Nevertheless, this summary would be incomplete without a cursory glance at the contrast of the nineteenth and the twentieth centuries in Hungarian history. This, to put it briefly, resembles the German process: a glorious nineteenth century set against the disastrous twentieth century. This contrast, in my opinion, is one of the main reasons for the important place of the 1848 Revolution in Hungarian historical consciousness. Not only liberals, but revolutionaries or nationalists too could find what they wanted in 1848. This applied to all those who have tried to identify at least one glorious period in modern Hungarian history. What else could it be than '48? – the revolution and its myth helped to create a bridge to a brighter future.

It would be tempting to end this chapter with a statement such as "After the changes in 1989-90, the events of 1848-49 are once and for all past, and daily politics can no longer overwrite history". But, as I have mentioned before, it is still not the case. The year 1848 – with its cockades, statements and other symbols – has retained a mobilising power, and (no wonder) politicians never hesitate to exploit "the power of March". This happened as recently as in the election campaign of 2002.

So, I would rather end with a fine quotation. In order to understand it better, I will refer to a not-so-old stereotype of Hungarian history. According to this – brought up recently by the Austrian-Hungarian writer Paul Lendvai – Hungarian history is "A thousand years of victory in defeat" *(Die Ungarn: Ein Jahrtausend Sieger in Nieder-lagen)*. Lendvai does not deny that he took the phrase from Géza Ottlik's delightful novel (published in 1959) *School at the border.* "Ottlik memorably sketched this unique relationship between the Hungarians and their defeats by the example of a class", says Lendvai. And now let us read Ottlik himself:

> "The 400th anniversary of the Battle of Mohács was approaching. It seems a remarkable thing to celebrate a defeat, yet the mighty Ottoman Empire, which could have celebrated its victory, no longer existed. All traces of the Mongols have also vanished, as indeed – almost in front of our very eyes – have those of the tenacious Habsburg Empire. We have, there-fore, got used to celebrating our own great lost battles which we survived. Perhaps, we also became used to regarding defeat as something exciting, made of more solid material, and more important than victory – at any rate to regard it as our true possession."

It may be taken for granted that Ottlik had the great Soviet Empire in mind when writing his novel. He died in 1990, in the year of the first free elections after the com-munist decades. The Soviet Empire collapsed the following year.

# Recent trends in historical research about the 1848-49 Revolution in Hungary

The flood of historical work on the Hungarian revolution of 1848-9 has not lessened in the last few decades. Here, I would briefly like to point out five themes where new results have been achieved and/or new questions have arisen. These are:

* the international relations of the Hungarian revolution;
* the problem with Austria;
* the question of the Hungarian nationalities;
* the policy of the Batthyány Government;
* the organisation and composition of the *honvéd* army.

## 1. International relations and comparisons

Several scholars (Domokos Kosáry, András Gergely, Géza Herczeg, Gábor Erdődy and others) have called attention to the significance of the German revolution and the possible German unification. Hungarian liberals – the members of the Batthyány gov-ernment and others – were aware of this fact, and were working towards an alliance with Frankfurt. This proved to be promising at the beginning, some German liberals also noticing the advantages of a German-Hungarian alliance – directed, no doubt, against some Slav peoples and Russia. Only later, with the hesitations of the Frankfurt assembly and the general comeback of the dynasties, did the chances of the Frankfurt–Budapest co-operation come to nothing.

A short but interesting comparison was drawn by Professor Gergely between two leading liberal politicians of 1848 – Heinrich von Gagern and Lajos Kossuth. These new achievements clearly demonstrate that the histories of "national" revolutions should be placed in a wider context.

## 2. Austria and the Habsburgs

Here I will only stress one important point emerging from recent research. Until the 1980s, all Hungarian historians agreed that the liberals of Budapest had to face a counter-revolutionary centre in Vienna, represented mainly by Count Latour, later by General Windischgrätz and Duke Schwarzenberg. The existence and fateful influence of this "damned camarilla" at the Habsburg court was taken for granted. The ground-breaking monograph of István Deák (New York University) showed that the old picture is simplistic and distorted. There was, in fact, no unified counter-revolutionary plot against Hungary, and clearly not from the beginning of 1848. Rather, there were competing forces in and around the court, and the Batthyány government was one of them. It was successful until July 1848. This view – put forward, not accidentally, outside Hungary – is now accepted by most scholars (though in several modified forms) and strongly contributes to a more sober account of the revolutionary year: not just positive (Hungarian) revolutionaries fighting against negative (foreign) reactionaries, but mixed forces in changing circumstances.

## 3. The nationalities question

Another constantly painful point has been the so-called nationality question. There are, of course, two ways of seeing this: one concerning the peoples of the whole Austrian monarchy, another concerning the peoples of the multi-ethnic Hungarian Kingdom. (In 1848, Count Széchenyi spoke of Hungary as a web of "nationalities".) This was (or is) the question where national histories based partly on national bias came most clearly to the forefront – during the decades of state-socialism, they had been swept under the carpet. And this is also the reason why Western historians – mainly because of misinformation – often gave rather distorted summaries. Nowadays, some promising works have been published which try to avoid prejudice and, instead of putting the blame on the other (nationality), make an attempt to reconstruct and understand contemporary situations. (Here again the names of D. Kosáry, I. Deák and perhaps Gy. Spira come to mind.)

Again, it was Professor Deák who began to break down the one-sided interpretations. Perhaps, it is worth quoting parts of his message. The first of these refers to the intellectual background of the Hungarian liberals' thinking (by no means unique in nineteenth-century Europe):

> "The Hungarian liberals were unable to fathom the depth of national sentiments among the non-Magyars. Why should free citizens of a free country suddenly be granted special status? Why should collective privileges be bestowed on a specific nationality, shortly after all corporate or caste privileges had been abolished? [Here follow the words of Kossuth ...] Neither Kossuth nor any Hungarian liberal or radical was ever willing to concede that the agitation of the national minorities was not necessarily reactionary." (Deák, 1979, p. 129)

And this is how István Deák does justice to both contesting sides:

> "To say that, in the spring of 1848, the Hungarians missed the chance to conciliate all their nationalities and, therefore, could not but lose everything, would be as wrong as to assert

that there was no chance whatsoever. Newly triumphant Hungary could not be expected, voluntarily, to divide the realm into self-governing territories, with the whole inevitably coming under the control of the non-Magyar majority, but the government huge could have arrived at a modus vivendi with some nationalities. The suppression of the Slovak movement, though immoral, was successful; the war against the Serbs and the Croats – as we shall soon see – had to be fought; the attempt to vanquish the Romanians was a terrible mistake." (Deák, 1979, p. 129)

Of course I do not mean to say – and neither does he – that, in interpreting historical problems, a halfway between extremes has to be found. However, he clearly wants to say that, instead of reinforcing black-and-white myths, situations and mentalities have to be analysed and interpreted. It must, however, be added that Deák's views on the nationality questions are not as widely accepted – at least in Hungary – as those concerning the "damned camarilla". It is nevertheless widely acknowledged now that all nationalities have their own "legitimate" 1848 with different views, even myths. Serious historians must be aware of this.

It is interesting to see that old views still find their ways into short summaries. To take one German example, Immanuel Geiss has devoted a few passages to the Hungarian problem: "Das Scheitern der Ungarischen Revolution am gross-magyarischen Chauvinismus 1848/49 und der Ausgleich von 1867 schufen wesentliche Bedingungen von 1914" (Geiss, 1990, p. 70). It is a question as to whether the Hungarian revolution failed and, if it did, whether the main or only cause of its failure had been "Great-Hungarian chauvinism". He himself partly contradicted this: "Tatsächlich geriet Österreich durch den Erfolg der Ungarischen Revolution in eine schwere Existenzkrise von der es sich nie wieder erholte" (ibid., p. 80). Geiss' views are unmistakably based on A. J. P. Taylor's witty and successful, but old and biased, monograph on the Habsburg monarchy, where the chauvinist Kossuth is the real troublemaker in the Carpathian basin. Nevertheless, it was a relief to see Manfred Botzenhart's new book *1848/49: Europa im Umbruch*, not least because, unlike all previous books, the Hungarian names have been written correctly. This, at least, gives hope for future understanding.

## 4. The Batthyány government

There have been important new results in the person and policy of the half-forgotten Hungarian Premier – and later martyr – of 1848, Count Lajos Batthyány. When not forgotten, he was shown as an opportunist rival of the truly revolutionary Kossuth. But his was the only revolutionary government, which remained in office for half a year (April to October). Now, after the publication of Aladár Urbán's huge biography, we know that Batthyány was always seeking compromise with the Habsburgs, but was always ready to defend the sovereign rights of his country. It has turned out that his views or his strategy were close to those of Kossuth, even if there were differences in their tactics and also in their dealings with public opinion.

In contrast to Kossuth – the orator–genius – Batthyány was an aristocrat who did not think it necessary to tell people about the dealings of his government. It has become clear that the existence of a well-equipped Hungarian *honvéd* army in 1848 was mainly the result of Batthyány's efforts. His policy meant that the country successfully faced her enemies for a whole year. He resigned only when he saw the hopelessness of his efforts for compromise and reconciliation. Thus, it is not just his martyrdom that deserves more attention and appreciation from posterity.

## 5. The *honvéd* army

Finally, due to the books and articles of Professor Urbán, Tamás Katona, Róbert Hermann and others, we know far more about the Hungarian *honvéd* army than before. The age-old myth of General Görgei's "betrayal" is buried forever; he is now recognised as the greatest Hungarian commander of the nineteenth century – the unjust charges against him originated from the writings of Governor Kossuth and his followers.

It is surprising to see the multi-ethnic character of the Hungarian army and also of its leaders. As for the latter, let me give one example: among the 13 Hungarian generals executed by General Haynau at the castle of Arad, one was a German duke from outside Austria, one a German from Austria, three were Germans from Hungary, one Croatian, one Serbian (remember, the Serbs and Croats were the most resolute enemies of the Hungarian revolution in 1848), two of Armenian origin(!) and four "pure Hungarians", of whom one hardly spoke any Hungarian at all. The same is more or less true of the whole revolutionary army, which is an another illustration of the complexity of the situation in 1848 and also of the circumspection that historians have to show in dealing with ethnicity and nationalities.

Even this short survey would be incomplete without some references to the recent discussions, as well as the gaps in our knowledge of 1848. To start with the gaps: the lack or neglect of local history is a constant feature in our historiography. It is probably linked to the centralistic character of Hungary. As for 1848, there are a few studies about Budapest, Debrecen (the "second capital" of the revolution) and the territory of Transylvania, but less about Pozsony (Bratislava, Pressburg) and few of any significance about other parts of the country. At least, they remain buried in their localities, making it more difficult to understand the real nature of events in 1848-49.

Of course, there are discussions everywhere, but perhaps the most constant of these concerns the character of the fundamental April Laws: whether they created a personal union of Austria and Hungary, or a stronger tie between the two countries, and whether they created a working system at all. If not, was it due to the old distrust between the two parties or to the unpredictable turn of events, which ruined the chances of a lasting compromise? Here, I think the questions are more and more precise, but the positions of historians have not come closer together. This clearly shows that the history of the revolution still provides a permanent occupation for historians – hopefully to the benefit of the public.

# Bibliography

Deák, István, *The lawful revolution. Lajos Kossuth and the Hungarians in 1848*, New York, 1979.

Geiss, Immanuel, *Der lange Weg in die Katastrophe*, Munich, 1990.

# Chapter 5
# The 1848 Revolution in the Romanian principalities: continuity and discontinuity

*Carol Capita, Alin Ciupala and Maria Ochescu*

## Introduction

In several historiographical traditions, revolutions represent both the end of one historical period and the beginning of another. Revolutions, unique and spectacular events, are historical facts that can, in particular, be used as chronological milestones in academic chronologies. But, in recent decades, research has demonstrated that revolutions are not the end or the beginning of historical periods. The new elements are integrated with long-term developments and the inheritance may be found next to the innovation, whether cultural (in the widest sense of the word), political or social.

In the former communist countries, this evolution of historical writing was pushed into the background or ignored. The ideological limits of the regimes that marked the evolution of East European countries in the second half of the twentieth century created a special image of these events; revolutions were seen as founding events and as facts that proved, beyond a shadow of doubt, the existence and inevitability of class struggle. Revolutions were thought of as proof of the battle of the bourgeoisie (in the nineteenth century, still a class related to progress) and the working class (sometimes still in its inception) against the feudal class. This entire construction was the result of a rather particular reading of Marxist texts, the result of contemporary ideological pressures rather than of the scientific endeavour. The idea that nineteenth-century revolutions were autonomous processes that had little to do with the continuing progress and affirmation of the working class was considered either heresy or a false idea. An honest analysis can easily prove the limits of this perspective on history. In fact, the elements of continuity play an important role, with a significance similar to the elements of innovation.

## The 1848 Revolution in Romanian historiography

Romanian historiography during the communist regime fits well into the pattern described above; the situation is possibly worse than in other countries of the region. There are many reasons for this. Firstly, many of the participants in the 1848-49 revolution greatly influenced Romanian politics until almost the end of the nineteenth century. As a result, this generation stands for the development of modern Romania; in at least one case, that of the Bratianu family, the revolution provided the basis on which their domination of Romanian politics was built until the communists took power. The members of this family dominated the Liberal Party from its beginnings until 1947. Secondly, the 1848 generation consisted mainly of intellectuals who greatly influenced Romanian culture. Romanian art and literature entered, with Rosenthal, Balcescu, Alecsandri and many others, the general framework of modern European culture. Thirdly, the historiography of the late nineteenth century, a romantic and nationalistic historiography (like all historical writing of the period), transformed this generation into a model of political action.

Last, but not least, were the pressures of the communist regime. The break between Bucharest and Moscow – at least at the level of declarations – had a curious influence on historical writing. Independence from the centre of the communist world (and its influence and "role" as the guiding country of socialist development) asked for the "discovery" of local roots for the political organisations of the working class, a special brand of counterbalance to the supposed unique character of the USSR and to proletarian internationalism. The result was the transformation of almost all social upheavals into actions in which the working class was, if not the spearhead, at least one of the groups that inspired it. That is why, in certain texts of the period before 1989, the first workers' strikes were thought to have taken place as early as the eighteenth century in a country where, at the end of the Second World War, the better part of its population still worked in the agricultural sector and in which a significant segment of the skilled workers were foreigners.

The result is rather discouraging when looking at traditional history texts. The events, while important, are still the main focus, but social developments are neglected. It is the same with cultural history. In our opinion, the best analyses were produced by historians of Romanian literature, not by researchers trained as historians.

In recent years, however, a new generation of historians has started to reflect on new types of sources, to introduce into the historical debate new areas of investigation (such as gender studies, the history of private life, the history of minorities, of clothing or of free time, and so on). This has caused a serious re-evaluation of the work already done, trying to select the positive results from those that were less acceptable.

## Continuities

The elements of continuity are visible. First of all, there is a continuity of personalities involved in the events of 1848. The more or less secret associations aimed at reforming Romanian society were the first place of "political exercise" for an entire generation. For example, the association called *Fratia* ("The Brotherhood"), active at the beginning of the 1840s, regroups most of the members of the future revolutionary government in Wallachia. Nicolae Balcescu and Christian Tell are among those who already had political experience. But this continuity is more profound. The leaders of the revolution were members of the great Romanian families, the aristocratic families that had shaped local politics even before this. It was the younger generation who considered that the time had come for new politics; they came from the same family environment, but with other policies – the result of contacts with French and Italian romantic circles.

But this was also the result of a more structural change which started in the eighteenth century. The bourgeoisie – created from elements of the lesser nobility, merchants who arrived from the Balkans and other regions of the Black Sea (Armenians are a good example) and intellectuals from Transylvania – was also a force involved in changing habits, with new clothing, new activities and new forms of entertainment, such as journals and theatres. It was a new world. The first journals and the first museum (for antiquities and natural sciences) were, like the creation of the state archives, signs of a modernity that brought access to information. This interest in knowing about other places and people also explains why some of the revolutionaries considered that the 1848 Revolution in the Romanian principalities was inspired by events in France (though they recognised that the European revolutions were the occasion and not the cause of the revolutions in the principalities). But, we stress again, these developments had started at least one generation before.

This model is duplicated by another on-going situation. At first sight, nothing might look further from the idea of continuity in 1848, than the problem of language (that is, the concepts and terms) used to transmit the revolutionary message and ideology. At a closer look, the issue can be dealt with from another perspective. The 1848 ideology was, throughout Europe, an essentially liberal ideology to which in some instances (as was the case in the Romanian principalities) national aspects were added. The Romanian revolutionaries, as well as their counterparts from other countries, used a new form of ideological expression shaped specifically for those to whom it was addressed, their level of education and their cultural conventions. The ideas were new, but, in order to become understandable for as many people as possible in the principalities, older forms of expression were employed. The most telling example of this was the constant drawing upon the Christian Orthodox religion and religious feeling, which was so important in a still traditional society. It was not just by chance that priests played such an important role in the development of events during the year of 1848, both in Transylvania (in the case of Greek Catholics and Orthodox Romanians) and in the Romanian principalities. In many cases, they were drawn unwillingly into the events by the constant appeal to the religious sphere and its link to the new society.

In the case of Wallachia, the priest Radu Sapca was called on to explain to the population gathered at Islaz (the place where the revolution started) the goals of the revolution, and, several days later, the metropolitan Neofit was even appointed as head of the revolutionary government. A similar situation existed in Transylvania, where the two Romanian metropolitans (Orthodox and Greek-Catholic) participated in events alongside the people. The symbolism of the 1848 Revolution in the Romanian principalities is saturated with Christian philosophy. The opponents of the revolution became the enemies of God; the cross and the Gospel became instruments of ideological warfare alongside the barricades and the gunpowder.

Another element of continuity was the idea of using diplomacy to attain their national goals. From the eighteenth Century, Romanians had asked the Western powers to intervene with the Ottoman Empire in favour of the principalities. During the peace conferences that ended regional wars between Russia, the Habsburg Empire and the

Ottoman Empire, delegations of Romanian nobles asked the great powers to give the Romanian principalities the statute of neutrality or to guarantee their autonomy. Since the Ottoman Empire was considered to be the major threat (and the religious factor also had a role to play), relations with the Christian powers were considered the better alternative. This attitude was apparent in the effort made by the revolutionaries in 1848 to rally public opinion in France and the German states to their cause.

## Discontinuities

The first and most visible change was in political action. The 1848 Revolution was the first occasion on which leading politicians found popular support for their proposals. True, in Romanian historiography, the 1821 uprising led by Tudor Vladimirescu was considered a revolution, but the debate over the character of this movement is still open and, in our opinion, it was too linked to the war of independence of the Greek people to be considered a strictly Romanian movement. In the eighteenth century, politics was still a matter of small groups of aristocrats representing the country. However, in 1848, the situation was different. In Iasi, capital city of the mediaeval and early modern state of Moldavia, the revolutionaries produced a text that outlined the reforms that were considered to be necessary to ensure progress in the country. This document, called the *Petitiune-Proclamatiune* ("petition–proclamation") was the work of a commission established by a vote at a meeting with about 1 000 participants; the document was presented to the ruling prince, Mihail Sturdza, by a delegation that considered that it represented the whole population.

Similar developments occurred in Wallachia and Transylvania. The gathering of people, sometimes tens of thousands, as in Transylvania, gave legitimacy to a political approach that was, for that time, essentially illegal. To the south of the Carpathians, in Wallachia, those taking part in the meeting from Islaz gave their approval to a document called "The Islaz Proclamation". This became the programme of the revolutionary government in Bucharest. In Transylvania, the Romanian revolutionaries acted in accordance with the decisions voted at the meeting in Blaj (one of the religious centres of the Romanians from Transylvania), including their opposition to the Hungarian revolution. It is significant that, even though small groups of people actually initiated the revolutions, the final approval was in the hands of these larger gatherings of citizens. In 1848 the Romanians discovered "the voice of the people", an element that influenced politics at least up until the First World War.

Perhaps the most significant break from the period prior to the 1848 Revolution was the definition given to the nation. Even if the effort to give it a political content failed, it nevertheless became a powerful idea that put its mark on the period that followed. The young Romanian intellectuals (most of them from well-to-do if not aristocratic families), members of the romantic current, understood the nation as a community which should reunite all Romanians: aristocrats and plebeians, rich or poor, intellectuals or ordinary people. The new criterion for accomplishing this solidarity was citizenship and the new allegiance was to the power of the nation and its political existence, not towards a prince, king or emperor. The modern Romanian state, which appeared in 1859 through the unification of Wallachia with Moldavia, would have the nation at its centre, a model not lacking in limits and contradictions. Already at the beginning of the nineteenth century, the members of the Romanian Enlightenment referred to the country and made appeals to patriotism, but the meaning given to these concepts was quite different from the meaning given by the 1848 generation.

For the former generation, the country was still considered to belong to the aristocracy, who had formed the intellectual and economic elite, those who owned land and held public office by virtue of a long and still-powerful tradition. The cultural and intellectual breakthrough introduced by the Enlightenment was not so great as to offer a new perspective on the structure of society, as occurred a generation later. The Greek aristocracy which had settled in the principalities, and from whom the Ottoman Empire had appointed princes to the thrones of Wallachia and Moldavia, after a period of cohabitation with Romanian nobles, entered into conflict with them for the supremacy of this region. But this phenomenon, accelerated by the arrival of new ideas from Western Europe, developed almost exclusively at the level of elites. Two decades later, things had changed. The 1848 generation broke with this tradition. In order to make himself understood by everybody, Nicolae Balcescu, probably the most important ideologist of the revolution in Wallachia, even developed a "textbook" of the citizen. After the defeat of the revolution in the Romanian principalities and Transylvania, the nation continued to represent the main model for co-ordinating the efforts of the Romanian people.

Another significant break with tradition related to the theatre of European politics. Until 1848, a significant proportion of the political actors and decision-makers viewed Russia as an ally that could help, at a cost, to counter-balance the influence of the Ottoman Empire. True, the loss of Bessarabia in 1812 was the result of the expansionist movement of Russia towards the Balkans, but the decision of the Ottomans to accept the territorial loss was taken under the influence of Romanian diplomats in the service of the Ottomans. Moreover, the loss of territories was perceived as a sign of the failure of the Ottomans. Russia, on the other hand, played an important role in introducing elements of political reform (in her capacity as protective power and occupation force after the Adrianople Treaty); however, these interventions in Romanian political life changed the opinions of local elites towards an alliance with Russia. The intervention of the Russian army against the Romanian revolutions (both in the principalities and in Transylvania) confirmed the Romanians' worst fears. From that moment on Romanian political life would be split between those in favour of an alliance with Russia and those who were against. Only the Franco-Russian alliance at the end of the nineteenth century somewhat changed Romanians' views about their powerful neighbour.

But the revolution determined the manifestation of yet another discontinuity, that between generations. The young aristocrats and intellectuals who had started to become known from 1840 as participants in more or less quiet efforts for reform, found in the revolution the opportunity to affirm themselves as a generation. Most of them were between 20 and 25 years old, but there were some – such as Ion Heliade-

Radulescu – who were over 40. What united these people was not only the shared goals and ideals, but their education, which had been completed in French, German and Italian universities. They came to know about the new ideas that were circulating in Europe, and were also introduced by their professors and peers into freemasonry. Their commitment towards new ideas was so great that, once they returned home, they brought with them the desire to modernise Romanian society. Quite naturally they became suspect in the eyes of the local police and civil authorities. But, even if they were called ironically "the bonjourists", they did not hesitate to adopt a new lifestyle, from clothing to manners, from literature to political ideas. As a result of their activities, politics became a daily activity, well hidden under the cover of cultural associations which edited publications of a pronounced political character.

Tensions appeared rapidly, not only in the public sphere, but also in the families of these young intellectuals. The sons understood their fathers less and less in a world that was increasingly split in terms of lifestyle, language and aspirations. Relying heavily on their estates, living in an oriental style (the result of Ottoman and Greek influences) and dependent on a political system that guaranteed their privileges, the fathers did not understand their children and regretted their departure from tradition. A shared social background – these young revolutionaries were all nobles – and blood ties could not ensure the stability of a society that had changed. The monument of the Golescu family in Bucharest is a reminder of this situation. The old Dinicu Golescu, a restless traveller in 1824-26, is resplendent in oriental costume and wears a long beard, a sign of his social position in society. He is surrounded by the busts of his four sons, all central figures in the 1848 Revolution in Wallachia, who are wearing Western clothing, sideburns and short trimmed beards.

In this battle between parents and children, the women, both mothers and wives, were sought as allies by both. In the decade before the revolution, the younger generation discovered the influence of women in politics and culture; the older generation acknowledged this role, even if grudgingly. Unlike the previous period, where women were totally (even symbolically) excluded from the political arena, the message of the 1848 generation was that women were seen as an integral part of the nation. When creating "Revolutionary Romania", the painter Constantin Rosenthal took as his model a woman draped in the banner of three colours (red, yellow and blue). She was none other than the wife of the revolutionary leader C. A. Rosetti. The revolution was also prepared in the ballrooms and literary clubs of the aristocracy, where women played a central role which went far beyond their duties as hostesses. The memoirs and letters of revolutionaries from 1848 are proof of this situation.

Romanian historiography speaks little of the attitude and involvement of the wives, sisters and mothers of the men of 1848, focusing only on their role. But, during the revolution, women played an active role – either as individual figures (such as Ana Ipătescu, who practically saved the revolutionary government) or as anonymous characters from the middle class. Their male contemporaries, such as Michelet and Garibaldi, wrote about their spirit of sacrifice, a message that many historians failed to understand. It is not too far-fetched to say that women made their entry into public life and politics during the 1848 Revolution, but their role decreased after 1859, when the peaceful process of modernisation began. What remains is their role as leaders of literary and political salons, in works of charity and, last but not least, in social work, seen as an important part of the public area of the second half of the nineteenth century.

## Conclusion

Looking at the 1848 Revolution, it seems to us that the significance of this event is precisely the combination between the new and old elements that made up Romanian politics in the middle of the nineteenth century. New perspectives on political action went hand in hand with a new perspective of Romanian society as a whole, but it was not a totally new world. The combination of the old and the new was, possibly, the first sign of modernity in Romanian politics.

## Bibliography

Albini, S., *1848 in Principatele Romane* ('1848 in the Romanian principalities'), Bucuresti, Ed. Albatros, 1998.

Berindei, D., *Revolutia romana din 1848-1849: consideratii si reflexii* ('The 1848-49 Romanian revolution: considerations and reflections'), Cluj-Napoca, Centrul de Studii Transilvane, 1997.

Maior, L., *1848-1849: Romani si unguri in revolutie* ('1848-49: Romanians and Hungarians in the revolution'), Bucuresti, Editura Enciclopedica, 1998.

Platon, Gh., *Geneza revolutiei romane de la 1848* ('The genesis of the 1848 Romanian revolution'), Iasi, Editura Universitatii "Al. I. Cuza", 1999.

Stan, Ap., *Revolutia romana de la 1848* ('The 1848 Romanian revolution'), Bucuresti, Editura Albatros, 1992.

# Chapter 6
# Liberty and unity: an impossible combination –
# The centenary celebrations of the 1848 Revolution in Germany

*Rainer Riemenschneider*

## Introduction

This chapter is based on a study that appeared in a collection published in 1989 to mark a number of centenaries celebrated that year (Riemenschneider, 1989). At that time, the history of commemorations, the politics of memory *(Geschichtspolitik)* and sites of memory were just starting to become a focus of German historical research. Dieter Langewiesche and Wolfram Siemann were undeniably the first to study the tradition of commemorating 1848. A vast array of publications came after them, particularly when the 150th anniversary of 1848 came round in 1998 – giving rise to celebrations and exhibitions the length and breadth of Europe, with commemorative books and catalogues too numerous to be listed here (see, for example, Siemann, 2000; Hettling, 2000; Gildea, 2001; Tacke, 2001). Schoolbook publishers obviously did well from this. For Germany alone, the bibliography prepared by the Georg Eckert Institute (2003) includes dozens of titles.

My study is based on an extensive survey of articles published in local and national dailies and weeklies, and of special books produced when Germany celebrated the 1848 centenary in 1948. These all make it clear that the general climate in 1948 was far from ideal for this kind of exercise. The many problems caused by war damage and the shortage of essentials were too pressing and too present for people to look back calmly to a distant national past. Everyone was too busy worrying what the next day would bring. The papers were full of stories about the black market, smuggling and trafficking in stolen goods: petty crime was rife, due to restrictions and rationing. Rationing indeed was so harsh that it provoked bitter strikes in the spring of 1948. In an article headed "Easter Eggs", one local paper reported that "An adult's monthly ration in April will comprise: 1 350g noodles, 9 000g potatoes, 425g meat, 600g fish, 265g fat, 62.5g cheese, 3 litres of milk, 1 500g sugar and 500g of dried fruit. [...] The rationing authorities say that, if all goes well, the bread ration – fixed at 7 000g – should go up 1 000g in Lower Saxony" (*Braunschweiger Zeitung*, 18 March 1948).

In spite of all these daily problems, just three years after the end of the "total war" that had been unleashed on Germany, preparations to commemorate the 1848 Revolution were well under way – and celebrations around the country were unexpectedly widespread (Siemann, 2000, p. 139). As Edgar Wolfrum points out, of the three anniversaries celebrated in 1948 – the tercentenary of the Treaty of Westphalia, which concluded the Thirty Years' War in 1648, the 50th anniversary of the death of Bismarck in 1898, and "1848" – only the last generated any notable political and public interest (Wolfrum, 1999, p. 39). The original plan was to turn the celebrations into a massive demonstration in support of German unity, but they ended by showing all too clearly that the gap between the two Germanys was becoming increasingly unbridgeable: the Cold War was already starting to freeze everything. Wolfrum shows that the birth of the two, mutually exclusive approaches to the writing of German history, which characterised the post-war period, can actually be traced to the rival celebrations, East and West, in 1948. This was forcefully illustrated in the three main centennial events: the Berlin demonstrations on 18 March, which commemorated the barricades of 1848; the relay-race that took runners through the western zones in mid-May, converging on Frankfurt-am-Main; and the Frankfurt Festival, 16-22 May 1948. In the following pages, I shall look at these three events.

## Dignity among the ruins: commemorating 1848 in 1948

### 1. Berlin, 18 March 1948

At its meeting on 9 January 1948, the Greater Berlin Council, representing the four sectors of the former capital, discussed plans to commemorate 1848, but failed to reach agreement on a joint celebration. As a result, two separate celebrations were held on 18 March 1948 to commemorate the same thing – the street fighting which marked the beginning of the Berlin revolution. The Socialists (SPD), Christian Democrats (CDU) and Liberals (FDP) staged a public rally on the square in front of the *Reichstag*, the old national parliament, while the SED, the party formed by merging the Communist and Socialist Parties in the Soviet zone, did the same on the Gendarmenmarkt. Commentators at the time saw these parallel ceremonies as "the most striking sign of the rift which has opened in Germany since the end of the war", since the two sides had first issued separate, mutually hostile declarations, with the tacit backing of the occupying powers (*Spiegel*, 20 March 1948). Even the preparations followed different tacks. On the Gendarmenmarkt, teams of young people from the state youth movement spent months clearing the debris with shovels, cheered on by rousing music in the background. On the Platz der Republik, in front of the ruined *Reichstag*, the approach was blatantly hi-tech, with bulldozers lent by the American and British armies shifting the rubble out of sight into an abandoned underground station – 30 000 cubic metres in the space of ten days.

The crowd on both sides also turned up in different ways. In the West, urged on by radio RIAS-Berlin, tens of thousands of people made their way to the venue individually, and listened in the pouring rain to speeches by representatives of the three political parties. In the East, 30 000 factory workers marched "in lengthy columns" to the Gendarmenmarkt behind the SED's red flag, to the sound of the *Internationale*. "Fear on the march" was *Spiegel*'s description (ibid.).

In these circumstances, memories of 1848 inevitably paled into a flimsy pretext for a rhetorical clash of a far more topical kind. This, at least, is what is suggested by contemporary newspaper coverage. One gets the feeling that Berlin was becoming a battleground for the two superpowers: "Now that democratic freedoms have been stifled in Bucharest, Budapest and Prague" wrote the *Sozialdemokrat,* a Berlin newspaper, "Berlin is the last outpost and the bridgehead of democracy in the world". It actually portrayed Berlin as the focus of East-West conflict, and spoke of 18 March 1948 as "the day on which the decisive battle between democratic freedom and medieval barbarism will be fought". It went on:

> "All those who believe in western culture and civilisation, in freedom of the individual, social progress and equality of the peoples will gather on the Platz der Republik; those who want to destroy our democratic freedoms and civilisation will meet at the Gendarmenmarkt." (*Braunschweiger Zeitung*, 18 March 1948)

Speakers in the West called repeatedly "for freedom – against people's democracy" (ibid.), those in the East wanted "unity and a just peace" (*Spiegel*, 20 March 1948). The two sides, which *Spiegel* was already calling "western" and "popular" democrats, used the words "freedom" and "unity" in ways that reflected their positions. The West's calls for "freedom" were clearly directed at the SED's efforts to reunify occupied Germany. The SED, on the other hand, was trying to give those efforts historical legitimacy when it declared: "The struggle for a united German People's Republic is 100 years old: it is up to the People's Congress to conclude it successfully" (*Braunschweiger Zeitung*, ibid.). And Wilhelm Pieck, one of the SED's most prominent figures, spoke of 1848 in these terms: "We are completing the Revolution which was left unfinished then" (*Spiegel*, ibid.).

Not everyone accepted this vision of unity, however: "We have no right to unite our country by selling off our freedom", declared the Liberal Karl Hubert Schwennicke on the Platz der Republik (*Spiegel*, ibid.). "Freedom" and "unity" were key concepts for both sides, but their incompatible versions of those terms generated separate visions of Germany's past, which in turn gave rise to irreconcilable interpretations of "1848". The political and ideological rift of 1948 had long-lasting effects, and I believe that the centenary revealed it. In *Spiegel*'s striking, perceptive and prophetic phrase, "the polemics on both sides turned the barricades set up on 18 March 1848 into a solid wall on 18 March 1948" (*Spiegel*, ibid.). Not the least irony was the fact that two separate publications on 1848, both of them commissioned by the Greater Berlin Council, were going to press.

Demonstrations identical to those staged in Berlin on 18 March 1948 began to take place all over Germany. Many towns and cities took their lead from the former capital. In Braunschweig and Nuremberg, for example, the political parties again took charge of the festivities – both versions, of course. As in Berlin, the Communists and Socialists demonstrated separately, although on different days (*Braunschweiger Zeitung*, ibid.). At these rallies, some of them held in makeshift venues (like the tram depots in Braunschweig which were, the papers reported, suitably decorated for the occasion), local celebrities, and sometimes regional MPs, made speeches, repeating the points their parties had made in Berlin, with personal variations. All of these events seem to have been incident-free, and to have taken place in a calm, if not solemn atmosphere – as if everyone had decided that Otto Suhr, Chairman of the Berlin Municipal Council, had been right when he said: "This day demands dignity".

## 2. The Relay Race

It is hard to say how many people turned out in the various towns in March 1948 – *Spiegel* speaks of "tens of thousands" in West Berlin and 30 000 in East Berlin, while another eye-witness puts the figure at 50 000 on each side (diary of Ruth Andreas-Friedrich quoted in Overesch, 1986).– but we do at least know that 20 000 runners took part in the relay race in mid-May, and that countless spectators lined the roads to see them pass. The race followed a star-shaped pattern – hence the name *Sternstaffellauf* (star relay race). The star had seven points, most of them close to the German borders – the Zugspitze, Ulm, Karlsruhe, Kassel, Berlin, Bremerhaven and Flensburg – where the main routes started, converging on Frankfurt, with side-routes joining on the way. The race began on 15 May, passed through nearly every town in Germany and ended in Frankfurt on the 18th, the day on which the German National Assembly had met in 1848. The 20 000 participants included leading athletes, such as Marga Petersen, the 100m champion, who joined the race in Bremen. The runners carried hollow batons, containing messages of support for Frankfurt and its 1848 Assembly from towns along the way.

The race – according to the press, the biggest mass event since the war (*Hannoversche Presse*, 15 May 1948) – was organised by local authorities, sports associations and choral societies. As far as the public was concerned, it seems to have had two aims: to mark the centenary of the National Assembly's session in Frankfurt in 1848 (Overesch, 1998) and also to be "a major demonstration in support of German unity" (*Hannoversche Presse*, ibid.). The Mayor of Braunschweig linked the two in his speech to the people of the city: the memory of 1848 should provide inspiration for Germany's political reconstruction. A short ceremony in front of the town hall marked the passing of the baton in the towns along the way: a speech by the mayor, surrounded by other dignitaries, a gymnastic display by local sports associations and songs from local choirs. The authorities certainly hoped that these associations, with their large memberships, would help to popularise the anniversary celebrations. The point was repeatedly made that the drive for national unity in 1848 had drawn some of its strength from these very associations: "In 1848, singers and athletes were the bearers of the message of freedom" (*Hannoversche Presse*, ibid.). The president of one local sports federation declared: "I hope that democracy will become as important for the whole community today as it was for the sportsmen then" (*Hannoversche Presse*, 19 May 1948).

A race on this scale, involving 20 000 runners and covering thousands of kilometres, called for perfect organisation and total discipline. Germans, however, are good in both departments – and one local paper was probably wasting its ink when it reported that the baton had been *pünktlich* arriving at Braunschweig town hall on Whit Sunday morning, just as the clock was striking 11.00 (*Braunschweiger Zeitung*, 19 May 1948). But there were occasional hitches. At Flensburg in north Schleswig-Holstein, which was strongly under Denmark's democratic influence, the race had trouble getting started. Kohlhoff, the 400m hurdles champion, had expected a big send-off – but this was spoiled by a line of furiously hooting motorists and a bell-ringing tram-driver, who simply wanted him out of the way. Further down the road, some of the runners cried off, giving work as an excuse. Finally, the baton was handed over to a motorcyclist, who had to stop for lunch to avoid reaching Schleswig too early. When he got there, the cathedral was locked, so another venue had to be found for the ceremony. Once Kiel had been passed, however, there were no further problems on the road to Frankfurt (*Spiegel*, 22 May 1948).

As a call for German unity, the race was at best a partial success, since it covered only the American and British zones. The occupying authorities in the French zone banned it for political reasons: "Germany's mini-Olympic race touched them on a raw spot" was *Spiegel*'s ironic comment. It added: "They were bent on keeping its federalist subdivisions intact, and this looked very like a demonstration for unity" (*Spiegel*, ibid.). The Soviets also banned the race. Having passed through the American and British sectors, the Berlin baton had to be flown to Frankfurt, and the Braunschweig section of the race could only start at Helmstedt, on the line between the British and Soviet zones. The SED shared the Russians' disapproval: for Wilhelm Pieck, the Frankfurt celebrations were simply dressing up the emergence of a western state (*Spiegel*, ibid.). In other words, the West's drive for unity in May was quite as unacceptable to the East as the SED's version of the same thing had been to the West in March.

## 3. The Frankfurt Festival, 16-22 May 1948

The Centenary culminated in the "week of celebration and culture", the title given to the Festival by the organising city, Frankfurt – "provisional capital of West Germany", as *Spiegel* called it (*Spiegel*, ibid.). The Festival owed its success to the commitment of the mayor, Walter Kolb, and it made him "Germany's best-known mayor". The week was rich in activities. It began with the opening of an exhibition on 1848 at the city's *Kulturverein* on Sunday 16 May, and continued with a performance of Mozart's *Magic Flute* (conductor, Bruno Vondenhoff) that evening. On 17 May, Mayor Kolb, Louise Schroeder, Mayor of Berlin, and Paul Loebe, President of the *Reichstag* under the Weimar Republic, laid wreaths to commemorate the revolutionaries who had died on the Frankfurt barricades in September 1848. That evening, Adolf Grimme, Minister of Education for Lower Saxony, addressed a youth rally on the *Römerberg*.

The biggest day was 18 May. It started with a reception, organised by the university and attended by representatives of various western universities and the rectors of all the German universities – except those in the Soviet zone (*Hannoversche Presse*, 19 May 1948). This was followed by a special ceremony in the *Paulskirche*, where the National Assembly had met just 100 years before. The weather was splendid, and people turned out in their thousands to see the relay runners arrive. Then, at exactly 3.15 p.m., the guests of honour walked in solemn procession from the *Römerhallen* to the *Paulskirche*, just as the members of the Assembly had done in 1848, while all the bells of the city rang out. The procession was led by Walter Kolb, accompanied by the writer, Fritz von Unruh, who had returned specially from his US exile to deliver the main address. Next came the presidents and ministers of the *Länder*, followed by church representatives and the university rectors in their ceremonial robes, and then a few uniformed representatives of the military government.

The organisers had hoped that the procession through the city centre, the vast public turn-out and the ceremony in the *Paulskirche* would recreate the sense of jubilation and the solemn hopes that had marked 1848. The preparations had been going on for a long time – particularly the rebuilding of the *Paulskirche*, destroyed in a March 1944 air raid, which had left only its outer walls standing. Rebuilding the church, regarded as "the home and symbol of German democracy" had been given top priority. As described by the mayor, the work had been a collective effort by all the people of Germany, with "wood from the forests of eastern and southern Thuringia, stone from Hesse and the Rhineland, iron and steel from the Ruhr, and money donated by workers in Berlin, Hamburg, Hanover, Munich and other German towns" (*Braunschweiger Zeitung*, ibid.).

Two basic ideas were at work in the project: the desire to give "German democracy" a religious character, and the feeling that the "common home", both literal and figurative, had been built by the efforts of the whole country – at least in theory. For contemporaries, both were of vital present-day importance, but needed to be taken further. They derived their legitimacy from harking back to the great founding event: "1848". All of this was to be symbolised by the rebuilding of the *Paulskirche* in 1948. The religious character of German politics was reflected in the building's dual function as *Volkshaus und Gotteshaus* – "House of the People and House of God". As one architect put it "The cross on top of the reconstructed church will set its mark on both political and religious action". As for the second aspect, underlined by the mayor – the fact that all Germany had contributed to the work – it is also worth noting that three of the bells which started pealing from the church at 8.00 in the morning on 18 May had been donated by the Protestant Church in Thuringia. Obviously, coming from a province which had been part of the Russian occupied zone since 1945, this gesture had both religious and political significance. The three bells from Thuringia actually reached Frankfurt on 20 March 1948, the day on which the Allied Control Council in Berlin broke up in total disagreement. The gap between the desire for unity and the realities of division could hardly have been wider.

Although the organisers tried to make the day a festive one, the disasters of the immediate past were too close to be forgotten. The mayor might speak of 18 March 1848 as the day on which German democracy – on which all energies should again be focused – had been born. But he could not help noting in his opening address in the *Paulskirche* that, instead of the beautiful, half-timbered houses of the *Römerplatz*, once the city's pride, the processional route had been lined by melancholy ruins, imperfectly concealed by the flags and the fir branches (*Braunschweiger Zeitung*, ibid.). *Spiegel* focused on the contrast between the immaculately organised celebrations and the disastrous realities which a saccharine evocation of the past was intended to drive from people's minds: "The ruins of the present were momentarily obscured by the pathos of the commemoration ceremonies, but the root causes the current problems of Germany, Europe and the world showed through all too often" (*Spiegel*, 22 May 1948). Fritz von Unruh, who had gone to the heart of the matter by attacking the many who were willing to serve all regimes without distinction, suddenly felt faint and had to break off his speech (*Braunschweiger Zeitung*, 19 May 1948).

Next day, on 19 May, the celebrations continued with the German Writers' Congress, which attracted some 400 poets and writers, and European Unity Day, with Henri Brugmans of the Netherlands as the main speaker (*Hannoversche Presse*, 20 May 1948). On Friday 21 May a football match between teams from north and south (excluding the French and Russian zones) was organised by Sepp Herberger, the federal German team's future trainer: this semi-national tournament drew 50 000 spectators to the Frankfurt stadium (*Spiegel*, ibid.). On 22 May, an "interzonal women's congress" marked the end of the festivities, which were rounded off with a huge fun-fair and final firework display.

## Conclusion: the festival that never was

All of this shows that 1848 was very much in people's minds in 1948. Organised by political parties and local authorities, the centennial celebrations took many forms, spanned much of the country and got wide press and radio coverage. My own impression is that mayors in larger towns played a bigger part in planning and running them than the *Land* Presidents, whose power-base was often not yet firmly established, due to the recent creation of these new states with few historical antecedents and the absence of a central government. The renascent political class saw the celebrations as an opportunity to raise their profile, and harking back to the democratic traditions of 1848 as a way of restoring democracy to a Germany which had lost its bearings after a decade of dictatorship and terror: "1848" served pedagogical purposes, and the commemorations were more of a study in political psychology than a traditional anniversary celebration.

Were the lessons learned? Was the message heard? True, there were vast turn-outs in Berlin in March – in the West, where people came voluntarily, and in the East, where they marched to order – and in Frankfurt in May. But did they really come to hear politicians hold forth on the subject of the barricades of yesteryear? Unlikely, one would think, as "1848" does not seem to have been a popular topic. In Nuremberg, for example, five people registered for an adult education course on the 1848-49 Revolution, whereas a course on Goethe's *Faust* attracted 250.

Some people have suggested that this contrast between enthusiasm for literature and lack of interest in "1848" reflected a certain political apathy (Overesch, 1986). This, I think, is going too far. We need to look elsewhere for the causes – at perceptions of 1848. My impression is that, in 1948, most people thought of 1848 as an unfinished revolution and – more importantly – were starting to think that leaving it unfinished had proved disastrous. An anonymous article on the Frankfurt ceremony, which appeared in a regional paper the day after, is a fairly typical example of this. Under the heading "Indivisible freedom", it declared: "The German people's failure to achieve a decisive revolution is the great tragedy of our history". The author went on to say that German history consisted of a series of botched or failed revolutions which marked the path "on which our people have trailed far behind other nations, which have made a far better job of securing freedom and democracy" (*Hannoversche Presse*, ibid.).

This argument had already been developed in another paper in March. Under the heading, "First freedom, then unity", the anonymous author highlighted the division caused in Germany by the nascent Cold War, and looked at the many reasons for the failure of the 1848 Revolution. He went on to discuss the effects of that failure, which had led to freedom being sacrificed to unity, and so – inevitably – to the "cliff-edge on which we are now standing". Seen from this angle, there was nothing to celebrate: "It would be wrong to celebrate the 1848 centenary with pride and satisfaction, as if this were a natural and accepted tradition, like Bastille Day in France" (*Braunschweiger Zeitung*, 18 March 1948).

In other words, one does not celebrate a botched revolution, any more than one celebrates a lost war. The centenary offered a chance, not so much to form a new picture of Germany's past – the professional historians had started doing that immediately after the "German catastrophe" of 1945 – as to use the media to bring that new picture to the attention of people far beyond the narrow circle of those academic historians. The comments in the press show how deeply today's concerns colour perceptions of the past. Our interpretation of the past is conditioned by our experience of the present, and our plans for the future. A truism for historians, this fact is again strikingly illustrated by accounts of the 1848 centenary celebrations.

## Bibliography

Georg Eckert Institute, Braunschweig, Germany, Thematische Auswahllisten von Unterrichtsmaterialien, No. 24: *Von der Restauration bis zur Revolution 1848*, 2nd edn, April 2003.

Gildea, Robert, "1848 in European collective memory" in Dieter Dowe, Heinz-Gerhard Haupt, Dieter Langewiesche and Jonathan Sperber (eds.), *Europe in 1848. Revolution and Reform*, New York and Oxford, 2001, pp. 916-37.

Hettling, Manfred, "Shattered mirror. German memory of 1848: From spectacle to event" in Charlotte Tacke (ed.), *1848 – Memory and oblivion in Europe*, Brussels, 2000 (Euroclio No. 19), pp. 79-98.

Overesch, M., *Chronik deutscher Zeitgeschichte*, Part 3/II, Düsseldorf, 1986.

Riemenschneider, Rainer, "1848/1948. Liberté et unité: un mariage impossible. Le centenaire de '1848' en Allemagne, 1948", extract from "Histoires de Centenaires ou le devenir des révolutions. Contributions à l'histoire des centenaires des révolutions de 1830, 1848, 1870 et 1871 en France et en Europe", in *Bulletin de la Société d'Histoire de la Révolution de 1848*, Paris, 1989, pp. 65-75.

Siemann, Wolfram, "Der Streit der Erben – deutsche Revolutionserinnerungen" in Dieter Langewiesche (ed.), *Die Revolutionen von 1848 in der europäischen Geschichte: Ergebnisse und Nachwirkungen; Beiträge des Symposions in der Paulskirche vom 21. bis 23. Juni 1998*, Munich 2000 (Supplement No. 29 of the *Historische Zeitschrift*) , pp. 123-54.

Tacke, Charlotte, "1848. Memory and oblivion in Europe" in Charlotte Tacke (ed.), *1848 – Memory and oblivion in Europe*, Brussels, 2000 (Euroclio No. 19), pp. 13-27.

Wolfrum, Edgar, *Geschichtspolitik in der Bundesrepublik Deutschland. Der Weg zur bundesrepublikanischen Erinnerung 1948-1990*, Darmstadt, 1999.

# PART TWO

# 1912-13 in European history

# Introduction to 1912-13

The choice of 1913 rather than 1914 as a possible turning point in recent European history may seem, at first, rather perverse. Many contemporary history textbooks, particularly those published in western Europe and the United States, often gloss over the Balkan wars of 1912 and 1913, except to include them within a list of factors and forces that contributed to the outbreak of the First World War.

However, our reason for including the events of 1912-13 in this series of key moments in recent European history was that the first and second Balkan wars were a significant part of a 200-year cyclical process of national liberation within the Balkans which began in 1804 with the first Serbian uprising against their Ottoman rulers and ended with the bloody conflict in the former Yugoslavia in 1991-5. As such the wars were part of a larger story of how the desire for national liberation, and the nationalist ideologies which fuelled those aspirations, shaped the political map of south-east Europe.

Serbia gained some measure of autonomy in 1817. Greece finally gained its independence from its Ottoman overlords in 1832. There were nationalist uprisings across the region in 1848. At the Congress of Berlin in 1878, Serbia and Romania gained full independence while Bulgaria became a self-governing province and the Habsburg empire took control over Bosnia, Hercegovina and the Sanjak of Novibazar. Now Ottoman rule in the Balkans was limited to Albania, Macedonia and Thrace and even parts of these territories were ceded to Greece in 1881 and to Bulgaria in 1885.

Undoubtedly, rapid population growth and internal structural problems pushed the rulers of the new states in the Balkans to seek to expand their territories and in this respect they began to covet the remaining Ottoman territories in Europe. But in each case aggression and internal resistance tended to be justified in terms of national liberation from foreign oppression. Montenegro, Serbia, Greece and Bulgaria legitimised the First Balkan War as a war to liberate Kosovo and Macedonia from Ottoman rule. Bulgaria, dissatisfied with its share of Macedonia, justified the Second Balkan War on the grounds that the people in the area of Macedonia it was claiming were Bulgarian. Serbia declared at the outset of the First World War that its main aim was to liberate the South Slav lands from Habsburg rule. Whilst the establishment of the Kingdom of Serbs, Croats and Slovenes in 1918 appeared to have achieved that, it was not long before the Kosovan Albanians rebelled, Macedonian nationalists set up the Internal Macedonian Revolutionary Organisation, many Croats and Slovenes began to see the Serbs as their new foreign rulers and national liberation movements emerged. Those divisions became even more apparent when the Axis powers occupied Yugoslavia in 1941.

Whilst the post-war Communist era under Tito kept a lid on nationalist aspirations, it was hardly surprising that the political leaders who came to power in Yugoslavia in 1990 adopted nationalist programmes. The problem, as it had been for most of the nineteenth and twentieth centuries, was that they were not only seeking to create nation-states; they were also seeking dominance over other national groupings in the same contested territories.

# Chapter 7
# The Great Powers and the Balkans, 1878-1914

*Ioannis Koliopoulos*

## The Great Powers and the Balkans in the build-up to the wars

Europe's south-eastern tip, which for several centuries was the western half of the Eastern Roman Empire of Byzantium, became the Balkans after the Ottoman Turks set foot in Europe and turned the region into the western part of the sprawling Ottoman Empire. The region has been associated with primitive ways of life, militant nationalism, instability and war – or so the West chose to depict the region, so as to satisfy its own intellectual or political predilections and needs (Todorova, 1997). However, the unruly and fierce Albanians, Serbs, Greeks or Bulgarians had their equivalent in the West not so long ago, and religious or national conflicts in the Balkans have never been as violent as they were in the West during the sixteenth and seventeenth centuries or, indeed, in the twentieth century. Inter-communal brutality and religious or national cleansing have been practised with equal intensity as much in the West of the continent as in the East.

The image of the troubled south-east corner of Europe influenced Clio's servants in their quest for truth and reality in the analysis of past events and developments, so much so that the principle of national self-determination (which in the West was accepted as a dominant and legitimate consideration for the American colonists against the English king and for the Italian or German subjects of the Habsburg emperor against their ruler) was not as readily accepted for the Ottoman Sultan's Greek, Serbian, Albanian or Bulgarian subjects. In 1912, the great powers of Europe were not inclined, for reasons of their own, to allow the Ottoman sultan and the Habsburg emperor to be deprived of lands like Albania, Kosovo, Bosnia, Epirus, Macedonia or Thrace by the nation-states of the region. These old and declining empires were kept alive for fear that their disappearance would create a power vacuum, causing dissension among the succeeding nation-states and the great powers supporting them.

These were not illegitimate fears and they did not only preoccupy Franz Ferdinand and Abdul Hamid. The polyethnic empire was not as useless or as defunct as most proponents of the nation–state maintained; so argued people with agendas other than those of the Habsburg emperor or the Ottoman sultan. The proponents of these empires, though not exactly representatives of the ancient regime or admirers of Prince Klement von Metternich, considered the empires of Central and Eastern

Europe useful, indeed vital, for maintaining a measure of peace and law and order in a region inhabited by a multitude of peoples with different creeds, tongues or identities. These views were behind some serious efforts in both empires to reform and shore up the declining structures, and the reforms under way further strengthened the position of those holding such views.

The reforms put forward in the Habsburg Empire were promulgated to shore up the two faltering empires and were aimed at making membership in the empire more attractive to the non-German districts rather than the prospect of a South Slav state nationhood offered by the Serbs, as well as the liberal reforms heralded by the Young Turks in 1908. Similar views with different preoccupations and serving different agendas were put forward in Greece by *déracinés* like Ion Dragoumis and a circle of like-minded men, who were disappointed with the Hellenic nation-state's performance and achievements, and sought a "solution" outside the nation-state in a restructed Ottoman Empire, in which the Ecumenical Greek Orthodox Patriarch would hold sway over all Greek Orthodox Christians of the empire.

These views, in favour of strengthening the declining polyethnic empires of Central and Eastern Europe, which were put forward in the first decade of the twentieth century from various quarters, sounded rather modern to those who had been condemning the nation-state as the cause of all the disastrous wars of the twentieth century. To the post-modernist enemies of the nation-state, and proponents of multicultural and multiethnic societies and state formations, the views of the early twentieth century in favour of the multinational empires of the region promised a benign restructuring of the empires and the various communities they sheltered.

## Greece

On the Greek side of the border with the lands claimed by the then existing nation-states of Greece, Serbia, Montenegro and Bulgaria – the states that formed the Balkan League in 1912 and dispossessed the Ottoman Sultan of most of his land possessions in Europe – there was not exactly a debate on the question of these lands, but rather unease and fears in intellectual and political circles about what the future held for the Greeks. A disastrous and humiliating war with the Ottoman Empire in 1897 had shown the limitations of the Greek nation facing the Ottoman Empire alone.

The protracted war of Greek and Bulgarian factions against each other, or against the forces which the Turks had at their disposal in Macedonia, did little to allay Greek fears about the future of Macedonia and the adjacent lands. Ion Dragoumis and a number of friends toyed with the idea of a "Greek Orthodox Empire" within a restructured and reformed Ottoman Empire. In the favourable climate produced by the Young Turk Revolt of 1908, such schemes did not seem extravagant or ludicrous, though in reality they were. The "Empire" comprising Greek Orthodox Christians under the aegis of the Greeks of the Ottoman Empire was also thought to have been the vision of the Phanariote elite before the Greek War of Independence of the 1820s. Arnold Toynbee, who envisaged this for the Phanariotes, apparently knew very little of that pre-national Greek elite; he seems, however, to have been influenced by the same events and interpretations of these events that influenced Dragoumis and his circle of Greek *déracinées*. Whereas Dragoumis considered the Greek nation-state defunct and useless, Toynbee regarded the state to be an elusive vision of Western Liberals, which could not possibly absorb Western liberal institutions (Dragoumis, 1985; Toynbee 1922, 1981).

Opposite Dragoumis stood a man quite different from him, not a visionary but a pragmatist, Eleutherios Venizelos, the great Cretan statesman who then embarked on a brilliant and turbulent political career in Greece. Venizelos had no illusions or doubts about what lay in store for the Greek state, as long as the men who served that state entrusted him with the necessary powers to lead the Greeks. He strongly believed that the previous unstable kingdom, which Dragoumis derided and despised, was a formidable instrument in the hands of able men under his leadership. Indeed, he was convinced that the Greek state was the only vehicle available which would propel the Greeks towards a solid future. In Venizelos' mind, the vision of the "Great Idea", which in the past had often seemed to favour the designs of those who envisaged a pan-Hellenic insurrection of the Greeks of the Ottoman Empire and union into a great Greek Empire, served only one purpose: the addition to the Greek kingdom of as much adjacent land as it could seize, hopefully in collaboration with the other kingdoms of the region, in order to better safeguard the seized territories (Veremis, 1980, 1989).

Venizelos, a revolutionary against established authority before moving his ambitions to the Greek kingdom, appeared to no longer place any faith in insurrections of the Greeks of the Ottoman Empire like the ones throughout the nineteenth century which the kingdom had stirred up in the Greek irredenta in the sultan's European dominions. He was able to grasp the essential weakness of these insurrections. They were condemned to failure, because they did not rely on regular armed forces of the state but rather on locally conscripted armed men of all descriptions, including brigands, and because the great powers of Europe would not allow the dismemberment of the Ottoman Empire.

Greece's protecting powers, Britain, France and Russia, especially the first two, were opposed to the Greeks disturbing peace in the region. This opposition led successive Greek governments to favour the use of irregular factions to promote the kingdom's irredentist designs by causing a revolt in the Greek irredenta which, in turn, favoured the growth of a formidable class of men of arms who put themselves forward as the nation's true army and who most of the time robbed the peasantry with impunity (Koliopoulos, 1987). Venizelos would have none of this, as he had set his mind on creating a strong and credible regular army, and he succeeded with the assistance of French officers, as soon as he assumed power.

Similar irredentist practices in Bulgaria and other nations in the region favoured the rise of men like Venizelos who wished to put an end to these old die-hard practices. This departure from disappointing past objectives and practices owed much to some of the profound changes in the European security system. The two alliances of

European powers, the Triple Alliance of Germany, Austria-Hungary and Italy, and the Triple Entente of Britain, France and Russia, had merged into two opposing military camps which, by threatening a general war in the continent, had forced the powers to avoid provocative actions. Peace was thus secured by the imminent threat of a general conflagration. This restraint by the great powers encouraged small states to pursue regional alignments aimed at settling local scores and hostilities.

## The Balkan League

The Balkan League of 1912 came into being in the context of this self-imposed restraint by the great European powers. The betrayal of the Russian tsar by the Habsburg emperor in 1908, when Austria-Hungary annexed Bosnia-Herzegovina without prior notice to Russia as had been agreed, left Russia humiliated as it had missed its chance to seize the Straits. Seeking some kind of compensation in the region, which Russia considered it deserved, the Russian Government encouraged the Slavic states of south-eastern Europe to count on its support for their common action against the Ottoman Empire. The Italian-Turkish War of 1911-12 acted as a catalyst: one of the powers of the Triple Alliance was at war with the Ottoman Empire, and the great European powers were faced with one more crisis in the eastern question (see Helmreich, 1938, Tricha and Gardika-Katsiadaki, 1993).

The alliance of Serbia with Bulgaria was the result of ample Russian encouragement, and obliged the two countries to prepare for common action against the Porte. Military objectives were left undefined; the fortunes of war were left to decide the division of the spoils, while the tsar's mediation in the event of disagreement over the spoils betrayed the alliance's interested patron. It was a Slavic alliance resting on Russia's wish to win a march against its rival Austria-Hungary, as well as Serbia and Bulgaria's wish to satisfy their territorial claims at the expense of the Ottoman Empire and, if necessary, at the expense of Greek territorial claims in the same direction.

Gone were the days of the Crimean War, when common action of all Orthodox Christians of the region under Russian auspices was seen as a sacred mission entrusted by God upon the Orthodox of the East. The states of the region appeared to be coming of age and learning the ways and means of their examples in the West. A new breed of men were dismissing the old rhetoric and sensibilities, and bracing themselves for action in the way men like Camilo di Cavour, Otto von Bismarck and Louis Napoleon III had done.

## The Slavic Alliance

The Slavic Alliance of 1912 made Greece extremely nervous and insecure, and justifiably so. More than the Bled Agreement of 1947 between Marshal Tito and Georgy Dimitrof for a Yugoslav-Bulgarian Federation and the union of Bulgaria's Pirin Macedonia to the then People's Republic of Macedonia, the Serbian-Bulgarian alliance of 1912 represented for Greece an unprecedented threat. It is worth noting that in 1912, unlike 1947 when Greece could count on the protection of Britain and the United States to counter the threat emanating from Communist Yugoslavia and Bulgaria, the country was virtually alone in what seemed to be a new round of imminent military action in the region to dispossess the Ottoman sultan.

Venizelos was in a position to discern the serious threat to Greek interests emanating from an alliance of Serbia and Bulgaria, and lost no time in opting for Greece to join the Slavic Alliance. It was no surprise to Venizelos that the country that heeded the Greek offer to join the alliance was Bulgaria. It was strong enough to accept Greece as a junior partner, with the Greek Navy as the only real asset. Bulgaria had by far the strongest army in the region and was expected to play a decisive role in the field. Bulgaria, moreover, had Russia's unqualified support and was seen as Russia's agent in the coming conflict in the region. In this sense, Greece joining Bulgaria against the Ottoman Empire was as much a defensive move vis-à-vis Bulgaria as an offensive one against the empire.

Events in the region moved fast, too fast for Greece to face alone. Greece's previous tenuous understanding with the Ottoman Empire to avoid the partition of the sultan's European dominions, because this was expected to be at the expense of both countries, was being diminished and undermined by a sense of power and a renewed mission infused in the Ottoman Empire by the Young Turks after 1908. The latter, moreover, did not hide their objective of restructuring the old edifice and turning it into a modern nation–state like the successor states in the region. In the Young Turks' design for the future there was no place for Greece.

## The war

War in the region came in October 1912 and, as expected, was forced upon the Ottoman Empire by the successor states. Serbia, Montenegro, Bulgaria and Greece took as much territory as their forces could gain in the field. There were some unexpected achievements and failures, most notably: Greece's advance from the south, deep into the Slav-speaking enclaves of Macedonia claimed by Bulgaria; Serbia's equally fast advance into Macedonia claimed by Bulgaria; Bulgaria's slow advance in the same direction as it faced the main brunt of the Ottoman forces in Thrace; and Italy and Austria's intervention on behalf of the newly-founded Albanian nation-state.

These unexpected turns of the war produced a radically new situation in the region. Triumphant Serbia and Montenegro moved deep into Bulgarian-claimed Macedonia and pushed the new Albanian state south into Greek-claimed Epirus. Serbia's gains in Kosovo were Greece's loss in Northern Epirus, which became Southern Albania. Greece compensated itself in Macedonia where it got the lion's share. Bulgaria lashed out against both Greece and Serbia in a second round of military action, in the summer of 1913, following an inconclusive conference in London. In addition to its former allies, Bulgaria was now also facing Romania and the Ottoman Empire. Bulgaria courted disaster, and disaster came not unexpectedly its way.

One state's gain was another state's loss as far as territorial gains and losses were concerned. The principal loser was the Ottoman Empire. Losses had been expected, though not of such magnitude. Bulgaria, too, was a loser, and unexpectedly so. Also unexpected was Albania's appearance, especially its southward push by Serbia. The Bucharest Treaty of August 1913, which ended military strife in the region, did little to allay Ottoman and Bulgarian grievances and left a formidable legacy of claims and counter-claims.

## The post-war situation

The two rounds of military action and the international treaty that put an end to that action represented the triumph of the nation–state against the old order in the region. In the space of less than a year, the political map of the region had changed beyond recognition; from the Danube to Crete and from the Adriatic to the Black Sea, bewildering changes were a reality or were about to be launched. Statesmen counted gains or losses of territory, while journalists and other observers tried to take stock of the new situation. (See, for instance, the eyewitness account of Crawford Price, 1915.)

A novel and a rather portentous reality represented the communities of "others" in all the states of the region, who came to be described as "minorities". Many centuries of peaceful or not so peaceful movement and settlement of peoples in the region had produced a rather mixed population, which tested the abilities and imagination of state authorities (Carnegie Report, 1914). The authorities did not appear to consider hetero-linguals an issue deserving of their attention and did not discriminate against foreign-language speakers. The struggle to win educational and ecclesiastical preponderance in Macedonia, in the period before the Young Turk revolt, witnessed the first serious acts of discrimination against foreign-language speakers.

Homogeneity of the nation–state was not exactly fashioned in the region, as recent Western criticism of ethnic cleansing practised in the 1990s seems to imply. The nation-states of the region were implementing national practices long in use in the West. Moreover, in the period under consideration and before the multicultural society in the West came to be considered an acceptable form of social composition, the linguistically and religiously homogeneous society of the state was considered the norm, not the exception. Homogeneity was a source of power and security, and all measures leading to homogeneity were not extraordinary or unacceptable.

The drive to secure the cherished national homogeneity assumed its grim and sinister aspects for at least two reasons, which are easily forgotten: i. the absence at the time of a regulatory international organisation to take an interest in or intervene to protect threatened minorities, and ii. the fact that most minorities in the region lived in border areas where a neighbouring state claimed them as brethren of its own nationals.

International legislation at that time fell far short of the regulations and instruments required for the effective protection of minorities. The international community, it seems, needed the gruesome experiences of two world wars to fashion rules and organs for the protection of vulnerable minorities. Recent experiences in the same region and elsewhere have shown how much more is needed in the same direction.

The Balkan wars of 1912-13 created many such border minorities in the region. These minorities were often victimised by unfriendly state authorities, not so much because their members were different from those of a state's majority but principally because they constituted or were perceived to constitute a threat to the security of that state. Claims from across the border of land inhabited by a minority linguistically or religiously akin to the majority in the neighbouring state undermined the position of the particular minority and, at the same time, retarded its incorporation and social assimilation into the nation-state.

## Conclusions

The terrible sufferings and humiliations of minorities in the successor nation-states of the region cannot possibly constitute an argument in favour of the rule of their predecessor. The nation–states of the region, which emerged from the Balkan wars stronger, did mismanage the minorities they acquired, on many occasions, but at the same time freed many more people from the despotic and tyrannical rule of an autocrat that had proved incapable of reform, and gave them something that was in short supply or even unattainable: pride, the pride of people free to cultivate their own language and culture, their own identity.

Political analysts, and sometimes historians, often favour the slippery road of drawing lessons from past events. Looking back to the objectives, the policies and actions of the states and their agents involved in the Balkan wars of almost a century ago, the historian is truly at a loss when it comes to drawing such lessons. One valid observation is that the changing fortunes of military strife and the outcome of the two rounds of confrontation did not meet the calculations and the expectations of the protagonists.

Another no less valid observation is that, if security considerations constituted a primary objective of the same protagonists, security and peace proved as elusive as they had been before the wars. Equally, and despite manifestations from most quarters to the contrary, the seizure of whatever land came one's way, proved the primary consideration, because seizure and holding of land has always been one of the principal features of wars between states. A related observation is that, once armies took the field, previous agreements and understandings were blown away by the winds of war. The allied states of the region learnt what Western states knew from long experience: that agreements will be broken as soon as national interest makes that imperative.

The Balkan League of 1912 was the first and last such league in the sense that it included all three main contestants for the Ottoman sultan's remaining possessions in the region, that is, Greece, Serbia and Bulgaria. Since 1912 those three nations have never been members of the same alliance at the same time. It is hoped that, sooner rather than later, Serbia and Bulgaria will join Greece as members of a European

Union equal to the challenging tasks confronting the Europeans and led by men with a vision for a Europe different from the one that bred wars like the Balkan wars.

## Bibliography

Carnegie Endowment for International Peace, *Report of the International Commission to Inquire into the Causes and the Conduct of the Balkan Wars*, Washington DC, 1914.

Dragoumis, Ion, *Phylla hemerologiou* ('Diary leaves'), ed. Thanos Veremis and J.S. Koliopoulos, Athens, 1985.

Helmreich, C., *The diplomacy of the Balkan wars, 1912-1913*, Cambridge MA, 1938.

Koliopoulos, John S., *Brigands with a cause: Brigandage and irredentism in modern Greece, 1821-1912*, Oxford, 1987.

Price, Crawford, *The Balkan cockpit*, London, 1915.

Todorova, Maria, *Imagining the Balkans*, New York, 1997.

Toynbee, Arnold, *The western question in Greece and Turkey*, Boston, 1922.

Toynbee, Arnold, *The Greeks and their heritages*, Oxford, 1981.

Tricha, Lydia and Gardika-Katsiadaki, Eleni (eds.), *E Hellada ton Valkanikon Polemon, 1910-1914* ('Greece of the Balkan wars, 1910-14'), Athens, 1993.

Veremis, Thanos (ed.), *Meletemata gyro apo ton Venizelo kai tin epochi tou* ('Studies on Venizelos and his time'), Athens, 1980.

Veremis, Thanos (ed.), *Eleutherios Venizelos: Koinonia – oikonomia- politike stin epoche tou* ('Eleutherios Venizelos: society, economy and politics in his time'), Athens, 1989.

# Chapter 8
# The Balkan wars, 1912-13: their effect on the everyday life of civilians

*Helen Gardikas-Katsiadakis*


## Research on the theme

To my knowledge there exists no study dedicated to the economic and social effects of the Balkan wars in Greece, let alone to their effects on everyday life, except for certain chapters in the works of the Greek Professor of Public Finance, Andreas Andreades. The nearest to it is the volume *Les effets économiques et sociaux de la guerre en Grèce*, in the series Histoire économique et sociale de la guerre mondiale published in 1928 by the Carnegie Foundation for International Peace. Indeed, such a task for the period limited to the Balkan wars would have been almost impossible.

Alexander Pallis, the Greek Delegate to the Commission for Refugees at the League of Nations, noted in his study on the effects of the war on the population of Greece:

> "From 1912 to 1923, Greece lived through a period of almost continuous wars. During these twelve years, she took part in five campaigns, which are: the First Balkan War against Turkey in 1912-1913, the Second Balkan War against Bulgaria in 1913, the European war in which Greece participated from 1917 on the side of the Entente, the expedition of Ukraine, undertaken at the request of the Allies against the Bolsheviks in 1919 and, finally, the Greek-Turkish war of 1919-1923." (Pallis, 1928, p. 131)

These wars, whether victorious, as were the first three, or disastrous, as was the last, resulted in vast territorial changes and the dislodgment of millions of people, affecting the everyday lives of ordinary people and transforming the demographic and the ethnological maps of the region. However, particularly in the field of social change, to distinguish the short-term effects of the Balkan wars from the long-term changes of the entire period is extremely difficult.

The demographic and ethnological issues are not the subject of this communication. Suffice it to mention that for Greece, the Balkan wars resulted in a major social or economic upheaval. Their consequences were dramatic, both in terms of the geographic and demographic expansion: Greece almost doubled her territory and her population.

|  | **1907** | **1914** | **% increase** |
|---|---|---|---|
| Land in sq. km. | 65 029 | 118 784 | 82.66 |
| Population | 2 631 952 | 4 881 052 | 85.45 |

Even more important, the character of the country changed as, for the first time since it became independent, it included sizeable ethnic groups other than the predominant Greek-speaking Christian Orthodox population. Indeed, in certain areas the Greek-speaking Christian Orthodox communities were in a minority.

To assess the effect of the wars on everyday life in Greece I will rely on narrative sources (memoirs, letters and so on) due to the lack of any other primary documentation.

## Two wars

For the regions of the pre-1912 kingdom – the "ancient provinces" as they came to be called after the territorial expansion of the twentieth century – the socio-economic effect of the wars on the average civilian was not dramatic. The average Greek of the pre-1912 kingdom was neither better nor worse off immediately after the war than he was before. The long war period of the First World War, its aftermath and its dramatic domestic repercussions tend to influence our judgment and tend to lead us to believe that the Balkan wars, though successful for Greece, had a damaging effect on everyday life. The two wars of 1912 and 1913 were two distinct wars of relatively short duration. Besides, even though the male population remained mobilised for a little over 13 months (from September 1912 to December 1913) the periods of actual fighting on the various fronts and at sea barely covered seven months in all. The social disaffection caused by long periods of mobilisation and by protracted, exhausting and unfortunate campaigns lay in the future.

This is a general assessment. I will now examine in as much detail as the available facts permit, the effect of the wars:

- at the front, on the mobilised troops and the population of the occupied territories; and
- in the rear, on the population in rural areas and in the cities.

In 1912 the male population of Greece responded to the decree of general mobilisation on 19 September with mixed feelings of national pride and apprehension. Memories of the previous unfortunate campaign of 1897 had been kept alive, though it was not the young conscripts of 1912 but their fathers who had experienced that humiliating defeat. It has been estimated that over the entire period of 1912-13 a total of 282 000 men were called to the colours. The strain on the workforce of the country was considerable. For the needs of the second campaign in particular, human resources had been so diminished that even orphans and emigrants were called to serve, and men serving behind the lines, guarding government or bank buildings for instance, were sent to the front.

Responding to the initial call, even emigrants who had settled in the United States returned to serve their country. According to some accounts, 57 000 emigrants served in the armed forces (Andreades, 1928). Some of them never returned to the States; others returned after the war.

Although censorship was established and dissatisfaction was not publicly expressed during the period of the campaigns, it is safe to assume that the wars were too short for any anti-war movement or massive desertions to occur. Public opinion on the whole supported the "patriotic" cause and the only criticism of the government came from excessively nationalistic circles. Letters from privates and officers contained pre-dictable complaints about the state of the army and the hardships of the campaign, the weather and sanitary conditions, but no widespread anti-war or anti-national feeling was evident (see, for instance, Gardikas-Katsiadakis, 1998; Tricha, 1993).

The second war, against Bulgaria, was shorter but much more violent than the first. Friendly and enemy troops were much more widely dispersed along an ill-defined front. What is more, the Second Balkan War was fought in mid-summer. Excerpts from several diaries describe the nature of the attacks, their cruelty and the exhaustion of the fighting troops. Above all, accounts describe the scalding heat and the thirst of the soldiers, and the experience of an unexpected, lethal enemy – cholera. A few days before the signing of the armistice in Bucharest, half the troops in the units involved in the campaign had been infected.

The descriptions are dramatic. A young Greek – who had left his village in the Peloponnese for the United States at the age of eight together with his two elder brothers, and who later settled permanently in Athens to found the first dairy factory, EVGA – Vasilios Sourrapas, recorded in his diary:

> "We got up in the morning at 5. We saw many of our colleagues lying on the ground. They rolled and kicked their legs like frogs. They were carried away to a spot far from the camp under the supervision of a doctor and a nurse. Many of them died and often the nurses carried others who had been infected by the mortal and terrible disease, cholera. At 8 a.m. one of our destroyers approached and navy doctors came out to the camp to visit the patients and determine the nature of the disease and they diagnosed that it was cholera.

> [...]

> We walked all day in the Nigrita plain. We walked in the unbearable heat and dust. And we suffered from dehydration all day long. We had been exhausted by fatigue and by diarrhoea on account of the disease. Two died on the road and many stayed behind. The doctor who observed all this complained to the major that, on account of their fatigue and exhaustion, the men could not possibly follow, but the major said: I will go to Nigrita, even if only three men can follow me. The sound of artillery grew nearer and reached our ears, the earth shook, and we could see the burnt villages, which the withdrawing enemy was looting and burning. Finally at 8 p.m. we reached Nigrita, but, alas, smoking ruins was all we found. The smell of smoke and the sight of the town were horrible. Everything was gone. The

beautiful and elegant buildings had collapsed. We passed among ruins, we bivouacked outside the ruins. All we found were a few old men and women, who stayed in the open. The
place was extremely fertile, with several fruit trees, vineyards and others. Vineyards exist to
the left, where a battalion of the 21st captured the 19th Bulgarian regiment and slaughtered
most of them. Only 7 000 they handed over to the Cross. They were delivered to the ships."
(Tricha, 1993, p. 187)

The cruelty of the war had succeeded in transforming a peace-loving and enterprising
civilian into a detached observer of atrocities. The perpetration of atrocities was a
distinctive feature of the two wars. The ill feelings and suspicion that had been bred
during decades of inter-communal strife in the contested areas must be attributed to
the exclusive character of the nation-building process that had emerged in the Balkans
in the nineteenth century. In fact, Vasilis Gounaris has convincingly argued that these
rivalries predated the appearance of ethnic differentiation in the region, originating
in most cases in intra-communal partisan disputes. And he quoted from a dispatch
written in 1904 by the Greek Consul General at Thessaloníki, Lambros Koromilas:
"But as usually happens in Macedonia, the first to appear in the villages is the rivalry
of interest – and then it is necessarily transformed into national rivalry" (Gounaris,
1993, pp. 200-1).

In the areas contested by several ethnic groups the intensification of this process had
led to outbursts of violence in the past. The practice was repeated when the liberating armies of the Balkan neighbours of the Ottoman Empire expelled the Turkish
authorities. To a degree, newly established local and military authorities managed to
maintain order until civil authorities were set up in the liberated areas. A soldier noted
in his diary at Elassona at the beginning of the war:

"The Turkish shops had been opened by the soldiers and some looting occurred, not so
much by the army, as by local people, who did this as an act of revenge against the Turks."
(Tricha, 1993, p. 42)

Despite mutual suspicion, there were no accounts of widespread ethnic violence
during the first campaign.

"I am sick and in the afternoon I obtain permission to go to the village. The inhabitants are
Bulgarian-speaking and eventually after many efforts I manage to buy two geese from a
villager." (ibid., p. 49)

During the Second Balkan War, however, ethnic violence assumed uncontrollable
proportions. The destruction of towns and bridges as troops withdrew was common
practice, condoned and often encouraged by military leaders, while there were cases
where regular troops participated in sheer acts of violence against inhabitants assumed
to be guerrillas or informants. The Commander of the Greek Army, King Constantine
himself, did not escape the prevailing spirit of cruelty. For him the war against Bulgaria was a war of annihilation, and he cabled to the government *"delenda est Bulgaria"*. This was the very same person who, at the beginning of the first war, had
whipped a Greek-speaking civilian in public for carrying weapons against the orders
of the authorities, in the newly occupied town of Servia (ibid., p. 47).

This is the darkest picture of the war and it went hand-in-hand with the destruction of infrastructure resorted to by retreating armies and with the continual movement of refugees to safety behind the shifting temporary borders. There are familiar images of distressed refugees on the road with their few belongings, with pictures of atrocities and widespread destruction in the war zone

## New territories

The acquisition of new territories imposed a fresh strain on Greece, since she had not yet fully incorporated into her social and legal framework the territories acquired in 1864 and 1881, the Ionian Islands and Thessaly. A number of important discrepancies in social and legal status between the old territories and the later acquisitions, the most important being the issue of land ownership, had not been settled in 1912. Indeed, the land question was aggravated by the acquisition of lands in Macedonia and Epirus. The problems were similar but not identical. In Macedonia, large underpopulated expanses lay uncultivated, while their tenants lived in small villages in the hills nearby. In these lands, the damage to lives, property and infrastructure was compounded by a large wave of emigration.

In the newly acquired areas, the drive for comprehensive reform that had marked the period after 1910 in the "ancient provinces" of Greece found a vast field of implementation, since the state undertook to integrate the new areas as rapidly as possible. The experience of Thessaly proved invaluable. With the expertise acquired there, the state adopted measures to improve conditions and to transform the economy and administration of the new lands.

Immediately after the conquest, in early November 1912, as soon as administrative authorities had been established in the major cities, teams of financial and administrative experts were sent out from Athens to review local conditions and the existing fiscal and legal status, and to propose measures for the assimilation of the new provinces (Demakopoulos, 1993). These missions produced a number of excellent surveys, published in 1914. Besides, the government passed laws prohibiting the transfer of property and it planned a comprehensive land-reform programme; this, however, was deferred on account of the First World War (Petmezas, 1993, pp. 210-14). The towns too suffered the consequences of the wars. Not only were some of them totally destroyed, but the larger ones were required to receive a wave of distressed refugees. To meet their needs, in June 1914, the government formed a new ministry, the Ministry of Communication, whose main task was to commission new town-planning projects.

The new "motherland" had a number of features with which the old administration and its citizens were unfamiliar. The old multinational state, where communities were identified by and administered according to their religious affiliation, was replaced by a "modern" national state, which was governed centrally and which intended to homogenise its population. A 1914 law (350/1914) for the "settlement of refugee fellow nationals in Macedonia and elsewhere" inaugurated a new system of corporate management of the land owned by the members of the community, laying the foundations for further legislation in the future. However, nowhere was this plan of homogenisation more pronounced than in the domain of town planning. Local authorities in larger cities that received waves of refugees from lands acquired by the other Balkan states commissioned foreign architects to draw new town plans. A number of medium- and smaller-sized towns, such as Serres, Kilkis, Amyntaio (Sorovitz) and Doxato, destroyed during the Second Balkan War, were among the first to benefit from the new wave of town planning (Karadimou-Gerolymbou, 1993).

The picture in the occupied islands was different. There, uncertainty was not so prominent and prevailing sentiments were different. Their Greek-speaking inhabitants rejoiced at the defeat and departure of the Turks and public jubilation was unanimous. Their joy was only offset by a tremendous rise in the price of commodities. An inhabitant of Chios, Stefanos Kynigos, wrote to his brother in the United States:

> "Don't ask what times we are going through. On the one hand we see the Greeks and on the other a rise in prices beyond all imagination. The double loaf of bread we buy at 18 metalikia, all goods, gas at 28 grossia the tin container. This month we have no money to go by."

Nine days later, their mother wrote:

> "Here, my dear George, we have a terrible rise in prices. Today bread costs 24 metalikia. As for other goods, it's best not to ask."

Prices dropped slightly after Christmas, but everyday life and business could not return to normal as long as the war lasted. On 24 February she wrote again:

> "Business began a little, but because prices are high it cannot return to its normal pace .... We hope that, when peace is signed and things improve, prices will fall."

Their main concern was to return to normal everyday life, to avoid conscription. When the second war began, Mother Kynigos, whose patriotism could not be questioned, wrote to her son:

> "And you will be taken into the army now, and I am distressed beyond words, my dear George ... The day before yesterday Stefanos went to the Governorship and found Mr George Bitsas, who used to serve at the Consulate, and asked him if there was a way to relieve you and he answered that because there is a war on it is very difficult. You must have great influence. The only thing, he said, that can be done is, when you present yourself and while you are serving, we can file a report, in which case something can be done." (Tricha, 1993, pp. 251-65)

In the case of the rural population of the "ancient provinces", there are no available figures to illustrate the effect of the Balkan wars. However, accounts in descriptive sources provide some indications. The mobilisation and the successive drafting of men in the rear for the needs of the campaigns deprived the land of manpower, while the requisition of animals and vehicles were an additional strain on the remaining population. The cost of the wars in human lives was not very high, compared to similar figures for the Bulgarian and the Serbian armies. The figures are in the following table:

|  | Soldiers | Officers | Total |
|---|---|---|---|
| Dead | 7 428 | 304 | 7 732 |
| Wounded | 42 191 | 628 | 42 819 |

(Source: Andreades, 1928)

The rise in prices that struck the occupied provinces did not seem to affect everyday life in the "ancient" Greek provinces as dramatically as it affected the war zone. Unlike the cases of Bulgaria and Romania, the drachma was kept at par, thanks to the fiscal reform legislation of 1910, the provisional domestic and foreign loans contracted through the mediation of the National Bank of Greece, and the overall stability of the economy. In fact, bank deposits increased during the war, the gold reserves of the National Bank increased also, and foreign commerce and public revenues remained stable (Andreades, 1928, p. 11).

## Economic and social conditions

Andreades attributes the stability of the economy, among other reasons, to a number of social factors: the spectacular number of Greek emigrants to the United States, who returned for the war, and the widespread financial assistance of Greeks all over the world, the wave of donations, and the willingness of the women peasants to substitute for the men missing in the war and thus sustain agricultural production (ibid., p. 12).

No figures are available to measure the immediate impact of the war on agricultural productivity, because the last pre-war survey was conducted in 1911 and the next survey was published in 1929. However, as the population had nearly doubled, while productivity in the war zone decreased, the overall short-term effect of the wars on Greece's balance of trade was negative, as shown in the following table:

| Year | Imports | Exports |
|---|---|---|
| 1911 | 173 510 | 140 902 |
| 1912 | 157 653 | 149 162 |
| 1914 | 319 000 | 179 000 |
| % increase, 1912-14 | 102.34 | 20 |

(Source: Andreades, 1928)

The effect of the wars on the urban centres of the "ancient provinces" was relatively mild. Usually wars result in a wave of domestic migration to urban centres, for a number of reasons (Kalitsounakis, 1928, p. 216). The population of the cities of "ancient Greece" increased. The first available post-war census, that of 1918, includes the migration of the entire First World War period. The population figures for the Athens-Piraeus conurbation provide a vague picture:

1907: 240 000
1918: 310 000

A natural consequence of the population increase was a marked shortage in housing. This had become a menacing problem in 1916, so that it called for legislation imposing a moratorium on rents. As early as 1912, however, urgent legislation had prevented the expulsion of tenants (Kalitsounakis, 1928, p. 216).

A distinctive feature of the war was the surge of patriotism that swept the country and that was most clearly articulated by members of the urban classes. For the female population of the upper-class families of Athens, the war offered an opportunity to express their patriotism and to socialise by serving as nurses in the campaign hospitals.

As Aspasia Mavromichali noted in her diary:

"I wanted to be useful at this hour and didn't think of myself at all … As soon as we arrived in Athens we enrolled, my sister and I in the Blue Cross, a League organised by Mr Alivizatos the Director of the Polykliniki and presided over by Princess Helen. Mother was Vice President. We were sent to a small outdoor operation unit … and at the same time we began lessons and practice. Oh, I was so exhausted that first day, to somewhat get used to the environment. The picture of calamity, of misfortune, of squalor was drawn in the most vivid colours. The patients who arrived, all of the lower classes, filthy as they are and in rags, emitted such a smell that caused revulsion."

When inspecting other outdoor hospitals with the princess, she wrote in her diary:

"The situation was horrible. They were all makeshift hospitals without enough beds, without nurses, with nothing. We heard nothing but moans, sighs and weeping. No one ran to help these wretched people … I asked permission to go up to the Princesses' room to freshen myself up a little. I washed myself with plenty of cold water and with renewed strength I ran down and we began to move the injured to the carriages. By that time several ladies from Larissa had arrived, most of them all powdered up and dressed in their Sunday clothes. They looked at us with amazement, as if we had fallen from Saturn."

One of them, the indefatigable Anna Papadopoulou, became a national heroine. Not all the ladies, however, had her stamina to endure stress:

"At a station we heard that the Princess, who had a heart condition, had suffered a crisis due to hard work and that Mr Alivizatos had made his utmost to relieve her. The train travelled at top speed, when in the absolute silence of the night we heard the alarm signal. Suddenly the train came to a standstill. We all rushed out … What had happened? Mrs Katsara had suffered a severe nervous breakdown and the doctor had to be summoned urgently." (Tricha, 1993, pp. 31-6)

# The impact of the war

As the news of the first victories of the Greek forces reached Athens, the population was overtaken by a wave of national euphoria that permeated everyday life in Athens. Newspapers increased their circulation and produced extra issues when extraordinary events, such as the naval battle of Limnos, occurred. Paper, printers and war correspondents were in short supply. The thirst of readers for thrilling stories was quenched by the appearance of a large number of popular publications with patriotic themes and titles like *The Turk-eaters of 1912*, *Our dolphins of 1912* or *The giant-fighters of Janina* (Demakopolous, 1993, p. 209n).

The official hierarchy attended formal religious victory celebrations. The populace expressed their excitement by attending a wave of popular theatre productions, vaudeville, comedies and dramas to celebrate the victories of the army. The popularity of these productions was such that even "serious" theatres were obliged to follow the trend in order to survive (Delveroudi, 1993, pp. 377-8).

Attempting to assess the impact of the war on the life of the ordinary citizen is not an easy task, both because comprehensive research on the matter is lacking and because the impact of the Balkan wars is over-run by the events that followed – mobilisation, domestic political crisis, the 1917-22 war years and the social disaster of the uprooting and resettlement of one and a half million refugees from Asia Minor.

Instead, I will borrow the words of a prominent liberal Greek author, George Drosinis, who describes in his memoirs the fate of a private secondary technical school he had been instrumental in setting up shortly before the Balkan wars in a large plot in Ambelokipi, then a green suburb underneath the Lykabettus hill, with a well-kept garden that he cherished:

> "In the spring of 1913 the garden had reached its heyday. Whoever came to the little house left with his arms full of roses and jasmines and honeysuckles, and friends picked its flowers to weave garlands for 1 May.
>
> But, first with the Balkan Wars, then with the European War and finally with the unfortunate Asia Minor campaign, the School, the garden, the Little House and all passed from requisition to requisition. In the two large rooms of the House the School's instruments and pictures were stored and I was left with only just a corner in the small room for my bed, so that I may still spend the occasional night there.
>
> No companions any longer. My presence at the school was useless, a fact that only gave me cause for sorrow – only to see the manner in which other people treated the items I had collected and combined so nicely. They lay broken, torn, scattered in the surrounding fields, like bones of dead animals; I stepped on them as I went to the School and I hardly recognised them. The garden existed no longer; only the trees remained, since they were tougher. The rest of the vegetation had been destroyed. ... What had survived human looting had been eaten or trodden upon by horses and carts that came and went unhindered.
>
> The poor School suffered so many transformations. Barracks for a thousand soldiers, warehouse for the clothing of conscripts, prison house for officers and, eventually, an Asylum for War victims, to which I gave the name "Shelter of the Motherland". ...With

the "Shelter of the Motherland" both the look of the School and the condition of the garden changed greatly. We began to cultivate the garden again with the help of some willing inmates. Although I could no longer settle myself comfortably in the little house, the hours I spent there were pleasant, so that I even stayed there overnight." (Drosinis, 1982, pp. 209-11)

The disruption of everyday life in the rear during the Balkan wars was indeed minimal. In 1914, after two successful wars, three advantageous peace treaties and the warm welcome home for the demobilised men, society faced the future with optimism, believing not only that recovery was at hand, but also that the enlarged state promised new opportunities. It was a period of euphoria, when politicians shared with society a belief that peace was necessary for Greece to "recover" from the war effort (a 500 million French francs loan was signed in Paris for the purpose) and make the most of its increased resources – and that this peace was possible. The "happy 1914", however, was nothing but a short spell of eight months between demobilisation and the outbreak of the Great War.

The year 1914 was also the 50th anniversary of the first major territorial enlargement of Greece, the acquisition of the Ionian Islands. The conference held to mark the occasion concentrated on issues related to the development of the region, and the post-Balkan wars spirit of euphoria imbued its proceedings. Things didn't work out as intended. The sequel to the story of Drosinis' technical school is instructive. It reopened in 1930 for a brief spell, but it did not fully recover until the early 1950s thanks to funds from the Marshall Plan and the overall post-war boom of the Greek economy (Belia, 1999, p. 236).

# Bibliography

Andreades, A., "Les finances publiques" in *Histoire économique et sociale de la guerre mondiale*, Paris, 1928, p. 11.

Belia, Eleni D., *Society for the Diffusion of Useful Books: A hundred-year course, 1899-1999*, Athens, 1999 [in Greek].

Delveroudi, Eliza-Anna, "Theatre" in *History of 20th-century Greece: the beginnings, 1900-1922*, ed. Christos Chadziiosif, volume Iii, pp. 377-8 [in Greek].

Demakopoulos, Georgios D., "The administrative organization of the occupied territories (1912-1914): A general overview" in *Greece during the Balkan wars, 1910-1914*, Athens, 1993.

Drosinis, G., *Loose pages of my life*, Vol. II, Athens, 1982 [in Greek].

Gardikas-Katsiadakis, Helen (ed.), *Leonidas Paraskevopoulos, Balkan wars (1912-1913): Letters to his wife Koula*, Athens, 1998.

Gounaris, Vasilis C., "Ethnic groups and party factions in Macedonia during the Balkan wars" in *Greece during the Balkan wars, 1910-1914*, Athens, 1993, pp. 200-1.

Kalitsounakis, D., "Législation ouvrière et sociale grecque pendant et après la guerre" in *Histoire économique et sociale de la guerre mondiale*, Paris, 1928, p. 216.

Karadimou-Gerolymbou, Aleka, "Towns and town planning" in *History of 20th-century Greece: The beginnings, 1900-1922*, ed. Christos Chadziiosif, Athens, 1993, Vol. Ii, pp. 242-6 [in Greek].

Pallis, A. A., "Les effets de la guerre sur la population de la Grèce" in *Histoire économique et sociale de la guerre mondiale*, Paris, 1928, p. 131.

Petmezas, Sokratis D., "Agrarian economy" in *History of 20th-century Greece: The beginnings, 1900-1922*, ed. Christos Chadziiosif, Athens, 1993, Vol. II, p. 82 [in Greek].

Tricha, Lydia (ed.), *Diaries and letters from the Front: Balkan wars, 1912-1913*, Athens, 1993.

# Chapter 9
# The Balkan wars: Russian military intelligence assessments and forecasts – Variants of old thinking in producing a new picture

*Arutyun Ulunyan*

In the run up to the First World War, Europe witnessed serious military and political conflicts which came to be known as the Balkan wars. They have been considered the catalyst that set off international confrontation and demonstrated the explosive nature of the Balkan region. N. M. Butler, acting director of the Carnegie Endowment for International Peace, wrote in February 1914 in the preface to the *Report of the International Commission to Inquire into Causes and Conduct of the Balkan Wars*: "The circumstances which attended the Balkan wars of 1912 and 1913 were of such character as to fix on them the attention of the civilized world" (Carnegie Report, 1914, p. iii). On the eve of these events, the situation on the peninsula attracted the persistent attention of different states outside the region, especially the Great Powers. Russia played an important role in this, due to her historical links with the Balkans and active involvement in the affairs of this region.

The Russian imperial bureaucracy being divided into two blocks, civil and military, attempted to influence the decision-making process concerning the Balkans and played an active role in either constructing political assessments of the situation or in making analytical forecasts of possible developments in the Balkans. By the early twentieth century, Russian military intelligence had consolidated its position in the information system by providing governmental structures with sensitive and important data. The officially separated structure of the military attachés represented an integral part of the whole intelligence service and was subordinated to the General Staff. According to their status and functional position, they fulfilled their missions abroad and were assigned to the foreign governments. They were responsible for collecting military and political information and for carrying out covert intelligence missions abroad (see Sergeyev and Ulunyan, 1999).

Throughout 1911, representatives of Russian military intelligence in the Balkan states were working on several levels determined by peculiarities and characteristic features of the countries in which they were posted. Thus, particularly in Romania, the military reforms and technical equipment of the national army, in particular, attracted the interest of the Russian attaché there. In Bulgaria the military attaché had to pay special attention to "political relations between Bulgaria and Turkey including her relations with Austro-Hungary" and to collect information "both on Turkey's military activity along the Bulgarian border and in the Bosporus in connection with the Turkish-Italian war". The military attaché in Serbia was ordered to get information and to carry out analytical research so as to clarify the "political attitude towards Turkey and Austro-Hungary because of the latter's activity in Bosnia and Herzegovina". A military attaché's activity in Montenegro included (as defined by the Main Directorate of the General Staff) monitoring the "political situation in connection with the Albanian insurrection and Austro-Hungarian aggressive plans", looking after the reorganisation process of the Montenegran army and monitoring the consumption of financial subsidies provided by the Russian government to Montenegro. A Russian military attaché in Greece was ordered to observe the situation in the Greek army and to follow the activities of foreign instructors assigned to the Greek armed forces. In Turkey, the military attaché focused on the Turkish attitude towards the insurrection in Albania and military preparations carried out by the Turkish authorities in the European part of the Empire and Italian-Turkish relations. (Russian State Military History Archive, RSMHA *F* 2000, In. I, File 7335) The allegedly-signed Romanian-Turkish convention was a key question which attracted the attention of Russian military agents in all Balkan countries since it was considered harmful in St Petersburg to have such a military alliance.

One of the most important problems faced by the Russian attaché in the Balkans was the intended railway construction, known as the Danubian-Adriatic project, and similar plans in the Asian regions of the Ottoman Empire. Due to contradictions between Belgrade, which supported a southern direction for the "Danubian project" and St Petersburg, which was keen that the railway line should take a northern direction, the Russian military's general assessments fell within the sphere of strategic intentions as they were defined on the basis of analytical proposals made by the Russian military attaché in the Balkans. Thus it was considered that the planned railway would "connect the Slav nations of the Balkan peninsula and the Slav nations with Russia" and this was to be a

> "serious political preparation for a joint solution of the strategic goals in the Balkans by these states. If policy has ever put before our strategy a goal 'to prevent the German world's invasion of the Balkan peninsula', particularly the capture by them [the Germans] of Thessalonica and Constantinople, this makes it easier to fulfill this mission with the existed 'all-Slavonic' railroad, going from the Black Sea to Adriatic Bulgaria, Serbia, the part of Turkey with the Serbian population and Montenegro." (RSMHA *F* 2000, In. I, File 7337)

As far as the second project was concerned, it was considered that any construction of the railroad in the Asian regions of the Ottoman Empire could be dangerous for Russia from a strategic point of view. Therefore, all political and military developments in the Balkan region were central to the Russian intelligence attention.

Serious momentum for analytical calculations could be provided by political events in the states situated in the region. The governmental changes in Romania in early January 1911 added new features to Russian assessments. Colonel M. Marchenko, who served as Russian military attaché in Vienna, considered that, following the failure of the liberal cabinet headed by Bratiano, the situation in Romania had changed because the new prime minister, Carp, was "a stubborn pro-German statesman with undisguised hostile feelings toward Russia and the Slavs" (RSMHA *F* 2000, In. I, File 3093).

Similar interests and concerns were expressed with regard to the situation in Montenegro and events on its borders, where the Albanian national liberation movement was more intense. Colonel N. Potapov, who was military attaché in Montenegro, stated in his special report to the General Staff that the Montenegrin ruler Prince Nicola

> "himself wants war against Turkey to 'save face' with the Albanians with whom the prince and his rather imprudent advisers so thoughtlessly instigated an imbalanced struggle against the Turks. There are reasons to believe that the Montenegrins, and not the Turks, are trying to find pretexts for waging war". (Mezhdunarodnye otnosheniya, MO, p. 117)

The so-called Austrian and Turkish factors in the Balkan situation were of interest to the Russian military attachés in the Balkans and incited them to obtain firm information on the possible plans of both empires. In a secret publication called "Collection of materials of the Main Directorate of the General Staff" which came out in the summer of 1911, the conclusion was drawn that Austria-Hungary was taking a break, not to resolve its finance problems, but rather to strengthen its army in the interests of any future aggression (June 1911, p. 16). Information received by the Russian military intelligence through different channels led some analytical experts in the regional military headquarters to the conclusion that the measures undertaken by the Austro-Hungarian authorities were not aimed "directly against Russia" (RSMHA *F* 1859, In. 6, File 139). As far as the Turkish plans were concerned, Russian military intelligence was taking them very seriously. The Russian military attaché in Sofia, Colonel G. Romanovsky, obtained confidential information in mid-1911 from the Bulgarian King Ferdinand who had actually made his point of view known by referring to an allegedly unstable situation in the Balkans. His view consisted of two inter-related arguments: one was based on Turkish preparations for war in the Black Sea; and the other based on his predictions of a possible war in the Balkans in the near future (RSMHA *F* 2000, In. 1, File 3067).

Thus, the so-called Turkish threat was taken more seriously by the Russian military intelligence than that of Austria-Hungary. Permanent rivalry between the two empires on a wide range of questions, including the problem of the Straits, Balkan politics, Caucasian and even Central Asian regions, influenced the logic and content of the analytical approaches adopted by Russian intelligence to the problem. It was demonstrated in dispatches by the military attaché in the Ottoman Empire, General-Major I. Kholmsen. In his special, highly confidential report addressed to the Chief of the General Staff he wrote about: 1. the Turkish plans to capture the Caucasus and Northern Persia; and 2. the Turkish desire to receive support from the Triple Alliance (RSMHA *F* 2000, In. 1, File 3819).

The Italian-Turkish war was unleashed on 16 September 1911 and represented a trial run for a possible conflict in the Balkans when one of the Great European Powers would plan to change the whole geopolitical map of the region. In late September 1911, some of the Russian military attachés presented their analysis of possible future developments in the Balkans. They noted several serious consequences of Turkish defeat in the war with Italy. They expected: 1. the build-up of the anti-Turkish coalition composed of small Balkan states; 2. attempts on the part of the Ottoman Empire to achieve results as a compensation in the Balkans for the failure in the war with Italy; 3. the intention of the Young Turks to keep power in their hands by using an attack on Greece and resolving the Crete question in Turkey's favour (RSMHA *F* 2000, In. 1, File 7382). During the Italian-Turkish war, according to the forecasts of the Russian military intelligence representatives in the Balkans, the

> "nervous atmosphere produced by the unsuccessful war on the Ottoman Empire is always fraught with new revolution which is capable of giving a signal for an unorganised movement against Turkey on the part of its neighbours in the Balkan peninsula and will inevitably lead to partition of the Turkish possessions in Europe." (RSMHA *F* 2000, In. 1, File 7382)

The autumn of 1911 became a critical period in the political history of the Balkans. The secret Bulgaro-Serbian negotiations, which were considered an important step towards concluding a secret military agreement, raised the very sensitive issue of the Russian reaction to an intra-Balkan agreement of that kind. The Russian military attaché in Bulgaria, Colonel G. Romanovsky, gave a detailed analysis of possible developments in the region and submitted several recommendations to his chiefs. He singled out the Bulgarian reluctance to hand over Silistra and Balchik with a "predominantly Bulgarian population" to Romania as a compensation in case of a Bulgarian enlargement in Macedonia. Bearing this in mind, Romanovsky had come to the conclusion that:

> "Under these circumstances our support to the Romanian aspirations could badly influence our prestige and could even result in the resignation of the current [Bulgarian] cabinet. The latter would seriously and unequivocally damage our interests here. The current government is composed of the parties which are the strongest and most loyal to Russia. Should the cabinet resign, it would be inevitably replaced by the Stombolists who would be joined by a group of adventurists and swindlers. Bearing in mind that the Bulgarian political situation is entering a new phase, this turn of events is not beneficial to us". (RSMHA *F* 2000, In. 1, File 3002)

Apart from the existing Bulgarian-Romanian contradictions, the military attaché predicted a deterioration of Bulgarian-Greek relations leading to both states wishing to obtain Thessalonica. To preserve either Bulgarian-Serbian relations or Russian influence in Bulgaria, and to promote the alliance between Greece and Serbia, it was considered prudent for Russia to refrain from getting involved in any conflict, either between Sofia and Bucharest or between Sofia and Athens.

The formation of a military alliance in the Balkans, where small states had regarded the Ottoman Empire as their common enemy, touched other powers which had their own interests in the region and bordered on it. It was the Austro-Hungarian Empire which traditionally played an active role in the Balkans trying to dominate the most sensitive sectors in it. Therefore the Russian military attaché in the Dual Monarchy, Colonel M. Zankevich, predicted in his secret report to his chiefs that Vienna's primary goal in the Balkans included the Austrian occupation of Novobazar Sanjak to pave the way to Serbia and Thessalonica. This turn of events, according to the military attaché's calculations, should have resulted in certain consequences, such as a war against Turkey, Serbia, Montenegro and against Russia who stood behind Belgrade and Podgoritsa (RSMHA *F* 1859, In. 6, File 139).

After having signed a series of secret agreements between Bulgaria, Greece, Serbia and Montenegro during the winter and spring of 1912 the so-called small Balkan countries (for the first time in history) formed an alliance on strong anti-Ottoman grounds but on very vulnerable and shaky principles. By the late summer and early autumn of 1912, Russian military intelligence activity in Bulgaria had been intensified. Regional policy in Sofia was considered the beacon of the future events and possible changes. Russian military intelligence officers noted the attempts of the "reasonable government" which made serious efforts to keep the country "from a formal declaration of war on Turkey" (RSMHA *F* 2000, In. 1, 7392). However, all those steps seemed to be useless since even the Russian intelligence obtained reliable information about the Bulgarian decision to take its chance with "the critical situation in Turkey and to start military activities against the Ottoman Empire together with the Serbs and Greeks in the second half of September [1912]" (RSMHA *F* 2000, In. 1, File 2987). Expectations of serious military conflict in the Balkans played an important role in the analytical forecasts made by the Russian military intelligence officers who were working in the region and influenced their assessments of the real situation. Thus, commenting on the unofficial offer of the German ambassador in Turkey to his Russian counterpart, and dealing with possible Austro-Hungarian occupation of Belgrade and Russian capture of Varna in order to prevent future war in the Balkans, the Russian military attaché in Greece, Colonel P. Gudim-Levkovich, wrote to his superiors that he was afraid "we could be pushed by our current policy into such a path" (RSMHA *F* 2000, In. 1, File 2994).

Despite all the information obtained, from open sources and through confidential channels, the Russian military intelligence could not give an answer to two principal questions until the middle of September 1912. The first question was who would start military activities and what would be the scheme of military co-ordination between the Balkan allies. The second question was the date of a possible war. The first and most important step on this road had been made by the military attaché in Montenegro, Colonel N. Potapov. On 15 September 1912, he sent to the headquarters of military intelligence a secret message which contained highly sensitive information and gave answers to both questions. According to Potapov, the situation would develop as follows:

> "First, military activities against Turkey should be started by the Allies simultaneously within five days of the ratification of the agreement; secondly, both sides [Serbia and Montenegro] should come together with a maximum concentration of their military potential; third, the allies' detachments would render support to one another on the border where military actions extend along the Novobazar Sandjak and across it, including Northern Albania and the Scutari region in which Montenegro is interested; fourth, neither side [Serbia and Montenegro] has a right to sign a peace agreement without the concession of the others; and fifth, in case of an Austrian intrusion into Sandjak, both sides are to send their forces to fight it." (RSMHA *F* 2000, In. 1, File 2989)

According to Russian intelligence the onset of the war was expected in the near future by officers residing in all the Balkan states except Turkey and a precise date for commencement of hostilities was even set for 1 October 1912. However, obvious contradictions existed between the information provided, on the one hand, by Russian military intelligence officers in Bulgaria, Montenegro, Serbia and Greece, and, on the other hand, by Russian military attachés in Turkey which prevented intelligence chiefs from forming a general picture of a possible turn of events. The Montenegrin declaration of war against Turkey on 9 October 1912, and the involvement of other small Balkan countries in military activity only nine days later, took St Petersburg by surprise. The war plans of the Balkan allies and possible territorial acquisitions became the central problem of Russian military intelligence. Constantinople and Adrianople were named among possible Bulgarian territorial demands (RSMHA *F* 2000, In. 1, File 7400). This question raised the interest of both Russian military and civil experts and concerned long-standing Russian plans in the Straits and Constantinople itself. The Military Minister, V.A. Sukhomlinov, expressed serious concerns about the possible reaction of Bulgaria and some of its allies to any Russian resistance in this area. The minister stated that, in the case of a negative Russian attitude towards Bulgarian aspirations,

> "the Balkan Slavic states will represent a special element unfavourably disposed towards us and thus we can hardly rely on them as allies in case of military confrontation with Germany and Austro-Hungary." (RSMHA *F* 2000, In. 1, File 3002)

The military activities of the Balkan coalition lasted until December 1912 and demonstrated both the strength of the Allies and their dependence on the Great Powers. According to military assessments carried out by the Russian General Staff, the Turkish defeat in Europe could change the balance of power in the Asian and Caucasian region but not in Russia's favour. Moreover, it was noted that if Constantinople and the Straits were to come under Bulgarian control, this would be detrimental to Russian strategic and political interests. It was considered in Russia that the conclusion of the ceasefire on 20 November 1912 could pave the way to a full-scale peace agreement.

Meanwhile, the situation in the Balkan countries strongly influenced their position after the peace treaty was signed. This fact was the focus of attention of Russian military intelligence in the region. As far as Bulgaria was concerned, the military attaché in Sofia had come to the conclusion that, despite the tsar Ferdinand's favourable attitude towards the "party of war", his country was not ready to carry out long-term military activity and was seriously dependent on foreign financial and food aid should the war continue (RSMHA *F* 2000, In. 1, File 2997). His colleague in Serbia also pointed out that in that country there were ardent followers of decisive policy toward Turkey and supporters of the Bulgarian move to Adrianopol and Chataldja (ibid.). All those observations and assessments made by the representatives of Russian military intelligence also included new issues which had not escaped their attention. Thus, by the end of 1912, a few military attachés were warning the General Staff of an imminent conflict between the Balkan countries. Relations between Bulgaria and Romania had deteriorated due to the rivalry between both Balkan states in their quest for domination in the peninsula. The Russian intelligence officer in Romania, Colonel

E. Iskritsky, analysed the situation in the region and wrote, in his reports to the Main Directorate, that

> "one of the basic principles of the Romanian foreign policy, following its independence in 1878, is to preserve the existing balance between Romania and Bulgaria, i.e. [its] desire to prevent any strengthening of the latter without simultaneous Romanian strengthening." (RSMHA F 2000, In. 1, File 2988)

Thus, as Iskritsky had foreseen, should the strong powers such as Russia, Austro-Hungary and Bulgaria increase their presence around Romania, the latter might feel her weakness and risk an imminent threat on their part.

While the London conference of ambassadors, which lasted from December 1912 until early January 1913, was dwelling on a peace agreement between the belligerent sides of the Balkan wars, any worsening of the situation in the peninsula was fraught with the danger of such an agreement failing. Information conveyed by Russian military intelligence to the military leadership of the country was causing the latter to fear a possible conflict in the Balkans. Bulgaria and Romania were listed among the primary instigators of any future regional skirmishes. In the meantime, there was a heightened political struggle in Turkey between the followers of the Young Turks' organisation *Ittihad ve taraki* on the one side, and supporters of *Hürriyet ve ittilaf*, which came to power on 9 July 1912, on the other. The decision of the Turkish government to agree to the demands of the Great Powers to hand over Adrianople to Bulgaria was considered by the Young Turks as betrayal on the part of the existing regime. On 10 January 1913, the leaders of *Ittihad ve taraki* carried out a coup d'état, displacing the former government and, after denunciation of the earlier agreements, resumed war.

Russian military attachés in the region continued their enquiries with the purpose of finding possible directions which the Balkan events could take. Initial information on a possible intra-allies conflict in the Balkans, particularly between Bulgaria and Serbia, came from Colonel F. Bulganin who was stationed in Rome. At the end of March 1913, he wrote to his chiefs, in a highly confidential message sent urgently to St Petersburg, that "there was a secret agreement between Serbia and Montenegro against Bulgaria" (RSMHA F 2000, In. 1, File 7400). Meanwhile, the dispute between Romania and Bulgaria, which was analysed in previous dispatches by a few Russian intelligence officers, was considered a link in a long chain of contradictions existing in the Balkans. Therefore, another conflict was foreseen, after the above-mentioned one, involving Bulgaria and Greece fighting to gain the upper hand over Thessaloníki (RSMHA F 2000, In. 1, File 3002).

As the work on the provisions of a peace treaty between the Balkan alliance and the Ottoman Empire was coming to its final stages, the relations between Bulgaria, on the one hand, and Serbia and Greece, on the other, were deteriorating. According to the London peace agreement signed on 17 May 1913, there were serious changes taking place in the Balkan peninsula. Albania had claimed its independence and Crete was reunited with Greece. All the Balkan possessions of the Ottoman Empire were added to the territories of the members of the Balkan Union except for a small part of Eastern

Thrace and Constantinople. Bulgaria, Greece and Serbia obtained different parts of Macedonia and Thrace. The distribution of those territories among the three allies was assessed differently in Athens, Belgrade and Sofia, but all of them were united in their dissatisfaction with the scale of the new acquisitions. Moreover, Romania, which had not taken part in the war, felt it necessary to gain Dobrudja as compensation for its neutrality.

The Russian military attaché in Bulgaria, Colonel G. Romanovsky, whilst observing the possible consequences of common animosity between the former allies, endeavoured to establish recommendations on how to settle the disputes between them. His plan, which was set forth in the dispatch addressed to the Staff, favoured the idea of applying pressure on Serbia in order to persuade Belgrade to refrain from war plans. Simultaneous disbandment of the Serbian and Bulgarian armies, according to the military attaché's explanations, should have served to that effect (RSMHA *F* 2000, In. 1, File 7407). A completely opposite point of view on the situation was put forward by Romanovsky's colleague in Serbia, Colonel Artamonov. In his coded cable sent to St Petersburg, the Russian military attaché mentioned the steadfast Bulgarian position on the territorial question, which was considered by this intelligence officer as conflicting with Russian Imperial interests (ibid.).

Meanwhile, on 1 June 1913, Greece and Serbia signed a secret agreement against Bulgaria and fifteen days later, Bulgarian troops attacked Greek and Serbian positions. It became evident to all foreign and local observers that Bulgaria was failing to wage war on two or even three fronts, that is, against its former Balkan allies as well as Romania and Turkey. Colonel V. Artamonov in Belgrade shared his assessments with his chiefs in St Petersburg and believed it possible that, after the defeat of Bulgaria and the re-establishing of the balance of power in the Balkans, the Balkan Union (with active Romanian participation) would be resumed (RSMHA *F* 2000, In. 1, File 3151). However, these utopian assessments seriously contradicted the evaluations made by the military attaché in Greece, Colonel P. Gudim-Levkovich, who resorted to ethnic and confessional arguments in an attempt to persuade his chiefs that there was a possible danger of a Bulgarian defeat due to, as he thought, the victory of the "non-Slavic coalition" where Serbia did not play a leading role and which was assessed in Greece as "the bankruptcy of the Russian policy" (ibid.).

The Bucharest peace agreement signed by Bulgaria with Greece, Romania, Serbia and Montenegro on 28 July 1913 led to serious territorial changes in the Balkans, which continued after the conclusion of the peace treaty between Bulgaria and Turkey. The end of the Second Balkan (or intra-allies) War led to the appearance of new features in the Russian military attachés' assessments of the Balkan situation. Their conclusions, which were based on developments subsequent to the Second Balkan War, embraced a wide range of assumptions and assessments. The Russian attaché in Bucharest, Colonel Iskritsky, predicted a possible Romanian-Serbian rapprochement, which he considered beneficial to Russia (RSMHA *F* 2000, In. 1, File 3048). Colonel G. Romanovsky, assigned to the Bulgarian Government, on the contrary considered that the loss by Bulgaria of its status as the strongest and most vital Balkan state negatively influenced Russian positions in the region and deprived Russia of a chance to use Serbia against Romania and Austro-Hungary in the event of an Austro-Russian war (ibid.). The military attaché in Turkey, General-Major M. Leontyev, warned about an imminent possible deterioration of the situation on the Bulgarian-Turkish border (RSMHA *F* 2000, In. 1, File 7410).

Despite all the contradictions in their assessments of the current situation, and their personal proclivities in favour of a specific mode of action, the representatives of Russian military intelligence in the Balkans were united in their opinion about the Balkan wars as forerunners of a much more serious conflict with a possible involvement of the Great Powers with a pan-European element. Throughout 1912-13, information received from the representatives of Russian intelligence in the Balkan region was carefully collected on the tables of both the Military Ministry and the Ministry of Foreign Affairs. Some of the documents were conveyed to the Tsar Nikolas II. But in many cases, political arguments overshadowed other reasons.

## Bibliography

Carnegie Endowment for International Peace, *Report of the International Commission to Inquire into Causes and Conduct of the Balkan Wars,* London, 1914.

*Mezhdunarodnye otnosheniya* ('Foreign relations'), Series No. 2, Vol. XVIII, Part 1, p. 117 (N. Potapov to Ya. Zhilinsky, 3 June 1911).

Russian State Military History Archive (RSMHA), *Fond* 2000, Inventory 1, Information from the Balkan department on the activity of military agents and Headquarters of the Odessa military district during 1911.

Russian State Military History Archive (RSMHA). *Fond* 1859, Inventory 6.

Sergeyev, E.Y., and Ulunyan, A., *Military attaché of the Russian Empire in Europe and in the Balkans, 1900-1914,* Moscow, 1999.

# Chapter 10
# The Balkan wars in recent Bulgarian historiography and textbooks

*Ivan Ilchev*

There is a clear pattern in Bulgarian historiography regarding the Balkan wars. It usually goes something like this:

The Balkan wars of 1912-13 were one of the loftiest peaks of Bulgarian national development. The Bulgarian nation and the Bulgarian army, united in a noble desire to liberate their brethren from the Turkish repression, raised the banner of freedom in October 1912. The unspeakable horrors of the everyday oppression, economic exploitation, murders, rapes of young girls and women alike, the arbitrary injustice of the Turks and the inability of the Ottoman state to reform itself in spite of efforts spanning the best part of a century, clearly showed that it was time to evict the Turkish invaders from the Peninsula.

The Bulgarian army carried the brunt of the war by defeating the major Turkish forces in Eastern Thrace and in the Rhodope mountains. Its allies met with only minimum resistance from the Turks who preferred to surrender to the Serbs and Greeks rather than to the valiant Bulgarians. The Bulgarian army took single-handedly the strongholds of Lozengrad and Adrianople which were considered unassailable by all the leading military experts at that time.

In the Balkan wars, the Bulgarian army was by far the most avant-garde; the Bulgarians were the first to use aircraft and air bombardment in warfare and introduced night attacks helped by field lights and artillery "fire mower" tactics assisting the attacks of the infantry.

While Bulgaria was fighting the Turks, Serbia and Greece were conspiring behind its back. The governments of the two countries, consumed by sinister nationalism, did not intend to fulfil their obligations as stipulated in the bilateral treaties. When their troops entered Macedonia in the autumn of 1912, they immediately started to persecute every show of Bulgarian national feeling, even in the parts of the region that were supposed to be given to Bulgaria. Priests and teachers were mistreated, as they were considered the embodiment of Bulgarian patriotism. Bulgarian national flags were lowered or torn down by drunken soldiers and Bulgarian city and village councils were immediately disbanded with military authorities ruthlessly ruling every aspect of the everyday life.

Unprovoked by Bulgaria, but driven by greed, Serbia and Greece concluded a secret bilateral treaty in order to keep the spoils of the war for themselves. At the same time, an envious Romania, which coveted territories where not a single Romanian lived, was preparing a treacherous attack.

The Serbians and Greeks seized their chance and attacked Bulgaria in the summer of 1913 during one of many insignificant military clashes. Almost simultaneously, the Romanian army invaded Bulgaria and the Turks, seeing this as a welcome opportunity, reoccupied Eastern Thrace, which had been given to Bulgaria as part of the London Peace Treaty of 1913 and overthrew virtually all the Christians in the region, Bulgarians and Greeks alike.

The former Bulgarian allies started to spread lies all over the world about the behaviour of the Bulgarian military, accusing them of atrocities towards the civil population and prisoners of war.

Encircled on all sides, the Bulgarians nevertheless fought bravely. They managed to survive the attack of the Serbs and even entered the territory of Serbia itself. At the same time, the Bulgarian army managed to surround the Greek army with King Constantine at its head and only the signing of the Bucharest Peace Treaty saved the Greeks from total defeat. The Bucharest Peace Treaty robbed Bulgaria of the fruits of its victories and Bulgarians in Macedonia fell prey to a repression even worse than inflicted by the Turkish. Eastern Thrace was violently debulgarised and Romania annexed Southern Dobrudja. This was a national debacle, a tragedy that threw a long shadow over Bulgaria's prospects for the future.

This is, if not the whole story, at least the gist of the most significant trends of Bulgarian historiography on the Balkan wars. A similar and even more passionate picture has been depicted in the extremely popular versions of history as recounted or suggested by popular television personalities – at least some of them historians by education and profession. A similar picture, if not so radical, is painted in the history textbooks, especially those for the higher grades.

The Balkan wars were, and continue to be, a topic of interest in Bulgarian historiography. From the very beginning, the question of the responsibility for the disastrous end of the war turned into a hot potato. All political parties were trying to draw a dividend and to persuade the potential voters that they were right in their forewarnings, The first books that tried to analyse what happened appeared as early as 1913. They were not a product of professional effort, but an attempt to use favourable circumstances to attack a political enemy. One of the masterminds of the Balkan union, the Prime Minister of Bulgaria, Ivan Evstratiev Geshov, published two books in 1914-15 including his memoirs, his analyses and a number of documents on the history of war. Then the First World War intervened and temporarily put an effective stop to any meaningful attempt to analyse the wars.

The inter-war years saw an upsurge of interest in the events of the Balkan wars. There are a number of reasons for this. In the first place, King Ferdinand, who led Bulgaria into two disastrous wars, was forced to renounce his crown. As the principal culprit was gone and did not wield enough restraining influence, it became much easier to dwell on the mistakes of foreign policy. Indeed, the wars were used as an important source of arguments for political polemics between left and right in the country. On the other hand, the wars turned into one of the few sources of national pride. They were popular and have remained so. They were one of the few examples of Bulgarian recent history when rulers and ruled were united in their efforts to pursue a common goal. This did not happen in the First World War and even less so in the Second World War. In a disillusioned society, painfully trying to reassert its values after the crushing and humiliating defeat of 1918, the memories of the victories in the autumn of 1912 had a stabilising effect. A plethora of books and articles were published, written by professional civil historians, military historians and military theorists.

A number of participants in the war, from members of the Cabinet, diplomats and generals, to privates, nurses and even military chaplains, published their memoirs of the fateful ten months from October 1912 to August 1913. The *Journal of Military History*, a real treasure trove on the wars, regularly printed articles on the movements, engagements and even skirmishes of the Bulgarian armies, from army corps down to the exploits of single platoons.

The crowning achievement of the military historiography of these years was the official history of the wars published by the Ministry of War. The best achievement in diplomatic history was the two volumes of history and personal memoirs of Andrei Toshev, the former Minister Plenipotentiary in Belgrade.

In the inter-war years, several main topics of research were defined and in subsequent decades they did not substantially change:

- The First Balkan War was considered almost unanimously to be a result of the national liberation movement in Macedonia and Adrianople, Thrace, which was Bulgarian by character and had, as an ultimate goal, the unification with Bulgaria or the gaining of autonomy as a stepping stone to future unification;
- It was a result of the inappropriate views of the Turkish ruling circles who could not reconcile themselves to the realities in Europe at the beginning of the twentieth century;
- It was a result of the struggle of the Great Powers for domination in the region;
- It was a result of the conviction of the power elites in the Balkan Christian states that procrastination might worsen the plight of the Christians in the Peninsula;
- It was unanimously accepted that the forming of the Balkan alliance was a mistake. For the first time ever, Bulgaria had to step back from its basic principle of never starting discussions on the division of Macedonia;
- The details of the military alliance were an additional slip-up. The Bulgarian military efforts were supposed to concentrate in Eastern Thrace while its strategic objective, Macedonia, was left in the hands of Greece and Serbia;
- Bulgaria had put too much faith in the goodwill of the Russian emperor and depended entirely on Russian policy in the Balkans to keep the peace in Romania;
- The Bulgarians tried to mollify their allies until this became virtually impossible;

- The attack against Greece and Serbia in July 1913 was decided by King Ferdinand and his sidekick in the army, General Mihail Savov, without consulting the political elite;
- The war itself, up to the attack on Chataldja, was a series of victories that astounded the world;
- Even after Chataldja, the Bulgarian effort and warfare supremacy were incomparable superior to those of Serbia and Greece.

As we can see, even in this brief list, the attention was focused on two major aspects of the war (the military and the diplomatic) with just an occasional nod towards ethnic conflicts.

Strange though it may seem, the situation did not change much with the communist takeover in the late 1940s. Many of the tenets of the old historiography were preserved, but the explanation of the established historical facts became radically different. There might have been fluctuations over the years, mostly as regards the state of relations with Yugoslavia but, in general, the new communist historians continued to follow the trodden path. Now, however, the monarch and the ruling elite were accused of irresponsibility, lack of attention and destroying the ideals of the nation.

The beginning of the 1980s witnessed a more responsible attitude towards the history of the wars. Especially at the time of anniversaries (1972, 1982, 1987), historical documentation on the topic was prolific, though the scope of scholarly interest did not change much. Only a number of collections of memoirs on the battle around Edirne and on the situation in the Rhodope mountains were worthy of note.

An attempt at a breakthrough (which never materialised) was a small book by Simeon Damianov on the Balkan countries during the wars of 1912-18. This was the first attempt in Bulgaria to look at the Balkan dimensions of the conflict from a Balkan angle. True, the angle was a bit distorted by the somewhat over-emotional patriotism of the author, but still the approach was a change. The book was published in 1982, in very limited numbers, by the Ministry of Defence. It was not sold anywhere and was in fact considered somewhat dangerous. This, and the death of the author who did not live to see it out of print, were the reasons that it passed almost unnoticed.

After 1990, in the turmoil that followed the fall of the Berlin Wall and the collapse of communism, history in Bulgaria became a possible escape from the problems of the present day. A number of professional historians and amateurs looked at history as a possible solace, at the victories of the past as a healing antiseptic for national pride, deeply wounded by the crisis in society. It is an adage that history is often not exactly a willing, but at least dutiful slave to politics; and the state of contemporary Bulgarian historiography on the problem reflects the problems of society itself.

According to incomplete data for 1989-2004, eleven books on the history of the Balkan wars and seven collections of documents were published, along with 46 articles and 16 memoirs. The topics of these books and articles could be grouped roughly as in the diagram below.

In brief, interest in the topic has never waned. Probably the best book on the history of the wars was the well-researched and well-thought-out monograph of Georgi Markov, which summarises the best achievements of Bulgarian historiography blending them with the author's own research. Georgi Markov's book is to date the only attempt to write a concise history of the strategy of the war.

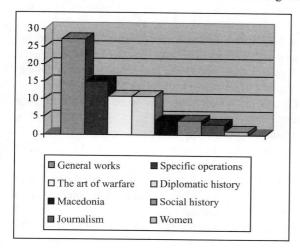

- General works
- Specific operations
- The art of warfare
- Diplomatic history
- Macedonia
- Social history
- Journalism
- Women

The problem of Bulgarian historians when dealing with the history of the Balkan wars is that they see it in a very traditional way – a clash of armies. All the other aspects of the war were considered, up to very recently, secondary and unimportant. I think that we could state that the pure military history of the war is on the brink of exhaustion as regards themes. On the other side, there is a wealth of problems touching on the social aspects of the wars that have barely been touched by the younger generation of historians. And by "younger" I certainly do not mean young.

Among the best attempts to look at the war from a different angle are two monographs by Sv. Eldurov on the Bulgarian church during the wars and on the plight of the Bulgarian-speaking population in Albania during these years. Eldurov has a knack for the factual and his books are very thoroughly researched. A monograph and a number of articles by R. Koneva on the fate of culture during the wars are worthy of mention; here the stress is rather on the state management of culture. Ivan Ilchev has written a number of articles and a monograph on the part played by propaganda in the conflicts. There are several good articles on the organisation of the army medical service, and there is a jewel of an exception to the lack of studies of the social history of the war period – an article on the role of women. Also, an attempt has been made to touch on one of the economic aspects of the wars – the role of the Bulgarian marines and the development of Alexandrupolis-Dedeagach during the war.

The social history of the wars however remains virtually untouched and there are numerous topics that I have been trying for years now to persuade my students to address:

- History of the ideas that led to the Balkan wars and the attempts of governments and lobby groups to shape the minds of the public according to their principles.

- The role of the modern state in creating modern nationalism based on the conception of a nation-state with its system of holidays, its martyrology, its saints, its established beliefs and so on.
- The Balkan wars in the context of individual and collective myth-making.
- History and problems of Bulgarian journalism during these years.
- The visual image of the "other" – the Balkan neighbour – with particular stress on political cartoons. This means visualising the war: postcards of real and imaginary battles, of heroes larger than life and vile enemies; military art, pictures of battles and the like.
- Nothing has been done to use the impressive resources of mass literature, which some historians consider to be of little value: songbooks, yearbooks, collections of primitive-sounding chauvinist poems that sometimes had a much greater impact on public imagination than literature of so-called higher quality.
- The strategic problems of the war, of which a number were due to erroneous decision making, remain obscure.
- Analysis of the obsession of Bulgarian politicians with Macedonia.
- The part played by Macedonian refugees in determining the general direction of Bulgarian policy.
- The predominant role that the country's capital, Sofia, with its large number of refugees from Macedonia (almost 50% of the whole population in some decades before the Balkan wars), played in the urban-rural ratio.
- Analysis of the neglect to attach any real importance to Thrace and access to the Aegean Sea.
- No meaningful attempt has been made to research the Bulgarian reasoning that lay behind the important decisions taken against politicians from neighbouring countries.
- Bulgarian historiography still cannot come to terms with the simple fact that the Turks have been living in the Balkans for half a millennium now and they continue to be treated largely as invaders or as an alien element in the Balkans.
- We still do not have, though attempts have been made, a real analysis of the so-called Russophile and Russophobe factors in Bulgarian policy.
- Nothing of real substance has been written on women and their part in the war effort, not only at the front (we have one or two articles on that), but behind the front lines. The predominant role of women in keeping the economy running during the wars is documented but not proved.
- Nothing whatsoever has been published on the problems of childhood during the war, the problems of growing up in the war years, the problems of socialisation in wartime.
- There is an encouraging trend amongst one or two younger historians who are interested in the state of the economy during the war years. The problem is that they concentrate mostly on the way the state was running the economy during the war, but they omit to address the psychological aspects of economic development and the ensuing troubles caused by war.
- Nothing has been written on the Bulgarian plans to develop Porto Lagos on the Aegean Sea into a major port.
- Nothing on the changes in the communications systems.

116

- Nothing on requisitions that fed the war effort and the crippling effect they had on a weak economy, or the psychological aspect of the distrust of the peasant in a state that made liberal use of the fruits of his labour.

The humanitarian aspects of the war have never been researched either:

- Nothing has been written on the precarious situation of Bulgarian Turks and Bulgarian Muslims during the war years, the fears they lived with and the psychological atmosphere that surrounded them.
- No documentation exists on how the Bulgarian Turks (and, in 1912, 18% of the population of Bulgaria was Turkish) reacted to the news of the war and what the state had been doing to keep them under control.
- Nothing on prisoners of war and the conditions under which they were held, how they were fed or the treatment they received. An encouraging note, however, is that a younger colleague has been working for some years now on soldiers' letters home, but she has not yet published anything.
- Nothing on the behaviour of Bulgarian troops towards their adversaries and towards the peaceful population in acquired territories. No research whatsoever has been done on the legal department of the army: how many Bulgarians were deserters, were any charges made against Bulgarian soldiers for rape or atrocities, and similar questions.
- There is one hopeful exception: an important volume of documents and a number of articles were published on the conversion of Bulgarian-speaking Muslims of the Rhodope mountains in 1912-13.

The refugees in Bulgaria and from Bulgaria are a problem of their own. Serious work has been done on the legal aspects. The refugee problem, as a part of the international relations of the country in the inter-war years, is more or less clear. Other important aspects, however, have yet to be touched upon: for example, the adjustment of the refugees to their new surroundings. Contrary to the well-established belief, rooted in arrogance, the welcome they got was rarely warm or, more to the point, was short-lived.

The problems of settling the refugees are a bit hazy. Some work has been done in land distribution but no research has been carried out on the plight of those who eventually chose the cities as a place to stay and look for work. We do not even know how many in the long run stayed in the villages and how many augmented the urban population of the country. And this is just the bare bones. No one has ever tried to research the impact of the change of educational patterns on adolescents.

It is a favorite self-delusion of Bulgarian politics (that seeped into Bulgarian historiography) that all Bulgarians, no matter where they lived, spoke the same language with very few regional characteristics. By the end of the Balkan wars, however, the official Bulgarian literary language had already been established and the children of the refugees, who had started their education using a different language, had serious problems adapting.

No research has been done on the Greeks who chose to leave the country after the Balkan wars and especially on the Turks and Muslims in general who started a new exodus, the second one since 1878 when modern Bulgaria came into being.

To sum up, Bulgarian historiography shows a general inability to let go of pomp and traditional rhetoric when discussing the Balkan wars. Bulgarian historians are brought up in a tradition of positivist political history and they still do not see the implications of social history. Even serious historians discard the value of soldiers' diaries and memoirs, with their painstaking effort to communicate their everyday thoughts, deliberations and activities, as unimportant and outside the main path of history.

While the wars are Balkan, the treatment is Bulgarian. One of the reasons for this myopia is a lack of documentation coming from neighbouring countries. Bulgarian historians, for example, have never been able to delve into the archives of Turkey, Greece or Romania on this topic, though the situation with Serbia is a bit better.

In a word, we have a history of the conflict itself but what we do not have is a history of the man in the conflict: his ideas, dreams, hopes and disappointments. Historians should refrain from mindlessly accepting and upholding stereotypical assertions like the one that the Bulgarian army has never lost a war and Bulgarian politicians have never managed to win one – as if wars were fought in laboratories under sterile conditions.

This means that, in the future, historians will not have to fear that they are going to lose their bread and butter, however meagre their ration might be. What we really need is to persuade our students that history is more than just a clash of armies, more than just intricate movements of diplomats, and more than the seemingly illogical decisions of the decision-making elite.

# Chapter 11
# The Balkan wars, 1912-13: a Turkish perspective

*Halil Berktay*

## The aspect of continuity

I would like to begin by noting that "a Turkish perspective" on the Balkan wars of the early twentieth century can mean at least two very different things. First, it can signify looking back from today to try to assess what those events (have) meant for the Ottoman empire and/or for Turkish society: the immediately political, and hence also the more complex social, cultural, ideological impact that they had at the time, and which may be said to have exercised a continuing, albeit non-linear, but irregularly pulsating, ebb-and-flow of influence over the succeeding nine decades or so. Then and now, such a perspective can also mean, and has actually meant, a specifically "Turkish" view of events – as opposed to other, comparably subjective views, such as "Greek", "Bulgarian" or "Serbian" takes on the alleged rights or wrongs of 1912-13.

In this second sense, it has to be not a Turkish but a Turkish nationalist perspective that we are talking about. In what follows, I would like to preserve and develop this distinction, starting with the first dimension, that is to say with my own appreciation of the Balkan wars as a modern historian of Turkey (who also happens to be Turkish, and therefore with an insider's knowledge and understanding of his country, though not necessarily as a nationalist), and then inevitably moving into the second dimension – since, as I would like to argue, not only was Turkish nationalism largely shaped and baked in the pressure-cooker of these Balkan wars, but it has also proved to be perhaps their most enduring legacy.

The Balkan wars of 1912-13 have been much more central to modern Turkish history than is often realised, both in themselves and as a crucial link between "the last wars of the Ottoman Empire and the first wars of modern Turkey." By this longish, cumbersome phrase, I mean:

(a) the war of 1911 that resulted from Italy's invasion of Tripoli;
(b) the Balkan wars of 1912-13;
(c) the 1914-18 war, the First World War itself, the Great War of European memory and the General Mobilisation *(Seferberlik)* of Turkish social memory, including of course Gallipoli very close to home as well as the more distant (and now ideologically distanced) Caucasian, Suez, Galician and Mesopotamian campaigns;

(d) the war of 1919-22, which is known to the outside world as yet another (and relatively small) Greco-Turkish War (see, for example, Overy 1999), but which for Turks constitutes their War of Independence *(İ stiklâl Harbi)*, through which they finally put the spectre of colonisation to rest and re-asserted their right to sovereignty, soon to be formalised by the 29 October 1923 promulgation of the Republic of Turkey.

As a result, and especially in Kemalist historiography, this War of Independence has come to overshadow all the other conflicts preceding it, and to be situated in a unique relationship with the Atatürk era.

## Transition

The long view, however, would be that each and every one of these wars constituted a link in a long chain of events and that, taken collectively, they were all part and parcel of the final phase of the so-called Eastern Question, during which the final agonies of the Sick Man of Europe somehow evolved or devolved into the birth pangs of a new nation-state. To put it another way, in the early twentieth century the Ottoman Empire was gripped by one big, protracted crisis stretching from 1908 to 1922, to which the Balkan wars were central in many ways, and which underlay the initial construction of Turkish national memory. For this, literary evidence is not hard to come by. In the "Spring 1941" opening scene of the famous Turkish Communist poet Nâzım Hikmet's verse epic "Human landscapes from my country" *(Memleketimden İnsan Manzaraları)*, there is a certain Corporal Ahmet who is described as having "joined [the army] for the Balkan wars / joined for the Great Mobilisation / joined for the Greek War" and whose motto: "Just bear up, pal, we are almost there" has become famous (Hikmet, 1987, p. 14). Some sixty pages later, we encounter a leftist university student who, after having heard a long yarn about Gallipoli from a companion on the Ankara train, muses that:

> "Just like a kind of fish
> a kind of tree
> or a kind of mineral
> there is also a kind of human being that inhabits this country
> for whom battles constitute
> his only worthwhile
> and unforgettable memory." (ibid., p. 79)

In Yakup Kadri Karaosmanoğlu's novel "The outsider" *(Yaban)*, the reserve officer who is recuperating in a remote Anatolian village after being wounded in the War of Independence epitomises both intellectual alienation and war-weariness. And, in recent scholarship, there is at least one example of regarding all the various military conflicts of 1912-22 as a single "ten-year war" on the basis of the overlapping generations of military personnel that they comprised (Görgülü, 1993).

So much for continuity, but what about the other side? How did the change occur – that is to say, what, if any, was the crossover point between "the last wars of the Ottoman

Empire" and "the first wars of modern Turkey"? How did an imperial consciousness shade into a national consciousness? Furthermore, if wars fought to maintain empire might in some sense be considered "unjust" while wars fought against aggression or for liberation might be regarded as "just", which was the last "unjust" war and which was the first "just" war on the Ottoman-Turkish side?

Such questions are probably easier to pose than to answer. Formulating them can help to pinpoint certain thorny problems while also underlining the general need to substitute multi-perspectivity for the obsolete egocentrism of a nineteenth-century type of national narrative. Nevertheless, apart from the logical apriorism (or legal essentialism) involved in trying to impose black-and-white definitions on the grey zones or furry edges of historical reality, clear-cut turning points of any kind can prove virtually impossible to identify.

Frequently, all we can do is to trace the process. The Young Turks' Revolution of 1908 brought the Committee of Union and Progress (CUP) to power – or at least into a share of power. As against the "despotism" (in Turkish: *istibdat*) of the Hamidian era, the CUP proclaimed Liberty *(Hürriyet)* for all. It also introduced a policy of "uniting the various elements" *(ittihad-ı anâsır)* of the empire around a common "Ottoman" identity. Instead, they were faced with a succession of both external and internal challenges, in response to which they drifted, gradually and perhaps even unconsciously, into a position of defending and fighting to maintain that very same empire against which they had proclaimed "Liberty" only a few years earlier.

What to go for: empire or revolution? Empire or reform? Empire or democratisation? At least, between February and October 1917, Kerensky may be said to have gone for empire, while Lenin went for revolution. In 1956, it was this same dilemma that also confronted (and overwhelmed) Khrushchev when, in response to pressure from the hardliners in his Politburo, he sent Soviet tanks to crush the Hungarian Revolution, thereby also sealing the doom of his own efforts at de-Stalinisation. In the mid-1980s, in contrast, Gorbachev sacrificed his own position and leadership in opting for glasnost and perestroika over empire. The Young Turks may be said to have opted for Kerensky's and Khrushchev's choice over Gorbachev's choice – and like the first two, it cost them their revolution.

In certain Balkan nationalist historiographies which are rather hostile to the Young Turks, the latter are regarded as having always been resolute Turkish nationalists, and only to have practised deception or dissimulation vis-à-vis the non-Muslim, non-Turkish communities of the Ottoman Empire, eventually revealing themselves for the wolves in sheep's clothing that they were said to have been from the very outset. This is too deterministic, too conspiratorial. It does not allow for the accidents of historical movement, for mutual and interactive "learning" processes, or for the contingency and mutability of "original" programmes or platforms. Empirically speaking, apart from wanting to restore the Constitution of 1876, the Unionists had hardly any blueprint in 1908. It would be difficult to find a more utterly unprepared bunch of twentieth-century revolutionaries. Instead, it was as they came to confront the Great

121

Powers' imperialist aims and the other Balkan countries' nationalist agendas, that they too rapidly developed into (imperialistically flavoured) Turkish nationalists.

This transformation occurred largely as a result of successive defeats, and not through any semblance of victory. For they lost in 1911, and then they lost very badly in 1912-13, only partly making good on a fraction of their losses in the Second Balkan War. In 1914-18 they lost virtually everywhere except at Gallipoli; and it was only with the War of Independence of 1919-22 that this catastrophic run was halted for good. Defeat was both general, in the sense that (despite many mutual atrocities and massacres on the way), it was the Muslim Turks of the Ottoman Empire that emerged as overall losers from the long nineteenth century (see, for instance, McCarthy, 1995, 2001), and also specific, with each individual disaster adding its own spoonful of bitterness to an already over-flowing cup. The Balkan wars loom very large in this regard. This was not just defeat by the (admittedly superior) Great Powers, but, worse, it was defeat at the hands of a number of small Balkan states, who were "our former subjects" to boot.

To some extent, therefore, it can be compared with the Porte's failure to put down the Greek Revolution of 1821, though this time it had much graver consequences. The Ottoman rout in the First Balkan War engendered natal deracination on a scale comparable only to the aftermath of the Russo-Turkish War of 1877-8. Again there was a huge influx of refugees, their abject poverty and misery compounded by a cholera outbreak, fleeing through Thrace to ferry-stops on the European side of Istanbul and then making their way across the Bosphorus into Anatolia. Hence, out of defeat there came a further step in the making of modern Turkey as a nation of immigrants expelled from the Crimea, the Caucasus, mainland Greece, Crete, the Balkans and (to a lesser degree) from the empire's former Arab provinces. Out of defeat there also came the Unionist putsch, the coup d'état of 1913 *(Babıâli Baskını)*, and thus the rise of a triumvirate of young, *arriviste* warlords (Enver, Talat and Cemal) to supremely non-accountable power.

By the same token, out of defeat there came the army reforms of 1913-14, when an older generation of Ottoman colonels and generals was replaced by a younger and much hungrier breed of Unionist officers. It was these reforms that made the Ottoman armies capable of fighting on, rather unexpectedly, for another four or five years in the Great War, and surprising the Entente with the tenacity of their resistance at Gallipoli. And while there seems to have been a strong connection between the horrendous Ottoman performance in 1912-13 and British expectations of a walkover in March-April 1915, the opposite connection appears to have been made even more explicitly by their Turkish rivals. Barely a week after the intensive fighting of the 24-25 April landings on the peninsula, Mustafa Kemal told his subordinates, while issuing orders for the 1 May 1915 counter-attack at Anzac Cove

> "I simply cannot accept that there are among us and among the troops we command those who would not rather die here than experience a second chapter of Balkan disgrace. If you feel there are such people let us shoot them at once with our own hands." (Steel and Hart, 1995, pp. 137-8)

Such links can be multiplied *ad infinitum*. After Mudros, as Istanbul came under British occupation, the surviving Unionist chain of command decided on Mustafa Kemal to lead a new nationalist resistance in Asia Minor, which thereby became the Valley Forge and the Yenan of the Kemalist revolution. But the idea of making a last stand in Anatolia may be said to have arisen not in 1918-19 but at least half a decade earlier, as Istanbul's extreme vulnerability was demonstrated when the First Balkan War stripped the empire of its Rumelian holdings and the Bulgarian army arrived at the Çatalca line.

In itself, this notion of one last stand, a final resistance, a sense of the Turks coming to the end of the road and growing bitterly angry, was not peculiarly Turkish. It came to be more generally shared, precisely because of the outcome of the Balkan wars. Aubrey Herbert was in Istanbul at the time, and during the winter of 1912-13, he was moved to write:

> "There falls perpetual snow upon a broken plain
> And through the twilight filled with flakes the white earth joins the sky.
> Grim as a famished wounded wolf, his lean neck in a chain,
> The Turk stands up to die." (quoted by Moorehead, 1985, p. 82)

Furthermore, this was no ordinary defeat in the usual kind of conflict between nation–states with clearly defined boundaries and ethno-politically compact populations, where "we" are inside, "the enemy" is outside, and the winning and losing societies are separated from one another. In 1912 the Ottoman Empire was still in the process of such separation, so that at least from the Turkish side, "the enemy" was inside as well as outside. Aubrey Herbert noted:

> "In 1913, when the Balkans gained one smashing victory after another over the unequipped and unorganised Turkish forces every Greek café in Pera shouted its song of triumph." (ibid.)

One can only begin to imagine the feelings of extreme humiliation that this entailed, the sullen tension and the accumulating hatred as Turks looked on.

## Nationalism

Perhaps more than anything else, out of defeat there came not only a huge nationalist upsurge on the day, amounting to nothing more or less than the first mass mobilisations of modern Turkish history, replete with rallies, contributions, volunteers, and poetic calls to arms – born, let us note, not out of any civic, domestic issues, involving class conflict or other forms of internal dissent, but out of a war and national defence emergency, with all its authoritarian-solidaristic implications – but there came also the tough, grim, vengeful, vindictive kind of Turkish nationalist ideology that all this gelled into in the longer run. At this point, of course, it was not (yet) the Kemalist variant of Turkish nationalism that the world has become accustomed to since the late 1920s, but the original, wild rootstock. Now to put all this into the theoretical perspectives used in contemporary nationalism studies, this Unionist *(İttihatçı, İttihadist)* or early Turkish nationalism may be said to have stood somewhere between the Hrochian third path of European paths to the nation–state, and the colonially contexted Asian or third-world nationalisms that were still to come.

Miroslav Hroch, and his former student Jitka Maleckova, have both pointed to three basic patterns of nation-state formation in European space: 1. A west European (British and French) trajectory of revolution or modernisation transforming the socio-political regime on the basis of a relatively stable territory and demography that had already been attained by the Late Middle Ages or during the Early Modern Era; 2. a central and south European (German and Italian) pattern of unification; and 3. a more east or south-east European model arising out of the break-up of empire. Let us leave the Habsburgs aside for the moment; very clearly, as the Ottoman Empire both retreated and disintegrated, it was being partitioned from the outside and the inside, that is to say not just by the Great Powers but also by the newly emerging Serbian, Greek, Bulgarian, Romanian, Albanian, Montenegrin and ultimately Turkish nationalisms that were engaging in an unbounded contest for space. It was this contest, culminating in the Balkan wars, that fundamentally shaped their mutual, multiple antagonisms, many of which have endured to this day.

But then there were also some asymmetries involved, which is why I find it necessary to try to add to or somewhat modify the Hroch-Maleckova third path. Ultimately, all these asymmetries had to do with the alignment of all the various other Balkan nationalisms against imperial power. First, it was because the Unionists found themselves in the driver's seat, so to speak, that, in open and direct confrontation with the Great Powers, Turkish nationalism acquired a proto-Third World dimension of generalised anti-colonialism that is largely missing from the other Balkan nationalist ideologies.

Second, as the Young Turks found themselves fighting to maintain empire, as against the liberation discourses of other Balkan nationalisms, Turkish nationalism acquired a heavy imperial-national overtone. Initially the imperial aspect stifled and obstructed the embryonic national discourse. Comparing the various mobilisation decrees of 1912, Fikret Adanır has shown how all the Balkan states were able to appeal directly and strongly to "faith and nation" while the Ottoman sultan was only able to call, weakly and lamely, for loyalty to the dynasty, the gains of the 1908 revolution, the Young Turks' reforms, and law and order.

At the time, this simply could not hold the line and, as it collapsed, Turkish nationalism developed in accelerated fashion, rushing in to fill a partial vacuum – inside the shell of empire. Third, as it did so, it was this same situation – exemplified by the Greeks cheering on the Pera in 1913 – that gave rise to the "enemy within" syndrome of Turkish nationalism, which continues to be obsessed with treachery or treason, or with "being stabbed in the back" – as recent events have demonstrated.

Fourth, and again mostly because of its different positioning with respect to Ottoman imperial power, Turkish nationalism emerged and developed later than most other Balkan nationalisms, which therefore became not only its rivals but also, paradoxically, its guides and instructors in the dark arts of how to create and homogenise a nation–state. In the late eighteenth and early nineteenth centuries, it was as if the Ottoman elite had decided to "do as the Europeans do" in order to be able to hold their own against Europe. Now, nearly a century after the launching of the Tanzimat, it was as if the Unionists were also saying that they should "do as the Greeks or the Bulgarians do" in order to be able to cope with these new and additional demons of early Turkish nationalism.

As W.H. Auden wrote in his "September 1, 1939":

> "I and the public know
> What all schoolchildren learn:
> Those to whom evil is done
> Do evil in return."

Not a chain of direct causation, perhaps, but a process of ideological interaction and escalation stretches from the Balkan wars of 1912-13, through the practically forced expulsion in 1913-14 of large chunks of the Greek Orthodox population of eastern Thrace and the north-west corner of Asia Minor, to the Armenian horrors of 1915-16. In the end, as with all blood-feuds, it comes to be predicated on "what they first did to us" – or at least on perceptions or narratives thereof.

Nowhere can such perceptual connections be seen better than in literature. Ömer Seyfeddin (1884-1920) was one of the pioneers of Turkish nationalism. The son of an army captain from a family that had been forced to flee the Caucasus in the face of Tsarist Russian expansion, he too became personally involved in the conflicts and convulsions of the last disastrous Ottoman decade. In 1903, he joined the army as a lieutenant, and was eventually posted as an instructor to the İzmir school for officers of the gendarmerie. In 1908, the year of the Young Turks' Revolution, he was transferred to the Third Army based in Ottoman Selanik (now Thessaloníki), seeing action in the Balkan wars, and surrendering to Greek army units during the siege of Ioannina. Released and sent back to Istanbul after a year in captivity, he left the army for good, and devoted the rest of his (very short) life entirely to literature.

As a publicist and essayist, Ömer Seyfeddin militated for a naturalised and essentialised nationalism, arguing that "if you are a Turk, you will think, feel and act like a Turk". Actually, of course, it was the other way round: By repeatedly writing and preaching about how Turks should think, feel or act, he and other members of his generation were busy constructing or inventing (modern) Turkishness.

For Ömer Seyfeddin and others, this went hand in hand with imparting a "national memory" to that initial, embryonic Turkish nation, that is, a certain canon about how it should "remember" itself, its past, and – most importantly – its enemies. Crucially, this intrinsically subjective element is lumped together with others that are more material or at least not so subjective, so that while the historical novelty of the nation may be generally recognised, it is the imagined, invented or constructed nature of the "common past" in question that comes to be vastly neglected or underestimated.

As I, too, have tried to show elsewhere, what actually happens is that a lot of the literati and dilettanti that make up the "small intellectual minority" of the Hrochian first phase of nationalism come to be involved in selectively recycling elements of a premodern, fragmented or heterogenous "social memory" into, now, an incomparably more compact and homogenised "national memory" that comes to be forged and disseminated, and to achieve hegemonic stature, through the memory-space of print capitalism. Furthermore, when such selective, imaginative, emotionally persuasive recycling occurs on a massive, genuinely popular scale, invariably it is fiction and poetry that offer the proper medium.

In Ömer Seyfeddin's case, too, this kind of construction of national memory was achieved not so much through his theoretical essays, addressed to his intellectual peers, but primarily through his popular fiction – through large numbers of superb short stories, largely unexcelled in subsequent Turkish literature, on which his claim to fame has come to rest. Particularly important in this regard are a number of stories that deal with incidents of the heinous persecution of Turks or Muslims resulting from Ottoman-Turkish defeats and the retreat of empire in the period 1908-18, in which "we" are the victims and "they" the villains are without exception the Greeks, the Bulgarians and the Armenians. By and large they are hate stories, all the more effective for not being pure figments of the author's imagination, but by being rooted in (part of) what was actually happening on the ground, for in this quite typical case of preferred, contested victimhood, Ömer Seyfeddin's selectivity consists of focusing on all the horrors that "others" were inflicting on "us", without ever going so far as to suggest what, at the same time, "we" are doing, were doing, or might have been doing to "others". In each and every one of these stories, furthermore, Ömer Seyfeddin is not just heaping abuse on "our enemies", but also admonishing Turks on what they should do or how they should behave.

Lest it should appear that Seyfeddin's perspective is unique, let me note that some of Nâzım Hikmet's early poems, penned during or in the aftermath of that same nationalist upsurge triggered by the Balkan wars, are just as stridently full of images of avenging "my heroic race", "our white-bearded grandfathers" or "mosques now crowned with crosses" that make for very uneasy reading today (see, for example, Hikmet, 1987, pp. 14, 19). Later, of course, Nâzım Hikmet became not only a Communist but a very major poet, perhaps one of the greatest poets of the twentieth century, many would say on a par with Pablo Neruda. More than a quarter century later, he was serving time in Bursa prison when he wrote his great "Human landscapes from my country".

Somewhere in the vastness of that epic tapestry is a likable person called Kartallı Kâzım, an honest man, a staunch Communist, who is described as having been a gardener before and having continued as a gardener after the War of Independence, during which he has fought both cleanly and courageously. And yet, this Kâzım is lovingly, compassionately presented by Nâzım Hikmet as having two weaknesses he cannot overcome: he still believes in God, and he still hates the Bulgarians – so much so that whenever he heard a fiery story about the deeds of Bulgarian revolutionaries, he would immediately fall out of sorts with the whole world, but then find quick consolation: "Either we were told lies about what this nation did to pregnant women during the Balkan wars," he would say, "or else, these revolutionaries must belong to some other Bulgarian tribe" (op. cit.). That is the only way Kâzım can reconcile himself to proletarian internationalism, to being told by his party that he must now regard Bulgarian Communists as his brothers. It is as strong an index as any of the impact of 1912-13 at the time, and of just how widely shared Turkish nationalism's initial demonology had become.

Then, however, came a fault-line, and a deliberate forgetting (or perhaps a semi-forgetting or a pseudo-forgetting). Following the final defeat of the Greek Expeditionary Army that had occupied western Anatolia, Turkey was declared a republic, before which the sultanate and after which the caliphate were abolished, paving the way for secularism as the main plank of a new platform of all-out Westernisation. Significantly, the slogan of "catching up with contemporary civilisation" *(muasır medeniyyet seviyesine ulaşmak)* became central to this Kemalist modernisation drive. What the Kemalists were re-affirming from the late 1920s onwards was not just an intention to catch up with, but also to come to belong to that once hated, but also envied, circle or family of "advanced" or "civilised" nations. In the sphere of international diplomacy, this quest for admission was reflected in a parallel slogan of "Peace at home, peace all over the world" as well as in strong support for, and an active role in, the League of Nations. It also went hand in hand with an explicit repudiation of the Unionists' Pan-Turkism or Turanism, or indeed of any other variety of Turkish irredentism. Ankara went out of its way to disavow all possible historical claims to territories beyond the border of the National Pact of 1920 as, in precocious pursuit of a policy of non-alignment, it kept pushing for a Balkan entente predicated on the multilateral recognition of the legitimacy and the territorial inviolability of all existing states in the region. In this context, the Balkans became Turkish (Kemalist) nationalism's forgotten realm of memory from the 1930s onwards.

Nevertheless, a bedrock remained of sediment deposited during that murderous "last wars" decade of 1911-22, extending like a tectonic plate from Unionism to Kemalism, and carrying along in slow, subterranean movement the original demonology of Turkish nationalism – of "our eternal enemies the Greeks, the Bulgarians and the Armenians" (aided and abetted by the Great Powers). The actual historical moment being no longer alive, this substratum of national memory is not perpetuated so much by literature – which cannot possibly reproduce the violent vibrancy of Ömer Seyfeddin's hatred – as by historiography and textbooks.

By historiography in this context, of course I mean not the sober sophistication of a number of Turkish academics – such as Fikret Adanır, Engin Akarlı, Şükrü Hanioğlu, or Stefan Yerasimos – who have situated themselves within the mainstream of historical scholarship as universally understood, but nationalist historiography, of which three main characteristics may quickly be noted. First, there is very little of it, due to both the redefinition of the Balkans as a forgotten realm of memory, and the Kemalist valorisation of both the Gallipoli episode during the First World War and the War of Independence of 1919-22 above all others. Second, most of what is available is not so specific to 1912-13, but prefers to deal more generally with a fused "long nineteenth century" continuum in which sudden attacks without any declaration of war (as at Navarine in 1827), or betrayal and abandonment (as in 1877-8), or being deprived of territory even in the case of victory (as with the loss of Crete in 1896-1900), tend to blend with 1911 and 1912-13 into a single story of unending woes and unfair persecution, while the varied clauses of the Treaties of London (1830), San Stefano (1878), Berlin (1878), London again (1913), Mudros (1918) and Sevres (1920) are also merged into a single meta-text of the piecemeal, but pre-planned partitioning of the Sick Man of Europe.

Third, this turns out to be a very thin, linear and schematic narrative, treated according to an extremely simplified scheme, which runs in terms of "their" ambitions, covetousness, treachery and onslaught, versus "our" innocence, good intentions, betrayal and victimhood. Turkish nationalist historiography begins by idealising the Classical Age, so-called, of the fifteenth and sixteenth centuries as a conflict-free realm of harmony between the state, the fief-holder and the peasant, and proceeds to provide us with an equally expurgated version of the late Ottoman *ancien régime*, which is said to have embodied the just and fair treatment of all ethno-religious communities *(millets)* by the Porte. All the various national and social revolts that came to shake the Balkans are regarded as fundamentally unjustified, and become reducible to banditry and brigandage. It would seem that the Turks had every right to make a Unionist and then a Kemalist revolution against Ottoman despotism, while all other nationalist-revolutionary movements were rising not against the same imperial authority, but somehow against the Turks as such. The corollary is that "we" were entirely within our rights as we tried to re-impose law and order, while "they" kept committing atrocities against us.

Many of the works on the Balkan wars are perfunctory in the extreme, having been written purely for domestic consumption, and without much thought for the standards of international scholarship – to the point where it frequently looks as if they are so cynically blasé about their subject matter as to be incapable of bothering to make a good argument beyond repeating the clichés of nationalist otherisation. Alongside such routine, rhetorical denunciations, there also exists another sub-set of primary and secondary narratives comprising memoirs, period accounts of various operations or campaigns, or official military histories commissioned by the Department of War History under the General Staff in Ankara. The last, in particular, are uniformly drab; written not by historians but by retired soldiers and intended to address not a general, intellectual readership but future staff officers. They are so full of technical details as to be incapable of addressing broader issues.

Much of this historiography of the Balkan wars loses track even of the historicity of Turkish nationalism, which is naturalised and eternalised to the point where it too loses its historical concreteness. We are left with no sense of the actual role of the Balkan wars in the original construction of Turkish national memory, nor of the complicated relationship between Unionism and Kemalism that then ensued, and which led to partial and incomplete erasures.

# Bibliography

Görgülü, Ismet, *On Yıllık Harbin Kadrosu 1912-1922*, Türk Tarih Kurumu, Ankara, 1993.

Hikmet, Nâzım, *Memleketimden İnsan Manzaraları*, Adam Yayınları, Istanbul, 1987.

McCarthy, Justin, *Death and exile: the ethnic cleansing of Ottoman muslims, 1821-1922*, The Darwin Press, 1995.

McCarthy, Justin, *The Ottoman peoples and the end of empire,* London, Arnold, 2001.

Moorehead, Alan, *Gallipoli London,* Ballantine Books, 1958.

Overy, Richard (ed.), *The Times atlas of world history*, London, Times Books, 1999.

Steel, Nigel, and Hart, Peter, *Defeat at Gallipoli*, London, Macmillan, 1995.

# Chapter 12
# The Balkan wars, 1912-13: an Austrian perspective

*Karl Kaser*

Regarding its political and military strategy, the situation for the Austrian-Hungarian monarchy on the eve of the Balkan wars was not an easy one. On the one hand, it considered the Balkan region its exclusive zone of influence and the only geographic-strategic area where it was able to try to emulate the other European Great Powers in their colonial attempts; on the other hand, it had been Russia that had created the war alliance of the Balkan states, which for Austria as a would-be colonial power made any influence on the alliance and its goals impossible. At the same time, the monarchy's room for manoeuvre was restricted in several ways: not just regarding its own economic and military resources, but most of all regarding the international political system of the increasingly dissonant "Concert of the Great Powers" and particularly regarding the existing and competing systems of alliances which made the "concert" into background music and gave priority to confrontation.

Keeping within the bounds of possibility, Austro-Hungarian foreign policy set itself realistic goals, which it could only partly realise, however, as the Balkan wars developed dynamics that the monarchy had not foreseen and which questioned its colonial strategy in the Balkans – particularly towards Serbia. The decisive political and military powers drew the conclusion from the Balkan wars that the foreign policy strategy of securing decisive influence on the Balkan countries in the context of the existing alliances could not be implemented any more by political, economic and diplomatic means. Finally, those voices would gain acceptance which already on the eve of the Balkan wars had demanded a pre-emptive war against Serbia in order to re-gain the political initiative in the Balkans.

The road towards this situation is analysed below under two main headings. Under the first heading, the possibilities and colonial goals of the Austro-Hungarian monarchy on the eve of the First Balkan War will be discussed. Under the second heading is a discussion from Austria-Hungary's perspective of the precarious strategic situation that had been created by the results of the two Balkan wars.

## The colonialist goals of the Habsburg monarchy on the eve of the Balkan wars

In this section, the situation of the Habsburg monarchy within the system of the European Great Powers must first be discussed. After this, the monarchy's colonialist concept of the Balkan countries will be discussed in general, and finally we deal with the concrete ideas of Austro-Hungarian foreign policy of the time after the First Balkan War.

From 1815 to about 1878, the "Concert of Great Powers", consisting of Great Britain, France, Russia and the Habsburg monarchy as well as Prussia/Germany, and completed by Italy in the second half of the nineteenth century, created stability in Europe. However, this stability was put in question by the formation of new Balkan states at the expense of the Ottoman Empire and by Russia's, Austria's and Italy's attempts to influence them. This gradually declining system of securing European peace was increasingly eclipsed by the two alliances of the European Great Powers, which led to an increasing danger of war in so far as one partner's war threatened to drag also the other partners into the war. Apart from this fact, this international policy of alliances of the Great Powers was accompanied by armament and investing in armament (Mann, 1998, pp. 185f, 192).

This change happened in two phases: 1. From the late 1880s to 1902 there were two areas of conflict divided from each other: the Triple Alliance (Austria-Hungary, Germany and Italy) versus the Dual Alliance (France and Russia); 2. During a second phase there was the consolidation of the two blocks of states: Germany's continuing rise and Russia's breakdown during the war against Japan lead to a re-orientation in so far as Great Britain partly joined the French-Russian Entente (Mann, 2001, p. 243).

Regarding war and peace, during these decades a "theory of realism" had been accepted. It was based on three assumptions: 1. States have "interests" or at least their "statesmen" articulate them; 2. Clashes of interests between states are part of everyday politics; 3. War is a common if dangerous means of pushing through or securing one's own interests. Thus potentially, as a rational instrument for achieving national goals, waging war became more and more likely (Mann, 2001, p. 238). In this regard, the small states in the Balkans were the Great Powers' equals in every way and the Balkan wars 1912-13 followed exactly this kind of logic.

In this context also the predominant national dogma, which gained acceptance during the late nineteenth century, must be taken into consideration – that is, "geo-policy". Its core was the conviction that the state was a geographic organism. "Vital", strong states were said to have the "natural" desire of extending their territories by colonialisation and conquest. Geo-politicians named four "vital" national interests:
1. defending one's own territory, as the predominant interest;
2. extending control of territories by geo-political formalism (forcing other states into "pacts of friendship" or making them economically dependent);
3. building up a colonial area of strategic control and rule; and
4. securing the first three issues by demonstrating economic and military strength within the system of states. (ibid., p. 241)

Striving for hegemony, rationality of war, geo-policy, the "objective" interests of the Great Powers and a certain constellation of alliances were the factors that led to the extension of a regional war towards a world war. Thus, a century came to its end in which Europe had enjoyed relatively long periods of peace. The Balkan wars were a pre-phase of the First World War in so far as by their results Austria-Hungary saw its interests only insufficiently considered.

Austria-Hungary's possibilities of realising its ambitions in the Balkans were declining at the beginning of the twentieth century, when the Concert of the Great Powers was increasingly ready to end the policy of putting a stop to the small and middle Balkan states' expansion against the Ottoman Empire – after centuries-old hostility one of the most important allies against the "Slavic threat". Thus, Austro-Hungarian foreign policy was orientated towards preserving the existence of the Ottoman empire as long as possible, in order to reduce Russia's influence on the region on the one hand and on the other hand to prevent the expansion of the Slavic Balkan states (which might also become a problem in home affairs). Thus, the monarchy got into conflict not only with the Balkan states themselves but also with the other Great Powers which already had given up on the Ottoman Empire or were working on its destruction. From the point of view of later historians, the monarchy became thus a burden for the European system of powers. By the annexation of Bosnia in 1908 it implied that it was trying to strike a harsher note for its Balkan policy (Kos, 1996, p. 10; Williamson, 1991, pp. 42f; Bridge, 1989, pp. 324f).

Austria-Hungary's relationship with its two partners in the Triple Alliance over the so-called oriental question – that is, the question of their attitude towards the Ottoman Empire or rather its breaking-up – was more or less critical due to different interests. Germany, which did not have any particular interests in the Balkans but concentrated on Anatolia, feared to be dragged into a Balkan conflict by the monarchy's foreign policy. Thus it was not ready to leave the leading role in oriental policy to Austria (Mommsen, 1991, p. 206). This conflicted with Austrian foreign policy, which considered the Balkans its very own sphere of influence. (Kos, 1996, p. 42). But German foreign policy supported those of Austria's interests, as formulated on the eve of the First Balkan War, that were not based on being enforced by military means.

The Italian attitude was different: Italy tried to preserve the status quo as long as it did not change into a direction conflicting with its own interests. Italian foreign policy interpreted Austrian-Hungary's interests as formulated by its foreign policy in such a way that after enforcing them in the Balkans the Habsburg monarchy would be economically superior and would profit to the disadvantage of Italian economy – particularly regarding Montenegro and the Albanian areas of settlement. But as, after the Ottoman-Italian war over the islands of the Dodecanese in 1911-12, Italy was strongly engaged in the Aegean Sea and increasingly in Northern Africa, it was not able to become considerably active in the First Balkan War (Kos, 1996, pp. 45ff).

On the side of the competing Dual Alliance of Russia and France, Russia had massive interests in the Balkans. Russian foreign policy tried to strengthen the Slavic Balkan states, on the one hand to weaken the monarchy, at least on the long run, and on the other hand to improve its own position in the region. While the influence of the monarchy was increasingly declining after the crisis of the Bosnian annexation in 1908-9, Russia succeeded in moving the competing Balkan states of Montenegro, Serbia, Bulgaria and Greece towards a war alliance against the Ottoman Empire (Rossos, 1981, pp. 8ff).

Habsburg colonial ambitions were torn between two kinds of colonial policy, between directly exercising power and imposing its cultural and administrative system – as was the case in Bosnia-Herzegovina after 1878 – and the attempted exploitation of economic resources, as was supposed to happen in the case of Serbia, the latter refusing the demands of the monarchy, however, which led to the so-called Customs War (1904-10) between the two countries. Basically, also the colonial policy of the Habsburg monarchy in the Balkans was based on the mercantile philosophy, as formulated as early as the eighteenth century, according to which one had to start out from the idea of a distributive share of powers in the face of overseas expansion, saying that the world's wealth was limited and its distribution was a zero-sum game: country A was only able to increase its wealth at country B's expense. This thought was supported by the obvious connection between a country's wealth and its ability to win wars (Mann, 1991, p. 357).

Thus, short but intensive colonial wars counted as rational actions; the victor took possession of disputed colonies, the loser had to be satisfied with what was left to him. From the decision makers' point of view these wars had the advantage of not happening on one's own territory. Thus, successfully waging war was to nobody's disadvantage in the victorious state (apart from rising taxes or a general mobilisation); probably it was even to the majority's advantage. For the sake of their own interests, the readiness of the wealthy classes to provide funds for financing aggressive foreign policy was increasing (ibid., pp. 358f).

Regarding this strategy, the task of the state was thus to open up and protect markets for its own enterprising bourgeoisie, with the help of its military potential. For its Balkan policy, the Habsburg monarchy pursued no other strategy – even in the face of the First Balkan War – if it did not want to decline as a Great Power in the face of the fact that Germany had been able to build up colonial empires during the previous decades and that Italy was about to do the same.

It was clear that the First Balkan War, if the Ottoman Empire was not to be victorious, could most probably produce only negative results for the Habsburg monarchy as in this case the Slavic allies as well as Greece would be victorious. A military intervention in favour of the Ottoman Empire would have resulted in Russian counteraction and also would have been strictly rejected by the German and Italian allies. Thus, for those responsible for the foreign policy of the Habsburg monarchy – if not for all its military leaders – it was clear that military intervention was not a serious alternative (Bridge, 1989, pp. 323ff). But still, the monarchy could hope for certain advantages, so to speak as a compensation for staying away from intervention.

On this, during the manifold discussions of experts, which had been called to the foreign ministry in the early autumn of 1912, there crystallised two central goals:

1. securing a decisive influence on the harbour of Thessaloníki and the railway line leading to it, as well as; 2. preventing any hostile power from establishing itself on the eastern Adriatic Sea in the area of Albanian settlement, such as Italy (rather unlikely) or Serbia (looking more probable). Thus, at first sight everything was mostly about trade and economic demands, but without being covered by political steps they could not be realised (Kos, 1996, p. 231).

Doubtless, these two goals were considered the preliminary stages of realising the great goal of military and colonial strategy – dominating the Balkan regions. Being the great loser in the field of the European Great Powers' colonial policy – and thus comparably far behind in its economy – for the medium term its economic resources were too small to keep up its status as a European Great Power (Kennedy, 1989, pp. 330ff).

When in the autumn of 1912 the situation was escalating and a war of the Balkan alliance against the Ottoman Empire seemed to be unavoidable, in the Austrian foreign ministry basically three possible developments were foreseen after war broke out: keeping up the status quo, if the Ottoman Empire were victorious; determining realistic goals, if the Balkan alliance were victorious; or accepting spheres of influence for the states of the Balkan alliance combined with partly keeping up the status quo (Kos, 1996, p. 19).

Now, regarding the second option one could not believe there was any chance of preventing the victorious powers from distributing the European part of the Ottoman Empire among themselves; and, with the exception of individual military leaders, no military intervention was (yet) being considered. For this case, the most important strategic goals were defined as: creating an autonomous or independent Albania; securing access to Thessaloníki (which was supposed to build a free port and if possible become an autonomous region, with the peninsula of Chalkidike, under international administration of some kind); hoping that unacceptable conditions for buying would not be imposed on those directing Austrian tobacco production in the area around the Thracian town of Drama or the harbour of Kavalla (Kos, 1996, pp. 20f). This way, Austria-Hungary could imagine remaining the decisive Great Power in the Balkans.

# Albania

The creation of an autonomous or if possible independent Albania, which was supposed to be under the decisive influence of the Habsburg empire, was directed against Serbia, which wanted access to the Adriatic Sea independently of Montenegro, and against Italy, which wanted to make the Adriatic Sea an Italian sphere of influence. The eastern part of the Adriatic Sea was bound to stay under Austro-Hungarian control for undisturbed merchant shipping.

Although during the Berlin Congress in 1878 the Albanian question was considered irrelevant by Bismarck, in the course of the following decades the Albanian-settled regions gradually became a factor also for international politics, particularly for

Austria-Hungary, Italy and Russia, whose spheres of interests were overlapping regarding the Albanian question. More simply, one could summarise the interests of these European powers as follows: Russia was trying to support the territorial enlargement of the neighbouring Slavic states at the expense of the Albanian regions (and thus indirectly the extension of its own power). Italy was striving for rule over the Albanian regions as a compensation for Austria-Hungary having been given the right of administering Bosnia and Herzegovina in 1878. Austria-Hungary was increasingly striving for independence for the Albanian regions to the greatest possible extent, to stop the expansion of the Slavic states of Bulgaria and Serbia towards the Adriatic coast.

Thus, in Italy and Austria-Hungary there were two influential powers which – if in a mutual alliance – intended to support independence of the Albanian regions in one way or the other due to different interests of their own. Regarding this question, these two states increasingly started to compete without, however, ending up in open conflict. This can also be explained by the fact that at this time neither of the two Catholic states was striving for direct control over the Albanian regions, as this would have confronted them with the problem of a Muslim majority. Particularly for Austria-Hungary this must have been a problem, as since 1878 it was confronted with conflicts between the muslim and christian parts of the population in Bosnia and Herzegovina. In the face of the threatening decline of the Ottoman Empire's power in Europe, the two states had spoken out for common action on the Albanian regions as early as 1876; there was agreement on supporting autonomy or independence for the Albanian regions if the Ottoman Empire were falling apart.

Regarding Albania, the diplomatic and military alliance between Germany, Austria-Hungary and Italy, existing after 1882, did not leave much room for manoeuvre for the two states. But in 1887 – when there were negotiations about prolonging the alliance – Italy succeeded in pushing through against Austria its demand for compensation in the Balkans if the existing status quo in the Balkans should change in favour of Austria-Hungary. Thus, this included a vague right of compensation regarding the Albanian regions.

Regarding the Albanian regions, the representatives of the two states decided at Monza in 1897 to try to keep the situation in the Balkans stable as long as possible. Should there still be a change of territories, the two states were to agree on common action. This agreement included a provision that both states formally supported Ottoman rule over the Albanian regions. But if the situation started to move, the two states would try to achieve understanding about the future status of the Albanian regions; this did not exclude the possibility of Albanian independence (Gostentschnigg, 1996, pp. 62f).

At the same time a kind of competition on the cultural level started for Albanian hearts and souls. However, it was and had to be restricted to the Catholic population in the northern regions of the Albanian area of settlement. The Catholic population was supposed to be a kind of ticket to the Albanian regions. The methods of the two states were rather similar: building and/or financing schools, influencing appointments of clergy, building churches and other larger or smaller presents that were supposed to keep the population happy. Austria-Hungary was able to point to its official function as a protective power of the Catholic population (the so called "cultural protectorate"). This way, there was a yearly influx of considerable financial support into the Albanian regions. Basically, however, this subsidy policy was a very restricted concept or instrument of foreign policy, not able to make any change one way or the other (Gostentschnigg, 1996, pp. 102-13).

It was clear that the decisive change had to come from the outside. A number of rebellions by the Albanian population had not really been able to endanger Ottoman rule over the Albanian regions. In most cases they were local revolts with very specific demands, such as resistance to the introduction of new taxes or against the despotic rule of single Ottoman administration functionaries. For example, in 1909-10 there were repeated rebellions in Kosovo against newly introduced taxes or recruitments. In the following year, a great rising in the northern Albanian regions finally led to handing over a memorandum to the representatives of the European Great Powers who were accredited in the capital of Montenegro, demanding rights of autonomy within the Ottoman Empire – but not independence; the Muslim parts of the population acted rather cautiously. Also in 1912 there was a similar situation, and again there were demands for autonomy.

Thus altogether, the Habsburg monarchy was able to express its vital interest in a dominating role by founding an autonomous Albanian administration area within the Ottoman Empire or an independent Albanian state. The rivalry with Italy over this question was not a problem a. o. due to the fact that the marriage of the heir to the throne (later King Victor Emanuel I) to the youngest daughter of the Montenegrin King Nikola I kept open an alternative option of territorial anchoring in the eastern Adriatic.

## Thessaloníki

As early as in the 1870s, Thessaloníki was considered by Austria-Hungary the most important gate of Austrian-Hungarian world-wide trade (the "Orient trade"). This attitude must be understood in the context of the building of the Suez Canal. On the question of the optimal (or at least the most reasonable) transport of goods, two schools of thought developed. One was in favour of increasing use of the cheaper but longer route for goods via Trieste. The strategic disadvantage of this option lay in the Strait of Otranto, which could be blockaded by Italy if that country wished to do so and was able to establish itself in southern Albania. The other opinion was in favour of increasing use of the more expensive but faster route via the harbour of Thessaloníki. Until the First Balkan War, the advantage of this option lay in the so-called Sandshak line: if this were built, the railway track would lie entirely on territory under Austro-Hungarian and Ottoman control.

In 1874 the stretch from Thessaloníki to Mitrovica (Kosovska Mitrovica) – built by the operating company Oriental Railways (in those days still financed by German capital)

– was opened; however, it was not yet connected to the Austrian railway network in Bosnia and Herzegovina. The Sandshak line project was to make the connection to the Bosnian railway system, which was exclusively narrow-gauge at that time. The Morava Valley line via Serbia would have been cheaper to build, particularly since in 1878 the monarchy had gained extensive rights on the Serbian railway network. But after the First Balkan War there was no argument left for a railway track via the Sandshak, because the latter had become Serbian (Kos, 1996, pp. 190-3; Riedl, 1908, pp. 10-13).

According to Austro-Hungarian foreign policy, Thessaloníki was to become a free port that would grant certain privileges to Austro-Hungarian trade, and the administration of the port was supposed to be given to an Austrian or Hungarian entrepreneur (Kos, 1996, p. 31).

## Kavalla

Kavalla was the export harbour for the tobacco-growing areas of the Thracian region of Drama, which lay north of the harbour. Particularly as regards transport the region was insufficiently opened up, and Kavalla was ideal as an export harbour in that the climate in and around the town was especially favourable for storage. In contrast to the competing harbour of Thessaloníki, Kavalla was protected from the north and thus not exposed to the cold northern winds. The "Vardarac" wind was able to considerably affect the quality of tobacco in the harbour of Thessaloníki. Already under Ottoman rule about 150 smaller and larger, mostly Austrian, companies had been established here, which bought tobacco from the Ottoman tobacco direction. But for the Austrian tobacco industry, the site of Kavalla was not essential, as 63% of the need could be satisfied by its own production (Kos, 1996, pp. 218ff).

Thus altogether we may conclude that Austria-Hungary was to look towards the results of the First Balkan wars with very limited prospects of success, as the hopes for the Ottoman Empire's further existence in Europe were dashed and the rising strength of the hostile powers of the Balkan alliance became a serious factor. With whom should or could Austria-Hungary form a coalition to enforce its anyway not very ambitious goals?

## First Balkan War and new facts

The strategic counter-offensive (from the monarchy's point of view) against the negative results of the Balkan War was the attempt by the Austro-Hungarian foreign ministry to break up the war alliance by trying to win over one of its members (Kos, 1996, p. 121). One wanted to try Serbia and Montenegro first, and after this Bulgaria. This attempt seemed to be made easier when at the beginning of the year 1913 it became apparent that the Balkan alliance was about to dissolve, as its members Bulgaria, Serbia and Greece were not able to agree on the distribution of Macedonia.

Already at the end of October 1912 – when the defeat of the Ottoman Empire became clearly apparent – Vienna saw three possible ways of enforcing its economic and political goals:

1. a customs union or far-reaching economic agreements with Serbia and/or Montenegro,

2. a customs union with several Balkan states or with the states of the Balkan union, or

3. a co-operation agreement with Bulgaria.

The monarchy tried to realise these options without co-ordinating its actions with the other Great Powers, since it considered this region its own exclusive sphere of influence (Giesche, 1932, pp. 16ff).

Regarding a customs union with Serbia and/or Montenegro, the then common trade agreements including a most-favoured-nation clause were not sufficient to guarantee a trade partner a privileged position on the contracting party's market. A customs union – abolition of the customs border between two countries – could have been a more efficient instrument: it would have secured sales of goods from Austria-Hungary with the contracting party/ies and cheap import of agricultural goods from the contracting countries. Right from the beginning, of course, there was also the thought that this way the Habsburg monarchy was trying to bring Serbia into dependency. At least these were the plans of the foreign ministry; the joint tax and finance ministry definitely rejected such plans of a customs union, as due to technical reasons they were difficult to realise, and a country like Serbia, they said, was not to be brought to its knees by them, as had been sufficiently proved by the so-called Customs War of 1904-10 between the two countries, which had been started on the question of exporting Serbian pork into the monarchy (Kos, 1996, p. 53).

## Serbia and the question of its access to the Adriatic

The already mentioned customs war with Austria-Hungary had resulted in re-structuring and diversification of Serbian exports (from livestock to grain and processed products). The Serbian export economy was dependent on access to the harbour of Thessaloníki, which was an insecure option as the Ottoman Empire had now and then blockaded the harbour. Thus, Serbia's plan for its own harbour in the northern or central Albanian region arose (Vojvodić, 1987, p. 247). According to this plan, a 40 or 50 km-wide corridor from Mrdare via Pristina and Djakova to Shengjin (north-west of Lezha) or Durrës was intended. Serbian demands for an Adriatic harbour of its own reach back into the nineteenth century; it was supposed to make Serbian trade independent of foreign countries. As an accompanying measure, a Danube-Adriatic railway through southern Serbia was to be built (Kos, 1996, p. 62). Realisation of this plan would have needed considerable investment, since both the harbours being considered had only a shallow-draught channel, being badly silted up (Kos, 1996, p. 64).

It was quite clear that any economic approach by Serbia to the Austro-Hungarian monarchy would be on condition of the latter agreeing to the building of an Adriatic harbour (Kos, 1996, p. 59). It was also clear that the monarchy could not agree to this. First, this would have endangered the formation of an autonomous or independent Albania; second, it would have given rise to the danger of a possible Italian-Serbian alliance – with the result that Italy might be able to establish itself on (southern) Albanian territory and thus control the Straits of Otranto, which would have affected the monarchy's access to worldwide trade as long as Trieste was the predominant export harbour.

Thus, the interests of the two countries were hardly to be harmonised. Austro-Hungarian policy intended to force Serbia into a customs union by on the one hand definitely preventing Serbia getting an Adriatic harbour and on the other hand bringing the harbour of Thessaloníki under Austrian control – thus cutting Serbia off from its export harbour (Kos, 1996, pp. 69f). The Serbian Government, however, firmly resisted this policy. Finally, the Austro-Hungarian foreign ministry offered Serbia a compromise, which did not include a customs union any longer but extensive trade relationships instead, as well as the use of a harbour on the Aegean Sea for Serbia (Kavalla, maybe Thessaloníki). The monarchy's advantages of such a solution seemed to be in Serbia being able to enforce the access to a harbour on the Aegean Sea only by the monarchy's diplomatic support. Moreover, Serbia's interests would have been shifted away from the Adriatic Sea, and Serbia would have got into conflict with Greece and Bulgaria, which might lead to a breaking-up of the Balkan alliance (Kos, 1996, p. 81). But this offer of compromise would have required the realisation of two conditions, viz surrender of Thessaloníki to Bulgaria and a friendly agreement between Austria-Hungary and Bulgaria, which then would have had both harbours under its control. But things did not develop that far, as the government of Nikola Pašić firmly rejected this offer (Kos, 1996, p. 82).

On the other hand, even Russia did not support Serbia's demand for an Adriatic harbour since, for the Russian leaders, this would not have been worth a war against the Habsburg monarchy. Thus, this Serbian idea could not be enforced any more, something which was also confirmed at the London Conference of Ambassadors where the formation of an independent and territorially coherent Albanian state was decided (Kos, 1996, pp. 90f; Bridge, 1989, p. 326). On the other hand, this also meant the end of Austro-Hungarian attempts at colonising Serbia by peaceful means. Thus the (vague) plans for a customs union with several Balkan states were also dropped; anyway they could only have been enforced against resistance from the two allies, for Italy feared a loss of its economic influence in the region: the Habsburg monarchy would have been able to secure a monopoly for itself. Germany feared to be dragged this way into resulting Balkan conflicts (Kos, 1996, p. 84).

The Habsburg monarchy's only success was the establishment of an independent Albanian state. In the First Balkan War, the Albanian territories had been occupied by the Balkan alliance. In the south, Greek troops occupied the northern Epirus; Serbia occupied the Kosovo, northern Macedonia and central Albania; and Montenegro occupied the town of Shkodra and its environs. After consultations with the Austro-Hungarian foreign minister, Count Berchtold, Ismail Kemal Bey, one of the Albanian leaders in exile, went to Durrës and on to Vlora, the last of the bigger towns not occupied by foreign troops. A quickly organised provisional government announced Albania's independence on 28 November 1912.

Everything else was now the matter of international negotiations by the ambassadors of the European Great Powers accredited in London. While the distribution of Macedonia led to quarrels among the former allies and finally to the Second Balkan War, there were negotiations about Albania's borders. Among all the negotiating parties, Austria-Hungary most determinedly supported a solution as generous as possible for Albania. On this question, Russia was the most determined opponent. A difficult problem was Shkodra, which was occupied by Montenegrin troops. In this matter, Austria-Hungary brought all its influence to bear and succeeded in pushing through a solution. But Austria-Hungary was not able to force through an agreement on the question of Albania's eastern border. Thus, the whole of Kosovo and western Macedonia came to Serbia (Gostentschnigg, 1996, pp. 74-7). Agreement on the debated southern border with Greece was reached as late as the following spring. Although the creation of Albania was doubtlessly a success for Austro-Hungarian diplomacy, it was a relative one, however, as at once the young state slipped into a lasting crisis.

## The question of an alliance with Bulgaria

Due to the failure of an alliance of any kind with Serbia, of the three strategic options that Austro-Hungarian foreign policy had considered, only the third one was left: an alliance with Bulgaria. This was a delicate matter, particularly as Romania was allied with the Triple Alliance and supported open territorial questions with Bulgaria in the form of claims to the southern Dobrudsha and the town of Silistra. On the one hand, Bulgaria was ready to accept an Albanian state, and the monarchy on the other hand was more willing to accept a Greater Bulgaria than a Greater Serbia. Bulgaria would have also accepted a free port at Thessaloníki – though only after the Greek army had marched into Thessaloníki – as well as the building of a railway line to Kavalla (Kos, 1996, pp. 122, 130).

The epitome of the precondition for an alliance of the Habsburg monarchy with Bulgaria was a Romanian-Bulgarian convergence. Bulgaria accepted – despite expecting negative economic aspects – negotiations with Austria-Hungary also because it was the only Great Power promising compensation for the loss of Silistra to Romania – the compensation being to bring Thessaloníki under Bulgarian control. For Russia had early spoken out for the port to stay with Greece. Furthermore, the monarchy also supported Bulgarian demands for Ohrid and Bitola to the disadvantage of Serbia (Kos, 1996, p. 159).

Bulgaria's economic concessions to Austria-Hungary, if Thessaloníki came under Bulgarian administration, were to be: 1. the harbour should have a free port zone for transit trade; 2. at the harbour the building of huge depots and warehouses as temporary stores for Austro-Hungarian use should be facilitated; 3. Austria-Hungary should contribute to administering the harbour in an appropriate way (Kos, 1996, p. 160).

Control of Thessaloníki, which had been occupied by Greek troops at the beginning of November, was disputed between Bulgaria and Greece from then on. From the monarchy's point of view it did not matter which of the two states controlled the city, if only the Austrian plans for access to the harbour could be realised. Basically, both states were willing to grant a special status to the monarchy. Austria-Hungary, however, in order to be able to realise its intentions of an alliance with Bulgaria, backed the Bulgarian horse, which on the one hand required the ceding of Silistra to Romania, and on the other hand compensation for Bulgaria (Kos, 1996, pp. 135ff).

On this, Austro-Hungarian foreign policy succeeded in developing some momentum about the end of January 1913 – a time when the Balkan alliance was under the threat of dissolution. The Austro-Hungarian Government decided to buy from Deutsche Bank the operating company of the Oriental Railways, which was also running the railway line from Thessaloníki to Mitrovica and which owned the majority of shares. This way, the monarchy's engagement in the Thessaloníki question was supposed to be emphasised (Kos, 1996, pp. 151f).

Subsequently, however, Austro-Hungarian foreign policy did not succeed in pushing through its point of view on the Thessaloníki question. On 31 March 1913, the St Petersburg Conference of Ambassadors started, with the representatives of the Great Powers being present, under the chairmanship of the Russian foreign minister, to solve the territorial conflict between Romania and Bulgaria. Already in the first talks, representatives of the Triple Alliance were unable to reach agreement on compensating Bulgaria's loss of Silistra by Thessalonica, since Italy and Germany voiced their opposition. Furthermore, Russia and France – as well as Germany – strictly rejected the Austro-Hungarian suggestion in the Conference of Ambassadors. Thus the monarchy's economic and political plans for Thessaloníki had to be abandoned (Tukin, 1936, pp. 164ff). For Austria, the Petersburg Conference was a heavy defeat. Bulgaria was not compensated by the ceding of Thessaloníki, which now was to become Greek for good – and thus Serbia, which meanwhile had reached an understanding with Greece, was to get access to the harbour of Thessaloníki. It became clear that the Greek government would not grant Austria-Hungary more favourable rights of access to the harbour of Thessaloníki than Serbia (Ebel, 1939, pp. 199ff).

Austria-Hungary's attempts to establish itself by diplomatic means as the decisive European Great Power in the Balkans had thus failed, due to the results of the First Balkan War. Although the monarchy could chalk up the founding of an independent Albania as a success, on the question of controlling Serbia – whether by economic dominance or by an alliance with Bulgaria – it had failed. For the first time, a violent (military) solution to the Serbian question was seriously on the Austro-Hungarian foreign minister's agenda (Tukin, 1936, pp. 164ff).

The results of the Second Balkan War worsened the basic strategic situation of the Habsburg monarchy in two aspects: first, Serbia's status was raised. Second, Bulgaria lost its access to the Aegean Sea or rather the Thracian tobacco-growing regions with the harbour of Kavalla. Austria-Hungary was interested in Bulgaria keeping the Kavalla region, which it had been occupying since the First Balkan War – less due to its economic significance (the cigarette industry), as this was only marginal, and more due to political considerations, to draw Bulgaria onto its own side against all odds (Kos, 1996, pp. 221f). During the Bucharest Peace Conference in August 1913, Russia and Austria-Hungary came into conflict with each other on this question, as Greece, supported by Russia, was not willing to give up the Thracian regions it had conquered during the Second Balkan War. The public considered the Bucharest Conference an Austro-Hungarian defeat (Kos, 1996, pp. 224f; Gostentschnigg, 1996, p. 74).

## Conclusions

Among the Great Powers, Austria-Hungary must be considered the great loser in the Balkan crisis of 1912-13, though Russia too had been unable to push through its ideas from a predominant position. But if for Russia the Balkans were only one theatre among others where it might pursue goals of expansion, for Austria-Hungary it was the only theatre, and thus the negative results of the Balkan wars were the more significant. On the one hand, Austria-Hungary had successfully contributed to the destruction of the Balkan alliance and had been able to strengthen its position on the Adriatic; on the other hand the monarchy had neither succeeded in tying Bulgaria to its side nor in eliminating or neutralising Serbia. Just the contrary: Serbia was strengthened by the crisis and the small state became a respectable middle power. Thus, both politically and economically, the monarchy had stayed far behind the goals it had set itself.

Due to this failure, in implementing the colonialist plans the military option came to the fore. As early as the eve of the Balkan crisis, senior officers as well as the heir to the throne, Archduke Franz Ferdinand, had spoken out for a preventive war against Serbia (Hantsch, 1963, pp. 360ff). After the First Balkan War, from the Austro-Hungarian point of view Serbia's economic subordination became improbable, and the foreign policy of the Habsburg monarchy was increasingly pushing towards direct confrontation with Serbia, while the foreign minister, Berchtold, at this time still recoiled from the consequences of such a step, namely, a probable war with Russia. Furthermore, the partners of the Triple Alliance were opposing a military engagement (Kos, 1996, p. 202).

After the Second Balkan War, Berchtold was not sure whether it would not have been better to engage militarily against Serbia and on Bulgaria's side. Now, he did not rule out any more the idea of a preventive war (Kos, 1996, p. 229) and he came to the conclusion that it was better to demand from Serbia withdrawal from certain regions, thus letting the quarrel escalate, and so reach a military solution this way. This change in his attitude must also be seen from the aspect that the alliance partner Romania was increasingly tending towards the hostile powers of the Entente and that an alliance between Greece and Serbia was becoming apparent (Kos, 1996, p. 231).

After the Second Balkan War, the conflict between Austria-Hungary and Serbia had reached a point of escalation that in the long run was to make a peaceful solution impossible for either side as both states were trying to rob each other's basis of livelihood. Austria could only imagine peaceful co-existence on the basis of a colonial relationship; Serbia could imagine it only if Austria gave up the attitude of a Great Power. In the face of the escalating conflict, on either side those politicians interested in conciliation had increasingly less chance of pushing through their ideas. While Serbia and Montenegro pursued a policy of "minor stings" towards Austria-Hungary, within the political and military elites of the Habsburg monarchy there was increasingly a tendency to make a fuss over trifles in order to provoke a military conflict (Kos, 1996, p. 235). The assassination of the heir to the throne, Franz Ferdinand, in Sarajevo on 28 June 1914 made possible a military solution.

# Bibliography

Bridge, F.R., "Österreich (-Ungarn) unter den Großmächten" in *Die Habsburger-monarchie 1848-1918*, ed. Adam Wandruszka und Peter Urbanitsch, Vol. VI: *Die Habsburgermonarchie im System der internationalen Beziehungen*, 1. Teilband, Wien, 1989, pp. 196-373.

Ebel, E., *Rumänien und die Mittelmächte von der russisch-türkischen Krise 1877/78 bis zum Bukarester Frieden vom 10. August 1913*, Berlin, 1939.

Giesche, R., *Der serbische Zugang zum Meer und die europäische Krise 1912* (Beiträge zur Geschichte der nachbismarkischen Zeit und des Weltkriegs, 18), Stuttgart, 1932.

Gostentschnigg, K., *Zwischen Wissenschaft und Politik. Die österreichisch-ungarische Albanologie 1867-1918*, Diss., University of Graz, 1996.

Hantsch, H., *Leopold Graf Berchtold. Grandseigneur und Staatsmann*, 2 vols, Graz, Vienna and Cologne, 1963.

Kennedy, P., *Aufstieg und Macht der großen Mächte. Ökonomischer Wandel und militärischer Konflikt von 1500 bis 2000*, Frankfurt, 1989.

Kos, F.-J., *Die politischen und wirtschaftlichen Interessen Österreich-Ungarns und Deutschlands in Südosteuropa 1912/13. Die Adriahafen-, die Saloniki- und Kavallafrage*. Böhlau: Vienna , Cologne, Weimar, 1996.

Mann, M., *Geschichte der Macht: Vom Römischen Reich bis zum Vorabend der Industrialisierung*. Frankfurt, 1991.

Mann, M., *Geschichte der Macht: Die Entstehung von Klassen und Nationalstaaten*, 2 vols, Frankfurt, 1998-2001.

Mommsen, W.J., "Österreich-Ungarn aus der Sicht des deutschen Kaiserreichs" in *Innere Staatsbildung und gesellschaftliche Modernisierung in Österreich und Deutschland 1867/71-1914. Historikergespräch Österreich – Bundesrepublik Deutschland 1989*, ed. von H. Rumpler, Vienna and Munich, 1991, pp. 205-20.

Riedl, R., *Sandschakbahn und Transversallinie. Ein Beitrag zur Geschichte der verkehrspolitischen Interessensgegensätze auf der Balkanhalbinsel.* Vortrag gehalten am 13. März 1908 im Niederösterreichischen Gewerbevereine Wien (1908).

Rossos, A., *Russia and the Balkans: Inter-Balkan rivalries and Russian foreign policy, 1908-1914*, Toronto, Buffalo and London, 1981.

Tukin, C., *Die politischen Beziehungen zwischen Österreich-Ungarn und Bulgarien von 1908 bis zum Bukarester Frieden*, Hamburg, 1936.

Vojvodić, M., "Serbia and the First Balkan War: Political and diplomatic aspects" in *East central European society and the Balkan wars*, ed. Béla K. Király and Dimitrije Djordjevic, Highland Lakes, NJ, 1987, pp. 240-59.

Williamson, S.R., *Austria-Hungary and the origins of the First World War* (The Making of the 20th Century), London, 1991.

# PART THREE

# 1919 in European history

# Introduction to 1919

The First World War did not end neatly. The armistice may have been signed on 11 November 1918, but hostilities continued in some parts of Europe, including the civil war in Russia. Also fresh conflicts quickly emerged between Poland and the Ukraine over eastern Galicia, between Poland and Germany over Posnan and Silesia, between Poland and Lithuania over Vilnius, and in the Russo-Polish war of 1920 and the Greco-Turkish War of 1921-22. Governments collapsed and empires disintegrated, leaving behind a political vacuum. This, in turn, encouraged national independence movements and socialist revolutionaries to attempt to seize power in the resulting chaos and confusion. This had already happened in Russia in 1917, but by 1918-19 other countries – including Bulgaria, Austria, Germany and Hungary – were experiencing similar developments.

It is perhaps inevitable that any attempt to bring together contributions on the events of 1919 – where those contributions reflect a multiplicity of historical perspectives, such as can be found in the following chapters – will focus to a large degree on the negative impact of the peace settlements, particularly Versailles, Neuilly, Trianon and Sèvres, and the resulting revanchist and irredentist aspirations of the defeated nations. It is also not surprising that a cross-national historical review of this kind highlights the mounting sense of disillusion and the unfulfilled hopes of the time – for example, the inability and unwillingness of European statesmen to replace the discredited idea of a balance of power by the Wilsonian concept of collective security, the growing isolationism of the United States after Wilson's death, the collapse of the Weimar Republic, the internal divisions that soon emerged in most of the newly-created states and the fact that most of them reverted fairly quickly to authoritarian rule, the rise of Fascism and National Socialism, the failure of the spirit of Locarno to resolve "the German problem", and the ultimate failure of the League of Nations to prevent the next world war.

However, it is also apparent in these chapters that the Great War and developments arising out of the peace process helped to set the agenda for, and impacted on, international relations for the rest of the century. The League of Nations may have failed in the 1930s, but the idea of collective security was not discredited and the search for effective international and intergovernmental institutions to replace the old system of alliances and the balance of power continued. Another lasting outcome of the Convenant of the League of Nations was the establishment of the Permanent Court of International Justice at the Hague in 1921. The Paris Peace Conference, through its reparations commission, also established the concept of war crimes, even if attempts to try alleged war criminals after the Great War proved abortive. Other elements of international co-operation and monitoring, which we now take for granted, also had their origins in the discussions in Paris in 1919-20, including the International Labour

Organization, arms limitation and verification, and attempts to control drug trafficking and the slave trade.

# Chapter 13
# The morrow of the Great War: France and the French in 1919

*Jean-Jacques Becker*

On 11 November 1918, news of the armistice led to scenes of almost unbridled enthusiasm in towns and cities across France, particularly Paris. But the undoubted euphoria of victory was coupled with an even greater sense of satisfaction that the war was at last over and the memory of appalling sacrifices. And this was particularly true of the soldiers at the front, whose enthusiasm was strictly measured, if only because the final weeks of the war had been very hard, with very heavy losses: 157 000 dead between August and November 1918.

## The period of mourning

Quite apart from the fact that the victory peals were all too often interspersed with the tolling of bells for the victims of the Spanish flu, many of the soldiers in the crowds wore black armbands to mourn the death of a close relative or colleague. What was immediately obvious in this France of 1919 was the sense of an enormous human loss. In fact the human cost of the war was still unknown. The figures had been veiled in secrecy and no one was really aware of the precise number of deaths, yet so many families had been plunged into mourning, so many young women knew that their husbands would not return, so many parents had lost an only son, or in some cases, two, three or even four sons, and so many children would never know their father.

It took time for the facts to emerge. It was only in 1920 that a report by the member of parliament for Nancy, Louis Marin, revealed that the number of dead and missing – who in other than a very few rare cases were unidentified dead – on 1 June 1919 was 1 383 000. Only much later was the calculation made that this represented an average of nearly 900 deaths a day since the start of the war. To the total of deaths must be added about five million injured, a figure that is not very meaningful since the scale of the injuries varied widely and some had been injured several times. What was significant, however, was the figure of one million with more than 10% invalidity, including 300 000 severely disabled, many of whom had been facially disfigured. The latter became a permanent feature of French society, as did the victims of poison gas, whose suffering was less visible in its effects but would continue until their death.

France in 1919 was above all a country of widows, orphans and cripples – a country in mourning.

This portrait of French society in 1919 would be gravely lacking if it failed to convey the enormous sense throughout the country that the war and its victims must not be forgotten, but must remain at the heart of the French soul. Everywhere, innumerable plaques recalled the sacrifice of the young men from a particular trade, government department or firm. And above all, there were the ubiquitous war memorials. From 1919 onwards they were erected for eternity in practically every town and village in France. The following year, at the insistence of the ranks of ex-servicemen, 11 November became a public holiday to commemorate not so much the victory as the immensity of the sacrifices made. On that same 11 November 1920, the tomb of the unknown soldier was inaugurated under the Arc de Triomphe in Paris.

## A bankrupt country

A country that had been bled dry, particularly as its long-established demographic weakness made the loss of its young men an even crueller burden than for other lands, was also an impoverished country that lay partly in ruins.

The cost of the war is very hard to calculate. There was the actual expenditure on arms and equipment, the upkeep of an enormous army and allowances to the civilian population. Then there was the cost of all the destruction, with a swathe of territory stretching over 500 km in length, and 10 km to 25 km wide, completely ravaged. Towns, villages, roads, railways, bridges, schools, churches, public buildings and factories all disappeared, fields became unworkable. Finally, there was the loss of earnings caused by the cessation of normal economic activity, the running-down of foreign investments and so on.

Viewed from the standpoint of the normal pre-war economy, the total cost was beyond imagination, and the calculation was made even more difficult by the depreciation of the national currency. Moreover, since it had not been possible to cover these costs through taxation, not least because a significant percentage of tax payers – more than 8 million men – had been mobilised, the war had to paid for by credit, in the form of internal loans of all sorts and external borrowing from the United Kingdom and (even more) the United States.

Paradoxically, whereas worries about how to cope with this situation should have been all-consuming, the entire population, including its leaders and particularly the finance minister, were seduced in the short term by the slogan "Germany must pay". The peace treaty should oblige the losers to pay reparations – thus giving a moral dimension to what were formerly called war indemnities – to cover the costs of the conflict. No one – or practically no one (at least in France) – asked whether a Germany that had also been ruined by the war, even if there was no destruction on its territory, was in a position to pay.

# The Revolution

Before the war, socialists like Bebel in Germany and Jaurès in France had predicted that any great war that took place would end with a great revolution. Their only mistake was about where it would happen. The Revolution had broken out in Russia where the Bolsheviks had seized power, but for them this was merely the first stage of a revolution that had to be on a European and then global scale.

While the war continued, the Russian Revolution had mainly been seen in France as the defection, if not treason, of its Russian ally, but how would it be once the war was over? The situation was quite different to that in Russia. There could not be a peasant revolution. Peasant farmers had suffered the greatest losses – 600 000 deaths, or nearly half of all fatalities – and the countryside had paid particular attention to Clemenceau's words about what was owed to the dead, but their material situation had somewhat improved during the war. They had been able to pay off their debts and purchase land. In fact, the improvements were partly a sham. The higher prices of agricultural products were a consequence of the weakness of the franc; and the cost of agricultural equipment, which now needed to be replaced since this had not been possible during the war, was also high. Nevertheless, there was very little likelihood in the short term that peasant demands would take a revolutionary turn, even if a certain number of younger peasants proclaimed their hatred of war and were tempted by Bolshevism.

Industrial workers' reactions might have been different, especially as viewed from afar the Russian revolution appeared to be a workers' revolution. They had suffered proportionally fewer losses than the peasant population but their incomes had fallen. They considered that their contribution to the war effort called for improvements in living and working conditions. Yet to a certain extent the opposite occurred. The women who had found factory work were rapidly sent home and many ex-servicemen found it difficult to recover their former jobs, despite the law, or even to find any job. Nor were matters helped by the difficulties of returning the economy from a war footing to peacetime production.

The result was a rapid growth in the membership of the general workers' confederation, the CGT, even though paradoxically leaders such as Léon Jouhaux, who before the war had been an anarchist and preached revolution, had now become reformists. They submitted a vast programme of reforms to the government, of which only one, albeit an important one, was accepted, in a law of 23 April 1919: a reduction in working time to eight hours a day, or forty-eight hours a week, with no loss of pay. This reform was not enough to assuage the growing agitation among workers, particularly as it took a long time to come into effect, and 1 May 1919 saw many disturbances. Significant security measures were taken, there were violent clashes between demonstrators and the police and a number of people died. In the course of the spring, there were multiple strikes on the railways, in steelworks and in the mines.

Moreover, once the war was over there was a growing hatred of war (particularly evinced by the slogan "never again"). At least part of the working class turned to the Bolsheviks, who had succeeded in extracting Russia from the war. How should the socialist party react to this situation? Before the war, it had openly preached revolution, even though it was more moderate in practice. During the war it had taken part in the so-called "sacred union", though as fighting drew to a close opponents of the union were in the majority. The conflict between supporters and opponents of Bolshevism caused deep divisions. The main debate concerned whether or not to join the Third Communist International. However, Bolshevism was of concern to more than just the socialist movement and the working class. It worried a substantial proportion of the population, particularly the middle classes, who feared that – as in other countries in Europe – preparations were under way for a revolution.

## A right turn

For most French men and women the main issue of the moment was the peace treaty, whose task was to ensure that such a cataclysm could never again come about. However, opinion on the matter was divided into very unequal parts. A fairly small minority soon realised that the negotiations had taken place in the absence of the defeated side, which would enable the Germans to conclude that they had been the victims of a *diktat*. This was far from the Wilsonian spirit of peace without victory, although the American president's views had in any case changed significantly since he had first used the phrase when the United States entered the conflict. On the other side, the overwhelming majority also came to the rapid conclusion that the peace terms would not be what they sought and the conditions imposed on Germany would be much less exacting than they would wish (even if at the same time in Germany they were deemed to be intolerable).

This was the background to the election of a new Chamber of Deputies. The existing members, who had been elected for four years in May 1914, had had their term extended until the end of hostilities. In fact, they did not end legally until parliament had ratified the peace treaty and the elections were finally scheduled for 16 November 1919. The resentment felt about an inadequate peace treaty for which France's allies were held responsible, the fear of revolution (typified by the most famous election poster of the campaign featuring a man with a knife between his teeth dripping with blood, symbolising Bolshevik Russia) and the difficult economic situation resulted in a marked swing to the right and the victory of the national bloc, whose policy was to extend the sacred union. The national bloc was not, as too often thought, simply the right. It also included the centre and even the centre left, but its victory was nevertheless remarkable as the right had been practically excluded from French political life for more than twenty years.

By late 1919, France and the French appeared to be deeply traumatised by a war they had just won and that now had to be paid for. They had wanted it to be "the war to end all wars", but they soon stopped believing this. However, they were sure they did not want to start again, hence the pacifism that would continue to grow over the coming years. They were sure that they did not want revolution, even though they still had reason to fear it the following year; but they were ready to resist it. Above all, they wanted life to begin again as before, and the war to be seen as merely a terrible interlude. However, wars of this sort are never mere interludes, but the starting point for formidable changes, and this the French did not wish to see. They failed to recognise that any return to former times was purely an illusion.

# Chapter 14
# The Weimar Republic: the burden of the Great War

*Gerd Krumeich*

The collapse of the first German Republic in 1933, leading to the European catastrophe of the Second World War, has given rise to a series of conflicting questions and answers on the reasons for this failure. There was a time after 1945 when historians explained Hitler's rise to power mainly in terms of international political issues and related aspects of the monetary system. At first, the primary cause was seen as the 1919 Versailles Treaty, which the Germans referred to pejoratively as the *Diktat* or, in more right-wing circles, the *Schmachfrieden*, the shameful peace.

Later generations of historians, particularly since the 1960s, have strongly challenged this explanation, and have instead emphasised the influence exerted on the Republic by the "continuity of élites" (to use the words of the famous historian, Fritz Fischer) between the Wilhelmine Empire and the Republic. "Continuity of élites" signifies that the leading strata of the former Reich, the army and the corps of senior civil servants and administrators, were not replaced or changed by the republicans, even though the latter had been in power since the fall of the monarchy in November 1919 and the proclamation of the Republic by the social-democratic leader Philipp Scheidemann, on 9 November 1918.

Since the 1970s then, "left-wing" or "democratically orientated" historiography has focused on the new political leadership's unwillingness to face up to the élites of the old order. This procrastination was seen above all in terms of the anti-revolutionary obsession of the social democratic leaders, who had been thrust into power in 1918 somewhat against their wishes. This has been argued particularly by the eminent historian Hans Mommsen. It is no accident that his great 1982 work on the Weimar Republic carries the provocative title *Die verspielte Freiheit* ('Freedom discarded'). This generation of 1960s historians had certain fundamental questions for its fathers and grandfathers: why had democracy been unable to free itself of the burden of the past, why had it chosen not to benefit from the "democratic potential" of the masses, why had it sought to repress rather than absorb the widespread trend towards direct democracy, represented above all by the workers' and soldiers' councils *(Arbeiter- und Soldatenräte)* that sprang up spontaneously throughout Germany in the dark post-war days? Would it not have been possible to secure the support of a majority of these councils for the democratic republic, rather than be engulfed by the Spartacist and then communist revolutionary movement, which the regime then subdued following the various uprisings of early 1919?

These were valid and necessary questions at the time and they reflected the previous generation's obstinate refusal to consider anything other than external factors to explain the collapse of the Weimar Republic. They undoubtedly cleared the way for a better understanding of the various political forces involved, particularly regarding the nature and importance (including the constitutional importance) of the workers' and soldiers' councils. It has to be said though that this generation of historians completely ignored the impact of the Great War and its political fallout on the Weimar Republic. We are now in a position to "re-open the case" and consider, in a non-partisan spirit, the war's impact on those who lived through it and had to draw the political consequences.

## The Weimar Republic

The first point to note is that the Weimar Republic was the child of the war. Its first steps, after its official inauguration, had massive political and moral consequences. It was the moment to come to terms with defeat. In October 1918, President Wilson of the United States had announced that peace would only be concluded with a parliamentary government and not with the former Prussian military caste. This parliamentary dimension was added to the monarchy when, on 1 November, the Chancellor, Max von Baden, formed a "parliamentary" cabinet based on the *Reichstag* majority. As early as 29 September 1918, a month before, General Ludendorff, the Quartermaster General or deputy chief of staff of the army, had called on the Kaiser "to bring those people into government who are largely responsible for things turning out the way they have".

Already we see the accusation, stated quite openly, that the victorious, or at least undefeated, army had been "stabbed in the back" by civilians who were weary of the war. The stab-in-the-back legend was a crushing initial burden to place on the Republic, particularly as, at the time, no one on the civilian side was aware of the lamentable state to which the German army had been reduced, in terms of both morale and *matériel*, after the collapse of the last great offensive of March 1918, which had been given the resounding name of "Michael". The army had subsequently suffered a grave crisis of morale. Soldiers started to walk away from the war, by failing to rejoin their regiments, refusing to go into attack and so on.

This only came to light later and many people at the time found accusations, levelled by the High Command, of communist intrigues easy to credit. After all, there had been a major strike of workers in the Berlin (and other) armaments factories in January 1918, which had been supported by the social democratic leadership made up of such centrist figures as the *Reichstag* member Friedrich Ebert. Ebert, Scheidemann and the others probably allowed themselves to be thrust into the leadership of the strike movement in order to abort it and counter the Spartacists, who wanted to transform the protest into a revolution. The centrist social-democrats may well have been trying to persuade the workers to return to their factories and not obstruct the work of their comrades in the trenches who lacked guns and ammunition. Yet the affair cast a cloud over Ebert for the remainder of his life. Although he was successively the head of government and then elected President in 1919, he never managed to convince the right and centre that he had not been a participant in the "stab in the back".

Throughout its entire existence, the Weimar Republic was haunted by the accusation that the left were really responsible for an undeserved defeat. For extremist propagandists, it was quite obvious that it was the "1918 revolution" and the establishment of a government of defeatists that had caused Germany to lose the war. Initially, Adolf Hitler was simply one protagonist among many. However, he and the Nazi party had one quite distinctive feature. They refused to accept any qualifications, arguments or distinctions. They were convinced that the stab in the back, the revolution and the signing of the Versailles Treaty had all been devised and implemented by "the Jew". Bolshevik or capitalist – it was all one.

It was under these doubtful auguries that the Republic took its first tottering steps, yet given the circumstances it was surprisingly successful. The first thing was to secure the return of the soldiers in good order. Admittedly since 9 November 1918, the date of the Rethondes armistice, some 7 million German soldiers had flooded back into their country, a return that was generally carried out in perfect order. But how would these armed men, embittered by "unmerited" defeat and confronted by the revolutionary movements, respond? The great worry was that there might be a putsch, an explosion of anger on the part of the returning men, a revolt with unpredictable consequences.

The Ebert government, which had entered office before the armistice, first had to deal with the sailors of Kiel, whose mutiny had started on 30 October 1918 and soon led to the establishment of soldiers' and workers' councils, first in Berlin, Hamburg and Kiel, and then in the great cities of the Rhineland and elsewhere. They saw their mission as being primarily to control the government and the democratisation of German society. The government saw its main task as bringing these councils, whose political structure was initially difficult to determine and which were suspected of strong revolutionary tendencies, under control.

So, faced with a massive influx of returning troops and a tense political climate, with the possibility of revolution, successive governments had just one priority, to create and maintain order sufficient to establish a properly constituted Republic and to elect a National Assembly whose task would be to draw up a democratic constitution. On 5 November 1918, Ebert announced that the main objective was to establish order. Four days later, the social democrat, Philipp Scheidemann, proclaimed the Republic on his own initiative from a balcony in the *Reichstag* building. He spoke of the "victory of the people" and of the "collapse of the old order" and of militarism, and called on the crowd not to allow any incidents to mar this victory. What was needed now, he said, was order, security and tranquillity.

# The Spartacist rising

There followed what was to become one of the running sores of the Republic, perhaps inevitable but nevertheless extremely inhibiting. In response to various, fairly minor disturbances, in particular the Spartacist rising in January 1919, the new government authorised a massive and brutal army response. The task was carried out on behalf of the Republic by the so-called free corps, units of former soldiers who had remained – or once more placed themselves – under the orders of their former military chiefs, regimental commanders and so on. It was therefore these seasoned fighters, armed with heavy weapons and commanded by officers, such as General von Lüttwitz, who mainly represented the former Prussian military élite, whom the young Republic entrusted – or was perhaps forced to entrust – with defending domestic law and order. Did they abuse this trust?

It is clear that the free corps' ruthless suppression of the Spartacists and striking workers was often carried out with exemplary brutality. To the ferocity of the class hatred felt by these soldiers returning from military defeat must be added the anger and bitterness they felt when suddenly brought face to face with those they largely held responsible for stabbing them in the back. The crushing of the Spartacist revolt in Berlin in January 1919 clearly reflects this hatred. The movement's two leaders, Rosa Luxemburg and Karl Liebknecht, were savagely tortured and "executed", and their bodies were thrown into a river. The assassins came out unscathed. This became one of the great, and ultimately insurmountable, fault lines within the new republic. Some 300 000 mourners attended the funeral of Karl Liebknecht and Rosa Luxemburg and vented their hatred of "military reaction".

Relations between the social democratic government and the communists suffered lasting damage. Until 1933 and the rise of Hitler, the parties of the left remained incapable of bridging the gulf between themselves and making common cause against a right united in its determination to overthrow the republican system. Throughout its life, the Weimar Republic paid heavy tribute for the disaffection of the working classes with the democratic republic.

The free corps were formerly dissolved on 6 March 1919, but their units remained at the service of whoever wished to call on them. Many of them were recruited into the army – the *Reichswehr* – which under the terms of the Versailles Treaty had been dissolved and then reconstituted as a force of just 100 000 men. Despite all the efforts of the allies, it also succeeded in establishing a reserve, or so-called black *Reichswehr*, made up of groups of these former soldiers. The most powerful organisation of this sort was the *Stahlhelm* ('the steel helmets'), with some 400 000 members. Another, much smaller group acted as bodyguards for a small workers' party founded in 1919, one of whose members was a certain Adolf Hitler, who had been seriously wounded in the war and awarded the Iron Cross, first class. His personal guard was called the *Sturm Abteilungen* (SA) and it received arms and training from elements in the

*Reichswehr*. In 1920, the SA comprised some 300 political soldiers, all devoted to their *Führer*. By 1933, their numbers had risen to 500 000.

Hagen Schulze, who has written a history of the free corps under the Weimar Republic, concludes that to their credit they preserved German unity and its form as a parliamentary and bourgeois republic. At the end of the Republic, however, these same forces served as its executioners.

Despite all this turmoil, the National Assembly was duly elected on 19 January 1919, with women also voting for the first time. There was a clear centre-left majority, which made it possible to form a government from which the right was excluded. Ebert, the uncontested leader of the social democrats, was elected President of the Republic, and the constitution that was debated and approved by the Weimar Assembly seemed capable of guaranteeing the continued existence of a strong and solidly based democracy. A sort of balance was created between president and parliament. The former was granted clear prerogatives, in particular that of using his powers under Article 48 to temporarily suspend fundamental rights and parliament's authority to legislate. The article was introduced to protect the nascent democracy against possible right-wing coups, but in 1933 it was to be the instrument with which those who wished to dismantle the last vestiges of the Republic could do so in complete "legality". However, in the circumstances of 1919, this was not seen as an imminent threat by a republic at odds with an extreme left whose revolution had been frustrated and an extreme right nourished on social sentiments and nostalgia, but also and above all on ferocious hatred for those deemed to be responsible for Germany's defeat and international subjection.

## Consequences of the Versailles Treaty

All in all, the Versailles Treaty was an enormous burden for a republic emerging from war. The victors were themselves exhausted, and had to fully heed their peoples' demands for recompense and reparations for damage suffered during the war. This is not the place to dwell on the details of the treaty, which reflected a Wilsonian commitment to restructuring international relations, for example through the establishment of the League of Nations and the International Labour Organization. But, from a more immediate perspective, the most important element was probably the infamous Article 231, which read:

> "The Allied and Associated Governments affirm and Germany accepts the responsibility of Germany and her allies for causing all the loss and damage to which the Allied and Associated Governments and their nationals have been subjected as a consequence of the war imposed upon them by the aggression of Germany and her allies."

There has been discussion since the 1930s on whether this article really constituted a moral indictment of Germany or was simply designed to secure the payment of reparations. Nevertheless, it is clear that in the climate of 1919 it certainly reflected a feeling among the allied peoples and their governments that they could finally have done with a country they believed had deliberately lit a conflagration in Europe, thus making itself responsible for millions of deaths and immense devastation, particularly in France and Belgium.

The reaction in Germany was total consternation and at first a categorical refusal to sign this "treaty of shame". Scheidemann, who had proclaimed the Republic just a few months before, expressed this view in symbolic terms: "may the hand wither that signs such a treaty". But the allies remained firm, and threatened Germany with military occupation and an end to the country's unity. On 28 June 1919, the treaty was reluctantly signed, in the presence of a delegation of French war veterans with severe facial injuries, symbolising still further the ills that Germany was accused of bringing on its neighbours, allied against its "barbarism".

During the fifteen-year lifespan of Germany's republican regime, there was no let-up in the protests against Versailles and the treaty of shame. Admittedly, some governments did try to comply with its provisions, create new international confidence and build on the foundations of the League of Nations, itself effectively based on the first article of the Versailles Treaty. This was particularly the case with Walther Rathenau, a great industrialist and philosopher, who had reorganised the war economy at the start of hostilities and who as head of government in 1922 resigned himself to a policy of executing the treaty. Likewise Gustav Stresemann, who two years later in conjunction with the French premier Aristide Briand, started to construct a peace policy and a European policy. However, all these attempts at international reconciliation were to be tainted by the shadow of Versailles. Right up to 1933, every German government opposed Article 231 and called for its repeal. Indeed the reason why Hitler was so well-known in the late 1920s, even among those who were in no way attracted by racism, was his determination to combat the treaty of shame.

Opposition to the treaty was thus a universal sentiment throughout Germany. However this did not lead to any unity of thought or action. Indeed, from the outset, the campaign against Versailles was weakened by the stab-in-the-back allegations. As early as November 1919, the highly popular wartime chief of staff General Hindenburg, whose status as hero was almost unchallenged, told a committee of inquiry on the causes of the defeat that it had undoubtedly been the result of communist agitation, a claim that was echoed by the nationalist right. The political radicalisation associated with "Versailles" and the naming of the "guilty parties" responsible for defeat led to an extreme polarisation of positions and a right-wing resurgence.

Nationalism took on a radical and a *völkisch* hue, extremely racist and with an emphasis on German excellence, in terms of blood and history. Hitler himself spoke constantly of German blood. A humiliated and subjected Germany, it was argued, must rise again in all its particular splendour. After Versailles the *völkisch* extremists had a much wider audience than hitherto. The *deutschvölkischer Schutz- und Trutzbund* ('association for the protection of the German people'), an extremely racist organisation that blamed Jews for the defeat and the Revolution, had more than 100 000 members by the end of 1919 and exercised growing influence on various veterans' associations, particularly the *Stahlhelm*. Even more significant, however, was the fact that the great centre-right party, the *Deutschnationale Volkspartei*, started to move in the direction of *völkisch* extremism. The party's 1920 platform expressed quite clearly its opposition to the "Jewish element", whose preponderant position in government and parliament was (it claimed) having an increasingly harmful effect.

## The rise of the extreme right in post-war German politics

As a consequence, the 1920 elections saw a marked right-left polarisation. The results were a clear indication of the rise of the extreme right since 1919. From then on, the so-called constitutional parties were never again to enjoy a parliamentary majority.

This extremely tense domestic situation was further aggravated by the decision taken in London on 5 May 1921 to set the sum owed by Germany in reparation for physical damage caused by the war at what seemed like the exorbitant figure of 132 billion Goldmarks. These were payable in instalments (lasting as far ahead as the 1990s), but in Germany there was an outcry. Throughout the country, hundreds of thousands of demonstrators proclaimed their refusal to accept this "enslavement of the German people". The government, which was well aware that acquiescing in this situation was the price to be paid for avoiding military occupation and the break-up of the Reich, was anathematised. For the right, both centre and extreme, there could be no greater term of censure than that of *Erfüllungspolitik,* the policy of implementing the treaty. When successive heads of government, Wirth and Rathenau, stated that they would continue to implement the treaty in order to demonstrate to the allies that Germany was physically incapable of paying the whole of its debt, the right delivered its thunderbolts.

Rathenau was a Jew and his valiant efforts to organise the war economy in 1914 no longer carried any weight. Right-wing gangs chanted in the streets the slogan "Walter Rathenau will not grow old: shoot down the damned Jewish pig". And he was shot down, on 24 June 1922, by two members of an organisation calling itself Consul, a secret society linked to the best known and most brutal of the free corps, the Erhardt Brigade. The Brigade had been established in 1919 and comprised some 2 000 officers of the former army. It was officially dissolved in 1920 but was then transformed into a secret organisation whose activities were generally tolerated by Bavarian officials, themselves increasingly at odds with the Republic and the *Reich.*

These incidents had a major radicalising effect in Bavaria. There was a strong reaction to the Law for the Protection of the Republic, which the parties of the left and centre placed on the statute book in response to Rathenau's assassination. This latter event had a significant galvanising effect on the republican parties and led temporarily to the establishment of a republican front. In Bavaria, where his violent activities were largely tolerated by the authorities, Hitler redoubled his organising efforts. Membership of the paramilitary group that protected the party's meetings and assaulted "communists and Jews" in bloody street brawls grew significantly: 300 SA, or brown shirts, in late 1921 had become 3 000 a year later. The head of the SA was a former army officer in Munich who since the end of the war had been trying to co-ordinate the army's activities with those of the so-called black *Reichswehr*, the almost ubiquitous free corps and other paramilitary groups left over from the Great War. He subsequently described his great ambition in his memoirs, published in 1928 – to give the front-line soldier the share of government that was his due. By late 1923, Hitler, the very prototype of the front-line soldier, thought he was sufficiently strong to attempt a putsch. It failed, following the "desertion" of the Bavarian state officials who had earlier encouraged him in his ambitions.

This post-war period was to end with the "battle of the Ruhr" in 1923, following the occupation of the region by French and Belgian troops on 10 January 1923. The French leader Poincaré had taken the decision because the Germans were looking for (and finding) any number of reasons for evading their treaty obligations and not making the required payments, in cash or materials, particularly coal. This "peaceful occupation" seemed very similar to a wartime equivalent. To a certain extent, the French and Belgians were paying back the Germans for what they had suffered during the occupation of 1914-18. Once again the shadow of the Great War weighed heavily over the Weimar Republic.

For a period it succeeded in freeing itself of this burden. The years from 1924 to 1928 were an astonishing interlude of political stability and cultural vitality. But, with the advent of the great economic crisis in 1928-29, starting with the New York stock exchange crash, the spectre of the Great War reappeared in all its force. It is interesting to note that it was only now that the great flowering of German war literature and films began, culminating in the famous controversy surrounding Erich Maria Remarque's great work, *All quiet on the western front*. As for Hitler, the economic crisis saw the transformation of his party into a mass movement. He himself remained the Great War soldier who never ceased to announce in every speech that his coming to power would signify the end of Versailles slavery and an end to all treason. He was greatly applauded, even by those who were not his followers, when in 1933 he withdrew Germany's signature from the Treaty of Versailles.

# Chapter 15
# Images of defeat: Hungary after the lost war, the revolutions and the Peace Treaty of Trianon

*Peter Bihari*

"Three teardrops on my eyelashes,
All the three so heavy and burning.
The first one, so hot, weeps over Upper Hungary.
The second, dearest of all, cries over the southern lands.
The third and heaviest one, runs for Transylvania.
Running for this or that part? – for the whole Greater Hungary."
(Revisionist poem, 1920s)

This chapter is less concerned with particular events – the revolutions of 1918-19 and the disastrous provisions of the Treaty of Trianon – than with their impact and afterlife, as displayed in public memory. Herein lies the main similarity: places of memory are not only a fashionable way of approaching history, but – in my opinion – particularly promising for history teachers (and students) who really want to connect our present to our past.

There is a similarity here between the Hungarian and the German situations around 1919 – apart from the sheer size, power and international importance of the two countries. Both were defeated, but reluctant to admit defeat which they attributed to a "stab in the back"; both developed radical nationalism – based on real or alleged grievances; both were utterly divided societies, united only in their desire to revise fully the "unjust" peace treaties.

As for what actually happened in Hungary in that hectic period 1918-20, let me quote the apt summary from Robert O. Paxton's recent book on the anatomy of Fascism:

"One may draw several conclusions from this story. First, that – no matter how strong the forces of left and right radicalism happened to be in Hungary – the country's fate was decided largely by the victorious Entente (and Little Entente) powers. Second, that no defeated country suffered comparable territorial losses and dismemberment, with the possible exception of Turkey by the treaty of Sevres, but that was rectified after the successful war of liberation in Lausanne, three years later. Third: no other country or population had to endure so many profound changes of the political system like Hungary – with the exception of the Ukraine .... All this took place in ten months. Add the loss of Great Hungary – already by 1919 – no wonder that the divisions, even cleavages of the nation proved to be so strong. One can experience these divisions even now, in the 21st century."
(IDÉZET /Paxton, 2005, pp. 24-5)

# Who could have thought?

This section of my chapter focuses on the consequences and the impact of the Treaty of Trianon on the Hungarian national consciousness – in other words, the "images of defeat" or Trianon as a "place of memory". We must certainly ask why the treaty caused such a tremendous shock and uproar in Hungarian public opinion – apart from the sheer numbers. I see three such reasons. Firstly, people were taken completely unawares – common people, intellectuals and also leading politicians. The right-wing Jesuit, Béla Bangha, writing as early as 1920, lamented:

> "And how suddenly did this end arrive! Five years ago, two years ago we would have laughed at anyone, even beat up anyone predicting that Hungary in 1920 would consist of merely 14 to 20 counties instead of 63, with Kosice, Bratislava, Timisoara, Arad, Cluj, Subotica abroad! [...] Who could have thought that so little is needed to ruin a thousand-year-old country, a country which had resisted Turks, Tartars and Western invaders – now being drifted to the brink of national abyss!"

Secondly, after 1920, Hungary found she had become one of the small and weak countries of Europe, whereas until 1918 she could regard herself as a great power, the key part of the Dual Monarchy, the thousand-year-old Empire of Saint Stephen. (Interestingly, nobody seemed to care that the break-up of the Dual Monarchy made Hungary – at least formally – now an independent state, after nearly 400 years of foreign rule.)

Thirdly, we must keep in mind that the dismembered territories were especially strongly attached to the nation's history. Upper Hungary and Transylvania retained Hungarian statehood during the Turkish period, and gave birth to a number of outstanding Hungarians from Matthias Corvinus to Béla Bartók. It was almost inconceivable that the birthplaces of such heroes could not be visited without valid passports – just like those of so many living and dead relatives.

Protests against, but also commemorations of, the Treaty of Trianon began the very day it was signed. On 4 June 1920, schools and stores remained closed. Several hundred thousand people held demonstrations in Budapest. National flags were kept at half-mast and remained like that for decades. Newspapers were published with black mourning margins, bells were ringing continously. This happened again in November 1920, when the National Assembly "discussed" and passed the bill – which, of course, was rejected by everyone. "This peace treaty, which aims at strangling an old civilised nation, is null and void before God and human beings" claimed MP Jenő Czetter in the parliamentary debate on the treaty. And, addressing himself to former fellow-nationals, he continued:

> "You should not forget, that your fatherland, the ancient Empire of Saint Stephen has always been the country of liberty, order, culture and the rule of law, where each race could develop freely, and every person could prosper according to merits."

It is not hard to discover a sort of golden-age myth here, a myth echoed in the most popular slogan of Hungarian revisionism: "Mutilated Hungary is no country – integral

Hungary is a heavenly country". Let me add here the other main slogan, a sort of national prayer: "I believe in one God, I believe in one Fatherland, I believe in one divine eternal truth, I believe in the resurrection of Hungary, amen". The prayer and the slogan were both selected through a nationwide "revisionary competition". The shortest slogan – "No, no, never!" – with its triple negative , was connected to the name of Tri-a-non.

## Symbols of revisionism and irredentism

Now to move on to the visible images of inter-war revisionism and irredentism in Hungary, I accept the opinion that "revision" in itself signifies a more moderate approach, since it can be legal and pragmatic, "irredentism" being more voluntary, arbitrary, aggressive and – usually – unrealistic. In Hungary the latter one prevailed, at least in public discourse and propaganda.

There are various pictures of the Central National Flag with Relic, showing the flag at half-mast at the Place of Liberty; at least one was sold as a picture postcard, with the prayer quoted above printed on the back (1928). The monument was overwhelmed with symbols and ceremonial inscriptions. The metre-long hand – raised to an oath – on the top of the rod, was modelled after Horthy's. The figures, of course, represent all strata of the population; the small pictures at each corner of the postcard image refer to four new monuments erected at the same place: "West", "North", "East" and "South": these symbolised the lost territories.

The statue of "Hungarian Sorrow" represented – not surprisingly – a naked woman. The famous writer Ferenc Herczeg – president of the Hungarian Revisionary League – spoke as follows, at the unveiling ceremony in 1932:

"We, Hungarians are the most sorrowful people on earth, because everything holy for us was mocked, whipped and crucified. And the mercenaries played dice over the inheritance of our ancestors. Our nation has been buried several times in the past, but it resurrected again on the third day".

This, in my opinion, is a very meaningful quotation. It is the voice of nationalism built on grievances, historicising national defeats, and – very significantly – deliberately using the language of Christianity. Hungarian suffering was equated with the passion of Jesus Christ, while succession states were quite often depicted as devils with nails and tails. The picture "Hungary crucified" – the cover of a famous multilingual book, *Justice for Hungary* – is another fine example of this parallel. Crucifixion was again recalled by a cross-shaped Trianon badge. Do I have to add that revision had its own Ten Commandments?

The image of Hungary standing alone among her foes, being regularly defeated, but always achieving resurrection, soon became a commonplace. This reflected romantic visions from the nineteenth century. In an article about "our national catastrophes", Albert Berzeviczy, president of the Hungarian Academy of Sciences, evoked the Tartars, the Turks and absolutist rule after the 1848 Revolution, concluding that "Trianon has united almost all the characteristics of our past national tragedies, thus being so far the gravest crisis which tests our vitality". Furthermore, he attributed the lack of proper defence to long-standing treacherous activity inside the country – he thus contributed to our own (latent) stab-in-the-back legend, already around in 1920. The analogy between the disastrous battle of Mohács (1526) and the Treaty of Trianon returned frequently; it even became the topic of final examinations in history at high schools in 1929. The title was simply: "Parallels of Mohács and Trianon".

Various irredentist memorials were not uncommon, even in humbler or just everyday surroundings. They could be seen in shop-windows in Budapest, for example, in the 1920s and the 1930s. Not that such things were expected by the powers that be – they were simply part of the public spirit, which even turned its attention to innocent objects of everyday life, such objects as a soda-siphon, an ashtray or a pencil-case. There was a "national drawing pin" and an irredentist watch; even advertisments for shoe polish carried the theme. Clothing was no exception either – though, interestingly, typically Hungarian dresses came into fashion only in the 1930s. Dress fashions extended to "Hungary in mourning". My personal favourite is from a hairdressers' competition, where the winning coiffure included the holy crown of Saint Stephen.

No opportunity was missed to reinforce the message: for instance, a revisionist foot-race was organised under the inscription "No, no, never!" You could buy a set of playing cards that carried illustrations "of the Hungarian fate" and there was an irredentist board game called "Let's regain Great-Hungary". This was from the late 1930s, when this programme was getting to take shape in reality.

One other important field must be mentioned: education. School days began and ended with the national prayer during the whole Horthy era. Subjects like literature, geography and history were overwhelmed with irredentist content and symbols. Records show irredentist drama being performed in school. I have mentioned high-school examinations, whose themes – directly or indirectly – were connected with Trianon or its revison. A detailed lesson-plan for 6th-grade pupils about "How to teach the Treaty of Trianon?" is very emotional, very one-sided, even extreme; it is offensive as well as insulting to neighbouring peoples, the nationalities who once formed part of Hungary.

## Conclusions

We have seen how Trianon memorials proliferated, mainly from the second half of the 1920s. Not surprisingly, many followed the pattern of First World War posters: the rise of official propaganda took place during the war years (and the following revolutions). Many, indeed most of these memorials used the symbols of romantic nationalism on the one hand and of Christianity on the other. The most effective ones successfully combined the two – which, essentially, had nothing to do with each other. We have seen how various forms of commemorations of Trianon and "integral Hungary" penetrated everyday life. As they were built on sore grievances, they certainly proved to be effectual. Nevertheless, already some contemporaries complained that the perpetual Trianon ritual was getting to be empty and hollow – in fact, even counterproductive and self-deceptive.

And yet – this is a crucial point – it had very important functions for the community. According to the French historian, Raoul Girardet, modern historico-political myths can be divided into four large groups: they are conspiracy theories or golden-age myths, or heroic apologies or unity myths of a community. It seems that all four united in the Trianon myth: Greater Hungary – kept together by the heroic and rightful Hungarian nation, resisting all its opponents alone – represented a golden age, but it was undermined by the conspiracies of internal and external enemies. Still, if united again to achieve complete revision, it would rise again and resurrect. As for unity, according to a young Hungarian historian: "revisionism was practically the only force to create national consensus in inter-war Hungary". He also added that it "bore the functions of a socio-psychological self-therapy" after the shock.

Let me add that previously – in the period of state socialism – historians somewhat one-sidedly over-emphasised the legitimising function of the Trianon-syndrome, namely that it helped, as nothing else, to stabilise the rightist-conservative system of Horthy and Bethlen. This view was biased, as it treated Trianon and revisionism as an artificially created problem, as a manipulation of the people by the ruling classes. But this appearance did have some substance. There are pictures that show this, for example one of Horthy, the Leader, or an election poster from 1931 showing the prime minister, Count István Bethlen, with the slogan "For the resurrection of Hungary".

Finally, I must briefly refer to some general features of Hungarian national consciousness between the two world wars. As in Germany, it turned definitely away from any traces of liberalism, and became chauvinistic and exclusive. It set itself against "imperfect" or "thin" Hungarians and treated them as internal enemies, thus becoming increasingly racist and anti-Semitic. In some ways it even turned against Europe – that is, Western Europe – which had brought nothing but undeserved miseries; it stressed the Eastern, "barbaric" origins of the Hungarians. A quotation from the right-wing radical Gyula Gömbös (Prime Minister, 1932-6) is revealing: "We have always protected Europe against our own Turanic brothers, and this very Europe is signing our death warrant now" he said in 1920.

His offended tone is exactly reflected in a picture with the inscription "For one thousand years for the West" and using the images of the apostolic cross and the "barbarian" warrior. Later, in the 1930s, the Hungarian Nazi movement – the arrow-cross men – used such "Turanic" symbols to mark the break with the West, but also a break with Christian tradition.

## Chronology of events

| | | |
|---|---|---|
| **1867** | Austro-Hungarian Compromise – Dual Monarchy created. | |
| **1913** | Count István Tisza returns as Prime Minister (until 1917). | |
| **1914** | Austria-Hungary enters the First World War against Serbia (until 1918). | |
| **1916** | Romania enters the war, attacking Transylvania. Count Michael Károlyi founds anti-war, anti-German independent party. Charles IV (I) succeeds Franz Josef. | |
| **1917** | Charles IV dismisses Tisza. Unstable minority governments follow. Debate on the "Jewish question" in periodicals (anti-Semitism grows). | |
| **1918** | Summer | The monarchy's last offensive at River Piave ends in disaster. |
| | 17 October | Tisza announces in Parliament that Hungary has lost the war. |
| | 24 October | Hungarian National Council formed of leftist opposition parties. |
| | 30-31 October | Victorious democratic revolution ("aster revolution"); Michael Károlyi Prime Minister. (Hardly any bloodshed, but Count Tisza murdered by unknown soldiers.) |
| | 3 November | Armistice of Padova signed with representatives of the former monarchy. |
| | 13 November | Hungarian representatives sign separate armistice in Beograd. |
| | 16 November | Hungarian Republic proclaimed in Budapest. |
| | December | Growing tensions and discontent. Communists and radical nationalists organise; Czechoslovak and Romanian armies cross the armistice lines. |
| **1919** | January | Károlyi becomes (temporary) head of state. |

| | | |
|---|---|---|
| | 20-21 March | Entente-note to Hungary demands further withdrawal – practically to the later Trianon frontiers. Government resigns, Soviet Republic created. |
| | April-June | Army of the Soviet Republic successfully withstands Romanian and Czechoslovak attacks, but yields to Clemenceau's ultimatums. |
| | July-August | Soviet Republic in crisis; Béla Kun's government resigns on 1 August. Romanian army enters Budapest. |
| | Autumn | White terror against Communists, Socialists, Jews etc. The Romanians leave Budapest; Admiral Horthy's troops enter the capital; he behaves as C-in-C. |
| **1920** | 1 March | The new National Assembly elects Horthy as Regent of Hungary (until 1944). |
| | 4 June | Treaty of Trianon signed. |
| **1921** | March, October | Former King Charles IV tries to return to the Hungarian throne (two "king's coups"). Little Entente powers mobilise; both attempts end in failure. |
| | April | Count István Bethlen forms government (PM until 1931). |
| **1922** | September | Hungary joins the League of Nations. |

# Chapter 16
# From balance of power to collective security?
# The League of Nations and international diplomacy

*Alan Sharp*

## A new order?

In December 1918 President Woodrow Wilson of the United States arrived in Europe to rapturous receptions, first in Paris, then in Rome and finally in London, where, at the Guildhall, he interpreted this enthusiasm as support for his policies. "I find in my welcome the thought that they [the Allied nations] have fought to do away with the old order and establish a new one, and that the key of the old order was that unstable thing which we used to call the balance of power, a thing which was determined by the sword which was thrown in on one side or the other, a balance that was maintained by jealous watchfulness and an antagonism of interests which, though it was generally latent, was always deepseated" (Shaw, 1919, p. 65).

What Wilson and a body of European and world figures were groping towards was a system of collective security, articulated by the president as the culminating of his Fourteen Points on 8 January 1918 – "A general association of governments must be formed under specific covenants for the purpose of affording mutual guarantees of political independence and territorial integrity to great and small States alike" (Temperley, Vol. 1, 1969, p. 435). The day after the president's Guildhall speech, the French premier Georges Clemenceau told an approving Chamber of Deputies in Paris "There is an old system of alliances called the Balance of Power – this system of alliances, which I do not renounce, will be my guiding thought at the Peace Conference" (MacMillan, 2001, p. 31). This obvious clash, between Wilson's belief in a new way and Clemenceau's continued faith in the old, means that there does indeed need to be a question mark in the title of this chapter.

Wilson may have believed that "the great game, now for ever discredited, of the Balance of Power" was no more (Temperley, op. cit., p. 439). His European colleagues were less sure, and whilst there was clearly strong popular and intellectual support during the First World War and beyond for a new system of international relations to replace the mechanisms that had failed in 1914, that enthusiasm was not necessarily shared by the political elites, though a strong sense of self-preservation increasingly prevented them from confessing this. Few were as open as Clemenceau about their continuing allegiance to the old system, and not all were irrevocably wedded to a system they perceived to have failed, but collective security represented an untried leap of faith with potentially fatal shortcomings.

The public, desperate for any organisation that could prevent a repetition of the Great War, expected its leaders to support the League. Those leaders were, for a variety of reasons, not entirely willing to do so but equally would not dissociate themselves from the League. One of the fault lines running through the whole system in the 1920s and into the 1930s was this dichotomy between what political leaders told their electorates and what they really believed. The year 1935 and the Abyssinian crisis would bring the British government, in particular, face-to-face with the consequences of this problem.

## The balance of power

The balance of power was defined by Emmerich de Vattel as "a state of affairs such that no one power is in a position where it is preponderant and can lay down the law to others" (Bull, 1995, p. 97). Balance of power as a system is most closely associated with the post-Napoleonic nineteenth century, with Britain's Lord Palmerston seen as one of its most adept practitioners. Palmerston's dictum that "It is a narrow policy to suppose that this country or that is to be marked out as the eternal ally or the perpetual enemy of England. We have no eternal allies and no perpetual enemies – our interests are eternal and those interests it is our duty to follow" encapsulates important aspects of the underpinning philosophy of the system. Governments must pursue their own interests and be prepared to defend them. They must also be prepared to be flexible, co-operating with or opposing any other members of the system as their interests dictated.

It was important to maintain a favourable balance of power on the side of yourself and your (temporary) allies. Yet, as the French diplomat Charles Maurice de Talleyrand pointed out, the system was artificial and required a moral dimension as well as military or economic muscle: "If ... the minimum of resisting power ... were equal to the maximum of aggressive power ... there would be a real equilibrium. But ... the actual situation admits solely of an equilibrium which is artificial and precarious and which can only last so long as certain large states are animated by a spirit of moderation and justice." The policy was particularly associated with the United Kingdom, or – as Eyre Crowe, in his famous 1 January 1907 memorandum would express it rather more narrowly – it was "an historical truism to identify England's secular policy with the maintenance of [the] balance of power" (quoted in Otte, 2003, p. 77). In 1923 Professor Pollard produced a rather more cynical and partisan definition of this relationship: "The balance of power in Europe was, in fact, a doctrine according to which Europe was to provide the balance and Great Britain to have the power" (Pollard, 1923, p. 60).

The era of Bismarckian alliances could be argued to have robbed the system of the flexibility it needed to operate. Although relationships were never exclusive, Austria-

Hungary and Germany were allies after 1879, France and Russia from 1894, with Italy allied (increasingly loosely) with Germany and Austria-Hungary, and Britain increasingly falling into the orbit of France and Russia, though without formal alliance ties. Palmerston's necessary fluidity was no longer in the system. It could also be asserted that Britain did not make it sufficiently clear that it would fight to prevent German dominance of the continent, but it seems unlikely that even the clearest statement (which, for domestic political reasons, Sir Edward Grey, the British foreign secretary, was never in a position to make) would have deterred Germany, particularly in the July crisis of 1914.

## A new approach to peace?

Wilson was not alone in blaming the outbreak of war in 1914 on flaws in the existing structures of politics and international relations, and demands for radical revisions grew as the enormity became more apparent of a war that did not end by Christmas 1914, 1915, 1916 or even 1917. Grey was convinced that the war could have been avoided if he had been able to force colleagues in Berlin and Vienna to attend, and abide by the decisions of, a European conference of great powers. As recently as 1913 the London conference on the Balkans seemed to indicate that the nineteenth-century Concert of Europe was still capable of preventing general war, as its admirers claimed it had done since 1815. But the system had always been voluntary, depending upon the willingness of the powers to participate, and it had no mechanism to force its members to consult one another. Grey was thus an early convert to the idea of a new international security architecture, with powers to demand consultation and delay before war could be declared, but it was when Wilson joined his voice to those of small, though influential, groups who were seeking change, that the idea of a League of Nations gained its most effective advocate, even if not its most influential designer.

The idea of a general alliance to preserve peace was not new. Maximilan Sully, adviser to Henry IV of France, had suggested a "Grand Design". The "Holy Alliance" after the Revolutionary and Napoleonic Wars, or Immanuel Kant's "Federation of Free States" were other earlier proposals with a similar objective. The nineteenth century had seen various international agreements to facilitate trade and communications and an increasing practice of the settlement of disputes by law or arbitration. In 1899 the first Hague Conference had established a Permanent Court of Arbitration, one of whose members, Léon Bourgeois, published in 1908 a book entitled *La Société des nations*, from which came the French name for the League, but little else. Almost all the great powers had agreements, either formal or informal, to submit their contested issues not involving national honour or security to some form of dispute-resolution procedure. Had there not been a general war involving all the great powers in 1914, twentieth-century historians might have written of the increasing internationalism and effective peace-keeping of the nineteenth century, which had come to full fruition in their own time.

Wilson came to Paris with one idea that was fundamental to his whole approach to peacemaking. He believed in the basic goodness of mankind. If the people were empowered this would produce a prosperous and peaceful future. The application of the principles of national self-determination and of democracy, which for Wilson were inextricably linked, would mean that people could choose the state in which they lived and then control the government of that state. Because they were good, they would choose wise governments. This would facilitate domestic harmony.

The extension of the influence of these rational and informed people to the realm of inter-national relations could be accomplished by the establishment of a League of Nations, an organisation designed not to outlaw war but to prevent a rapid slide into conflagration such as had happened in the summer of 1914. Making the world safe for democracy would make the world a safer place, because democratic governments would heed the warning voices of their informed public opinions and not allow disputes to deteriorate into war. In Wilson's own words – "My conception of the League of Nations is just this, that it shall operate as the organised moral force of men throughout the world and that whenever or wherever wrong and aggression are planned or contemplated, this searching light of con-science will be turned upon them, and men everywhere will ask "What are the purposes that you hold in your heart against the fortunes of the world?" (Armstrong, 1982, p. 9). Georges Clemenceau was less convinced: *"vox populi, vox diaboli"* he growled, whilst paying Wilson the dubious compliment of referring to *"la noble candeur de son esprit"* – *candeur* meaning naivety (Duroselle, 1988, p. 738).

Given that Wilson was perceived to be the great champion of the League, it is surprising that he was not more active in creating drafts and plans before his arrival in Paris. Rather it was in Britain, with the Phillimore report in May, and in France, with the findings in June of a committee chaired by Bourgeois, that the first practical proposals appeared in 1918. Phillimore's League would be a close relative of the Concert of Europe. It would emphatically be an organisation of sovereign states. However Lord Justice Phillimore, invoking the Anglo-Saxon concept of the "hue and cry", proposed that any member that went to war without exhausting the League's procedures "will become ipso facto at war with all the other Allied states". This automatic and unequivocal sanction represented the heart of the idea of collective security and its fate would be crucial in determining whether the League would become a revolutionary new force in international diplomacy. The French report shared many common ideas with Phillimore, but Bourgeois proposed that the League should have teeth, an international military force. He was also anxious to restrict membership to the existing wartime allies, thus raising Anglo-American sus-picions that France really only wanted a perpetuation of the wartime alliance to enforce the peace against Germany (Egerton, 1979, pp. 65-9).

Only after these reports, with which he claimed to be unimpressed, did Wilson begin to draft his own first proposals, with the aid of his friend and confidant Colonel Edward House. His early thoughts did include the *ipso facto* war sanction, an idea shared by the preliminary drafts submitted by Jan Smuts, the South African war minister and member of Lloyd George's war cabinet, and Robert Cecil, a leading member of the Conservative party and formerly minister for the blockade of Germany. Wilson's first draft stated

"Should any Contracting Power break or disregard its covenant ... it shall thereby *ipso facto* ... become at war with all the members of the League". This encapsulated the central idea of his alternative international organisation, collective security, an automatic guarantee by all the members of a universal alliance of the political independence and territorial integrity of other member states in the face of unprovoked aggression. Wilson's wording, however, exposed the central problem of the system – the clash between the sovereignty of the member states and the requirement that any guarantee be absolute, unconditional and automatic. Here the most fundamental decision for any sovereign government – that of going to war – would be taken for it by another government which had broken its international pledges. As his secretary of state, Robert Lansing and one of his leading legal advisers, David Hunter Miller, pointed out to the president, such a provision was incompatible with the constitutional right of the United States Congress to determine any American declaration of war.

It was equally unwelcome to any of the other major states and Wilson's changed wording eventually became the basis for Article 16 of the Covenant. This stated "Should any Contracting Power break or disregard its covenant ... it shall thereby *ipso facto* be deemed to have committed an act of war against all the members of the League". This restored to each individual member government the discretion to determine its own response to any such breaches. In the contest between a League superstate and the national sovereignty of the potential membership there was no doubt that the states would win, but this did rob collective security of the immediacy upon which any credible guarantee depended (Sharp, 1991, pp. 42-76).

Thus, when the League members promised in Article 10 "to respect and preserve as against external aggression the territorial integrity and existing independence of all members of the League", Robert Cecil expressed the view of many when he asked "Yes, but do any of us mean it?" Cecil himself had highlighted that "For the most part there is no attempt to rely on anything like a superstate. What we rely upon is public opinion ... and if we are wrong about that, then the whole thing is wrong". The French delegate to the League commission, Ferdinand Larnaude, was heard to remark: "Am I at a Peace Conference or in a madhouse?" (Sharp, ibid., pp. 57, 62).

The reality was that the main members of the League did not perceive it as a replacement, but more as a development and improvement of the existing system of international relations – and the ambiguities to which this gave rise were already apparent in 1919. The League was supposed to offer its members an absolute guarantee of their territorial integrity and yet be the vehicle for peaceful change. Britain in particular was insistent that a system that did not allow for flexibility and change over time would simply be destroyed by its own rigidity and thus itself constitute a threat to the world peace it was designed to deliver.

Wilson consoled himself that, though the peace conference would undoubtedly make mistakes, these could be corrected over time by the League mechanisms. If, however, some of the many new frontiers of Europe were defined, under Article 19, as "international conditions whose continuance might endanger the peace of the world" then, presumably, the remedy would be to alter them. But, in such cases, what would become of the territorial guarantee in Article 10? Who did the League insurance policy protect, and to whom did it only apply under certain conditions not very clearly spelt out in the small print? If, for example, France believed in collective security as embodied in the draft Covenant of February 1919, why was there a need for the guarantees against renewed German aggression offered by Lloyd George and Wilson in March? If a great power like France felt the need for added protection, why should lesser states put their national security entirely into the hands of others? Could the aggressor in an international dispute always be recognised? Would such states, like the villains in early cowboy films, conveniently wear black hats to make their identity clear?

## The League of Nations

The League was never the universal body that its mission demanded that it be. In 1920 it had 32 founder members, mainly the victorious powers together with some states that had been neutral in the recent conflict. The major enemy states were excluded whilst the uncertainties of the Russian situation left another pre-war great power outside the new organisation. At its peak, League membership rose to 63 states but in the course of its existence 17 states either withdrew or were expelled, including Japan, Germany, Italy and the USSR. There was never a time when all the great powers were simultaneously in membership and the loss of the United States from the very outset dealt the organisation a crippling blow. Not only would the League be deprived of American power and counsel, but those states expected to provide the muscle for League decisions, most notably Britain, had to ask themselves, before acting, what was the potential for confrontation with the United States in, for example, the enforcement of a naval blockade against an aggressive member with whom the Americans still wished to trade?

The freedom of the seas in time of war had always been a sensitive subject in Anglo-American relations, playing a major role in the outbreak of the 1812-15 war between them and threatening further conflict during the American Civil War and in the First World War. Stanley Baldwin, the later conservative British Prime Minister, said that he would always discuss any such blockade with Washington before allowing the Royal Navy to become the League's enforcer. As with the post-war settlement in general, America's withdrawal from the execution of policies in whose creation it had played a vital role, left Britain and France as the main players and Geneva, where the League established its headquarters, became yet another arena in which their contested visions clashed. Salvador de Madariaga of the League Secretariat suggested that "Everything went on as if, for lack of any common adversary, France and Britain had chosen the League as the arena in which to fight each other" (Henig, 2000, pp. 138-57).

America's absence left Canada with serious concerns about the implications for its own relationship with its powerful neighbour and led to four Canadian attempts to either delete or dilute Article 10. Perhaps inaccurately and certainly undiplomatically, one Canadian delegate declared that Canada lived "in a fire-proof house far from inflammable materials" and hence saw little need to contribute to an international fire brigade. Although the Canadian initiatives technically failed, the reality was that, as a British Foreign Office memorandum acknowledged in 1926, members' obligations under the Covenant would be limited by their "geographical situations and special conditions"; it would be for each state to decide its contribution to any collective security operation, and sanctions under Article 16 were not mandatory (DBFP, 1966, Series 1A, Vol. 1, pp. 847-8).

Collective security was not – as Gilbert Murray, the chairman of the League of Nations Union in Britain pointed out – very secure. "The obligation in Article 10 is at once too widespread for any prudent nation to accept, and too vague for any prudent nation to bank upon. As the Covenant now stands, no nation would be really safe in acting on the supposition that, if it were attacked, the rest of the League would send armies to defend it" (*Daily News*, February 1923, quoted by Henig, 2000, p. 148). Attempts to strengthen collective security under first the Treaty of Mutual Assistance and then the Geneva Protocol were resisted fiercely in Britain by the Foreign Office and the service departments, who believed these could result in undefined and unacceptable military commitments. Optimistic advocates of these proposals to make collective security more effective argued that this would enable and encourage mutual and continuing disarmament. The pessimistic and paradoxical doubts of their opponents were neatly summarised by the British Committee of Imperial Defence in November 1935: "It is almost impossible to forecast the nations with which we might be brought into conflict owing to a breach of the Covenant … It is also difficult to calculate what the composition of our … [armed] forces should be, as no reasonable warning of the conditions under which we might have to operate can be given. Consequently … [a]s the result of the principle of collective security we must be more instantly ready for war than before" (Dunbabin, 1993, pp. 440-1).

Although the League was itself a product of the post-war peace settlement, and the 26 articles of the Covenant formed the first part of all the treaties negotiated in Paris, it became clear at an early stage that the British and French did not intend to let major aspects of treaty enforcement slip into its hands. In the aftermath of the March 1920 Kapp *putsch* in Germany, and in retaliation for what it perceived to be an illegal incursion of German troops into the demilitarised Ruhr district, France occupied unilaterally five German towns, Frankfurt, Darmstadt, Hanau, Homburg and Dieburg on 5-6 April 1920.

Lord Robert Cecil suggested that these German troops in the forbidden area represented a threat of war and thus, under the terms of the treaty, should be referred to the League. The Foreign Office found his case strong, but was not prepared to follow this policy – such matters were for the allied governments to settle, not the League. Cecil wrote to Curzon, Balfour and Lloyd George on 12 April 1920, arguing that the German troop movements could be construed as contraventions of Articles 42 and 43 of the Treaty constituting a threat of war and hence the League should be summoned. Sydney Waterlow, an official in the Foreign Office, commented "Either we must sooner or later find an occasion to promote recourse to this machinery, or we must reconcile ourselves to the Covenant becoming a dead letter" (191340/4232/18 in FO371/3783, British National Archive, Kew). The League had its uses, for example in sidestepping the principle of self-determination when it was felt necessary to provide France with the coal of the Saar, and Poland with the use of Danzig as a port, without awarding either state sovereignty over the inhabitants affected. Minority protection in eastern and central Europe could helpfully and conveniently be passed to the League.

The request by Britain and France to discover a solution to the impasse they had reached in interpreting the results of the 1921 Upper Silesian plebiscite into actual frontiers was an unusual and exceptional involvement of the League in treaty execution. It was not necessarily one with a happy outcome for Britain, since the eventual frontier favoured Poland to a greater extent than London wished. The disparaging description of the committee by the British cabinet secretary, Sir Maurice Hankey, as consisting of "A pro-French Belgian, two Dagos and a Chink" did not suggest great respect and reflected British disappointment (Hankey to D'Abernon, 2 October 1921, D'Abernon Papers, Add. MS 48954, British Library). More normal was the Anglo-French rejection in 1921 of the League as a credible replacement for the Inter-Allied Military Mission Control Commission as the major enforcer of German disarmament and their continued scepticism about its potential as a future monitoring agency, despite the provisions of Article 213 of the treaty.

The League did enjoy some successes, most notably in the Aaland islands problem in 1920 and in the Greco-Bulgarian dispute of 1925 but, significantly, both were in relatively accessible parts of Europe, were between minor states, and did not involve the direct interests of a great power. The League's beneficial role in inhibiting slavery, international prostitution, and the trading of drugs, or in promoting the protection of refugees and minorities, was acknowledged at the time and by later historians. What is not entirely clear is whether the "new diplomacy" achieved substantially different results than the "old" might have done in similar circumstances.

The League was much less effective where any of these criteria did not apply, for example in the Bolivia-Paraguay confrontation of the early 1930s, or in 1920s incidents such as the Polish seizure of Vilna. The Franco-Belgian occupation of the Ruhr in 1923 was a further example of the exclusion of the League from matters arising from treaty enforcement. In the same year the Corfu incident indicated that the exigencies of the international system, great power politics and prestige could all play a role in undermining League involvement (Dunbabin, 1993; Henig, 2000). When the incident was remote and involved a great power, such as in Manchuria in 1931, the League struggled to make any impact and its problems were not eased by the difficulty of clearly identifying Japan as an aggressor (Armstrong, op. cit., pp. 28-32). It was, however, in Abyssinia in 1935 that the demands of the old and new diplomacies came into the sharpest confrontation.

In December 1934, Italian and Abyssinian forces clashed at Wal-Wal in Abyssinia (Ethiopia). On 3 January 1935, Abyssinia appealed to the League under the auspices of Article 11, but nine months later Benito Mussolini, Italy's fascist leader, used this

180

incident as an excuse to invade Abyssinia on 3 October 1935. Such behaviour might have been acceptable to the other great powers (though clearly not to the invaded peoples) in the nineteenth century, but it was not so in 1935. There was no doubt that Italy had acted aggressively and in contravention of its obligations towards a fellow member of the League (whose membership Italy had, ironically, sponsored). There was equally no doubt that Abyssinia, already well known in Geneva for its dubious dealings in slavery, was not an ideal test case as a deserving cause for international solidarity, but the circumstances meant that the credibility of the League and the "new diplomacy" became inextricably linked with the response to this problem of its major players, Britain and France.

Their position was, however complicated by the demands of the "old diplomacy". Increasingly concerned about the actions of Hitler's Germany in renouncing disarmament and introducing conscription, Britain and France were anxious to retain Italian support in Europe. Italy had an impressive modern fleet and Mussolini boasted of the power and size of his air force. He did nothing to harm Italy's claims to be an actor of great significance in the European theatre when his troops advanced to the Brenner frontier and deterred Hitler from further intervention in Austria after the murder of Chancellor Dolfuss in July 1934. Italy was thus perceived to be an important component in any European balance of power. An Anglo-French-Italian meeting at Stresa in April 1935 seemed to Britain and France to have consolidated an anti-German bloc, whilst Mussolini's perception was that Anglo-French indifference to the fate of Abyssinia was the *quid pro quo* for Italian support. (For the general European diplomatic background, see Marks, 2002; Steiner, 2005.)

On the one hand, therefore, stood collective security, the League and international morality and on the other, considerations of balance of power and an amoral approach to international diplomacy that measured ends, not means. Britain, perhaps to a greater extent than France, was caught between these two conflicting visions. As the crisis in Abyssinia developed, so did the pressures on the British decision-making elite, torn between the public's continuing support for the League and their own scepticism and preference for the unpalatable alternative. Robert Vansittart, the Permanent Under-Secretary at the Foreign Office, neatly summed up their unenviable situation in a typically acerbic minute on 8 June 1935: "The position is plain as a pikestaff. Italy will have to be bought off – let us use and face ugly words – in some form or other, or Abyssinia will eventually perish. That might in itself matter less, if it did not mean that the League would also perish (and that Italy would simultaneously perform another *volte-face* into the arms of Germany, a combination of *haute politique* and *haute cocotterie* that we can ill afford just now". He predicted "a horrid autumn" (Adamthwaite, 1977, p. 138).

The British government faced an election that autumn. The total electorate was 31 379 050. Of those eligible to do so, 21 997 254 voted in that November's general election. Earlier in the year the League of Nations Union (whose membership was itself in decline from its peak of 407 000 in 1931 to 377 824 in 1935) organised an early example of a public opinion poll, asking about British perceptions of the

League. Nearly 11 million people, or over half the number that would vote later in the year, responded to a series of questions which had increasingly tough implications for employment in the armaments industries and, ultimately, about whether the British public would fight to preserve peace. To the first question, as to whether Britain should remain in the League, 10 642 560 said yes, and 337 964 said no, an unsurprising 97% yes vote. The next three questions asked about the desirability of all-round disarmament and the prohibition of international arms trading. The fifth question, in two parts, first asked whether an aggressor should be compelled to desist by economic and non-military means, and 9 627 606 or 94.1% said yes, whilst 60 165 said no. The second part asked about public support for, if necessary, military sanctions against an aggressor. Altogether, 6 506 777 said yes, 2 262 261 voted no, still giving 74.2% approval for the ultimate sanction of war. No British political party that wanted to secure election could ignore this public endorsement of the League, no matter how sceptical its leaders might be about collective security.

Thus Britain did press for sanctions against Italy, but backed away from the two that would be most likely to deter Italy (or, more alarmingly, provoke Mussolini into what British leaders called "a mad dog act", for example a surprise attack on British naval forces in the Mediterranean) – an embargo on supplying oil to Italy and denying it the use of the Suez Canal. This may have been sufficient to maintain the government's credibility in the eyes of the electorate, and the coalition National Government, in which the conservatives were the dominant partners, was comfortably re-elected, but the international results were less happy. The sanctions against Italy were not sufficient to prevent its conquest of Abyssinia, a fact reluctantly recognised by the League in the summer of 1936. The League was thus perceived to have failed and became an increasing irrelevance in international diplomacy, small states looked to their own security, or, like Ireland, became neutral, and the larger states reverted to their more familiar policies of alliances and rearmament. When the Austrian *Anschluss* destroyed the independence of a member in 1938, the League was not even informed. Italy became the ally of Nazi Germany, driven away from the Stresa camp by a policy that had achieved the exact opposite of its intentions. Britain had secured neither collective security, nor re-established the balance of power.

## Conclusion

The reality was that, unless the major powers – especially Britain and France – were prepared to give full support to the League, collective security could not succeed and small powers could feel aggrieved that their faith in the system had been betrayed. On the other hand, there was the question of who would bear the brunt of League action. As Sir Samuel Hoare, the British foreign secretary, told the League Assembly on 11 September 1935 "my country stands … for the collective maintenance of the Covenant in its entirety, and particularly for steady and collective resistance to all acts of unprovoked aggression" but he had, significantly, presaged this remark by stating "One thing is certain. If the burden is to be borne, it must be borne collectively. If risks for peace are to be run, they must be run by all. The security of the many cannot be ensured solely by the efforts of the few, however powerful they may be" (Hoare, 1954, p. 170). It was, a cynic might point out, both to the advantage of smaller states that the League should be successful and that the costs to themselves should be minimal. During a dispute between Colombia and Peru in 1932-3, the Irish delegate to the League, Sean Lester, proposed an arms embargo on Peru. In Dublin Sean Murphy (the Assistant Secretary at the Department of External Affairs) reminded Lester that Ireland was neither an arms manufacturer nor exporter. "The Minister wishes to avoid a situation in which the Irish Free State would be too prominent in the acceptance of an obligation the burden of which falls not on the Irish Free State but upon other states" (Kennedy, 1996, p. 179).

The lessons of Abyssinia were painful. On 30 June 1936, the Abyssinian emperor Haile Selassie addressed the League's Assembly. "I ask the Great Powers, who have promised the guarantee of collective security to small states – those small states over whom hangs the threat that they may one day suffer the fate of Ethiopia: What measures do they intend to take? Representatives of the world, I have come to Geneva to discharge in your midst the most painful duties of the head of a state. What answer am I to take back to my people?" (Kennedy, ibid., p. 220). For followers of *realpolitik* the answer was obvious, as Colonel Henry Pownall, then serving in the secretariat of the British Committee of Imperial Defence declared: "So much for Collective Security and 'moral forces' and all the rest of that stuff ... It's no good thinking that Articles 10 and 16 of the Covenant can remain. People who rely on them for safety will be let down as Abyssinia was let down. This the smaller nations are particularly alive to and are saying so vociferously in their press. So ... we now know where we stand, the Experiment has been made and failed. How lucky that it has been tried out in this minor test case, lucky for all except Abyssinia" (quoted by Dunbabin, 1993, p. 441).

Robert Cecil's Great Experiment had ended in failure. It had been based on too many paradoxes: the attempt to create collective security in a world of sovereign national states; the hope of international democracy in a world dominated by great powers; the aim of deterring a potential aggressor and maintaining the peace with the ultimate threat of war; a guarantee of territorial integrity combined with an agency for territorial readjustment; in short a revolutionary basis for future international stability. Yet it had set a precedent that would be followed again in 1945, with the establishment of the United Nations, an organisation that has had its own difficulties in applying the concept of collective security. Indeed in the UN's case perhaps collective should be spelt with a "k", since it is only in Korea and Kuwait that successful operations have been mounted. The League represented one of the more noble aspects of peacemaking at the end of the First World War and his experiences as the deputy to the first secretary-general, Sir Eric Drummond, may well have had an important influence on the future thought of Jean Monnet, whose suggestions for European co-operation after the Second World War would combine the international characteristics of the League with additional supranational competencies. Monnet had a great belief in the power of institutions, often quoting the nineteenth-century Genevan diarist, Henri Frédéric Amiel, "Each man begins the world afresh. Only institutions grow wiser: they store up the collective wisdom; men subject to the same laws will gradually find, not that their natures change but that their behaviour does" (Duschene, 1994, p. 401).

The League may be judged not to have been an absolute failure if it helped to foster the idea of international law and contributed towards future international institutions, but in the inter-war period it never replaced the concept of the balance of power in the mental maps of most of the leading statesmen. The tragedy was that their attempts, whether sincere or cynical, to appear to be supporters of collective security delivered neither unity nor security, and undermined their preferred, but now politically discredited, alternative.

# Bibliography

Adamthwaite, A., *The making of the Second World War*, Allen and Unwin, London, 1977.

Armstrong, D., *The rise of the international organisation: A short history*, Macmillan, Basingstoke, 1982.

Bull, H., *The anarchical society: A study of order in world politics*, 2nd edn, Macmillan, Basingstoke, 1995.

DBFP, *Documents on British foreign policy*, HMSO, London, 1996, Series 1A, Vol. 1.

Dunbabin, J.P., "The League of Nations' place in the international system", *History*, 1993, Vol. 78, No. 254.

Duroselle, J.-B., *Clemenceau*, Fayard, Paris, 1988.

Duschene, F., *Jean Monnet: The first statesman of interdependence*, New York, 1994.

Egerton, G., *Great Britain and the creation of the League of Nations: Strategy, politics and international organisation, 1914-1919*, Scolar, London, 1979.

Henig, R., "Britain, France and the League of Nations in the 1920s" in A. Sharp and G. Stone, *Anglo-French relations in the twentieth century: Rivalry and cooperation*, Routledge, London, 2000.

Hoare, Sir Samuel, *Nine troubled years*, Collins, London, 1954.

Kennedy, M., *Ireland and the League of Nations, 1919-1946: International relations, diplomacy and politics*, Irish Academic Press, Dublin, 1996.

MacMillan, M., *Peacemakers: The Paris Peace Conference of 1919 and its attempt to end war*, John Murray, London, 2001.

Marks, S., *The ebbing of European ascendancy: An international history of the world, 1914-1945*, Arnold, London, 2002.

Otte, T.G., " 'Almost a law of nature?' Sir Edward Grey, the Foreign Office and the balance of power in Europe, 1905-1912", *Diplomacy and Statecraft*, 2003, Vol. 14, No. 2.

Pollard, A.F., "The balance of power", *Journal of the British Institute of International Affairs*, 1923, Vol. 2.

Sharp, A., *The Versailles settlement: Peacemaking in Paris, 1919*, Macmillan, Basingstoke, 1991.

Shaw, G.B., *Peace conference hints*, Constable, London, 1919.

Steiner, Z., *The lights that failed: European international history, 1919-1933*, Oxford University Press, Oxford, 2005.

Temperley, H.W.V. (ed.), *A history of the Peace Conference of Paris*, 6 vols., Oxford University Press, Oxford, 1920 (reprinted 1969).

# Chapter 17
# Yugoslavs at the Paris Peace Conference and the legacy of the First World War

*Tvrtko Jakovina*

## The First World War and its legacy among the South Slavs

A colleague of mine, a teaching assistant in American history at Georgetown University, gave a quiz to his students. The task was to make a list of the five greatest American presidents. To my surprise, Woodrow Wilson, the 28th president, was not chosen by any of his students. To his big surprise, Wilson (I think) would have been a likely choice by most European pupils given a similar list. However naive and idealistic, a Messiah and statesman ahead of his time, Wilson laid the foundations for at least three cornerstones of modern world politics: national states, democracy and collective security (see, for example, Sheffield, 2002, p. 278; Best et al. 2003, pp. 39-41). The end of the First World War marked a definite beginning of the new era. Although the results were far from perfect, and although some national elites (Croatians, for example) later referred to the nineteenth century as their (more) "golden age" rather than the century that followed, the consequences of the Great War proved to be victorious, positive and enduring.

The First World War drastically changed the position of the South Slavs and the political geography of south-eastern Europe. Of the Fourteen Points drafted by Woodrow Wilson in January 1918, three are in direct connection with that area. Although all of the Yugoslavs finished in the same state, the Kingdom of Serbs, Croats and Slovenes, and therefore shared the consequences, the legacy of the First World War was and is not equal among the former Yugoslavs. Even shortly after the war, it meant much more for the Serbs than for the rest. The whole range of villages named after the regent Alexander Karadjordjevic was founded in the eastern part of Croatia (Slavonia), Vojvodina (today northern Serbia) and Macedonia (then called Southern Serbia), areas where land was given to Serbian war veterans. Other measures were far from popular. The territory of the Kingdom of Serbs, Croats and Slovenes that used to be part of Austria-Hungary was bigger in size, with a larger and better-off population than that of Serbia (with Macedonia and Montenegro). Those people were dissatisfied with the decision to exchange former Austro-Hungarian crowns to dinars by 4:1 ratio (see Tudjman, 1993, pp. 298-302; Pirjavec, 1995, p. 20).

After the end of the Great War, previously separated Southern Slavs were finally united in one state and under one, Karadjordjevic, dynasty. Therefore the legacy of the war was celebrated. Although the Yugoslav idea was originally Croatian, it was embraced by the Serbs and many others. The Serbian army and Serbian politics, together with Slovene, Croatian and Serbian politicians from the Austro-Hungarian Empire, can be credited with the foundation of the new state.

After the Second World War, in Tito's socialist Yugoslavia, the official line was similar to the one expressed by the left wing (that is, communist intellectuals) during the inter-war period. Yugoslavia as a state and unification of the South Slavs was positive. Nothing else, of course, was right: the capitalist system, monarchy, dictatorship, the unsolved national question. That, together with the historiography which always insisted on "historical distance", meant that books on the Great War were relatively few, especially in some Yugoslav centres. Macedonians were generally disappointed with the results of the First World War. During the war Bulgarians were trying to uproot any trace of Serbian influence. After the War, Serbs were doing the same in the opposite direction.

In retrospect, though they did not recognise it at the beginning, Macedonians were pleased with the foundation of the Yugoslav state. During the Second World War and in Tito's Yugoslavia, they were given elements of statehood. Therefore their reading of Versailles was identical to the official line during the socialist period. Kosovan Albanians were never particularly happy with Serbian rule or the instability with repression that preceded and followed military operations. In spite of the fact that the war started after the assassination of Archduke Franz Ferdinand in Sarajevo, the fighting happened relatively far from Bosnia-Herzegovina. For Muslims and Croats there, the assassination of the archduke by Gavrilo Princip – a member of the organisation "Young Bosnia" supported by a secret association of Serbian army officers called the "Black Hand" – was extremely negative. Nevertheless, after the First World War the bridge over the River Miljacka in Sarajevo was renamed after Gavrilo Princip. In Yugoslav textbooks he was mostly portrayed as a patriot, one of the oppressed classes, somebody who did a desperate but understandable act of patriotism. Today the name of that bridge is *Latinska ćuprija* again, as it was before the Great War. The monument in remembrance of the slain royal couple was demolished shortly after the war, never to be raised again. On the spot where Princip was standing at the moment of the murder, his footprints were marked and became one of the places to visit in Sarajevo.

Croatians fought on several fronts. At the beginning all of them were in the Austro-Hungarian army, fighting on the Serbian, Galician and later Italian battlefields. Thousands fought as volunteers on the so-called Saloniki front established in autumn 1918. Those, like, for example, future Croatian cardinal Aloysiye Stepinac, or the future Ban of Croatia and the last royal prime minister Ivan Subasic, were always regarded as more devoted to the Monarchy and to Yugoslavia, at least for the time being. However, without the Croatian writer Miroslav Krleza and his novels (and, later, television dramas and films based on his works), the First World War would hardly exist in everyday memory in Croatia. Even monuments commemorating soldiers who died in battle are few. Croatian historiography never dedicated much attention to the period, stopping with the Sarajevo assassination or starting with the development of the newly-founded kingdom. Works on different phenomena that took place in political life during the war, the work of the Yugoslav Committee or the political parties in the Croatian *Sabor* (parliament) during the war, were usually portrayed mostly through their state-building efforts. With the end of the Cold War and the collapse of the Yugoslav Federation, mention of Yugoslavia in Croatian public discourse was always accompanied by some descriptive term, usually "Greater Serbian" or "communist". The third most common description was "Yugoslavia – offspring of Versailles". It embodied the feeling of a huge conspiracy against the Croatians and their right to be independent. Since the goal in 1990 was to leave Yugoslavia, everything connected with that state, especially its very foundation, was negative.

Slovenes were far less frustrated by the fact that their country was part of Yugoslavia. Much more realistically than the Croatians, they understood that the odds of solving the situation in 1918 in any way more favourable to their "national cause" were non-existent. Italians, who won the war and finally managed to cross the Soča (Isonzo) River, acquired huge chunks of Slovenian (and Croatian) national territory through the secret London Treaty. Elements of the Serbian army helped to halt the Italians from taking even Ljubljana (Krizman, 1989, p. 338). First in the Kingdom, and later in Tito's Yugoslavia, the Slovenes, the most educated and developed of all South Slavs, managed to strengthen their position. Areas lost to Italy in 1919 were partly regained in 1945. The western part of Slovenia is full of monuments and graveyards dedicated to the First World War, together with the beautiful museum in Kobarid (which, a few years ago won an award from the Council of Europe as the best museum that year). As for the Croats, the end of the First World War meant for the Slovenes the end of a centuries-long unity with the Habsburgs.

Montenegro is in a rather peculiar position. One of the occupied countries, one of the allies and countries explicitly mentioned in Wilson's Fourteen Points, whose long-lived ruler was grandfather of the Serbian regent and future Yugoslav king, continued to be deprived of his throne and his country was stripped of its sovereignty. People of Montenegro, orthodox by religion, favoured the united state. However, not everyone was happy with the methods used to achieve the unification of Serbia and Montenegro. The Whites, named after the colour of the leaflets used to propagate their ideas, as opposed to the Greens – those loyal to the Montenegrin dynasty of Petrović – called the elections for the Grand National Assembly of Montenegro, which deposed Nicholas I and proclaimed unification with Serbia. All subsequent attempts to change the situation, like the Christmas Rebellion of 1919, were in vain (Tudjman, 1993, pp. 250, 273). The glorious history of the long-independent and well-connected, if poor, principality remained the inspiration for many Montenegrins, even those who felt that part of their national identity was Serbian. Those who felt more or only Montenegrin glorified their dynasty, opposition to the Ottomans and independence. Today, with Montenegro striving for a referendum, which might restore full sovereignty to

Podgorica, the unconditional unification with Serbia in 1918 is more and more often viewed in a negative light.

For the Serbs, the First World War was one of their crucial and also glorious historical events. Not very many nations were faced with so much hardship, in such a short period of time, as the Serbs. First there were two Balkan wars, then a world war, all in less than three years. Serbs managed to win a series of battles against the Austro-Hungarian forces in 1914; after defeat, they moved their government and army to the south, staying politically strong, respected and facing a bright political future. The choice was whether to gather areas regarded by them as undoubtedly Serbian (Greater Serbia) or to strive to achieve a larger, Yugoslav, solution. The newly founded Kingdom of Serbs, Croats and Slovenes was Serb-dominated and, in a way, represented a glorious ending of the century-long development and territorial growth of the Serbian state. The problem was that the Serbian elites were intoxicated by victory, and acted more as occupiers or masters, than as brothers. Croats were especially dissatisfied by the loss of the institutions and autonomy they had enjoyed during centuries of Habsburg rule. In the second half of the 1980s, more and more Serbian historians started to question publicly the choice made in 1918. According to them a mini-solution would have been far better for Serbian national interests. Such a state would have included two-thirds of Croatia with all of Bosnia-Herzegovina, Montenegro and Macedonia.

In 1914, when the war erupted, the future Yugoslav president and leader, Josip Broz Tito was a corporal in the Austro-Hungarian army. The first battles in which he participated and fought bravely on the Serbian front were eventually erased from his official biography. Many years later, while travelling in that part of Serbia, he mentioned the places where his unit had been fighting. Alexander Rankovic, the strong man of Serbia during the early years of Tito's Yugoslavia, warned him not to say too much about all that (Ridley, 2000, p. 71). During the war between the NATO alliance and Serbia in 1999, the monument dedicated to France, in memory of their joint effort during the Great War, was covered over since France was also participating in the attacks on Serbia. One of the "friends of the court" in the case of former president of Serbia, Slobodan Milosevic, at the International Hague Tribunal mentioned Tito's career on the Serbian battlefield in 1914. He was stopped by the judge and his remarks disregarded as irrelevant. The incident is, however, very indicative. History in the south-eastern part of Europe is still very much alive and (mis)used in political debates.

## The First World War

Southern Slavs include nations divided from the rest of the Slavic block by Hungarians and Romanians; Bulgarians, Serbs and Montenegrans were the only ones who were independent before the First World War erupted. Inhabitants of Macedonia were under Ottoman rule until 1912, when historical Macedonia was divided between Greece, Bulgaria and Serbia. Bosnia and Herzegovina was Ottoman until 1878, but only became Austro-Hungarian officially in 1908. After that the Croats and Slovenes were subjects of Vienna, as well as those Serbs who lived in Vojvodina, Croatia and Bosnia-Herzegovina. The Austro-Hungarian Empire was facing a serious problem with discontented Slavs, not only those in south-eastern Europe. Although the problem of nationalities was getting stronger every day, the challenge of nationalism was withstood. All the Slovenes, divided between several historic provinces, together with the Croats in Dalmatia and Istria, were in the Austrian half of the Monarchy. The rest lived in the Hungarian part and managed to preserve their autonomy and parliament *(Sabor)*.

Military forces on the territory of Croatia–Slavonia were part of the Hungarian *honved*, but the language of command in Domobranstvo, as it was called, was Croatian (and had been since 1868), officers were Croatian, uniforms bore Croatian insignia and the flag was framed with Croatian national colours (Ćutura and Galić, 2004, pp. 39-40). Although probably flattering to the Croatian national elite, the practical problem of how to command an army with three languages was probably the most serious one in such a organisation. No matter how dissatisfied with the whole situation, they were divided, weak, small and poor. Serbs had their own state and that was worrying Vienna. Belgrade had an ambition to become the Piedmont of the Southern Slavs.

"The Monarchy must take an energetic decision to show its power of survival, and put an end to intolerable conditions in the south-east" commented the Hungarian Prime Minister following the assassination of Archduke Franz Ferdinand in Sarajevo on 28 June 1914 (Best et al., 2003, p. 266). Whether or not the Serbian Prime Minister Nicholas Pasic knew of the plot is irrelevant (MacMillan, 2003, p. 113). After the ultimatum given to the Serbs, the war erupted. Austro-Hungarian dreams of crushing Serbia, humiliating Russia and breaking up the Entente were futile. The majority of soldiers who attacked Serbia were Croats and Serbs from the Monarchy. The first battles were won by the Serbian army, but soon Belgrade was lost. When Bulgaria entered the war on the side of the Central Powers, Serbian and Montenegrin territory was divided and held by these two powers until the very last days of the war.

Italy remained neutral at the outbreak of war, only to join the Entente in May 1915. After months of negotiations with both sides, the Italians secured the secret London Agreement, which promised them large parts of Albanian, Croatian and Slovene territory, as well as Southern Tyrol. The Italians launched four attritional Battles of the Isonzo (Soča) in 1915, trying and failing to break through Austrian positions towards Trieste and then eventually to Vienna and Budapest (Sheffield, 2002, pp. 326-31; Boban, 1991, p. 17). The plan was to meet Russian troops somewhere in Hungary, but Italian forces were too weak to do anything. The endless campaigns of 1915 continued in 1916.

There were no major outbreaks on the front in 1917. The commander-in-chief of the Austro-Hungarian forces there was the Croatian General Borojević. When the revolution erupted in Russia, the Soviet foreign service denounced secret diplomacy and published all secret agreements known to the tsarist diplomats. What the People's Commissariat for Foreign Affairs did helped the Austro-Hungarian cause. The war propaganda office in Vienna reprinted as leaflets the maps of lands allocated to Italy by the London Agreement of 1915. Slovenes and Croats, who were the majority of soldiers on the Soča front, were outraged. The first stunning victory by the Italians, helped by the British and the French, was achieved in Vittorio Veneto between 24 October and 4 November 1918. Trieste was finally lost. Together with the victories on the Saloniki front in the south-east, South Slavs were on the way to founding a united state for the first time ever. There were many ideas about how to organise it, but only one army and one dynasty was in charge.

In 1919, French colonial troops came to Zagreb. One battalion was situated in the very centre of the city. They were Vietnamese, though citizens of Zagreb called them "Chinese", and they performed popular operas and dances for the citizens (Suvar, 2001, p. 31). But the Vietnamese were just temporary guests. The Great War was a real historic break. After a thousand years in a political union with the Magyars and half a millennium with the Habsburgs, Croats found themselves in a new state where they were not one of the least, but one of the most developed and richest. The capital was new, as was the dynasty and the dominant religion. The system was less western, but the people in charge were regarded as brothers and their language was similar. Many Croats and Slovenes were not included within the borders of the newly-founded state, but all Serbs were now living under their own rule. Ideas about how to organise the new kingdom were numerous, and differed between the Serbian, Croatian and Slovene national elites, as was obvious during the war.

When the war erupted, the head of the Serbian state was King Peter I, often regarded as one of the most liberal in Serbian history. The head of government was Nicholas Pasic, a politician often considered as one of the most capable in the history of modern Serbia. Already in September 1914 Serbian politicians stated that their goal was to form a strong state that would include all Serbs, all Croats and all Slovenes. That goal, which claimed more than just liberation, was confirmed once more in early December 1914 in the southern city of Niš (Dimić, 2001, p. 11).

On the other side, part of the Croatian political elite left the country and organised the Yugoslav Committee. The seat of that political body was in London. Its president was a Croatian, Ante Trumbić, from Split in Dalmatia. Their idea was to form a common state with Serbia and Montenegro. Frano Supilo, member of the Committee, allegedly one of the most capable Croatian politicians ever, had the idea of forming a federal state, rather than a centralised one. That is where Supilo was in sharp conflict with his Serbian counterparts. Disappointed with the attitude of Pašić, and with the Entente after he learned of the London Treaty, Supilo resigned. Representatives of the Yugoslav Committee after all managed in 1917 to sign the Corfu Declaration with the Serbs, which was in tune with the federalist concept.

The future state was to be a constitutional, parliamentary, democratic monarchy. Three flags, three religions and two scripts were to be guaranteed. This change of attitude by the Serbian authorities was short-lived, inspired by the revolution in Russia and complications in political relations (Goldstein, 1999, pp. 110-11; Boban, 1992, p. 8). Croatians, Slovenes and Serbs who stayed loyal to the Habsburgs and continued to participate in political life in the Austrian half of the Monarchy in 1917 adopted the so-called May Resolution. This demanded a separate South Slavic unit within the Monarchy. They formed their Yugoslav Club with Anton Korošec, a Slovene, as the president. Croatian parliamentary and historical traditions were also invoked (Dimić, 2001, pp. 21-4; Krizman, 1989, p. 342). Following that decision, when the end of Austria-Hungary was close, delegates of the Slovenes, Croats and Serbs founded a National Council *(Narodno vijeće)* in Zagreb. On 29 October 1918, Vijeće proclaimed independence and the State of Slovenes, Croats and Serbs, with its capital in Zagreb, was founded. Unrecognised, without military forces and confronted by the Italian army – which was penetrating areas promised to them by the London Treaty and far beyond – the State of the SCS was in deep trouble. Pushed by the Croats from Dalmatia, who were directly endangered by the Italians, and dismissing the calls of Stjepan Radić and Dr Hrvoj, who warned the delegates not to go to Belgrade "like geese into the fog", the delegation led by Dr Ante Pavelić (a dentist) left for Belgrade. The Address of Unification was read to the regent, Alexander Karadjorjdevic, on 1 December 1918.

## Paris 1919

The conference in Versailles started in January 1919. The defeated countries, those that still existed, were not invited. Although there were as many as 58 different committees at the Paris conference, the decisions of the Council of Five – and, even more, of the Supreme Council, composed of the prime ministers and presidents of the United Kingdom, France, the United States and Italy – were law (Kissinger, 1994, p. 232). And even they did not share the same values and the same vision of how to organise the peace.

The Paris peace talks were taking place in conditions of continued fighting. The Great War did not, in fact, end in 1918. On the contrary, British, French, American and Japanese troops were still fighting with the Reds in Soviet Russia. Russians were fighting a civil war. Some years later, and after the counter-revolutionary forces had been repulsed, one of their leaders, General Wrangel, together with thousands of Russians, came to the newly-founded Kingdom of Serbs, Croats and Slovenes, and died in Belgrade where he was buried. At the same time there was a Russian-Polish War. Hungarians were still fighting on two fronts in modern Slovakia and Romania. The Irish were pushing for independence. There were widespread communist revolts and insurgencies. People across the Continent were completely worn out by the conflict, with huge loss of life and huge property damage. Those were the conditions in which the talks were taking place and to which the talks were, up to a point, responding. The re-arranging of borders was one of the hottest issues. Some, like those of Poland's eastern frontier, were revised on the battlefield.

The talks, therefore, served in part to legitimate changes being made by force. They offered the prospect of pushing for referenda and plebiscites. Referenda were held in Burgenland (Austria), Schleswig-Holstein and Silesia, but there were no plebiscites in the South Tyrol, Alsace-Lorraine or Danzig and the Polish Corridor. The reason, of course, was that in these areas the Big Four had a preferred outcome and they could predict that plebiscites in these areas would produce outcomes opposite to what they preferred.

The priorities of the Big Five differed. Japan wanted international recognition of its mopping-up of German colonies in the Pacific. Britain was concerned about its empire. France wanted revenge. The USA wanted national self-determination and the creation of a League of Nations. Italy wanted to implement the London agreement of 1915. Greece was also making a bid, both diplomatically and militarily, to restore some version of the Byzantine Empire, at the expense of the Ottoman Empire. The Paris peace talks recognised the so-called Balfour Declaration of 1917 and the Sykes-Picot Agreement.

All those facts played a crucial role when we talk about the territories of Yugoslavia, or the Kingdom of Serbs, Croats and Slovenes, as the country was called from 1 December 1918. The Kingdom of the South Slavs already existed before the Versailles conference started. The only unsolved problem was its borders. The Yugoslav delegation at the conference consisted of representatives of its various peoples. The majority were Serbs, but the minister of foreign affairs was a Croat from Dalmatia, Ante Trumbić, president of the Yugoslav Committee. Although Trumbić signed the Act of Unification in Cyrillic and was pro-Yugoslav, opposed to any idea of the continuing Austro-Hungarian Empire, he was not, to say the least, politically correct when talking about the Serbs. He told a French writer:

> "You are not going to compare, I hope, the Croats, the Slovenes, the Dalmatians whom centuries of artistic moral and intellectual communion with Austria, Italy and Hungary have made pure occidentals, with these half-civilised Serbs, the Balkan hybrids of Slavs and Turks."

On the other hand, one Serbian member of the delegation told his British counterpart: "for the Serbs everything is simple; for the Croats, everything is complicated" (MacMillan, op. cit., p. 113). While some in the delegation were much more interested in securing southern borders and orientating the state toward the Balkan peninsula, others worried about the fate of those who stayed within Italy, Austria or Hungary (Boban, op. cit., pp. 17-19).

At the end of the Paris Peace Conference, Bulgaria seized parts of her national territory near Strumica, Caribrod, Bosilegrad and an area east of Titmok to Serbia. The Neuilly peace agreement with Bulgaria was signed on 27 November 1919; the Kingdom of SCS signed it on 5 December. Romania was promised the whole of Banat. Eventually, Velika Kikinda, Veliki Bečkerek (Zrenjanin), Vršac and Bela Crkva also were given to Serbia. The final agreement was signed in 1924. Hungary lost Međimurje, Prekomurje, Prekodravlje (Gola, Ždala i Repeš) and Baranja, areas which were inhabited almost exclusively by Slovenes and Croats. The agreement was signed on 4 June 1920. Although Yugoslav claims included Klagenfurt, Villach and Volkermarkt, only Maribor and Radgona eventually finished up in Yugoslavia. The most painful was the division between the Kingdom of SCS and Italy. At the very end of 1920 in Rapallo, an agreement was signed. Everything west of Snježnik and Idria in Slovenia, the whole of Istria, the islands of Cres, Lošinj, Lastovo and Palagruža, together with the former capital of Dalmatia, the city of Zadar, became Italian. The city of Rijeka (Fiume) was not promised to the Italians by the London Treaty, but the flamboyant adventurer and great Italian poet Gabriele D'Annunzio occupied the city with an irregular, private army in 1919. Rijeka was established as a separate city-republic, but was annexed by Italy (Boban, op. cit., pp. 17-19).

## Conclusion

Was the First World War the key event of the twentieth century, from which everything else flowed, as Gary Sheffield claims? (Sheffield, 2001, pp. 264, 274). Some of the leading experts even claim that it was a tragic and unnecessary conflict. Others think that it was tragic, but necessary, since it was fought against militarist, aggressive autocracy. Not all countries became democracies, collective security through the newly created League of Nations proved useless, new nation–states were far from being that (the Czechoslovak state contained 10 million Czechs and Slovaks, 3 million Germans, 700 000 Hungarians, 500 000 Ukranians and 60 000 Poles). The Paris peace talks and the Treaty of Versailles were not the direct cause of the Second World War, but the treaty being so imperfect it certainly contributed to the outbreak of the new war. The peace agreements reached in Paris in 1919 did not end all wars. But without the victory achieved in the Great War the victory of liberal democracy would not have been possible.

The Kingdom of Serbs, Croats and Slovenes was the best possible solution for everyone. For Slovenes and, especially, the Croats, anything else would have been less favourable. Unity with the Serbs saved huge chunks of national territory, which would otherwise have become Italian (Antić, 2004, pp. 15-21). Croatian hopes that, since they were more developed, their position in the new country would be dominant, at least economically, proved to be futile. Serbs, though just a tiny majority, wanted to dominate everything, which then implied coercion.

Was the end of the First World War, and the revolutionary movement that won the battle in Russia and briefly touched so many European cities, the beginning of the Cold War? If the Cold War was, primarily, a battle of ideas, then the answer is yes. The new rulers of the Kingdom of Serbs, Croats and Slovenes organised a network of "internment camps" in different parts of the new kingdom. Not all the people interned were potential Bolsheviks or former prisoners of war captured by the Russians, but included Habsburg loyalists, members of national minorities and others (Miloradović, 2004, pp. 267-74). All in all, 80, 000 people passed through these camps, 57 000 of whom had been captured in Russia. Politically, the move was extremely unpopular.

That, together with so many other things, was the "beginning from which Yugoslavia never recovered" (MacMillan, op. cit., p. 117).

# Bibliography

Antić, L., "Prvi svjetski rat i Hrvati" in *Hrvatska Revija*, Year 4, No. 2, Zagreb, 2004.

Best, A., Hanhimäki, J.M., Maiolo, J.A., Schulze, K.E., *International history of the twentieth century*, Routledge, London, 2004.

Boban, L., *Hrvatske granice od 1918. do 1992. godine*, Školska knjiga/Hrvatska akademija znanosti i umjetnosti, Zagreb, 1992.

Čutura, D., and Galić, L., "Veliki rat: vojnopolitička situacija uoči rata" in *Hrvatska Revija*, Year 4, No. 2, Zagreb, 2004.

Dimić, L., *Istorija srpske državnosti, Srbija u Jugoslaviji*, SANU/Beseda/Društvo istoričara južnobačkog i sremskog okruga, Novi Sad, 2001.

Goldstein, I., *Croatia: A history*, Hurst and Co., London, 1999.

Kardum, L., *Europska diplomacija i Prvi svjetski rat (prvi dio)*, Zagreb, 1994.

Kissinger, H., *Diplomacy*, Touchstone, New York, 1994.

Knock, J.T., *To end all wars:Woodrow Wilson and the quest for a new world order*, Princeton University Press, Princeton, NJ, 1992.

Krizman, B., *Hrvatska u prvom svjetskom ratu, Hrvatsko-srpski politički odnosi*, Plava biblioteka, Globus, Zagreb, 1989.

Kola, P., *The search for Greater Albania*, Hurst and Co., London, 2003.

Macmillan, M., *Paris 1919: Six months that changed the world*, Random House Trade Paperbacks, New York, 2003.

Miloradović, G., *Karantin za ideje, Logori za izolaciju "sumnjivih elemenata" u Kraljevini Srba, Hrvata i Slovenaca 1919-1922*, Institut za savremenu istoriju, Beograd, 2004. [in Cyrillic]

Petrinović, I., *Politička misao Frana Supila*, Književni krug Split, 1988.

Pirjavec, J., *Jugoslavija, Nastanek, razvoj ter razpad karadjordjevićeve in Titove Jugoslavije*, Založba Lipa, Koper, 1995.

Ridley, J., *Tito: Biografija*, Prometej, Zagreb, 2000.

Service, R., *Lenin: A biography*, Harvard University Press, Cambridge, MA, 2000.

Service, R., *A history of twentieth-century Russia*, Harvard University Press, Cambridge, MA, 1997.

Sheffield, G., *Forgotten victory, The First World War: Myths and realities*, Review, London, 2002.

Smodlaka, J., *Izabrani spisi*, Književni krug, Split, 1989.

Šuvar, M., *Vladimir Velebit – Svjedok historije*, Razlog, Zagreb, 2001.

Tuđman, F., *Hrvatska u monarhističkoj Jugoslaviji, Knjiga prva 1918.-1929.*, Hrvatska sveučilišna naklada, Zagreb, 1993.

# Chapter 18
# The Great War and the Treaty of Neuilly: real and imaginary legacies in the public debate in Bulgaria

*Ivan Ilchev*

In something like 35 years in the twentieth century – to be precise between 1912 and 1947 – or in less than half of a usual life span – the Bulgarians fought four wars and lost three of them. This is a record unrivalled, I think, and (one is tempted to say) not a cause of envy in any other European state. In fact, it was quite possible for an 18-year-old conscript in 1912 if he was lucky – and if you call this luck, of course – to fight in all these conflicts.

It was inevitable that these wars – and especially the defeats and the subsequent peace treaties – would leave deep scars on the national psyche, scars that were very obvious and still are visible, at least to a certain extent.

The only war from which the country managed to emerge victorious was the First Balkan War of 1912-13, which ended in the Treaty of London of May 1913. This rare victory is why it looms in the national memory as a triumph of the collective effort of Bulgarians. But they did not have the time or the opportunity to reap the fruits of their labours. The disastrous Second Balkan War of the hot summer of 1913 followed on its heels. The defeat on the battlefields was sealed by the Bucharest peace treaty.

Two years later came the First World War. Bulgaria holds the dubious distinction of being the only state in the whole world to succumb to the persuasions of the Central Powers after the autumn of 1914 (and the Ottoman Empire was the only state before us to do it at all), while more than twenty countries chose the side of the Entente.

The dreams of revenge, the dreams of glory, soon turned into monotonous lice-picking at the front or, worse in heaps of mangled bodies, thrown without much fuss somewhere into the rocky soil of Macedonia. The Salonica armistice of September 1918 and then the peace treaty of Neuilly of 27 November 1919 marked rock-bottom in Bulgaria's collapse.

## A small state

The tables of the pre-war balance of power in the Balkan peninsula were overturned in 1919. At the beginning of the century, Bulgaria was the largest Christian state south of the Danube. It was widely deemed to be the fastest-developing Balkan state, with a booming economy, an infrastructure rapidly changing for the better, a country with a progressive legal system, with up-to-date social legislation. Its army was deemed the best disciplined, best armed and probably the best motivated in the peninsula. The French military attaché in Sofia sent a report in 1911 in which he claimed that one Bulgarian infantry battalion was worth three Romanian ones. In autumn 1912 the former American president, Theodore Roosevelt, wrote a fiery article on the recent history of south-eastern Europe, calling Bulgaria "the Japan of the Balkans" – not only because of its military prowess but because of its rapid economic and social development.

After 1919 Bulgaria became the smallest Balkan country (apart from Albania), its territory less than half that of Yugoslavia or Romania; its economy stagnated for almost 15 years and its political life was marred by numerous crises and violence. The victors followed its every move in the diplomatic or military field with suspicion. It was considered a potential source of conflict. From an international point of view, for almost two decades, it was kept in the freezer. On numerous occasions, its neighbours publicly humiliated Bulgaria. Sofia had no choice. It had to apologise, to recoil with clenched teeth.

Unlike the above-mentioned conflicts, the participation of the country in the Second World War was not voluntary. Up to the last possible moment, the Bulgarian King Boris III tried to keep outside the emerging conflict between the Great Powers. This, however, turned out to be impossible. Germany needed Bulgaria to keep the whole peninsula under its iron heel. It wanted to use its territory as a springboard for aggression against Yugoslavia and Greece. And the so-called democratic countries – Great Britain, France and the USA – did not lift a finger to help the Bulgarians in their predicament. Sofia was considered to be the lawful prey of Germany, an undisputed part of the German sphere of political and economic influence.

There was some kind of consolation. By adroit manoeuvering, Boris managed at least to avoid direct participation in the war. This was not enough. At the end Bulgaria lost again and on 10 February 1947 signed the Paris Peace Treaties along with Italy, Romania and Germany's other allies. When we have all this in mind, it is striking that (on the surface) the country did not fare as badly as might be expected. When it entered the Balkan War in the autumn of 1912 its territory was 96 000 sq. km. After three consecutive defeats, in 1947 it was 15 000 sq. km bigger.

Bulgaria's human losses in all the armed conflicts of the first half of the century were generally much smaller than those of its neighbours. Furthermore in all these wars the Bulgarian army fought outside the borders of Bulgaria proper. Apart from the bombing in 1943-44, the country was spared the ravages and the devastation which, at different times, almost ruined Serbia, Greece, Romania or Turkey. Why then were the Bulgarians complaining and whining about a result that might even be considered a success by a number of other countries?

This kind of positive reasoning did not – and still does not – have much chance of success in Bulgaria. Most Bulgarians blamed the military defeats and the peace treaties as one of the main reasons for the comparative backwardness and weakness of the country. And the Treaty of Neuilly, one of the Paris peace treaties of 1919-20, was considered to be the main wrongdoer. In the public mind, the treaty was elevated to the position of a status symbol, a stereotype that could explain all the recurring problems with the vindictiveness of Bulgaria's neighbours, helped by the vileness of the Great Powers. For instance: Why was the economy not running smoothly? Because of the treaty. Why did social unrest not calm down? Because of the treaty. Why were politicians corrupt and unreliable? Because of the treaty. Why did the rate of divorces skyrocket? Because of the treaty. Why did morale plummet? Because of the treaty.

Stereotypes in general, as we know, play a substantial role in domestic politics and international relations. According to the founder of the modern theory of stereotypes, Walter Lippman, the fundamental merit of the stereotype lies in its function as a classifier of realities. This merit, however, often turns into its essential disadvantage. This happens when the stereotype is either not up to the standard any more, or when it classifies objects and phenomena according to non-essential secondary characteristics. Lippman himself mentions that "it is not necessary for the stereotype to be false". This sounds more like an excuse. Indeed there are quite a few scholars who believe that the stereotypes are untrue by nature and that they are "widely spread misleading information, traditional nonsense". And why not, by the way! Another researcher, Vaineke, later claimed that it is not actually so important whether the stereotype is true or false. What really matters is whether one believes in it. And this conviction – the stability of the stereotype, which can hardly be shaken – is one of its distinguishing features. That is why knowledge often "hardens" and turns into dogma, which keeps on functioning long after it has proved epistemologically groundless.

The most enduring stereotype in Bulgarian history for the last century and a quarter is what I call the San Stefano syndrome. According to this syndrome, in March 1878 victorious Russia made the defeated Ottomans accept the justice of Bulgarian claims. In the San Stefano preliminary treaty a spacious Bulgarian principality was created, with a generous outlet on the Aegean sea coast, including most Bulgarians within its boundaries.

San Stefano Bulgaria was stillborn, but it had a long and glorious life in the public imagination and political rhetoric. It was discussed and analysed in a plethora of books and thousands of articles appearing in newspapers, journals and solid scholarly publications. No one dared to express even a vestige of a doubt about the justice of the imaginary frontiers drawn in the outskirts of the capital of the Ottoman empire.

The unpleasant truth, however, was quite different. The Bulgarians had to live confined within the boundaries – the "cage" as they used to say then – that the Great Powers drew up in Berlin in the summer of 1878. San Stefano became a powerful political slogan but also a guiding beacon in Bulgarian foreign policy. Up to 1912, the

San Stefano stereotype put Sofia politicians at odds with all their neighbours, none of whom shared the dream of a mighty Bulgaria in the centre of the peninsula, with virtual strategic control of the most important lines of communication.

The stereotype of San Stefano Bulgaria was shattered during the wars. In fact, Bulgarians themselves abandoned it in 1912, when – in the Bulgarian-Serbian agreement – they acquiesced in the Serbian demand for a division of the apple of discord, Macedonia.

The stereotype of the Neuilly Peace Treaty took the place of San Stefano in 1919. According to the Bulgarians, the Neuilly Peace Treaty was unnecessarily harsh and it stood in contrast to the lofty moral principles declared by the Allies. The treaty itself took a year in the making, though most of the belligerents had started to prepare their claims for the future peace conference as early as 1914. In general, the experts of the Entente abided by similar principles. They did not question the ethnic, strategic or economic grounds of the Bulgarian irredenta. The politicians, however, thought differently.

The experts could afford the luxury of suggesting viable strategic solutions aimed at a peaceful Balkan peninsula in the distant future, whereas politicians across Europe were victims of an inbred myopia. The furthest they could see were the next elections. Their seats in parliament hung on the whims of the voters. And the voters in western Europe and the Balkans were adamantly anti-Bulgarian.

In late 1918 and early 1919, the Foreign Office in London was inclined to let Bulgaria keep the whole, or at least part, of the so-called uncontested zone in Macedonia according to the Serbian-Bulgarian Treaty of 1912, plus Eastern Thrace up to the Mydia-Aenos line and southern Dobrudja. "To make Bulgaria relinquish its legal aspirations would doom the dreams of Balkan unity" prophesied one high-ranking British diplomat.

The so-called Committee of Inquiry in the USA, made up of experts who had to prepare the grounds for the future peace, thought that Bulgaria had rights over eastern Thrace, southern Dobrudja and even a substantial littoral on the Aegean Sea coast. Macedonia, according to the committee, was without any doubt a Bulgarian region, but the events of recent years – *realpolitik* – were all against antagonising Serbia.

France was in favour of harsh punishment for the Bulgarians – *les petits boches*. At the same time, Serbia demanded a belt 30 to 40 km wide on the border of the two countries; this would have moved the frontier to within 20 km of Sofia. The Greeks insisted on the whole of Thrace and the Rhodope mountains.

In the long run, their opinion prevailed – though not entirely. According to the final text of the treaty, Bulgaria once again lost southern Dobrudja to Romania. The ratio between Bulgarians and Romanians living there was 23 to 1. It also lost several enclaves on its western border with Serbia. The Serbs clamoured for them on strategic rather than ethnic grounds. And they could hardly do that without blushing. In the Tzaribrod region out of 21 000 inhabitants only 79 were Serbs; in the Bossilegrad region there lived 21 000 Bulgarians and 12 Serbs. Villages, cemeteries and even individual houses were cut in two by the border.

But the most important loss from a territorial point of view was the outlet to the Aegean Sea. Thrice in its recent history Bulgaria has managed to win a precarious hold on the Aegean coast and three times it has lost it. This doomed the country to a semi-landlocked position and directed its economic interests towards central Europe – that is, Germany.

The country was flooded with refugees. Nobody knows how many there were – estimates differ, ranging from 150 000 to 400 000. For years they were a quandary for all Bulgarian governments. They had to be fed, given jobs, helped to acquire decent housing. Loans were negotiated with international financial institutions, but their impact upon the plight of the refugees was negligible. Private donors also tried to help, with varying degrees of success.

Bulgaria was left without a conscript army. Instead she was generously permitted to hire a professional army of 30 000. This meant that it would have the distinction of having the smallest but the most expensive army in the Balkans. It was also forbidden to possess military aircraft, tanks and, in a twist of malicious humour, even submarines. Bulgaria, like all the other vanquished countries, was burdened with reparations.

## The impact of the Treaty of Neuilly

The Treaty of Neuilly had a lasting psychological impact. It helped to develop even further the pragmatic scepticism that has always been part of the Bulgarian national psychology: "Values and ideals count for nothing! Strength and power are the important factors! Guns form the decisive argument." In Bulgaria, as elsewhere in Europe, a generation bereft of ideals and attracted to a cynical view of life emerged. The sons did not understand. What is more, they openly mocked their fathers for their mistaken belief in great ideas like patriotism, fatherland, justice and morality.

The Treaty of Neuilly ruined the reputation of the traditional ruling elite, a part of which actively participated in making the disastrous choice in the autumn of 1915. Those who opposed it did not attempt resolutely to thwart the decisions of King Ferdinand and his pliant servant, the prime minister, Vasil Radoslavov. The elite as a whole tried to move the burden of responsibility for the defeat on to the shoulders of the soldiers who had left the front in September 1918 and thus brought on the catastrophe. The soldiers in their turn developed the useful myth that the soldiers of Bulgaria had never lost a battle, but the Bulgarian politicians had never won a war.

The Treaty of Neuilly strengthened the already ingrained belief that Bulgaria was at all times the victim, the sacrificial lamb of the Great Powers, who were always ready to lay it lovingly on the altar of their interests, in order to cut with a bloody knife the choicest pieces of its national patrimony. This feeling, by the way, is shared by most Balkan peoples.

The Treaty of Neuilly blemished the somewhat idealistic picture that had existed previously in Bulgaria of the so-called democratic countries. France and Great Britain were the ultimate villains, while the USA turned out to be weak, meek and faltering in its decisions. This attitude precipitated the slide towards Germany in the 1930s.

The Treaty of Neuilly contributed to the development of a mindset of losers amongst many Bulgarians. The most cherished dream of Bulgarian foreign policy, its ultimate goal in the inter-war years, became to avoid another thrashing. The fear of the Great Powers' cudgel was at the bottom of some apparently illogical moves by Bulgarian governments in the 1930s, when they moved to establishing closer relations with Yugoslavia, the country which in popular mythology had stolen Macedonia from the Bulgarians.

The Treaty of Neuilly had a lasting negative impact on Balkan relations. It poisoned them almost to the point of no return, as several futile attempts at agreements in the 1930s convincingly proved. It predetermined the axes of enmity and possible friendship in the peninsula. At the beginning of the 1930s, Yugoslavia made some tentative attempts to include Bulgaria in the so-called Balkan Entente but they failed. "You could hang us, but do not ask us to put the loop on our necks ourselves" was the reaction of the Bulgarian minister in Belgrade. He had in mind the goal of the proposed Entente – to keep existing borders intact.

The Treaty of Neuilly left Bulgaria in the inconvenient situation of a major power bent on revenge in the peninsula – at least, according to the neighbouring Balkan politicians. This was only theory. In practice, the country was too weak, the army was severely restricted by the peace treaty, and it was poorly armed. In a word, it was not a military threat to any of its neighbours. The truth was that Bulgaria might become a probable danger. It could ally itself to any major power bent on revenge.

In 1938 the Balkan countries, alarmed by the worsening situation in Europe which threatened war, tried to redress the situation. According to an agreement signed in Salonica, Bulgaria was given the right to a conscript army. It could fortify its boundaries, it could rearm itself with modern weapons. If it could afford them, it could even have submarines. The agreement, however, came too late to mend the already broken fences.

The Treaty of Neuilly revived the murky, painful feeling that Bulgarians were not accepted as real Europeans. That the west Europeans thought of them as a people hovering on the brink – belonging and yet not belonging to Europe. A humpty-dumpty sitting on the fence between Orientalism and Europeanness.

The Treaty of Neuilly put the Bulgarians living in Serb or Greek Macedonia in a much worse situation than before the Balkan wars. No one was allowed to consider himself a Bulgarian. Owning or reading a Bulgarian book was a capital offence. Terror almost eradicated all that the Bulgarian intelligentsia had painstakingly created through the ages.

The Treaty of Neuilly changed the attitude of many Bulgarians to the so-called Macedonian movement. For forty years the Bulgarians sacrificed money, did not spare their efforts and started wars for the dream called Macedonia. All was in vain. The Bulgarians were ashamed to acknowledge it, but they started to tire – the national dream lost its credibility, the new leaders of the Macedonian movement did not have the aura of the old ones. The situation was not helped by the internal strife and indiscriminate murders in the Macedonian organisations in the 1920s.

The Treaty of Neuilly turned Bulgaria into a fertile ground for the spread of left-wing ideologies. Bulgaria was one of the few European countries where communist ideas gained ground and communists became a political power with which to be reckoned.

Was the Treaty of Neuilly as bad as its contemporaries and as a majority of historians considered it to be? No doubt, it was a severe treaty, but no more callous than the Bulgarians' own plans, had they managed to tip the balance in their favour. In 1916, when it looked as if the Central Powers were gaining the upper hand, the Bulgarian foreign ministry suggested dividing the whole of Serbia between Austria and Bulgaria – so as not to create any problems in the future. No one dared to remember or mention this fact after 1919.

In the inter-war period the Treaty of Neuilly was one of the most powerful weapons to use in public debate in Bulgaria. All political camps – from the far left to the far right – delved into its woes for short-term political advantage. Every 27 November was the occasion for street demonstrations, processions of refugees, political demonstrations and pub brawls.

It turned out to be a very useful stereotype. Even after the Second World War, history textbooks treated it much in the same vein as it was treated before the war. The years have moved on, however, and the stereotype has begun to lose its attractiveness. Immediately after 1989, many political groups tried to revive it. In the beginning, they met with some success born out of nostalgia, but now it seems that the Treaty of Neuilly has passed irrevocably from the sphere of public rhetoric and political usage to the domain of historians. They still continue to argue with each other, but their discussions do not really interest ordinary Bulgarians any more. Not that the historians are too active either. Notwithstanding its lasting negative impact, the Treaty of Neuilly has never been the subject of more than a handful of scholarly books.

# Chapter 19
# Images of women, 1914-20: the ideals and the realities

*Ruth Tudor*

This chapter looks at the representation of women in government propaganda posters from the First World War and its aftermath, across Europe and in the United States of America. The main focus is on:

- How were women portrayed in government propaganda during the war and afterwards? What were the realities behind these images?
- When did the ideal match the reality and when did it not? How can we account for the discrepancies? What national differences can be identified?
- What can we learn from the idealised representations about ideas and beliefs regarding women's nature at this time?

The following useful questions in relation to the topic of 'women and war' are also touched upon:

- How far was the First World War a catalyst for change in women's lives and for how long?
- To what extent did the war change all women's lives?
- What was the contribution of women in wartime? What variety of roles did they have?

## Methodological challenges

The methodological challenges involved in this topic include making the distinct experience of women in the past visible and avoiding the dangers of imposing a progressive, emancipatory interpretation on women's history. This is what Ute Daniel has called the "wishful thinking model" (Daniel, 1997, p. 273). In relation to the First World War, we must avoid the assumption that – because women's suffrage was achieved at the end of the war in the USA and in some European countries, including Britain, Germany and Russia – women's war effort had political motives and that the suffrage was a consequence of their support for and participation in the war.

The "wishful thinking model" of women's history is particularly apparent in school history textbooks, which tend to focus on war as a catalyst for change without following up the experiences of women after the war. "Women and war" is a popular topic in European secondary school history textbooks, but it risks oversimplifying the experiences of women in terms of their diversity and often fails to look at the impact of ideas about gender on women's war experiences and on representations of women in propaganda. Daniel (ibid.) has underlined the need to stay very close to the sources in researching women's history. In addition, there is a need to be aware of the diversity among women across Europe, and across the USA, and in terms of social class.

War is commonly a catalyst for change for women because it gives them opportunities to take up roles and have experiences that have been denied to them in peacetime. In particular, women often gain greater social and sexual freedom and greater physical mobility during wars; they do new types of work, for example, in heavy industry; and they demonstrate new skills, for example, managerial and organisational skills. Before the First World War, the common traditional view of women across Europe and in the USA was that they could not carry out these roles or behave in this way because it was not in their nature to do so. This belief about women's essential nature was used to justify their exclusion from political power.

As Grayzel (2002) and Shover (1975) have shown, the First World War was one that demanded the participation of women as well as of men. The First World War demanded the mobilisation of the whole population. The importance of women in the war effort in the USA, for example, is shown in the thousands of images of women that were produced as part of the selling of war, in order to get support and participation (Dumenil, 2002). During the First World War, women were vital both as supporters and participators in the war effort. The nature of propaganda images produced by the various governments involved reflected national conventions and cultures, including commercial conventions, as well as beliefs about gender. Indeed, governments deliberately used culturally-familiar images in order to make their propaganda more effective. It is necessary, therefore, to analyse images of women during the war in the wider context in order both to make sense of these images and to make a judgement about the extent to which they accord with the reality of women's experiences.

Shover (ibid.) has identified the following dilemma faced by governments during the First World War. These governments needed women to respond to wartime needs. At the same time, governments wanted to preserve the traditional view of women as passive. There was, therefore, no intention of permanently changing gender relations and the government had a delicate balancing act to negotiate in order to get women's active participation while at the same time upholding the traditional social order.

## Roles and images

An important function of women, especially at the start of the war, was to support the mobilisation of men, usually as combatants. This was especially important in a country such as Britain, which had no conscription or military service and initially relied entirely on volunteers. In the early years of the war, women's function was to put emotional pressure on men to participate. Early images show women as vulnerable, as victims, and often associate women with children. In the British poster *Women of Britain say "Go"!* the private sphere of the home is represented by the woman and child who are shown as soft, clinging and passive, and clearly distinct from the public sphere

MERCI !

represented by the male soldiers marching away. The men are shown as homogeneous and active, and the straight lines of their guns, uniforms and marching formation contrast with the image of the women. These types of images were directed at both women and men. The role of women was to encourage men to go to war and the role of men was to go. A similar image is shown in the French poster *Merci*. The differences between the women in this French image and those in the British one are minimal. However, in other images French women tended to be shown as less direct and less substantial than British women, and it is likely that this is because of the influence of Protestantism and the tradition of liberal individualism in Britain, compared to France, where gender relations were still deeply influenced by the Catholicism enshrined in the Napoleonic Code.

Images like these, whose function was to motivate women to act as mobilisers for the war, did not challenge traditional ideas about women. These images often showed women as victims and as passive onlookers. They were, therefore, in danger of contradicting other images designed to get women to participate in the war as workers,

particularly in heavy, dirty and dangerous jobs. Further images of women as the victim include the Russian poster where the female victim appears as a piece of seemingly incidental detail in the bottom right-hand corner (Jahn, 1995). A German soldier is holding a Russian woman by the hair and another German soldier is laughing. There is more than a hint that this woman is about to be raped and almost certainly is being humiliated.

A British poster *Men of Britain! Will you stand for this?* attempts to get men to enlist by informing them of the 78 women and children killed in a naval attack on Scarborough in 1915. Another, *Enlist,* shows a helpless woman and baby drowning as a result of the sinking of the *Lusitania.* A German poster, *Farmers, do your duty; the towns are hungry!*, showing hungry women and children, is intended to mobilise men as farmers. In common with some other German posters, this image is more realistic than many of those from other countries. In contrast, *Collect combed-out women's hair*

shows a ghostly and very feminine woman offering up her long hair – the symbol of her femininity – against the background of a red cross. This poster comes from Germany in 1918, by which point the British blockade had forced Germany to find substitute materials, for example, hair instead of leather or hemp (Shover, ibid.).

All these images were designed to make men feel protective towards women and they did not challenge traditional ideas about men or women. A rather different style, however, is shown in *The Austrian went to Radzivily*. This is a Russian poster which shows a strongly-built Russian peasant woman effortlessly defeating Austrian soldiers. This image is directed at the mobilisation of men, but attempts to do it in a different way from the majority of images at this time. In this poster the woman's actions are supposed to shame the man into signing up – even a woman can deal with the enemy and all she needed was a pitchfork! However, this image was not challenging traditional Russian ideas about women. If we look at the wider context we find that the poster's style is that of the *lubok*, a traditional genre which showed peasant women as capable, earthly and maternal (Petrone, 1998). Although the *lubok* style was very common in Russia in 1914 and early 1915, it then began to decline and Russian propaganda images became much more similar to Western images.

Images that showed woman as a sexual victim were also designed to mobilise men to fight. In these images the woman commonly appeared as a powerless victim of a sexual predator and not as someone who was aware of herself as a sexual being or who enjoyed her own sexuality. These images were entirely in keeping with industrial-era ideals of women in western Europe. The very few images that did portray women as consciously sexual aroused criticism at the time. The US image *I Want You for the Navy* from 1917 was part of a range created by one artist, Christy, whose designs were criticised for lacking dignity. The image is an unusual example of First World War propaganda because it works by using sexual provocation. However, it does not challenge the idea of woman as dependent upon man, and it

denies the reality of women in the navy at this time (Grayzel, ibid.).

Far more acceptable and common was the type of image shown in *Destroy this Mad Brute* (1917), also from the USA, where the woman needs the man to join up in order to protect her honour. The poster shows the woman as being abducted for sexual use by a beast. While the beast represents the enemy, the woman represents the USA's honour, purity and civilisation. A similar image is shown in *It's up to you*. This 1917 image from the USA very strongly suggests that the woman is to be a victim of rape.

Red Cross
Christmas
Roll Call
Dec. 16–23⁻

*The*
GREATEST MOTHER
*in the* WORLD

Images of women as mothers were very common. Such representations of women were entirely acceptable both because they were in keeping with traditional ideas about women's nature and their role within society, and because women as mothers had a crucial role during the war. These posters portrayed women as clean, gentle, caring and lacking in sexuality. The woman in *The greatest mother in the world* is an unusual representation of a woman in wartime posters because she's so large (Dumenil, 2002). In her arms she holds a tiny wounded soldier. As a mother, therefore, it seems that a woman can be shown as large and powerful. Women as mothers did not challenge traditional ideas and were important, both because women were needed to nurture and care for soldiers and children and also to reproduce the next generation at a time when the present generation was being decimated.

In reality, contemporary beliefs about mothers and war, and the different attitudes of women towards war, were diverse and complex. Dr Aletta Jacobs, in the Netherlands, argued that mothers could not support war because the grief experienced as mothers was too great. She called for future control of foreign policy by an international group of men and women, and this type of pacifism became a feature of feminism in the 1920s and 1930s (Macdonald et al., 1987). Ellen Kay in Sweden had similar views and said that women who supported war were unnatural (Macdonald, ibid.). Early on in the war, in the United Kingdom, mothers orchestrated the "white feather" campaign, an aggressive and public act towards men aimed at shaming them into joining up to fight. By contrast, in Malawi, Africa, there was resistance by women to being asked to encourage their men to join up. Eventually women in Malawi were taken as hostages in order to force men to volunteer (Grayzel, ibid.). Across the world, only a very small minority of women participated in the war as combatants. The Russian "Battalion of Death" was formed by women to shame men into fighting and was praised by Emmeline Pankhurst, a British feminist and suffragette (Macdonald, ibid.).

Posters that portrayed women as nurses were among a very small group of images where men were allowed to look dependent on women (Shover, ibid.) while at the

same time the men remained looking manly. The image seen in a Belgian Red Cross poster is typical. Women are gentle, caring and in the case of this Belgian poster, literally angelic. Images of women as nurses did not challenge traditional ideas about women, and women were shown as traditionally feminine unless they were the enemy. In *Red Cross or Iron Cross*, the German nurse cruelly pours water on the ground in front of an incapacitated, thirsty soldier. She is portrayed as an "unnatural" woman and this is acceptable because she is from the opposing side in the war.

As the war progressed, the range of women's roles became broader and this is reflected in the images. Women were needed to participate in heavy industry and to act as managers in ways that challenged their traditional roles. Government posters portrayed women's war work as cleaner, safer, easier and lighter than it really was. Women in industry tended to be portrayed as young, presumably because this was less threatening to traditional ideas about the role of women within the family. Furthermore, there was no suggestion that these changes in women's work would be permanent; in fact some women, for example in Germany, would not take up new opportunities because they were only temporary (Daniel, ibid.). In the British poster *These women are doing their bit,* the soldier in the background serves to remind the viewer both why women should make munitions and also that he will return; and in the British *God speed the plough and the woman who drives it*, agricultural work is shown as easy and romantic. The Russian poster *Everything for the war* also portrays women's work in industry as easy and attractive. By contrast, the women shown in *German women work for victory!* look miserable. This image from 1918 is more grimly realistic than comparable images from other countries. By 1918, German women were involved in huge strikes in industry and in food riots, many initiated by women. This poster may be seen, therefore, as a reflection of morale in Germany in 1918. The radicalisation of urban working-class women was one of the causes of the 1918 revolutions (Daniel, ibid.).

## The realities

The realities of women's war work are more diverse and complex than the posters suggest. In many countries women were eager to take up opportunities for new types of work, but because of better pay and conditions, not for patriotic reasons. A minority of these women entered traditional male areas but most of these women had to give up their jobs in 1918. Overall, there does not appear to be a significant increase in the number of women in paid work post-1918 compared to pre-1918. Although there was a shift in the type of work done, this accelerated a trend already going on. In the United States of America, for example, the war accelerated a trend from 1870 onwards of more women going into paid work and into different types of work. In particular increased numbers of women went into office work and the metal, chemical and electrical indus-

tries, while fewer were employed in domestic service (Weiner Greenwald, 1980). In the United States of America, the First World War gave some women, mainly poor and black women, new opportunities in better-paid jobs, for example, with the railways and in metalworking. There is a danger of assuming, therefore, that because the suffrage for women followed the war in many countries that women's war work was aimed at emancipation. In many cases the women took the opportunities for financial reasons.

Condell and Liddiard (1987) show a 1918 photograph of women putting TNT into shells at Woolwich Arsenal, Britain. Before 1914 there had been 10 women employed at Woolwich. By 1918 there were over 24 000 women working there. However, these changes did not last beyond the war. Some women in 1918 went on strike to try to keep their jobs, but most gave up work relatively easily. In part, some women were willing to give up work because of the double burden of work inside and outside the home which they had struggled with during the war.

Women frequently appeared as symbols in First World War posters. This use of images of women to represent the nation, particularly its purity and honour, was traditional in most countries. These images served to remind nations of the righteousness of their cause in the war and also inspired men to enlist to protect the nation. It is important to note that women as symbols are often portrayed as both powerful and sensual. This is allowed because they are not real women. In a 1917 US poster, *The sword is drawn,*

*the navy upholds it,* Columbia wields the sword of justice and calls to men to uphold it. It equates the national honour with female honour. In the distance we can see the navy, and the address of the US Navy recruiting station is given at the bottom of the poster. In an Italian poster of 1917, *Subscribe to the loan*, Italy is represented by a powerful woman who is not at all frightened of the advancing Goth, who has dropped his club in shock at the strength that she possesses. In a similar poster campaign, *Subscribe to the fifth Austrian war loan* (1916) shows a heraldic female national figure holding up a sword decorated with laurels of victory. One of the most powerful female allegorical figures is that of the French Marianne. In a typical poster, she is shown as a very formidable female warrior, complete with Gallic headgear and sword, urging the French public to do its duty. *Russia for truth* (1914) shows a similar image of a woman. In another Russian poster, three figures of women are used to show the unity between Russia, represented by *Vera* (Faith), France, represented by *Liubov* (Love) and Britain, represented by *Nadezhda* (Hope). An Italian poster captioned ... *And what was ours is ours again* refers to the territories incorporated into the Austro-Hungarian empire, and also portrays Italy as a powerful and sensual woman.

One apparent exception to the general trend in First World War posters is the 1917 US image of a woman drummer, drawn in a natural style. The woman is shown as a peasant type, attractive, fairly young and confident. The text of the poster is *The spirit of woman-power. Women, serve your country where you can.* This image, chosen for the poster by a US women's organisation to promote the war effort, comes originally from a painting of peasant women in the French Revolution. The fact that the women are not American and not contemporary lessens the apparent challenge to traditional ideas about women in America.

## After the war

In 1919, images of women virtually disappeared from government propaganda. During this period countries concentrated their efforts on reconstruction and on grieving. Both memorials and posters in 1919 ignored the contribution of women as workers in the First World War. Almost all the war memorials constructed after the war show soldiers. Those that do include the figure of a woman show her as a grieving mother who represents the grieving nation, as on the memorial in Veliko Turnovo, Bulgaria. The mother was seen as very important after the war, partly because she symbolised the grief of the nation but also because of concerns about the birth rate and the high mortality rate. Pressure was put on women to reproduce the next generation. A notable exception to these memorials is in Peronne, France, where the woman in the memorial is portrayed as angry.

A French poster of 1919 is an appeal for investment in national reconstruction. It shows three male workers nailing up the French flag over territories previously occupied by Germany. In another 1919 poster from France, *Day of the liberated areas. After victory, to work!*, a demobilised soldier with a cockerel on his shoulder goes to work on reconstruction. In communist Russia, women were commonly shown in posters because they had a vital contribution to make in industrialising Russia: *What the October Revolution gave the woman worker and the peasant woman'* shows a young Russian woman happy and eager to contribute to the Russian economy.

In conclusion, the posters were idealised images and generally did not accurately reflect the reality of women's contribution to the war effort. The vast majority of images showed women as dependent, domestic, self-sacrificing, gentle and caring. Exceptions to these occurred only when the women were allegorical or the enemy, or when the woman portrayed fitted in with traditional ideas within a particular cultural context. Women were not portrayed as a diverse group. Most women shown in the images looked financially well-off and not as though they were motivated by economic need. The nature of propaganda, therefore, enabled governments to mobilise women for war while at the same time not challenging traditional gender relations.

## Bibliography

Bonnell, V.E., *Iconography of power: Soviet political posters under Lenin and Stalin*, Berkeley, University of California Press, 1997.

Condell, D., and Liddiard, J., *Working for victory: Images of women in the First World War, 1914-18*, London, Routledge & Kegan Paul, 1987.

Cooke, M., and Woollacott, A., (eds.), *Gendering war talk*, Princeton, NJ, Princeton University Press, 1993.

Daniel, U., *The war from within: German working class women in the First World War*, transl. Margaret Ries, Oxford, Berg, 1997.

Dumenil, L., "American women and the Great War", *OAH Magazine of History* No. 17 (October 2002), Organization of American Historians.

Gervereau, L., and Prochasson, C., (eds.), *Images du 1917*, Paris: BDIC, 1987.

Grayzel, S.R., *Women and the First World War*, London, Pearson Education, 2002.

Grayzel, S.R., *Women's identities at war: gender, motherhood and politics in Britain and France during the First World War*, Chapel Hill, NC, University of North Carolina Press, 1999.

Hill, J.A., *Statistics of women at work, 1900*, Washington, DC, Government Printing Office, 1906.

Jahn, H.F., *Patriotic culture in Russia during World War One*, Ithaca, NY, Cornell University Press, 1995.

Kleinberg, S.J., "Women in the economy of the United States from the American Revolution to 1920" in S.J. Kleinberg (ed.), *Retrieving women's history: changing perceptions of the role of women in politics and society*, Oxford, Berg/Unesco, 1988.

Macdonald, S., Holden, P. and Ardener, S., (eds.), *Images of women in peace and war: cross-cultural and historical perspectives*, Basingstoke, Macmillan Education in association with Oxford University, 1987.

Paillard, R., *Affiches 14-18*, Reims, Impr. Matot-Braine, 1986.

Paret, P., Irwin Lewis, B. and Paret, P., *Persuasive images: Posters of war and revolution from the Hoover Institution Archives*, Princeton, NJ, Princeton University Press, 1992.

Petrone, K., "Family, masculinity and heroism in Russia war posters of the First World War" in Mellman, Billie (ed.), *Borderlines: genders and identities in war and peace, 1870-1930*, New York, Routledge, 1998.

Rickards, M., *Posters of the First World War*, London: Evelyn, Adams & Mackay, 1968.

Shover, M.J., "Roles and images of women in World War 1 propaganda", *Politics & Society*, 1975, No. 5, pp. 469-86.

Weiner Greenwald, M., *Women, war and work. The impact of World War I on women workers in the United States*, Westport, CT, Greenwood Press, 1980.

Woollacott, A., *On her their lives depend: munition workers in the Great War*, Berkeley, CA, University of California Press, 1994.

# Chapter 20
# The year 1919: its global dimension

*Odd Arne Westad*

This chapter proceeds from the need to see European history as international and global history. It adds the colonial perspective to the discussion of the significance of the year 1919, but it also adds – in a colonial context – some of the social history of the epoch. It is, in a certain way, about the history of that momentous year in European history seen from below and outside.

There are two main trends that 1919 symbolises for the world outside Europe and North America. The first is the process of decolonisation in Asia, Africa and the Caribbean, which can be said to have had its origin in that year. The other is the radicalisation of anti-colonial movements in the Third World in the direction of Marxism and Communism. While the first trend was a result of the war and the way it ended, the second was a result of the failed peace, which did not bring about any of the results that the colonised world had been hoping for.

## Decolonisation

In 1919 Europe as a continent was brought to the edge of the abyss by the consequences of the Great War. Its weakness, observed with particular acuteness outside Europe itself, was not only economic and material, but also political and moral. To the many millions of Africans and Asians who experienced European internecine warfare – as participants in Europe or elsewhere – the war showed a continent intent on tearing itself apart. As a result, many members of the local colonial elites in the Third World lost the sense, widespread before the war, of European purpose as being the key element in colonialism. One of them was the Indonesian nationalist Sutan Sjahrir, who before the war had written

> "For me, the West signifies a forceful, dynamic, and active life. It is a sort of Faust that I admire, and I am convinced that only by a utilisation of this dynamism of the West can the East be released from its slavery and subjugation. The West is now teaching the East to regard life as a struggle and a striving, as an active movement to which the concept of tranquility must be subordinated ... Struggle and striving signify a struggle against nature, and that is the essence of the struggle: man's attempt to subdue nature and to rule it by his will."

In 1919 none of this admiration was left, for Sutan or most other educated leaders in the Third World. From the beginning of that year on, an increasing number of nationalist movements put full independence on the agenda for the first time.

The flourishing of anti-colonialism in the Third World, which the radicalised nationalist movements could build on, had begun during the First World War. Not only did the war signify a European loss of purpose, but it also provided opportunities for local organisations that pre-war repression had been able to contain. From 1914 on, with the attention of the imperial authorities turned elsewhere, local nationalists strengthened their parties and movements, and recruited in most cases many times the number of adherents that they had had before the war started. By 1919 many nationalist organisations, in India, China, and Indonesia – to mention just a few countries – were ready for more large-scale political offensives.

The content of those offensives was much decided by events in the year 1919, when the great powers met in Paris to discuss the peace settlements. In India, February 1919 marked the start of Gandhi's campaigns for an independent country, while the British response to these campaigns – including the Amritsar massacre of 13 April – and Gandhi's non-violent protest against the violence propelled him to a national leadership position. To Gandhi and many of his pacifist followers, the failure of the peace conferences to address colonial issues on the victorious side was a sign that nationalists would have to rely on themselves and their own actions to gain independence.

In China the consequences of 1919 were even more earth-shaking. As inhabitants of a semi-colonial country, in which the imperialist powers had taken over parts of the territory – the so-called 'concessions' – rather than setting up a full colonial state, many Chinese hoped that President Woodrow Wilson's declarations about full national sovereignty would also count for them. When the question of the concessions was not discussed at Paris except in terms of those held by Germany, Chinese public opinion was infuriated. And when it was decided to award the German concessions to Japan, rather than returning them to China, the sense of insult and denigration boiled over into a massive protest movement, known to all Chinese today as the 4 May movement, after the day in 1919 when Beijing students took to the streets in protest.

The 4 May movement became the starting point for modern Chinese nationalism and for the two parties that came to dominate its twentieth-century history – the Kuomindang and the Chinese Communist Party. The slogans the students had launched about uniting with the people around the country, about women's emancipation and about creating a new vernacular literature, reverberated in China's development up to 1949 and beyond. Over four hundred journals and newspapers date from the 4 May era, making 1919 both a cultural and political watershed in China's modern history. The young Mao Zedong wrote in 1919:

> "Since the great call for world revolution, the movement for the liberation of mankind has pressed forward fiercely, and today we must change our old attitudes toward issues that in the past we did not question, toward methods we would not use, and toward so many words we would have been afraid to utter. 'Question the unquestionable. Dare to do the unthinkable. Do not shrink from saying the unutterable. No force can stop a tide such as this.'"
> (Schram, Vol. 1, 1995, p. 318)

It was not only in China, though, that Chinese protested against the agreements reached at Versailles. In Paris, street protests – though on somewhat smaller scale than in Beijing – were led by Wang Jingwei, who had worked in Paris during the war (and who later went on to become China's foremost collaborator during the Japanese occupation after 1937). These demonstrations were joined by people from France's colonies in South-East Asia, among them a young Nguyen Ai Quoc, a Vietnamese who later would join the communists under the name Ho Chi Minh.

For the young Ho, three years Mao's senior, the years immediately after the First World War were crucial for his future course. Having appealed in vain for US support for democratic freedoms and political autonomy in Vietnam at the Versailles Peace Conference, the 30-year-old photo retoucher living in Paris became bitterly disappointed with Wilsonian diplomacy and turned towards Marxism as a solution to his country's ills. To show how fluid the colonial situation was at the beginning of the twentieth century, on first arriving in France in 1910 Ho had sent a letter to the French president requesting admission to a training school for colonial administrators:

> "I would like to become useful to France in relation to my compatriots, and would like at the same time to help them profit from the benefits of instruction." (Quinn-Judge, 2002, p. 24)

Ten years later, Ho explained to the 1920 congress of the French Socialist Party at Tours:

> "The hydra of Western capitalism has for some time now been stretching its horrible tentacles toward all corners of the globe, as it finds Europe too restricted a field of action, and the European proletariat insufficient to satisfy its insatiable appetite." (Quinn-Judge, op. cit., p. 32)

Criticising the French socialists for not doing enough for the liberation of the colonies, Ho voted for the party to join the Communist International, and later became an itinerant agent for the Comintern in many countries in Europe and Asia before leading the Vietminh – the communist-led Vietnamese resistance movement – in the 1940s.

## Communism

Although set up in 1919 primarily to promote revolution in Europe, the Third International – also called the Communist International or Comintern – came to play as important a role in the Third World as it did in the continent of its birth. But although the promise of 1919 was for the Comintern to symbolise the promise of world revolution – a kind of reverse Versailles where all countries and peoples had a deserved and just place – the organisation in the 1920s came to function chiefly as an organ of Soviet control over the international communist movement and thereby in the end came to defeat its own promise.

The Comintern emerged from the three-way split in the socialist Second International over the issue of the First World War. A majority of socialist parties, comprising the International's "right" wing, chose to support the war efforts of their respective national governments against enemies that they saw as far more hostile to socialist aims. The "centre" faction of the International decried the nationalism of the right and sought the reunification of the Second International under the banner of world peace. The "left" group, led by Vladimir Lenin, rejected both nationalism and pacifism, urging instead a socialist drive to transform the war of nations into a transnational class war. In 1915 Lenin proposed the creation of a new International to promote "civil war, not civil peace" through propaganda directed at soldiers and workers. Two years later Lenin led the Bolshevik seizure of power in Russia, and in 1919 he called the first congress of the Comintern, in Moscow, specifically to undermine ongoing centrist efforts to revive the Second International. Only 19 delegations and a few non-Russian communists who happened to be in Moscow attended this first congress; but the second, meeting in Moscow in 1920, was attended by delegates from 37 countries. There Lenin established the Twenty-one Points, the conditions of admission to the Communist International. These prerequisites for Comintern membership required all parties to model their structure on disciplined lines in conformity with the Soviet pattern and to expel moderate socialists and pacifists.

The administrative structure of the Comintern resembled that of the Soviet Communist Party: an executive committee acted when congresses were not in session, and a smaller presidium served as chief executive body. Gradually, power came to be concentrated in these top organs, the decisions of which were binding on all member parties of the International. Moreover, Soviet domination of the Comintern was established at an early stage. The International had been founded by Soviet initiative, its headquarters were in Moscow, the Soviet party enjoyed disproportionate representation in the administrative bodies, and most foreign communists felt loyal to the world's first socialist state.

In the Third World even many non-communists felt that communism might be an idea whose time had come. The young Indian Jawaharlal Nehru wrote in 1919:

> "Today the spectre [of communism] has materialised and is holding the western world in its grip. Russia and Hungary have ended the age-long domination of the capitalist and the owner of property. Horrible excesses are ascribed to the Bolshevists in Russia. But if this is so then it is difficult to imagine how millions of human beings should prefer this terror and degradation and should voluntarily labour to bring it into existence. We are a communal people and when the time comes perhaps some form of communism will be found to suit the genius of the people better than majority rule. Let us prepare for that time and let our leaders give thought to it." (Gopal, 1972, pp. 140-4)

The Comintern was to be the vehicle through which the communists should set off rebellions against colonialism. For many of those in the Third World who opposed foreign domination, the Russian revolution had been a signal event. Not only did the Bolsheviks want to set up a new state of their own that did away with colonial oppression and ethnic domination, but they also promised to support all movements worldwide that had the same aim. And, most important of all, the communists had both a model for how to overthrow the former regime and a pattern for a new state that was just and modern at the same time. The image of the October Revolution that

Comintern propagandists spread worldwide was one that many young organisers and intellectuals found immensely attractive as a future for their own countries.

No wonder, then, that by the early 1920s communist parties had been established in most key states in the Third World – China, India, Indonesia, Turkey and Iran all saw communist parties established in 1920 or 1921. The leaders of these parties – those who had not already been arrested or shot by the regimes in power – congregated in Moscow for the Comintern congresses, as did European communist leaders. Records of the meetings show not only how diverse the early communist movement was, but also how difficult the encounters between the Russians and Marxists from other backgrounds turned out to be.

The Soviets had expected opposition (and not a little condescension) from western European Marxists who attended the first Comintern congresses. What surprised them more was the ability and willingness of Third World Marxists to stake out independent positions on the understanding of social developments and the political course of communism. While in no way presenting a uniform critique of Soviet socialism, the voices of these leaders described some of the difficulties that would prove impossible to overcome in their Third World policy for later generations in the Kremlin.

The young Indian communist Manabendra Nath Roy, for instance, criticised Lenin at the Second Comintern Congress for being too reluctant to give Third World communist parties a leading role in the anti-colonial revolutions in their countries. While agreeing with the Soviet leader that the communists had to ally with the local (or 'national') bourgeoisie against the colonial power, Roy believed that the communists had to propagandise independently among, and recruit from, all social layers for their own party, which would form a "vanguard of the working class" even in areas where that class was very small relative to the peasant masses. Claiming that an alliance with the Soviet Union could help Third World countries avoid capitalist development altogether, Roy saw the possibility, at least in some areas, of communist parties coming to power before the working class was fully developed and therefore having to carry out both "petty bourgeois reforms, such as the division of land" and the construction of proletarian power simultaneously (Schmidt-Soltau, 1994).

Even worse from a Soviet perspective was the critique voiced by the Bashkir communist Mirsaid Sultan Galiev. Born in 1892 into an ethnic group that had been colonised by Russia, Galiev argued for the revolution as first and foremost meaning the liberation of enslaved peoples. As founder of the Militant Tatar Organisation of Socialists-Internationalists, Galiev had already in 1914 called on Tatar and Bashkir soldiers in the tsar's army to rebel, since the cause of the war was that "Russians, not content to have conquered the Tatars, Bashkirs, Turkestanis, the [peoples of the] Caucausus, etc., wanted to conquer the Turks and Persians as well" (Rorlich).

Galiev joined the Bolsheviks in Baku in 1917, and soon became the most prominent party leader with a Muslim background. As Stalin's deputy as Commissioner for Nationalities, the Bashkir communist argued that "all colonised Muslim peoples are proletarian peoples" without strong class contradictions, and that the liberation of the colonies was an essential precondition for revolutions in the West. Galiev stressed that

"So long as international imperialism … retains the East as a colony where it is the abso-lute master of the entire natural wealth, it is assured of a favorable outcome of all isolated economic clashes with the metropolitan working masses, for it is perfectly able to shut their mouths by agreeing to meet their economic demands."

Understandably, as Stalin's star rose within the government, Galiev's fell. He was expelled from the party in 1923, accused of wanting to organise a separate anti-colonial International and for claiming a progressive role for Islam in the liberation of Asian peoples (Rorlich; Bennigsen and Lemercier-Quelquejay, 1960, 1986; Bennigsen and Enders Wimbush, 1979; Carrère d'Encausse and Schram, 1969).

Sultan Galiev was arrested in 1928 and, predictably, shot in prison in 1941. By the time he was executed, much of the promise of 1919 had disappeared from world communism for those who primarily identified themselves in terms of the anti-colonial struggle. If it could be argued that Wilsonian anti-colonialism failed in 1919, then Lenin's anti-colonialism failed progressively as the Soviet Union established itself as a state with its own colonial population. In this sense, at least, 1919 as a turning point was perhaps as fundamental to the anti-systemic movements as it was to the imperialist countries that tried to establish peace amongst themselves.

## Bibliography

Bennigsen, A., and Lemercier-Qelquejay, C., *Les Mouvements nationaux chez les Musulmans de Russie* ('National movements among Russia's muslims'), 2 vols, Paris, Mouton, 1960-64.

Bennigsen, A., and Lemercier-Qelquejay, C., *Sultan Galiev, le père de la révolution tiers-mondiste*, Paris, Fayard, 1986.

Bennigsen, A., and Enders Wimbush, S., *Muslim national communism in the Soviet Union: a revolutionary strategy for the colonial world*, Chicago, IL, University of Chicago Press, 1979.

Carrère d'Encausse, H., and Schram, S.R., *Marxism and Asia: an introduction with readings*, London, Allen Lane, 1969, pp. 178-80.

Gopal, S. (gen. ed.), *Selected works of Jawaharlal Nehru*, Vol. 1, New Delhi: Orient Longman, 1972.

Quinn-Judge, S., *Ho Chi Minh: The missing years*, Berkeley, CA, University of California Press, 2002.

Rorlich, A.A., "Mirsaid Sultan Galiev and national communism" on website at http://www.yeniturkiye.com.

Schmidt-Soltau, K., *Eine Welt zu gewinnen! Die antikoloniale Strategie-Debatte in der Kommunistischen Internationale zwischen 1917 und 1929 unter besonderer Berücksichtigung der Theorien*, 1994.

Schram, S., "Manifesto on the founding of the Xiang River Review (14 July 1919)", *Journal*, 1995, vol. 1, p. 318; original in *Mao Zedong zaoqi wengao* ('Mao Zedong youth manuscripts'), Changsha, Hunan.

# Chapter 21
# The Great War as cultural watershed

*Dimitri Vezyroglou*

Cultural history is wary of watersheds. Whether it is concerned with representations, artistic forms, intellectual fashions or attitudes, cultural history prefers to focus on long-term trends and slow changes, rooted in a system of contexts, whether social, political, ideological or technological, whose own development has a sometimes concordant, sometimes discordant impact on cultural life. Nevertheless, a historical phenomenon as exceptional from every point of view as the Great War offers cultural historians an opportunity to consider and deal with this notion of watershed or clean break. Firstly, because such an event represents a clear boundary, even in the minds of those who lived through it, between a before and an after. Whether or not such a feeling is justified, the societies of the 1920s and 1930s viewed the first global conflict as the brutal point of entry into the modern era. Equally, though, the period of mourning that had such a profound impact on this long post-war period represented a major cultural extension of the war.

The purpose here is to consider the Great War from the standpoint of the cultural history of the early twentieth century, rather than offer a cultural history of the Great War (see, for example, Becker, 2005), even though certain aspects of the latter must be taken into consideration, as must the debate between the "consent" and "coercion" schools for explaining the violence of the war, at the heart of which is the notion of brutalisation, which links up to the themes of cultural history.

## The case for the Great War as a cultural watershed

### 1. A lasting influence on the culture of war

The First World War had a massive impact on all aspects of culture, both popular and elite. From novels to postcards, from films to opera, and in all types of music and popular song, every means was used to transmit a culture of war combining patriotic symbols, exaltation of combativeness, a spirit of sacrifice and the transformation of war into a combat to defend race and civilisation (Audoin-Rouzeau and Becker, 2000).

Apollinaire, the poet of love and desire who volunteered for the French army, found in the war both a subject for marvel and a metaphor for desire. In *Calligrammes* (1913-16), a collection of poems mainly written during the conflict, when Apollinaire was at the front, several works draw a constant parallel between war and the act of love; they betray a genuine sense of wonder at the spectacle of war. For example, in *Fête* he writes, in Oliver Bernard's translation:

"Skyrocket burst of hardened steel
A charming light on this fair place
These technicians' tricks appeal
Mixing with courage a little grace
…
The air is full of a terrible liquor."

In a poem with the highly significant title *Merveille de la Guerre* (Marvel of war) he talks of the beauty of a night sky lit up by shellfire. The poet is seduced by his fighting experience, both as a spectacle and as an act, which induces in him a feeling of wonder, intoxication and, in the strongest – sexual – sense of the term, fascination. In the poem "Désir", he says that his desire is in front of him, behind the *Boche* (Kraut) lines. The unique experience and facility of expression of a poet like Apollinaire should not blind us to the fact that the culture of hostilities extended to all the belligerent countries, whose peoples were compelled to experience the same intoxication with and fascination for the act of war. As Stéphane Audoin-Rouzeau showed in France (1993), and Sebastian Haffner (2000) in such a vivid way in Germany, even children's cultural environment was invaded by the war. Whether in school, games or family life, the war was omnipresent in children's universe, both as a context and as an object of fantasy. Haffner, who was born in 1907, describes this with great clarity.

For him, the war was a great exciting game in which nations confronted each other. It provide greater entertainment and more satisfying emotions than anything peace had to offer. This is what a whole generation of German school pupils experienced between 1914 and 1918. Naturally, you went to school, learned to read and count, and later learned Latin and history. You played with your pals and went for walks with your parents, but was all this enough to fill your existence? It was the military operations that really added spice and colour to your life. When major offensives were under way, with hundreds of thousands of prisoners, fortresses taken and large quantities of equipment captured, this was a time to celebrate, to let your imagination run wild, to live intensely, as you would later when you fell in love (Haffner, op. cit., pp. 34-9).

Such a culture of war could not just suddenly disappear once the armistice was signed. Firstly, because the children of the period of conflict became the adolescents and then the adults of the 1920s and 1930s. The age at which their minds were opening up to the world – which would determine how they would perceive that world – was marked by the war, and their culture would forever bear its traces. In addition, certain elements of the war culture continued to affect post-war Europe, as evidenced by the omnipresence of a patriotic, and even nationalist, discourse in a continent where the nation had been enshrined as the highest form of political organisation. The culture of war was also prolonged by the all-persuasive war veterans' spirit, which prevented a resurgence of painful memories. The culture of war made it an absolute taboo for individuals to internalise and accept the violence of war.

The sudden emergence of the culture of war, so all-pervasive in the years 1914-18, therefore transformed European society and its perception of its identity, and led to a cultural watershed. This break with the past was particularly striking in the artistic domain.

## 2. A shattering of cultural forms and objects

During the Great War, a generation of artists entered into radical confrontation with all the traditional art forms. The best example is the Dada movement, not only because of its determination to overturn the traditional artistic order but also and perhaps above all because of its strong links with its spatio-temporal context.

Dada originated in Zurich in 1916. In this island of peace in the heart of a Europe ravaged by war, as the Battle of Verdun raged, Tristan Tzara launched a movement that would gradually extend throughout the continent – and beyond – and whose starting point and rallying call was a rejection of all the old aesthetic, historical, social and national foundations of art. Dadaists saw all the arts, from poetry to painting, from sculpture to music, as the means to and elements of a radical revolt aimed not just at abolishing established cultural categories but at shaking and even bringing to its knees a European culture deemed to be ossifying and ossified. Duchamp's "ready-mades" are a good illustration. By placing their signature on everyday consumer products, artists were being trebly provocative: they were denying the superiority of artistic forms over that of functional objects, thus blurring the distinction between art and triviality; they were dispossessing themselves of the laborious process through which, at least since the Renaissance, artists had established the individuality and value of their works; and finally they were overturning the fine arts tradition that had been patiently built up over the eighteenth and nineteenth centuries, which isolated artistic production in a body of rules deemed to be fixed for all time.

It was no coincidence that the movement emerged during the First World War. The war, seen as the apocalypse of European thought, was the main trigger of this revolt, whose destructive nihilism seemed to be justified by the surrounding and all-pervasive violence. Dada reflects deep disillusionment in response to the self-destruction of a civilisation, but that self-destruction also offers it the opportunity and pretext for its own destructive enterprise. Dadaism's international and cosmopolitan character – the movement extended to the whole of Europe, as well as the United States and Japan – can also be viewed as a reaction to the dead weight of nationalism that descended on Europe in 1914, the most obtrusive manifestation of which was the culture of war. There is no doubt that Dada emerged from the experience and memory of the conflict (Becker, A., 2002).

The war was thus both the source of and the setting for a fundamental fissure in the artistic order. But the old European conception of culture also had to give ground to new forms of mass culture.

## 3. The arrival of mass culture

The Great War, which to many represented the arrival of modern culture, coincided with the start of mass culture. This trend towards cultural communion and the introduction of technology also helped to burst open the traditional and elitist representation of culture inherited from the *beaux arts* or fine arts school. The inter-war period saw the triumph of two of the most typical elements of twentieth-century mass culture: sport and the cinema.

In the field of sport, the great cycle races, football and boxing matches were watched by vast crowds. In 1921, 120 000 people watched the Dempsey-Carpentier fight in Jersey City, while in 1923 up to 200 000 spectators squeezed into the newly inaugurated Wembley Stadium in London for the final of the FA Cup. The first football World Cup was held in 1930 and from its first European edition in 1934 it became a major symbol of the new popular culture.

The cinema also gained a large popular audience during the First World War. It was the main leisure activity for those who remained at home and highly appreciated by the men at the front. After the war it spread to the most remote rural areas. It was also the focus during the war for one of Europe's major cultural revolutions, the discovery of America. From 1915 on, the European market was flooded with American films, for reasons both short-term (decline in European production because of the fighting, mobilisation of personnel, the requisition of factories) and structural (the failure of European cinema to keep abreast of new trends and developments since the 1900s). The results were unambiguous: in 1914, more than two-thirds of the films shown in the world were French, whereas by 1918 more than two-thirds were American.

But the change was not just an economic phenomenon. Discovering the films of David W. Griffith, Thomas H. Ince and Cecil B. De Mille came as a shock to European film-goers and film makers, not to mention the revolution caused by those of Charlie Chaplin. Their use of editing, close-ups and long shots, their camera movements and their innovations in the direction of actors added up to a complete break with the past, lessons that the European cinema would henceforth have to learn. It is particularly noteworthy that these directors were fascinated by the war as an aesthetic vehicle: Griffith, in *The birth of a nation* (1914) and *Intolerance* (1915), Ince in *Civilization* (1916) and De Mille in *Joan the Woman* (1916) made the portrayal of war a test-bed for experimentation as part of the revolution in film making. For the general public and avant-garde film-goers it was the American model that now dominated, aesthetically and commercially.

The transition during the war years to the era of mass culture was accompanied then by a growing fascination in European popular culture with the United States. While jazz and its derivatives became part of European life, and American films achieved ever-growing popularity, certain major sporting events also brought America regularly to the forefront of the European cultural stage. The victory of the American boxer Jack Dempsey in Jersey City on 2 July 1921 over his French opponent Georges Carpentier had undoubted symbolic value.

Yet how reliable is this notion of watershed or a clean break, in other words of a classification of European culture into distinct periods strongly linked to contemporary perceptions?

## The case against the Great War as a cultural watershed

### 1. An artistic and cultural modernisation process already well under way

Clearly, the fragmentation of older art forms, of which Dada is the most striking and visible example, did not occur all at once. The first cracks in the traditional order appeared in the mid-nineteenth century. Several works offer powerful symbols of these changes, this gradual shaking-off of the canons of traditional art. Just to take certain French examples, Manet's *Olympia* in 1863 defied the rules for portraying the female nude, the man in Rodin's 1876 *Bronze Age* seemed to presage the dawn of a new era of humanity, while Manet's paintings depicting the Gare Saint-Lazare in 1877 forcibly introduced tangible signs of modernity into a pictorial tradition that had consistently ignored them.

Similarly, Dominique Kalifa has demonstrated clearly that the birth of mass culture goes back to the mid-nineteenth century or even the 1830s, a period in which European societies were experiencing profound cultural changes linked to the growing role of technology and images (Kalifa, 2001). These changes were reflected in increasing "cultural industrialisation" in response to mass audiences (something that applies equally to the press, publishing, the theatre and – at the end of the century – the cinema) and led to an acceleration in the tempo of society and a greater emphasis on spectacle (Schwartz, 1998).

However, the real revolution that gave birth to modern culture came at the turn of the twentieth century. In literature, the examples are legion. One such is *Les mamelles de Tirésias* in 1903, Apollinaire's unfinished work presented for the first time in 1916 in which he invented the word – and the notion of – "surrealism". The same Apollinaire opened his collection *Alcools* (1912) with a poem, "Zone", whose very first verse starts "You are weary at last of this ancient world". The work proclaims the poetry of the modern world and exalts a mystique and aesthetic of triviality. Apollinaire's verse shattered the old poetic forms and heralded the birth of a new and liberated world whose beauty he sought to celebrate.

A similar revolution took place in the theatre between the 1870s and the 1900s, in the writings of Ibsen and Chekhov, and in the productions of companies such as Stanislavski's Moscow Arts Theatre, Antoine's Théâtre Libre in Paris, and then Max Reinhardt's German expressionist theatre. This end-of-century movement, which was the first to free itself of the classical theatre canons, undoubtedly provided the wellspring for the theatre of the twentieth century, of whom Brecht and the French directors Jouvet, Dullin, Baty and Pitoëff were early representatives.

The end of the nineteenth century was also a major turning point in painting. After the impressionist revolution, artists like Munch, Ensor and Van Gogh continued and broadened the search for a representation of subjectivity with connotations of pessimism, pain and even violence, so clearing the way for the various expressionist schools that were to characterise the early modernist movement. These different elements coalesced into a system of pictorial representation with the formation of groups such as Die Brücke, centred on Kirchner, then the Blaue Reiter in Munich with Kandinsky and Macke. This same turn-of-the-century period saw the Viennese Secession of Klimt and the Viennese Workshops of Schiele and Kokoschka. The same period was marked by the sudden arrival of Cubism, exemplified by Braque and Picasso, signalling the start of the reign of artistic abstraction and itself a major turning point. All the new developments prepared the way for the radical artistic revolt of Dada and the New Objectivity of Grosz and Dix, by providing them with the necessary tools, syntax and even themes.

Despite its radicalism and its almost violent rejection of the ancient world, Dada cannot be seen as a movement without kinship or genealogy. As early as 1909, Marinetti employed similar violence to condemn the same sclerosis of artistic thought. His first *Manifesto of Futurism* proclaimed:

1. We want to sing the love of danger, the habit of energy and rashness.
2. The essential elements of our poetry will be courage, audacity and revolt.
3. Literature has up to now magnified pensive immobility, ecstasy and slumber. We want to exalt movements of aggression, feverish sleeplessness, the double march, the perilous leap, the slap and the blow with the fist.
4. We declare that the splendour of the world has been enriched by a new beauty: the beauty of speed. A racing automobile with its bonnet adorned with great tubes like serpents with explosive breath ... a roaring motor car, which seems to run on machine-gun fire, is more beautiful than the Victory of Samothrace.
5. We want to sing the man at the wheel, the ideal axis of which crosses the earth, itself hurled along its orbit.
6. The poet must spend himself with warmth, glamour and prodigality to increase the enthusiastic fervour of the primordial elements.
7. Beauty exists only in struggle. There is no masterpiece that has not an aggressive character. Poetry must be a violent assault on the forces of the unknown, to force them to bow before man.
   [...]
9. We want to glorify war – the only cure for the world – militarism, patriotism, the destructive gesture of the anarchists, the beautiful ideas which kill, and contempt for woman.
10. We want to demolish museums and libraries, fight morality, feminism and all opportunist and utilitarian cowardice. [...]

Violence and aggression thus become vitalist principles of art. Within that framework, futurism constituted a form of spiritual brutalisation that was in certain respects a precursor of the culture of war but also laid the groundwork for Dadaist nihilism and the revolutionary voluntarism of Russian constructivism.

If there was a watershed or breakdown in the artistic order, therefore, it did not coincide with the Great War, which represented rather the culmination of a movement that had been under way in all the arts since the outset of the twentieth century.

## 2. A doubtful watershed

The place of Dada and its lesser imitators in the history of art should not be confused with its situation in the artistic world of its time, which was essentially marginal – a position that in any case it actively laid claim to and cultivated. The immediate post-war period in the cultural field was in fact marked by a return to normal, based on a denial of modernism, an essentially normative and moralising discourse, and a quite conspicuous return to the classical canons (see, for example, Silver, 1991). Hence the scandal caused first by Dada and then by surrealism. The very reason for this outrage and scandal was that society was not yet ready for this call for the abolition of old artistic forms.

This return to normality in the arts also reflected a genuine blurring-over of memories of the war. The great majority of artists and writers drew a veil of silence over the traumatic memory of the conflict (Audoin-Rouzeau and Becker, op. cit., Dagen, 1996). They refused to acknowledge and discuss the personal dimension of the brutalisation engendered by the war. The rejection suffered by the few works that tried to deal with this subject, such as Henri Barbusse's *Under fire*, confirms the strength of this taboo.

From all standpoints, the dominant cultural discourse of the post-war period was concerned with society's return to an established order. If a breakdown did exist, it was strongly denied by a dominant culture that was not prepared to give way to the assaults of artistic revolutionaries

# The Great War as a cultural stage

## 1. The war as a cultural reference point and symbol

Denial of war-induced traumas by the dominant discourse did not prevent the arts from returning almost obsessively to the war. In the pictorial arts, the Germans Grosz and Dix made the war a recurrent motif of their work, which in turn enabled them to cast a spotlight on the fundamental violence of modern society, as revealed and accentuated by the experience of war. War literature, as in the novels of Barbusse *(Under fire)*, Remarque *(All quiet on the western front)* and Dorgelès *(Les Croix de bois)*, provides many examples of war's impact on the imagination and its transformation into a major and essential element of the modern narrative. In the cinema, following the example of American film makers, in particular King Vidor (*The Big Parade*, 1925), European directors also sought to portray the unportrayable, and used a new aesthetic to depict this new and paroxysmal form of violence. Examples in France include Léon Poirier's *Verdun, visions d'histoire* of 1928 and Raymond Bernard's *Wooden crosses* (adapted from Dorgelès' *Les Croix de bois*) in 1932. One of the most successful of numerous examples in Germany was undoubtedly G. W. Pabst's *Comrades of 1918 (Westfront 1918)*, released in 1930.

Each of these works reflects a burning desire to depict the impact, pain and grief of the war. They are often also concerned with the impossibility of repeating such unspeakable brutality. Yet it is rare to find artists who, like Dix in a number of his drawings and self-portraits, or Cendrars in his work *J'ai tué* ('I have killed') of 1919, succeed in expressing the anguish of those who not only suffered the violence of the war but were also willing participants in it. Dix, for example, shows on his own face the rictus of the bloody brute that the war had turned him into. Such lucidity was exceptional, but it is clear for all that in both form and content post-war cultural works carried the imprint of their authors' experience of the conflict.

## 2. The complex time-scale of attitudes

The timeframes of cultural history remain a complex subject. The Great War was of course a critical moment in the development of European attitudes, but any assessment of the scale of the changes requires a close examination of the phenomenon of cultural demobilisation (A. Becker, op. cit.). The "continuation of the war in the mind", to use Gerd Krumeich's expression, varied in rhythm and intensity according to country, milieu and generation (Krumeich, 2002). Cultural demobilisation was certainly a slower process than its military counterpart, but the pattern was a complex one.

Besides, the great artistic watersheds and the moral cataclysm of the era have to be seen in the context of a powerful and sustained social, cultural and moral conservatism. The post-war *années folles* or "roaring twenties" – a dizzying age of jazz and sensuality – are a myth. The reality of women's status, for example, reflects the return of the former moral and social order. European women did secure the vote in certain countries and at least the illusion of a change in their social status, thanks to their contribution to the war effort. In reality though, for women the post-war period meant a return to the kitchen and in sexual matters they were subject to strong conservative influences, witness the French law of 1920 outlawing contraception and abortion. In fact another half-century had to elapse – that is, towards the late 1960s – before this conservatism started to crumble.

## 3. Mass conflict, mass culture

While mass culture did not originate with the First World War, the inter-war period undoubtedly saw a massive growth in the phenomenon. It was then that Europe entered fully the era of large-scale industrialised culture and great cultural manifestations. In the cinema, Chaplin was adulated as never before – or since – by élites and masses alike. Pending the arrival of television, radio broadcasting created a mass audience for great sporting events.

These two phenomena – the growth of mass audiences for and increasing industrialisation of the new cultural forms – provide strong echoes of the Great War itself, the first war to be fought on such a mass and industrialised scale. It is as if the mass era had arrived simultaneously in the military, cultural and political spheres.

So, finally, the Great War represents less a watershed or clean break – a somewhat ambiguous concept, ill-adapted to a cultural context – than a decisive stage in the process through which Europe entered the era of cultural modernity.

At a time when it seemed bent on self-destruction, Europe made a discovery that changed its relationship with the world, the discovery of American culture, through cinema and music. This discovery, which was to lead in the following decades to an Americanisation that was both acknowledged and feared, was in the end the only genuine cultural watershed in Europe in the years 1914-18. Unless, that is, one adds another cultural revolution, this time in the political sphere, namely the birth of the notion of collective security, whose application did not take practical effect for a long time but which as an idea, and thus as a cultural phenomenon, represented a genuine break with the pre-1914 world.

## Bibliography

Audoin-Rouzeau, S., *La Guerre des enfants 1914-1918. Essai d'histoire culturelle*, Paris, Armand Colin, 1993.

Audoin-Rouzeau, S., and Becker, A., *14-18, Retrouver la Guerre*, Paris, Gallimard, 2000.

Becker, A., "Créer pour oublier? Les dadaïstes et la mémoire de la guerre" in *Démobilisations culturelles après la Grande Guerre, 14-18 aujourd'hui – today – heute*, May 2002, No. 5, pp. 128-43.

Becker, J.-J., *Histoire culturelle de la Grande Guerre*, Paris, Armand Colin, 2005.

Dagen, P., *Le Silence des peintres. Les artistes face à la Grande Guerre*, Paris, Fayard, 1996.

Haffner, S., *Geschichte eines Deutschen*, Stuttgart and Munich, Deutsche Verlags-Anstalt, 2000.

Kalifa, D., *La Culture de masse en France. 1. 1860-1930*, Paris, La Découverte, 2001.

Krumeich, G., "Où va l'histoire culturelle de la Grande Guerre", *Démobilisations culturelles après la Grande Guerre, 14-18 aujourd'hui – today – heute*, May 2002, No. 5, pp. 7-13.

Schwartz, V.R., *Spectacular realities. Early mass culture in fin-de-siècle Paris*, Berkeley, Los Angeles and London, University of California Press, 1998.

Silver, K.E., *Vers le retour à l'ordre. L'avant-garde parisienne et la Première Guerre mondiale*, Paris, Flammarion, 1991.

# PART FOUR

# 1945 in European history

# Introduction to 1945

In 1945 came the end of a war that had caused human disaster on a scale never previously seen. Air raids and artillery had reduced many European cities to rubble. Economies were depleted and many industries, roads, bridges and railways had been destroyed. Over 40 million people had been killed, many of them civilians. Millions had been systematically exterminated in the concentration camps. All over Europe there were orphan children who needed to be identified and reunited with their surviving relatives. Soldiers were trying to get home, or were being held in prisoner-of-war camps. Everywhere there were refugees and displaced persons. Many were trying to get back to their homelands while millions of others – including German residents in other countries, Crimean Tatars and Chechens in the USSR, and other ethnic minorities – were being forcibly expelled from the towns and villages they had regarded as their homes.

By the time the three Allied leaders, Roosevelt, Stalin and Churchill, met in the Crimean resort of Yalta in February 1945, they knew that the war in Europe was almost won. American and British troops had crossed the Rhine and were advancing on Berlin from the west. Soviet troops were in Latvia, Poland, Bulgaria and Romania, had crossed Germany's eastern frontier and were just 50 km from Berlin. Consequently, though it was still necessary to maintain co-operation to bring the war to an end as quickly as possible, the Yalta Conference was rather more concerned with planning for the peace. During the course of a week the leaders agreed that a defeated Germany should be divided into occupation zones, that the French would be one of the occupying powers, that the USSR would enter the war against Japan and that the Polish borders would be moved westwards to reduce German territory and increase that of the USSR.

Given that the chapters in this section of the book were first presented as papers at a conference in Yalta in 2003 and that, thanks to the Ukrainian Ministry of Education and Science, one of the sessions was held in the meeting room of the Livadia Palace, it is not surprising that most of authors spent some time considering the significance of the original Yalta Conference. There is no doubt, as Professor Borodziej pointed out, that Yalta has had a lasting significance for many Poles, and other central and east Europeans. The sense of betrayal may have diminished with each generation but, like the Ribbentrop-Molotov Pact for the Baltic States, Yalta continued to colour people's perceptions right into the 1980s. At the same time, as Professor Westad points out in the first chapter in this section, the division of Europe was not determined by the Yalta Conference, but by the military situation in Europe at the end of the Second World War. Or, as Stalin said to Milovan Djilas,

"This war is not as in the past. Whoever occupies a territory also imposes on it his own social system. Everyone imposes his own system as far as his army can reach. It cannot be otherwise."

As several authors in this section observe, the Cold War did not begin with Yalta – its roots went much further back than that – but the end of the war did mean that Europe switched from being an arena defined by the threat of fascism to one defined by the military, diplomatic, economic and ideological competition between two superpowers.

# Chapter 22
# The Yalta Conference and the emergence of the Cold War

*Odd Arne Westad*

## The Yalta myths

There are many myths about the 1945 Yalta meeting – some had already developed at the end of the war and some are more recent creations. In a few countries in Europe, these myths serve as a cover for other discussions that might be more worthwhile than overall debates on Great Power decisions, but which are also more painful, because they imply discussing national myths about decisions taken at the time when the World War was developing into a Cold War. Examples of topics associated with such myths are the exodus of German refugees from the East, the crushing of the Warsaw Rising, and – not least – the fate of the countries incorporated into the Soviet Union. In many contexts – not least in classrooms – it is then easier to discuss the interactions of Great Men at Yalta.

The key myths about Yalta are two: Europe was divided up at Yalta; and the Cold War started at Yalta.

## "Europe was divided up at Yalta"

In reality, there was no such decision. The division of Europe was the result of a European civil war that had gone on since 1914. By 1945 the main protagonists of these wars – Britain, Germany and France – had all ceased to be powers that could determine the future of the continent. The Soviet Union and the United States were left as the only real Great Powers (or superpowers, as we later came to call them) at the end of the Second World War. Both the ideological and the strategic aims of these two states were on a collision course well before 1945; the division line between their European regions of control was determined not by the Yalta Conference, but by the military situation in Europe at the end of the Second World War.

## "The Cold War started at Yalta"

Again, the Cold War had different and rather more fundamental origins than the conflicts that were visible during the Crimean conference – or the specific clashes that developed in the inter-regnum between the Yalta meeting (4-11 February 1945) and the next (and final) conference of Allied leaders (Potsdam, 17 July to 2 August). The character and timing of these origins of course depends on which area of Europe one is talking about.

The confrontation between Communism and its opponents in Europe and the United States started not in 1945, but in 1917. If one asks the Poles, the Cold War was certainly in full swing in Poland in 1944 – maybe even in 1920. I believe some Ukrainians would strongly feel the same way. In most other areas, the coming of the Cold War was a much slower process, where several causes – military, diplomatic, social and ideological – together created a climate of confrontation.

If these are the Yalta myths, what then were the "Yalta realities", as seen by the main participants?

## The realities of Yalta

When Franklin Roosevelt, Joseph Stalin and Winston Churchill met in Yalta, a great war was about to end. Everyone present knew that – though they did not know how long the war's final phase would take, or what the military positions would be when their opponents, Germany and Japan, collapsed. The conference was therefore about both ending the war and organising the peace. The two aspects were closely related, because all three leaders believed that if they succeeded in working together in ending the war, they also had a very good chance at working together in organising the peace. This is what could be called "the Yalta attempt": winning the war and organising the peace in a way that did not lead to imminent conflict within the wartime alliance.

If the Yalta Attempt was a joint effort by the three leaders, why was it then ultimately so unsuccessful? The traditional explanation is of course that the three did not really mean what they said – while talking about co-operation, what they really were angling for was unilateral advantage. In other words, the attempt at co-operation was just rhetoric, not reality.

This interpretation is almost certainly wrong, not because of its insistence that advantages to the leaders and their countries did play the key role in decision making, but because of its claim that these perceived interests could not go along with a perceived potential for co-operation (or at least an absence of conflict). We now have a great deal of the internal materials from before, during and after the Yalta Conference, from all three sides. Among Stalin's papers in the Russian State Archive of Contemporary History in Moscow there are substantial files on Yalta, as well as Molotov's papers in the Foreign Policy Archive of the Russian Federation. The internal materials from all three sides and the records of the discussions show that none of them saw conflict inside the Alliance as being in their interest, at least not in the short run.

Most historians who have looked closely at the international situation in 1945, after the new documentary evidence from the former Soviet Union became available, agree that the issues at stake – and the way they evolved – were more important for the breakdown of co-operation than any ill intent against negotiations as such on any side of the wartime alliance. The political and military situation in Europe and in East Asia simply moved too fast between Yalta and Potsdam for workable compromises to take hold, given the ideological gulf that separated the Soviet Union from America and Britain at the outset. With Germany gone, all the matters of reconstructing Europe were on the table. And each of the former partners wanted to see their idea of Europe come into being, even if it meant risking overall co-operation in the process. The stakes for the future were too high to risk compromise.

Such a type of explanation, connecting structural preconditions to rapidly evolving political situations that no single power was able to control, seems increasingly to be the favoured tool for historians in interpreting the Cold War. One major reason for this is the increasing weight that new historical accounts of this period put on the role of ideologies, both on the American and the Soviet side. These two powers were in their essence defined by their ideologies – capitalism and liberal democracy on the US side, and Marxism and collectivism on the Soviet side. In a situation where these two powers dominated the negotiations (both at Yalta and at Potsdam the British were the "poor relations" at the table), the ideological divide made compromises hard to achieve and demanded, both in Washington and in Moscow, a clear political determination to seek compromise over conflict if any form of co-operation were to continue.

## The issues at stake

If this is the perspective used, one will need to look at the key issues at stake at Yalta and Potsdam (and beyond) in order to understand the origins of the Cold War at the diplomatic level. It is particularly important to look at the reactions of key leaders as events unfolded, given the background of what I have already said about ideologies and how ideologies function. Preconceived ideas do not determine how people solve their problems, but they influence (and sometimes strongly limit) the options that are seen as being available. All the leaders involved in these negotiations were cautious and careful people. But their carefulness worked in two directions. One way, their caution told them that they needed each other, at least as long as the war was still on. The other way, it told them not to trust the motives of an ideological enemy, who – in the last resort – wanted to see his political system triumph over yours.

Let me then first say a little bit about the three key figures at the Yalta Conference, about their mindsets and their approaches to diplomacy.

### Franklin Delano Roosevelt

The US president, born in 1882 into one of the wealthiest and most well-known families in the United States, had during his presidency become the most important progressive leader in American history. His public programmes, such as the New Deal, had helped Americans overcome the worst social effects of the Great Depression and he had allowed left-wing technocrats to move the administration's policy towards creating an unprecedented role for the state in the US economy and public life. There is reason to believe, however, that for FDR these policies were primarily expediencies to overcome the crisis and win the war, as his biographer William Leuchtenburg has pointed out. FDR's greatest task was to overcome the challenges to American ideology, both domestically and internationally, to defeat authoritarian rule, and by implication to extend American freedom in a global sense – in other words, complete the agenda that had been left unfulfilled after the First World War.

Even though weakened by illness at Yalta, the president stuck to that agenda and to his belief that such a programme could better be achieved by getting his interlocutors to co-operate, rather than resist. He was very aware of the US position of power – nothing could be done at Yalta or anywhere else for that matter on the Allied side unless the Americans agreed, in FDR's estimation. By appearing to be the balancer between Churchill's old-time imperialism and Stalin's Communism, the American President found his opportunities to influence both almost limitless. As he himself had put it to some of his closest aides in May 1942:

> "You know I am a juggler, and I never let my right hand know what my left hand does … I may be entirely inconsistent, and furthermore I am perfectly willing to mislead and tell untruths if it will help win the war."

## Joseph Stalin

The Soviet leader was born in 1879 as the son of a poor cobbler in the provincial Georgian town of Gori in the Caucasus, then an imperial Russian colony. A man of limited intellect who rose through the ranks of the Communist Party through an enormous capacity for hard work combined with a limitless appetite for intrigue and what we today might call networking, Stalin saw Marxism as his main working tool for governing the Soviet Union and understanding its relations with the outside world. Having misjudged the intentions of his previous ally – the Germans – he believed his wartime alliance with the United States and Great Britain to be more lasting, because the rivalries between his two imperialist allies for a long time would be more severe than those between the two of them and the Soviet Union.

Stalin's perspective, therefore, at both the Yalta and Potsdam conferences was that, even though war between the Soviet Union and capitalist states would be una-voidable in the long run, the material basis of power relations strongly implied that at the moment the war ended it was the re-division of imperialist hegemony that preoccupied Washington and London, not confronting the Soviet Union. If Moscow played its cards correctly – in other words, if Stalin made it possible for the two others to accept the Soviet Union as a legitimate power with its own security interests – then war could be postponed and socialism could be made stronger before the ultimate showdown with imperialism. A talented actor, Stalin saw his role at the conferences as that of the statesman alongside other statesmen, insisting on his legitimate share of the spoils and through that very behaviour avoiding suspicions about his basic aims.

# Winston Churchill

The British Prime Minister, the oldest of the key participants at Yalta, was born in 1874 at Blenheim Palace, into one of the most prominent families of England. He was old enough to have stood for office in the nineteenth century, and kept throughout his twentieth-century career many of the ideals of the previous century with him. While Roosevelt and Stalin both, in different ways, liked to think about other countries in terms of the content of their political systems, Churchill believed a mix of culture and geo-strategy determined international relations. He therefore believed strongly, for instance, that the shared culture of Britain and the United States would gradually bring the two countries closer together. In spite of his distaste for socialism, he also saw Stalin – to begin with – as pursuing reasonable security interests in Eastern Europe. But, already at Yalta, Churchill had begun to feel that Stalin's demands went far outside the very limited role London had assigned to Moscow in the post-war settlement.

Acutely aware of Britain's reduced power and influence, Churchill was hoping that the United States would support the retention of both the British Empire and American forces in Europe, so that the balance of power of the continent would not tip too much in Russia's favour. But – rather surprisingly, given his background – Churchill was enough of a realist to see that if a choice had to be made between these two priorities, Britain's first priority had to be Europe, not the empire. Having tried to get Stalin's agreement to an outright division of Eastern Europe into spheres of interest during his visit to Moscow in October 1944, Churchill knew that Stalin's signature on a piece of paper was not enough; only American power in Europe could prevent a gradual extension of Soviet influence towards the West.

None of the approaches of the leaders who met at Yalta was, in the long run, much suited to compromise over complex diplomatic issues or, for that matter, to respect for the sovereignty of others. But, at the same time, given the short-term perspectives of Roosevelt, Stalin and Churchill at the particular time when the conference met, it must have seemed unlikely that the Grand Alliance would descend into conflict and mutual acrimony less than a year later. In order to understand the speed with which the alliance dissolved, one has to study not only ideas and perceptions, but also the concrete issues that faced the conference participants who met in the Livadia Palace on 4 February 1945.

For our purpose, I would like to concentrate on two key issues at Yalta: the negotiations over Poland's territorial and political future, and the talks concerning Soviet entry into the war against Japan.

## The Polish question

This was part of the origins of the Second World War, but it was seen in very different ways from London, Moscow and Washington. For Churchill, the fate of Poland was one of the key causes of the world war, and his government saw a clear need to re-establish some form of Polish independence after the war was over. For Stalin, Poland was first and foremost a yardstick to measure how far the alliance would hold. Even though Polish territory was important to Moscow in security terms, Stalin had spent little time during the war discussing what kind of political system Poland was to have in the post-war period. Basically, he would take as much as he could get without endangering the alliance: a Communist-dominated government if possible, a coalition government if necessary. For Roosevelt, Poland was territory for negotiations. He cared less – much less – about what might happen in Warsaw than about keeping the alliance together for the foreseeable future. Even though he suspected that Stalin, through his attempts at excluding the Polish government-in-exile from any role in post-war Poland, was playing for keeps already in 1944, the president still hoped that through his own negotiating skills he could find some form of compromise with the Soviet leader.

The territorial rearrangements with regard to Poland had been discussed between the Allies on several occasions towards the end of the war, and the debate at Yalta was relatively brief, fixing its Eastern border slightly east of the Curzon line, which had been first proposed as the Soviet-Polish border in 1920. The western borderline was to give Poland compensation from Germany in the form of Prussian territory east of the Oder river, but the final decision was to be left to the future peace conference. At Potsdam the three allied powers agreed on a "temporary" borderline – subject to a final peace conference between Germany and Poland – including all German territory east of the Oder and Neisse rivers (except those parts of East Prussia that went to the Soviets) as part of Poland, and implicitly sanctioned the mass expulsion of the German population from these territories. The peace conference was of course not held until 1990.

The key debate at Yalta was over the political future of Poland. Stalin had tried to present a *fait accompli* by unilaterally recognising the communist-led Polish Government in Lublin before the Yalta Conference even met. But both the Soviets and their Western allies knew that the Soviet action was a negotiating ploy rather than a firm decision – what really counted, as Churchill to his frustration kept reminding himself during the conference, was the Red Army's positions inside Poland. Determined as he was to "rescue Poland from the Soviet clutches", the Prime Minister knew even before the conference began that the best that could be achieved was – as he put it – "a dirty little compromise". And even though Roosevelt wrote to Stalin before he set out for the conference, letting him know that he was "disturbed and deeply disappointed" at the Soviet decision to recognise the Lublin government, the president also saw that the United States would be negotiating from a position of weakness, with its forces hundreds of miles from the country over which negotiations were taking place.

The final outcome on Poland at Yalta was certainly a compromise, however, and it was probably Stalin who gave most on paper, by allowing a reorganisation of the Lublin government to include representatives from the London-based government-in-exile. But Poland also showed the weakest aspects of the Yalta Attempt, because on a matter as vital as what kind of government would control the lands between Germany and

Russia, neither the United States nor the Soviet Union was much set for compromise in the long run. "Do not worry. We can implement it in our way later," Stalin told his Foreign Minister Molotov after the agreement had been made. "It is the best I can do for Poland at this time," FDR told his chief military aide, Admiral Leahy.

The whole debate over Poland therefore showed how differently the three Great Powers within the alliance viewed the world. Issues of legitimacy, though deferred, would come back to haunt the compromise over Poland almost as soon as the Crimean conference ended.

## Soviet entry into the war against Japan

These key differences in perceptions were also evident in the discussions about the possibility of Soviet entry into the war against Japan, an issue that is not often discussed in connection with the European dispositions at Yalta, but which is of central importance for understanding how the pressures of regular diplomacy interacted with the world views of the main leaders. For Stalin, it was self-evident that the Soviet Union would have to attack Japan at some point – but only after the war in Europe had been won, and preferably after the war in the Pacific had so weakened the Japanese Imperial Army that victory would be a walkover. What is often forgotten is that as late as January 1945 Stalin and the Soviet General Staff still saw a Japanese attack on the Soviet Union as a distinct possibility, and knew that Soviet resources were already spread so thinly that such an event would have catastrophic effects on its strategic dispositions, not to mention on its ability to influence the end of the war in Europe through combined political and military pressure. War with Japan was unavoidable, Stalin postulated, because Japanese capitalism saw the Soviet Union as its deadly enemy (whatever conflicts it happened to be involved in with the West).

But on the US side, such a Soviet-Japanese war was not taken as a foregone conclusion. On the contrary, President Roosevelt believed strongly that the United States needed to tempt the Soviet Union into entering the war. There were three strong reasons why most planners in Washington saw such a need – and none of them is the *naïveté* the President has sometimes been endowed with by historians. The first reason was that the Soviet entry was a precondition for avoiding American losses in the final part of the war on a scale that would dwarf even the high rate of the US Pacific campaign. The second was that even if the United States was developing a new weapon that according to its proponents "would revolutionise warfare", there was no guarantee that an untested atomic technology would actually yield results. Without such a weapon, the invasion of the Japanese home islands could be become a long and arduous affair. And third, if the Soviets did not enter before Japan was defeated, not only would the relative US position in East Asia be weakened because of the losses it would have had to take, but such a continued Soviet neutrality would also leave Moscow free to improve its positions elsewhere, including in Europe and the Middle East, as the war was drawing to an end.

In other words, the United States needed compromises with the Soviets to be made at Yalta, in order to better pursue its own interests in the final stage of the war and beyond. That Stalin was, in the end, willing to commit himself to an entry into the East Asian war after the war in Europe had been brought to a close was seen as a major victory for US diplomacy. It showed that the Yalta Attempt was based on the needs of the Great Powers in the final period of war as the main participants sixty years ago perceived them to be. But just as the ideological gap became too wide to bridge in Europe as concrete peacetime policies had to be constructed, so did the perceptions of the roles of the other side go through a dramatic change in East Asia between the Yalta and Potsdam conferences. At Yalta, Soviet military force was seen as a common resource for the alliance, in spite of the generally held mistrust of Stalin's motives. Six months later, the Red Army was fast becoming a threat more than an ally.

## Conclusions

The Yalta Attempt – and then its failure – was about bringing Russia into some form of co-operation with the rest of Europe and with the United States. I have spoken at length about the reason why this failed in 1945 and could only re-start with the end of the Cold War. But, beyond the Cold War, there were also broader reasons why this project was, and is, difficult. Like the United States, the development of Russia as a state was based on continental conquest, on having a special position that made it the natural centre for the regions that surrounded it. Nowhere, of course, is that more evident than in the Crimea, where the three leaders met, especially if one thinks in a 200-year perspective. I think that overcoming the division of Europe can only succeed if Russia, through its own, internal processes of change, moves from being an empire to being a state that wants, for its own reasons, to be integrated into Europe. This is a process that is not unknown to other countries and it is a process that will take time.

# Chapter 23
# Yalta, Potsdam and the emergence of the Cold War: an overview from the United Kingdom in the light of the latest research

*Martin McCauley*

In November 1917, Arthur Balfour, the British Foreign Secretary, wrote a letter to Lord Rothschild, the English head of the Jewish banking family, pledging Britain's support for Zionist efforts to establish a Jewish home in Palestine. In a recently discovered document, Balfour states that Britain never had any intention of honouring this pledge. It had been a tactical move to win support for Britain during the First World War.

During the Great Fatherland War (1941-45), Stalin followed in the Balfourian tradition. He made many promises he had no intention of keeping, first and foremost concerning Poland. His pledges were tactical moves to strengthen the security of the Soviet Union. Churchill did the same, as indeed did Roosevelt.

## The Yalta Conference

What was Britain's perception of its interests at Yalta? What goals did it set itself and to what extent were they realised?

The key to Yalta is the military situation. Indeed military issues dominated. The Red Army was already on German territory, in Romania, Bulgaria, Poland, Czechoslovakia and Hungary, and it was preparing to take Vienna, the capital of Austria. The Ardennes offensive (the Battle of the Bulge, December 1944 to January 1945) had surprised the Western allies and spread gloom among many commanders. Germany would be much more difficult to take than envisaged. Indeed, so optimistic had General Eisenhower been, in the second half of 1944, that he bet General Montgomery that the Allies would be in Berlin and the war over by Christmas Day, 1944.

Edward Stettinius, the US Secretary of State, underlines the reality of the situation:

> "It must never be forgotten that while the Crimean conference was taking place, President Roosevelt had just been told by his military advisers that the surrender of Japan might not occur until 1947, and some predicted even later. The President was told that without Russia, it might cost the US a million casualties to capture Japan [British military estimates were half a million killed and half a million wounded]. It must also be remembered that at the time of the Yalta Conference it was still uncertain whether the atomic bomb could be perfected and, that since the Battle of the Bulge had set us back in Europe, it was uncertain

how long it might take for Germany to crack … It cast a deep gloom over the confident expectations that the German war would soon end."

For Roosevelt there were three important issues at Yalta: to defeat Germany; to defeat Japan; and to establish the United Nations Organisation. On the UN, no sanctions could be imposed unless the permanent members of the Security Council were unanimous. According to Roosevelt: "The most important thing is to maintain the unity of the three Great Powers, to defeat Germany, then get them all around a table to work out a world organisation."

Where did all this leave Churchill? On the sidelines. Churchill wanted to co-ordinate a joint approach before the conference, but Roosevelt was not interested. From Soviet sources there are some unflattering references to Churchill. Sergo Beria, Lavrenty Beria's son, who was part of the eavesdropping team at Yalta, reports that the Soviet guards respected Roosevelt but made jokes about Churchill. The latter found it difficult to sleep and consumed quite a lot of alcohol. He knew that everything was bugged and took delight in producing quintessentially English phrases which would give the translators a hard time.

Roosevelt had made up his mind about his policies and Churchill was not going to change them. Franklin Delano Roosevelt (FDR) simply refused to discuss issues with him. Churchill was walking beside the jeep carrying FDR and trying to take up certain questions, but Roosevelt's reply was that everything had been discussed and decided. Part of the problem was that FDR saw the Soviet Union as a partner in the post-war management of the world. The USA wanted to dismantle Britain's colonies, and in this Moscow and Washington had more in common than Washington and London.

Poland was the main problem from the Western point of view; the problem was that Soviet domination of Poland had been conceded at Teheran. In the October 1944 percentages agreement between Churchill and Stalin, there was no mention of Poland but the rest of eastern and south-eastern Europe was carved up into spheres of influence – notably Greece (90/10% for the West), Romania (90/10% for the Russians), Bulgaria (75/25% for the Russians), Yugoslavia and Hungary (both 50/50%). FDR and Churchill did get Stalin to accept some London Poles in the Lublin government. Churchill wanted eight or ten, but he could not confront Stalin on his own. He tried to get FDR to do so, but the latter wished to work with Stalin and could not afford to fall out with him. Churchill therefore had few cards he could play at Yalta. Even so, at the end he was more or less satisfied with the outcome, as was FDR.

Stalin was much better informed than either Churchill or Roosevelt. Burgess and Maclean were providing documents on British policy and Kim Philby was providing intelligence. Alger Hiss, the Soviet agent in the State Department, was a member of FDR's team at Yalta. Stalin knew exactly what FDR was willing to concede to get Russia involved in the war against Japan. Roosevelt did not pick up the signs that Stalin was keen to get into the war.

From Churchill's point of view, Yalta produced the Declaration on Liberated Europe which spoke of democracy, freedom, sovereignty and so on. From the Foreign Office documents, it is clear that it thought that this declaration superseded the percentages agreement of October 1944. Stalin did not. Another issue on which Churchill was pleased was Spain. Franco was to stay. If he were removed the communists could take power. This would then pose problems in the Straits of Gibraltar. Russia had ambitions in Libya and Tangier. In terms of cards, at Yalta, Stalin probably thought he held three aces; perhaps FDR thought he had two or even three aces. Churchill held no aces. Indeed he probably only held the two of clubs and the two of spades!

The Americans knew the Russians needed reparations from Germany, but did not agree to any sum at Yalta. They also thought the Soviet Union would need substantial US loans after the war. Britain had been almost bankrupted by the war and knew it needed US loans after the war.

One of the reasons why the British delegation was pleased with the results of Yalta was the extraordinary impression that Stalin made on them, from Churchill downwards. Alexander Cadogan, Permanent Under-Secretary in the FO, remarked:

> "I have never known the Russians so easy and accommodating. In particular he has been extremely good. He is a great man, and shows up very impressively against the background of the other two ageing statesmen."

Stalin had been so accommodating. He had agreed, after initial opposition, to allow France a zone and a seat on the Allied Control Commission. Again, after a show of dissent, he had agreed to the American voting formula for the Security Council, thus ensuring the creation of the UNO. Churchill was ever mindful of Neville Chamberlain, the British Prime Minister who was duped by Hitler. "Poor Neville Chamberlain believed he could trust Hitler. He was wrong. But I don't think I'm wrong about Stalin."

## Between Yalta and Potsdam

British attitudes changed radically after Yalta. Disillusionment set in. Britain found that the Russians would not help to resolve questions on the European Advisory Commission. The conclusion was that the Russians had thought that by the end of the war they would be at the Rhine, and had been surprised at the rapid advance of the Allies. They had decided to hold on to everything they had. One British Foreign Office official lamented that "democracy" and "co-operation" had different meanings in Russian. Democracy was "guided democracy" while co-operation meant that each power did as it liked in its zone and the others acquiesced.

Russia emerged as a future potential enemy. This is articulated for the first time by the Chiefs of Staff on 2 October 1944. It reappears in May 1945. The Chiefs of Staff were instructed by Churchill to report on the possibility of taking on Russia militarily should trouble arise in Britain's future discussions with it. On 24 May 1945, Churchill expressed anxiety about the Russian bear sprawled over Europe. He instructed the Chiefs of Staff to examine from the military point of view the possibility of driving the

Russian bear back to Moscow before the Americans and the British had demobilised their forces. By 11 June 1945, Churchill is presenting a gloomy review of the situation in Europe. "The Russians are all powerful in Europe."

Churchill would have liked the Allies to remain where they were at the end of the war in order to negotiate a favourable agreement on access to the Western sectors of Berlin. However the Americans were not prepared for a confrontation with Stalin because they wanted the Red Army as allies in the war against Japan. Instead, the Allies withdrew to their agreed zonal boundaries and entered Berlin only in early June. The faulty agreement on Western access to Berlin (and the right of West Berliners to travel to West Germany) was eventually to cause much friction between the wartime Allies.

## Potsdam

Churchill took the fateful decision not to attend Roosevelt's funeral. It is still a mystery why he failed to grasp the opportunity to meet Truman and attempt to influence him. Truman hero-worshipped Churchill. Roy Jenkins, in his biography of Churchill (2001), suggests that there was never any real warmth between Churchill and FDR. They were tactical allies. This may explain, in part, Churchill's decision not to travel to Roosevelt's funeral. Whatever the reason, it was an extraordinary lapse by Churchill who normally had such a fine nose for public relations. Truman suggested that he should meet Stalin at Potsdam, and Churchill could come in at the end. This neatly illustrates Britain's role: it was not the "Big Three", but the "Big Two and a Dwarf".

On 2 July 1945 Alexander Cadogan, Permanent Under-Secretary at the British Foreign Office, wrote to Churchill:

"We are hoping to prepare for you a list of cards that we and the Americans hold in our hands. There are not many. The most important is American credits. Our possession of the German fleet, industrial plant and resources in the West. The German archives. Any concession which Stalin may wish to extract from us, for example, on the Straits or Tangier."

Truman, of course, had the atomic bomb. Before Potsdam, Stalin thought he held three aces, but the atomic bomb changed all that. Now he had only two. Truman probably thought he had three aces, one of them being the A-bomb. At last, Churchill thought he had an ace.

General Alanbrooke reports Churchill's reaction to the news of the explosion of the bomb on 23 July 1945:

"It was no longer necessary for the Russians to come into the Japanese war; the new explosive was enough to settle the matter. Furthermore we now have something in our hands which would redress the balance with the Russians! The secret of this explosive, and the power to use it, would completely alter the diplomatic equilibrium which was adrift since the defeat of Germany! Now we had a new value which redressed our position (pushing his chin out and scowling), now we can say that if they insist on doing this or that, well we can just blot out Moscow, then Stalingrad, then Kiev, Kuibyshev, Kharkov, Stalingrad [sic], Sebastopol, etc. And now where are the Russians!!!"

Truman was impressed by Stalin: "I can deal with Stalin. He is honest – but smart as hell."

## Britain's attitude to the Soviet Union

Britain was always aware that the Soviet Union was a military giant and Britain a military dwarf. From a military point of view, negotiations at Teheran and Yalta were defensive and almost apologetic. Politically this placed Britain in a weak position to defend its interests and resist the domination of Europe by the Soviet Union after the war. In a perceptive analysis dated 17 April 1944, the Foreign Office considered the goals of Soviet policy and the likely consequences for Europe:

> "Stalin rejects the American view that peace can be maintained by an organisation of international co-operation. Capitalism means wars. Stalin wants peace and will stay out of wars, if possible.
>
> The Soviet Union is busy constructing a *cordon sanitaire* along its western frontier. The aim is a group of small states tied to the Soviet Union by treaties, if possible. Moscow will oppose any federation because this would make it more difficult to influence the individual states. These states should claim territory from their neighbours – East Prussia to Poland, Transylvania to Hungary, etc. thus making them dependent on Moscow for security.
>
> Russia needs 25 years of peace to become a great economic power and over the next 10 to 25 years will attempt at all costs to avoid hostilities with Britain and the US.
>
> The Soviet Union will avoid socialist revolution in Europe at all costs because it would destabilise the region and the new regimes could become insubordinate and therefore difficult to control."

What difference did the change in leadership make on British policy? Was Attlee better disposed towards the Soviet Union? No. The Labour Party's analysis of the Soviet Union's policies after 1945 was almost the same as that of the Conservative Party. It expected the Soviet Union to concentrate on domestic affairs and not to become a military threat to Britain or Western Europe. Ernest Bevin had considerable influence as Secretary of State for Foreign Affairs. Bevin hated communists as he had fought them during his trade union days. He could not stand Molotov. Labour's foreign policy was the same as New Labour's foreign policy. The foundation of it was the alliance with the United States. This caused conflict with the left wing of the Labour Party, but Attlee brushed this aside. Some members of the parliamentary Labour Party were providing information to Stalin through Soviet agents.

The key factor was that Britain was weak, militarily and economically, and needed US aid.

## Germany

Great Britain was concerned to ensure that Germany did not become a threat to peace as it had twenty years after 1919. Germany was the bogey until 1946, when views changed and the Soviet Union came to be viewed as the coming threat. The same view prevailed in Eastern Europe. President Eduard Benes of Czechoslovakia was willing to make concessions to Stalin in return for security against a resurgent Germany. The Czechs and Slovaks were always better disposed towards the Russians than the Poles. That all changed after the Warsaw Pact invasion of Czechoslovakia in August 1968.

## The British understanding of Stalin and the Soviet Union

A major concern for the Foreign Office was to analyse the personality and policies of Stalin and the Soviet Union. Was Stalin essentially a Marxist or a pragmatist, or a combination of the two? Churchill's approach to diplomacy was personal. If he could meet a head of state personally, then a possible deal could be struck. Foreign policy came down to fashioning personal relationships in which trust was the key element. If this could be established, then wide-ranging policy decisions could be taken. Only in this way could one ensure that agreements were actually implemented.

Churchill concluded that Stalin was a man he could do business with. He would keep his word. This meant that he believed he could understand Stalin's thought processes and therefore he could fashion policies which could succeed. Churchill dismissed Molotov and the other leaders as "Bolsheviks". In other words there was no way one could fathom how they arrived at decisions and, by extension, no way one could influence them.

British diplomats believed that Stalin was under pressure from his Politburo or Council of Ministers and that he might have been scolded from time to time for giving away too much. Some even thought that Stalin had to carefully take into consideration what his military leaders proposed.

Churchill's conclusion when he encountered problems with Stalin was that the Soviet leader was the problem. In an interesting analysis, dated 14 August 1942, Churchill mused over why Stalin was accommodating one day and the opposite the next. He concluded that Stalin might have been putting his views on record for future reference and to please the commissars (government ministers).

> "We asked ourselves what was the explanation of this performance and transformation from the good ground we had reached the night before. I think the most probable is that his Council of Commissars did not take the news I brought as well as he did. They perhaps have more power that we suppose, and that he was putting himself on the record for future purposes and for their benefit, and also letting off steam for his own."

Where does the idea that Stalin was not master of the Kremlin come from? From the agents and fellow travellers in the Foreign Office? Unfortunately there are no documents which provide a clear answer. On the other hand, one finds the same type of analysis being proposed by American diplomats and analysts, and also by the Canadians.

The reality was that Stalin was the master of the Kremlin but, of course, he discussed approaches and tactics with his aides. Molotov, on occasions, argued strongly against Stalin's view and sometimes the master changed his mind. On other occasions, if Stalin judged that Molotov's decisions at a meeting with the Western Allies were misguided, he would submit him to ferocious verbal assaults. On one occasion Molotov broke down and wept under the strain. The same applied to the military. However it should be underlined that Stalin never allowed a majority to form against him so that he could be over-ruled.

## The origins of the Cold War

Is it possible to identify a single event that precipitated the Cold War? No. The Cold War was a process, which gradually gathered momentum. From the beginning of the Grand Alliance between the Soviet Union, the United States and Great Britain there were sources of tension. However, until the autumn of 1943 Stalin was on the defensive. Afterwards he gradually gained confidence (this can be dated from late 1943, when the *Internationale* was dropped as the Soviet national anthem and a Russian national anthem replaced it). By 1945 Stalin was very sure of himself. Molotov, in his old age, conceded that Stalin was conceited in 1945 and overstretched himself. Great Britain, in its relations with the Soviet Union, was on the defensive until Potsdam. Indeed one can say that London was always on the defensive. The United States always believed itself to be the dominant partner but regarded co-operation with Stalin after hostilities as the key to securing and maintaining world peace. Hence Great Britain played a minor role in the drama that led to the Cold War. This conflict was essentially one between the two powers that became superpowers, Russia and America. Every other state was a bit player in the drama.

Stalin's personal archive provides many insights into his personality and decision making. He suffered bouts of illness, which must have reduced his ability to master all the details of a problem and then decide what to do. He had a stomach complaint from at least 1936 and he arrived one day later at the Potsdam conference, apparently having suffered from a recurrence of the stomach problem.

He was very jealous of other decision makers, for example, Molotov and Zhukov. The British interpreter, Hugh Lunghi, thought he treated Molotov insultingly, "like a dog". The aim was to ensure that Molotov remained subordinate to Stalin and did not take any decisions on his own initiative. Of course, it was impossible for Stalin to control Molotov like a robot since on many issues the latter had to use his initiative. Stalin adopted the same attitude towards all other officials who might impinge on his powers of decision making. He refused to share power with anyone. Given the expanded influence and power of the Soviet Union, it was simply impossible for one man to take all the important decisions. A superman could not have done it.

Given his desire to arrogate all power to himself, a partnership with the United States after the war would have imposed enormous pressure on him, at a time when his health was failing. No single decision maker could have coped with the multitudinous problems seeking solutions. He could have imposed a general line, but could not have checked if every official was carrying out his will.

The same applied to domestic policies. It crossed his mind that the Russian soldiers and civilians who had defeated Napoleon and ended up in Paris brought many of the foreign ideas back with them in their rucksacks and heads. The Decembrist Revolt, an attempt to remove Tsar Nicholas I in 1825, was one of the results of this ferment of ideas. This is one explanation for the deportation of returning Soviet prisoners-of-war to Siberia and not permitting them to rejoin their families.

Stalin had hoped for US credits, which would have made reconstruction easier. When these failed to materialise he was obliged to raise the capital in the Soviet Union itself. The population was exploited to rebuild the country quickly. In order to galvanise citizens and eliminate opposition, he chose to promote Russian nationalism, especially its anti-Western and xenophobic aspects.

Montefiore's book (*The Court of the Red Tsar*, 2003) provides many insights into Stalin's thinking and method of decision making. He regarded himself as an intellectual – he read an enormous amount of world literature – and therefore felt he had the right to interfere and pronounce on any subject he deemed important. "Important" here means anything with a political impact. He was very tired after 1945 and often spent months in the south, mainly in Georgia, but had to be kept informed on every issue that he regarded as important. He went through mountains of paper every day and carefully formulated decisions and orders, which were then relayed to Moscow. He wrote letters and memoranda on a gargantuan scale and was always asking if so-and-so had carried out orders. He hated gossip and chatterboxes but wanted to be kept informed about the latest details of the personal lives of his associates. It was as if only he were to be allowed to collect gossip so that, probably, he could use it against the person at some time in the future. One of his aides commented that he knew six Stalins, so complex was the master of the Kremlin. It required great skills from his subordinates to divine which Stalin was addressing them. The wrong response could mean that the wrath of the leader descended on them, which could terminate their careers.

He was also a consummate actor and could charm at will. This explains why the impression that Stalin made on his interlocutors varied from person to person. Sometimes he chose to insult Churchill. For instance, during the October 1944 negotiations, which resulted in the percentages agreement, Stalin was so rude that Churchill was on the point of abandoning Moscow. Stalin then invited him round to his apartment for a family dinner and worked his magic on him. Churchill left wreathed in smiles. On other occasions he set out to charm him – and always succeeded. The impact the Soviet dictator had on Churchill is quite extraordinary, given that the British leader was a life-long hater of communism.

Stalin had the same impact on Roosevelt, but then the American leader wanted to believe that America, in partnership with Russia, could rule the world after 1945. Churchill was always aware that, after 1943, Britain was facing a Europe that could be dominated militarily, and possibly politically, by the Soviet Union after the war. On its own, Britain could not resist the advances of the Russian bear.

FDR, on the other hand, always presented an air of effortless superiority vis-à-vis the Soviet Union. It was neither a military nor a political threat to America. He bothered little about the ideology of Marxism-Leninism, always assuming that liberal capitalism and democracy would prevail. Whereas Stalin was convinced Russia would become the promised land, FDR knew that America already was the promised land.

## Reasons for the Cold War

First there was Stalin's overconfidence after 1943. Then there was his desire to retain control of the Soviet Union: a partnership with the USA would have resulted in many Soviet decision makers and Stalin could not have imposed his will on each and every matter. He was very jealous of other Soviet decision makers, from Zhukov to Molotov.

The United States wanted a partnership, but became more and more frustrated since they thought they had three aces and should decide policy. They thought that the Soviet Union needed their capital to recover.

Stalin had a low opinion of Truman – "not educated and not clever". It is surprising that such a cautious decision maker did not take more pains to cultivate the US President, who was impressed by Stalin.

Stalin was tired and often ill after 1945.

Stalin did not rate Attlee very highly: Great Britain was not a factor in starting the Cold War, but they were happy to see the USA stay in Europe: the Marshall Plan and NATO were godsends for Great Britain.

There is no single event that one can discern that can be identified as the beginning of the Cold War. It was a gradual process. However, from the outset of his presidency, some of Truman's advisers, such as Averill Harriman and George Kennan, took a very negative view of the Soviet Union, They did not mince their words about the perceived threat the Soviets posed to Europe and America.

FDR and Churchill did not "give away" Eastern Europe at Yalta. At Teheran, they conceded a leading role for Russia in Poland and after the Red Army occupied Poland it was almost a *fait accompli* that Moscow would dominate its neighbour. The percentages agreement of October 1944 revealed that Churchill was willing to trade zones of influence. He recognised that the Soviet Union would henceforth dominate Eastern Europe. At the back of Churchill's mind was always the fear that a resurgent Germany could again attempt to dominate western Europe. Having the Russians in Eastern Europe was one guarantee that this would not become a reality.

# Chapter 24
# The Crimean Conference and the origins of the Cold War

*Alexander Chubaryan*

## The growth in Cold War historical research

Recent years have witnessed a rapidly growing interest in Cold War history among historians and political journalists all over the world. Concentration on this topic is related to a number of reasons.

First, there is now an opportunity to use huge bodies of new documents, primarily archival ones. Previously inaccessible archives of the former Soviet Union are of paramount importance in this connection. In spite of researchers' explicit discontent with the fact that some archival materials are still inaccessible, generally one can say that even the documents that are now available and used by scholars do permit us to define the main stages of transition to the Cold War and confrontation, to understand the essence of Soviet intentions, to trace the decision-making process, to assess Stalin's role and the logics of his policy, as well as the correlation between ideological and practical *Realpolitik* issues. As researchers also have access to US, British, French and German published and archival documents, they can reconstruct the whole picture of Cold War developments by comparing sources from both sides and drawing from a rich memoir literature as well.

Second, it is worth noting that, since the mid-1990s, hundreds of conferences and meetings dealing with different aspects of the Cold War have taken place, including those where actual witnesses were present. In the early 1990s, the International Cold War History project was launched by the Woodrow Wilson Centre in Washington. Apart from dozens of conferences and seminars, its framework included a special Bulletin (12 issues have been already printed) where archival documents previously unknown to the academic world are published regularly. Apart from Washington, centres for Cold War studies were created in many countries – in Russia (at the Institute of Universal History of the Russian Academy of Sciences), in Britain (at King's College, London) and in Germany (at the University of Essen); dozens of conferences were organised in France, Italy, the Czech Republic, Slovakia, China, Japan, Vietnam and other countries. As a result, a kind of network has taken shape, uniting hundreds of scholars specialising in Cold War history.

Third, during the last decade hundreds of books and articles have been published, shedding light on various aspects of the Cold War's origins, development and end. The authors' points of view often differ radically, which gives grounds for discussions and comparisons.

Fourth, research in this field is facilitated by the fact that the process is now over, that the Cold War itself had come to an end, so it is possible to analyse this phenomenon in its finished form. Therefore, we have a complete picture of the Cold War, including the assessment of its reasons, the analysis of its stages and the factors determining its end. Researchers can compare the participants' aims at the beginning with the real results of their actions.

And, fifth, Cold War history should be placed in a broader context. As we know, as a result of the Second World War a new international political system, the Yalta-Potsdam one, was formed.

In fact, only a few global international systems emerged during the nineteenth and twentieth centuries – the Vienna system (after the Napoleonic Wars and the defeat of France), the Versailles system (after the First World War) and, finally, the aforementioned Yalta-Potsdam system.

Historians have an opportunity to compare these systems' evolution and the circumstances of their emergence and functioning, and to define their typology, common features and peculiarities. The study of the Yalta-Potsdam system's role is today additionally facilitated by the fact that it ceased to exist together with the Cold War itself.

Previous research of the Cold War and Yalta-Potsdam system's phenomena has also revealed the need for an interdisciplinary approach, for a concerted effort by historians, political scientists, legal experts, sociologists and economists. This need is especially acute, as it is practically impossible to understand many aspects of these topics without an analysis of the economic and legal factors.

Moreover, studies of the last forty years' history have demonstrated the remarkable efficiency of a systemic approach, of analysis involving the methods applied by political scientists to various systems, including the international ones.

Finally, the need emerged to include within the framework of Cold War research specialists on various countries' internal histories. Many aspects of foreign policy – that of the Soviet Union, for instance – can be understood and explained only in the context of internal processes taking place within the Stalinist system, the interconnection between political and ideological factors, the peculiarities of the genesis and role of the Soviet military-industrial complex, and comparison of this complex with those of the USA and other countries.

All the aforementioned circumstances have predetermined both scholarly interest in the topic in various countries and the quite substantial results and achievements marking the studies of post-war history during the last ten years.

It is worth noting that these historical problems have also attracted the interest of a wider public. A documentary series on Cold War history, produced jointly by the British and the Americans, was shown on television in many countries, including Russia. Many other television programmes and films on the same topic have been created recently in various countries in Europe and Asia; a number of popular books and brochures covering these issues have been published. Now the question of producing a secondary school textbook on Cold War history is on the agenda.

In 1999, on the initiative of Russian and British specialists, a special international journal – *Cold War History* – was founded in London. It has a joint British-Russian editorial group and a representative international editorial board. So far, 12 issues of the journal have been published. Another periodical on Cold War history is published in the USA, based at Harvard University.

## The Cold War and the global system of international relations

This part of the chapter discusses the issue that has long been attracting specialists' attention – the relationship between the Cold War and the whole global system of international relations that existed from the end of the Second World War up to the late 1980s. If we use this approach, we will see that the Cold War was an important, decisive element, but still only an element in the general development of international relations and the whole post-war international political system. This approach, in my opinion, is an extremely fruitful and interesting one.

During the last decade a number of problems related to the history of international negotiations at the final stage of the Second World War, as well as those of Cold War history itself, have been raised in the course of numerous discussions and in publications. In a single presentation it is impossible even to list all the problems that were the focus of scholarly attention. Therefore, I shall discuss only some of them – the most debated ones.

First of all, there is the issue of the Cold War's starting point. There is a well-known idea, existing in American historiography since the publication of Fleming's book, that the Cold War started immediately after the Russian revolution of 1917. This point of view is shared, as a rule, by "left-wing" historians. However, the overwhelming majority of scholars, including the author of this presentation, think that the Cold War began after the end of the Second World War.

Another subject of debate is the question of when the first omens of future confrontation between the Allies appeared. Historians have found a memo, addressed to Stalin by the NKVD (People's Commissariat of the Interior) in summer 1943. The authors name the United States as the Soviet Union's main adversary after the war, and emphasise the need to take this into account and prepare accordingly. At the US National Archive, scholars also found wartime memos and other documents defining the Soviet Union as the principal future adversary.

When we talk about inter-allied relations, we must keep in mind that their wartime differences – on the opening of the Second Front, Lend-Lease shipments and so on – had become considerably aggravated by 1945, as victory was coming closer. Gradually the main lines of disagreement took shape; later they developed into severe confrontation. The destinies of east, south-east and central European countries, liberated from German occupation, were the main point in this connection. Moscow planned to take these countries under its control and, using Soviet troops deployed there, bring left-wing Communist governments, obedient to the Soviet Union, to power.

Western Allies tried to prevent this kind of development and to preserve these countries within the orbit of the Western world. All aspects of this struggle were concentrated in the discussion of Poland's future. Every government post was contested. Using the tactics of gradual steps and surface compromises, the Soviet Union finally managed to establish communist-dominated governments in Poland, Czechoslovakia, Bulgaria, Rumania, Albania and Yugoslavia. Soon these countries declared their intention to build socialism on the Soviet model with all its attributes (such as *de facto* one-party rule, nationalisation of industries, mass purges of dissidents and ideological criticism of the capitalist system).

In current Western (especially American) historiography, there are a number of books criticising Roosevelt for "surrendering" eastern Europe to the USSR. Of course, in retrospect we can say that Roosevelt and Churchill did give way to Stalin on the issue of the power structure in east European countries. But it is equally obvious now that this compromise, reflecting the level of co-operation between the members of the anti-Hitler coalition, was in reality a forced one. Soviet troops were already present in all these countries; Moscow had all the instruments of influence there. Roosevelt and Churchill had no real means or opportunities to prevent this kind of development, except a direct armed conflict (which was both impossible and meaningless). The Western Allies had to resort to oral rhetoric and efforts to bargain some concessions.

The countries of central and eastern Europe that had – together with the Soviet Union – constituted the "socialist camp" adopted the Soviet model of internal development and joined the general competition and confrontation with the West. Later, especially in the 1970s and 1980s, as the new documents show, these countries, contrary to previous assessments, often displayed much more independence from Moscow than in the earlier period. Their leaders either had even more hard-line ideological and political ambitions, or were bold enough to adopt a more flexible approach towards the West.

The German Question also was a contested point. Here inter-Allied differences revealed themselves in a rather sharp form as early as the end of 1945. The two parts of divided Germany went in different directions; Germany was the place where the former Allies' different value systems and political interests collided. The German Question was a permanent source of crises, often putting the opponents on the brink of an open clash.

Both sides, however, were afraid of German reunification: the USSR regarded it as a threat of a revived bourgeois and anti-Soviet Germany, and the western countries were alarmed by the prospect of the East German totalitarian system spreading to the West. In Germany the Cold War was symbolised by the Berlin Wall, and its destruction became an equally symbolic image of the Cold War's end. From the ideological point of view, the situation in the German Democratic Republic presented difficulties for the Soviet leadership as well, as the East German ruling elite was distinguished by extreme dogmatism and an uncompromising hard-line approach.

The arms race was a principal element of the Cold War. At first, its nuclear monopoly gave the United States a serious advantage in its confrontation with the Soviet Union. The latter compensated for this by a considerable preponderance of conventional forces and armaments deployed in Europe. Later, the development of atomic and hydrogen weapons by the USSR restored the balance.

The resulting nuclear arms parity was among the main features of the "bipolar world", and both sides spared no effort to maintain this balance. It should be mentioned that, in spite of certain arms-limitation measures, put into effect as a result of protracted negotiations, nuclear parity was maintained at a rather high level, which had a disastrous effect on the Soviet economy. It was extremely overburdened, and this fact was displayed with the utmost clarity by the systemic crisis of the Soviet economy in the late 1980s.

The Cold War, having Europe as its "ground zero", spread to the whole world. Africa and Asia also became arenas of confrontation or struggle for influence. Very often this competition resulted in protracted conflicts of a national or ethnic character, or to direct clashes between the two systems, as happened during the Korean War. Later the Cold War led to a prolonged confrontation in Angola, Mozambique and Ethiopia. Therefore, Cold War confrontation became in fact global. It also covered various spheres, including the activities of international organisations. The United Nations is the most obvious example in this connection.

Ideology played one of the central parts in the general framework of confrontation. Today, after several years of lively discussions and the search for new documents, historians are still debating the issue of which element was the dominant one in the Cold War's emergence and evolution, especially as far as the Soviet Union was concerned. Among American historians, to say nothing of the Europeans, two opposing concepts took shape. One of them identifies ideological aims and ambitions – combining the ideas of "world revolution" with the "eternal" aims of Russian imperial expansion – as the basis of all actions taken by Stalin and his entourage. According to the other concept, Stalin and his collaborators were driven, first and foremost, by purely pragmatic intentions, known as *Realpolitik*.

In the author's opinion, both these concepts have some basis and at the same time suffer from a one-sided approach, as the aims of Soviet foreign policy strategy in reality were more complex. Documents discovered in Russian archives show that as early as the autumn of 1945 Moscow, on Stalin's personal instructions, had launched an active anti-Western ideological campaign. In November 1945 its main edge was directed against Britain, but soon the United States became a target as well. The rights of Western journalists, accredited in the Soviet Union, were restricted; the circulation and sales of Western periodicals, distributed in the country during the war, were cut down drastically; and other measures of a similar kind were introduced.

This campaign against Western influence reached its peak during the so called "struggle against cosmopolitanism". Thousands of Soviet intellectuals – cultural figures, artists, scientists – were subjected to severe criticism for the propagation of Western ideas, or for "servility" towards the West. Many of them lost their jobs; others were purged. These large-scale campaigns continued up to Stalin's death in March 1953.

Even after that, during the whole Cold War period, the ideological component continued to play a dominant role. It provided arguments for purges against dissidents and general campaigns to subdue non-conformism. It is worth noting, however, that ideology did play quite a significant part on the Western side as well. Senator McCarthy's campaign persecuting people in the USA for their communist views, a general offensive against the idea of communism and constant talk of the Soviet threat constituted a considerable part of the West's confrontation with the USSR.

Studies of this aspect of the Cold War enable us to make more general conclusions about the role of ideology and its relationship to politics. They also involve issues concerning the genesis of the so-called "other's image" and the consolidation of stereotypes, both in the thinking of the elites and in the mass, everyday mentality. Deeply rooted stereotypes are quite stable and their dismantling is a difficult, and often rather controversial, process.

The so-called leaders problem should also be added to the list of causes for transition to the Cold War. For the Soviet leader his relations with the British and US heads of state were a completely new experience. For decades he had been facing *de facto* isolation. Then suddenly Stalin found himself in a situation of an equal partnership with Roosevelt and Churchill. They expressed their respect and even admiration for him. Together with Churchill, Stalin divided spheres of influence in eastern Europe in 1944; in 1945 the three leaders jointly constructed the post-war international political system. All this increased the Soviet leader's prestige and self-esteem radically. Many people were interested to see whether the co-operation and mutual trust that had developed between the Big Three members could be preserved after the war. But the situation in this respect changed suddenly and radically.

Roosevelt died on the eve of the Potsdam Conference; while the summit was going on, Churchill's party suffered an electoral defeat and he lost his post as Britain's Prime Minister. In Potsdam Stalin had to face completely new Western counterparts, with whom he had never had any contacts with before. According to eyewitnesses' accounts, Stalin was extremely irritated by this; he was losing confidence and treated the new partners with distrust. Moreover, behind the Soviet leader's back, the President Truman had carried out the test of the atomic bomb, which sharply increased Stalin's animosity towards him.

This kind of development created a new personal, psychological atmosphere between the Allied leaders, which had a certain influence on inter-state relations as well. We have already mentioned Stalin's instructions, issued in November and December 1945. It is worth adding that in his "letters from the South" (where he was spending his vacation) Stalin made extremely sharp personal comments about Churchill, accusing his closest lieutenants in the Politbureau of "bowing down" to the British leader and the West in general. In those very days *Pravda*, the CPSU central newspaper, published Churchill's speech in Parliament, where the retired Prime Minister praised Stalin and his role in the victory over Nazism. The latter reacted sharply: he wrote that he did not need to be praised by a well-known representative of Britain's imperialist circles and an old enemy of the Soviet Union. Stalin's wrath received new fuel and arguments after Churchill's speech in Fulton, Missouri, which Soviet propaganda denounced as a Cold War manifesto. Therefore, the personal psychological factor had also played a part in the transition to Cold War and confrontation.

For many years historians, diplomats and journalists exchanged accusations, placing the responsibility for the Cold War on the other side. In the 1950s and 1960s, "revisionist" American historians started to talk about US responsibility as well; then, during the period of *détente*, Zbigniew Brzezinski wrote about a fatal combination of circumstances leading to the Cold War. And, in spite of new attempts to lay the blame on the other side sometimes made even today, we share the view of those who think that the Cold War was a result of the two sides' clashing intentions, aims and actions, which contributed to mounting mutual criticism, and the adoption of a hard line, tending towards confrontation and struggle. After that, the Cold War acquired a logic of its own, with the struggle and confrontation reproducing themselves and increasing international tensions.

Historians and political scientists now discuss the substance of the Yalta-Potsdam system and the extent of its relationship to the Cold War – whether the former was the cause of the latter or whether it just continually impelled it onwards.

The Yalta-Potsdam international political system was a complex and controversial phenomenon. Its founders tried to build a new global order that would exclude any repetition of the terrible war that had just finished. To achieve this aim the United Nations Organisation was created as the main guarantor of peace and security. At the same time, this system was based on the new balance of forces that was taking shape as a result of victory over Nazi Germany.

Decisions taken in Yalta and Potsdam fixed the joint agreed principles and positions, and at the same time led to future sharp controversies. The authors of those decisions confirmed a certain status quo between the Soviet Union and the West (the USA first and foremost). It is generally accepted that the system was to a large extent based on the bipolarity principle, which existed up to the end of the Cold War.

Sharp confrontation and the Cold War were the most visible and obvious components of the Yalta-Potsdam system, but its substance was not limited to that. From 1945 to the late 1980s the world witnessed a lot of rises and falls in the development of international relations. Sometimes it was at the brink of a military conflict, as happened in the Cuban missile crisis of 1962 or earlier, during the Berlin crisis of 1948. But the system's framework also included the first *détente* after Stalin's death and the other, longer period of *détente* in the late 1960s and early 1970s, which gave rise to a lot of hopes and was manifested in a really important achievement – the Helsinki Final Act and the so-called Helsinki process as a whole.

The Yalta system and its attribute – the bipolar world – apart from precipitating global confrontation, created a certain stable balance as well. One cannot escape an impression that the main participants of the game had developed certain rules (intentionally or accidentally), making it possible to avoid a general conflict. It seems that confrontation stopped at the very border of a collision (some ideologists and statesmen even defined this situation as "policy at a brink of war"), but this border was never crossed.

A lot of local conflicts and even wars, sometimes quite bitter, broke out during the 40-year-long Cold War period, but the main actors – the USSR and the USA, together with their allies – managed to prevent a large war and avoid a direct collision.

Arguments in favour of deterrent and containment policies were elaborated by theoreticians and ideologists from both sides. Occasionally the world faced situations of extreme tension, but every time the main opposing powers had enough common sense and will to avoid precipitating a global nuclear war.

The post-war period was characterised by a close interconnection and intertwining of external factors, which was revealed in the late 1980s with utmost clarity. The collapse of the Communist regimes in the countries of Central and Eastern Europe, the beginning of radical changes in the Soviet Union leading to the establishment of a new system, completely turned the tables in the sphere of international relations as well. The Cold War was over, the Berlin Wall went down, and the former socialist countries of Eastern Europe returned to something like the pre-war social order.

## Conclusion

With the collapse of the Soviet Union, the Yalta-Potsdam international political system came to an end too. Hard-line global confrontation is becoming a thing of the past, not just ideologically and diplomatically, but in the military-strategic sphere as well. With Russia's transition to a liberal market economy and political democracy, the age of sharp ideological confrontation was over.

Humanity is facing new threats and challenges, and international terrorism is the most serious among them. There are a lot of complicated, sometimes even sharp, problems between Russia and the West, but they are solved by different methods and in different forms. The content of international affairs has changed dramatically; humanity is challenged with the task of building a new international political system, reflecting the global objectives and balance of forces of the early twenty-first century.

# Chapter 25
# Yalta seen from the Polish perspective

*Włodzimierz Borodziej*

There are two questions that probably all the contributors to this book had to address before writing their chapters: What exactly is the topic here? And is there any "latest research" on Yalta that can change our perception of the Yalta Conference? Or is it rather the "revolution" of 1989 that now influences our thinking about the recent past?

The research on this subject in Polish is exhaustive, most of it based on published American and British records. Polish archives provide an important appendix, because they show us the alternatives and arguments both of the Polish exiles in London and of Polish society in the still partly-occupied country. But my guess would be that the real relevance of all these documents is not that they allow us to reconstruct concrete measures or paths not taken; even Yalta seems much more interesting as deception than as decision, and later not so much a geo-political system as a myth which shaped the imagination of two generations of Poles and created a clouded horizon for public discussions until 1989. So my aim is to show, in the short space I have, the interaction between myth and reality in 1945 and in the following decades.

Except for the Soviet archives, all the relevant records have been exploited by historians since the 1950s; in the 1990s, many of the Stalinist files became accessible too. For this reason one is hardly able to present new findings – if we are talking about documents, facts and figures. On the other hand – and this leads us probably to the more important point – even a well-established knowledge of the facts rarely means that interpretations cannot change. They do and they have, most importantly in American historiography, which played and still plays the role of leader in our subject. As we know, this development started in the early 1950s with the total rejection of Yalta as something shameful and regrettable, went through a decade of relative stability, became the subject of investigative accusations in the 1970s portraying the USA as the main malefactor and finally ended in a kind of new consensus documenting both the merits and failures of Franklin D. Roosevelt.

Polish historiography did not change quite as fast; in fact one could even risk the thesis that it did not change at all. To the exile, Yalta from the very beginning was considered a symbol of evil and treason. In the official historiography of the Polish People's Republic, Yalta was not considered a real topic. Potsdam – as a symbol of the decision on Poland's western border – aroused much more interest, bringing together fundamental political and border change. In the 1980s, so-called independent historians (publishing beyond the reach of censorship) took a new look into the matter. Not surprisingly, they came up with conclusions reminiscent more of the exiles' historiography than that of the Polish People's Republic. With the arrival of this national consensus, Yalta ceased to be a topic of interest any more.

As we all know, the Polish question was one of the core issues of the Yalta Conference, the "headache of the world" as Roosevelt put it, debated in most plenary meetings. I shall try first to explain why it was such a headache; then follows a presentation of Polish reactions in early 1945; and the last section of my chapter will be devoted to the myth of Yalta's impact on Poland in the Cold War.

# From the Molotov-Ribbentrop Pact to the Yalta Conference

There would have been no Polish question in the Second World War if Russia, as an ally of Germany, had not attacked Poland and then annexed more than 50% of the Polish Republic's territory in September 1939. The alliance between the Nazi Reich and the Soviet Union was already creating an awkward situation in 1940-41, when the British kept insinuating to Moscow that they would be willing to accept the new Soviet western border if the Kremlin decided to join the allies' camp. The Polish government-in-exile protested more than once against these British approaches, since it considered the *restitutio ad integrum* of the pre-war Republic as its main war aim and constitutional obligation. The German attack on the Soviet Union complicated the situation even more, though London did not accept Moscow's idea of a secret protocol guaranteeing the new Russian western border, a proposal which they presented to Eden in December 1941. A few days earlier, the Polish Prime Minister General Władysław Sikorski had also ignored Stalin's suggestion they should talk about border issues between Poland and the Soviet Union. His host wanted to change the border, if only "a little bit" this time (with German troops nearly visible from the Kremlin windows).

Sikorski did not take advantage of the weakness of the Soviet Union, probably counting on the imminent collapse of Stalin's empire and the entry of the United States into the European war. But the empire survived the crisis of 1941 and Washington never considered Poland a touchstone for American-Russian relations; so the terms of trade for the Polish government-in-exile became worse and worse. When in 1942 the Polish army was formed from former Soviet prisoners who had left the Soviet Union, relations with Moscow deteriorated; and they became nearly hostile when in April 1943 Berlin broadcast the news of mass graves of Polish officers found near Smolensk. As the Polish government-in-exile supported a motion to have the graves examined by a commission acting under the authority of the International Red Cross, Stalin used this opportunity to break off relations with the "Polish émigrés in London".

In Moscow a Polish committee composed of communists and a division under Polish communist command were organised. When in summer 1944 the Red Army crossed the new Soviet-Polish border, the communists were installed as the new administration. The anti-German resistance, which to this point had been loyal to the government-in-exile, was disarmed, and many officers were either shot or deported to the Soviet Union. This made the creation of parties who were not under communist control impossible. In January 1945 the National Liberation Committee, which already claimed the role of the highest and only state authority, changed its name to the Polish Provisional Government.

The events of 1944 in the liberated Polish territories reduced the government-in-exile to a marginal force. The cabinet was unwilling and unable to negotiate the border issue. After the Katyń affair, Moscow denounced the "Polish émigrés' circles" as reactionary and pro-fascist. The only solution it offered was to add to the Polish communist committee some "progressive" and "truly democratic" emigrants and politicians from the underground, on condition that these individuals accepted the new Soviet-Polish border. In October 1944, at the same time as Churchill drew up his famous percentage agreement over the Balkans, negotiations with the Polish Prime Minister Stanisław Mikołajczyk collapsed. Mikołajczyk left office a few weeks later, the reshaped cabinet of his successor understood themselves to be a "government of national protest" and were not treated as a real partner by either London or Washington. So in January 1945 Poland had a government-in-exile, recognised by nearly all states except the Soviet Union, and an acting Provisional Government, recognised by hardly anyone except Moscow. The ruined country had no internationally accepted borders on the east, west and north; only in the south-east – the old border with Hungary and, since 1918, with the Czechoslovak Republic – was its border not disputed.

## From Yalta to the establishment of a Stalinist regime in 1948

This is the shortest possible background to the proceedings at the Crimean conference regarding the Polish question. I wish to stress only four important points.

Obviously, Yalta was neither the first nor the last time the Big Three debated Poland. Already in Moscow in October 1943 it had become obvious that Soviet arguments were prevailing over the weak line of defence presented by the British. The following month in Teheran, Stalin had reached a general consensus with his partners to move Poland westwards. Churchill fought for the Polish government-in-exile and was apparently convinced that a fair outcome was still possible; Roosevelt did not object to Stalin's plan and only asked him to postpone the final decision until after the US elections. During the previously mentioned Moscow meeting in October 1944, it became clear that the Polish government-in-exile had no part to play in future negotiations, since the Teheran decision on the border issue definitely undermined the cabinet's position and left them no room for alternative policies. In early 1944 one of the envoys of the government-in-exile was already being told by British politicians: "You Poles, you are very much like the Irish. You are able to think only in terms of the past." Stalin, said the British, does not want to swallow Poland, and besides Russia after the war would have no choice but to co-operate with the West (Dülffer, 1998, p. 28). Seen from this perspective, Yalta did not bring any changes to Poland's eastern border; it only made the Teheran decision public. The conference was another important step in settling the question of the future government of Poland, to the detriment of the government-in-exile, but it did not deliver definite decisions on the question of the western border, which was settled only six months later in Potsdam.

Secondly and surprisingly, the Western border was discussed by the Big Three as if it were not connected with the German question. At this point it was only the British who had investigated the problem of population transfer thoroughly. They knew at least roughly the figures of millions of people involved and used this argument against Stalin's plea for the western Neisse; but apparently they understood the question firstly as a tactical tool and secondly in practical terms, as a matter of future occupation policy in the British zone of Germany. Still none of the participants, Stalin included, seems to have addressed the profound dimension of the problem: the more German territories that were promised to Poland and the more Germans who were expelled to the remaining territory, the smaller the chances for a German communist experiment became. In this sense Wilfried Loth's thesis of the future East German state as "Stalin's unwanted child" still seems to be worth debating.

Thirdly, though the issue of the western border remained unsolved, on paper the decisions on Poland's future may even have been considered a good solution. Democracy and free elections, the amendment of the Provisional Government by leading politicians from exile and from the underground, under American and British supervision – all this could be understood as a promise for Polish half- or even three-quarters sovereignty. A democratic Poland within the Soviet sphere of influence, an influence which would probably be limited to foreign affairs and security policy – in a one-world vision where co-operation between the Big Three would clearly prevail over already visible tensions – such a vision could still be understood as the best solution for the "endless Polish imbroglio" (Yergin, 1980). In the weeks following the conference, this reading of the Yalta decisions became irrelevant – first of all because of the arrest and trial of exactly those resistance leaders who wanted to negotiate with Moscow on the basis of the Yalta agreement. This and all the following breaches of Yalta show how limited the influence of the Crimean conference was. Still it remains worth stressing that these were unilateral actions and decisions by Moscow, clearly counteracting the letter and spirit of the agreement.

Fourthly, let us now ask: how did the Poles react to the pronouncement of the decisions in February 1945? We may distinguish three types of reaction. The communists responded with delight: their international standing would be soon improved by recognition, the formula of an "amendment" of the government clearly indicated that the core of the existing construction was to be preserved. At the other pole we find the government-in-exile. "Yalta" confirmed even in the written version (without the specific implementation which would follow soon) their worst fears: Poland was going to lose some 50% of its pre-war territory, the amount of compensation by German territories remained uncertain and the government-in-exile, still the official and only internationally recognised authority, was put aside as if it didn't exist. The Crimean decisions, they warned, "create a situation where the remaining rest of Poland is forced to become a satellite state of Russia" (Kersten, 1989, p. 103; Dülffer, 1998,

p. 101). That was exactly what George F. Kennan had predicted previously, in telegrams which no one in Washington apparently took seriously or, to put it more precisely, considered to be important enough. British censorship withheld the quoted cable from the underground leadership, like many other communications from the government-in-exile, but the policy of "national protest" – this time against the "new partition of Poland" (Kersten, op. cit., p. 104) – was continued; not surprisingly it ended with the withdrawal of recognition by the UK and the USA in July 1945.

The most interesting and politically important reactions were articulated by the Peasant Party (to which Mikołajczyk belonged) and the Socialist Party in the underground. The Peasant Party was probably the strongest in the underground and held a key position amongst the exiles. They hoped for an overwhelming victory in the promised free elections. The Socialists were less important in terms of numbers, but had a substantial ensemble of well-known politicians for whom dealing with Russia was always of primary importance. Both parties had suffered comparatively small losses under German and Soviet occupation. The Peasant Party decided to comply with the Yalta agreement, hoping that the return of Mikołajczyk and free elections would bring the peasants' representatives to power. The socialists in exile decided against; those in Poland supported the line of the Peasant Party. The Council of National Unity, the highest civil authority of the resistance, voted on 22 February in favour of accepting the Yalta decisions. The country was too exhausted to stand up against the invading Soviets; after the end of the German occupation, the people waited for guidelines to return to normal life; and if Stalin and the Polish communists accepted other Polish politicians as partners in forthcoming negotiations, maybe something could be done to diminish the foreseeable losses in the east.

In the following months, the implementation of the Yalta decisions distorted most of the hopes of many Poles. Poland, which may be called a founding member of the anti-Hitler coalition, was prevented from taking part in the first session of the United Nations Organisation in April. The leaders of the anti-German resistance who emerged from the underground to start negotiations with the Soviets were arrested and condemned in Moscow; the chief of the civil resistance and the commander-in-chief died in a Soviet prison soon after, the other convicted leaders were released from prison and returned to Poland, where many of them would be arrested again, this time by Polish secret police. At the same time as the trial of the leaders of the underground was taking place, the talks between Mikołajczyk (as the leader of the exile Poles) and the communists began. It was during these negotiations that the secretary of the Communist Party phrased the famous sentence: "We shall never return the power once we've gained it". The people of Poland did not know of this confession; and, judging from the enthusiastic reception Mikołajczyk was given on his arrival in Warsaw a few days later, many still believed that somehow Poland could be saved from Soviet domination. All these hopes vanished with the police terror and merciless suppression of anti-communist opposition, with the faked referendum of 1946 and the faked election of 1947, and definitely with the establishment of a fully fledged Stalinist regime in 1948.

# The communist era and the legacy of Yalta

Thus for Poland the Yalta agreement became the symbol of betrayal. Actually one cannot overstress this shift of opinion between 1945 and 1947: those contesting the Crimean conference in spring 1945 protested against the letter of the conclusions, against the loss of the eastern provinces and the loss of sovereignty. The violation of these official decisions, the beginning of the Cold War and life on the wrong side of the Iron Curtain resulted in a different opinion on Yalta, which in fact went much further than the doubts expressed in spring 1945. The Crimean conference began to serve as a symbol for much more: for betrayal not only by the Soviet Union but also by the Western powers, who took no risk by implementing the letter of the agreement. Internally, Yalta became the explanation for the refusal to talk with communists and for the refusal to trust anything they said. It cemented in place the division into "us" (society) and "them" (the authorities), which was to shape the political history of Poland at least in the late 1970s and 1980s: if you cannot rely on anything the other side says, virtually no negotiations are possible.

Apart from this practical impact, "Yalta" became a symbol of the hopelessness of Poland's place between East and West in the whole Cold War period. Timothy Garton Ash starts his book about Solidarity and the Polish Revolution with the following impression:

> "When I first came to Poland I kept hearing a very strange word. 'Yowta', my new acquaint-ances sighed, 'yowta!', and conversation ebbed to melancholy silence. Did 'yowta' mean fate, I wondered, was it an expression like 'that's life'?"

"Yalta" (Polish pronunciation 'yo'wta') is the first fact of life in contemporary Poland. "Yalta" is where the story of Solidarity begins. "Yalta" for the Poles means that, after their army had been first to resist Hitler, after Britain had gone to war in defence of Poland's independence and Polish servicemen had fought courageously in defence of Britain, after some six million of their compatriots (one in every five citizens of the pre-war Polish Republic) had died in the war – after all this, their country was delivered up by their Western allies, Britain and America, into the famously tender care of Uncle Joe Stalin.

While it can be argued that Churchill and Roosevelt had no alternative, since – when the Big Three met at Yalta in the Crimea in February 1945 – the Red Army already occupied the territory of the former Polish Republic; and, while in the final communiqué of that meeting Stalin solemnly promised "the holding of free and unfettered elections as soon as possible on the basis of universal suffrage and secret ballot", such a deliverance was an equivocal blessing for anyone. But to understand why it was in Poland that the first workers' revolution against a "Workers' State" erupted in August 1980, you must understand why the prospect of Soviet "liberation" was so particularly appalling to the great majority of Poles in 1945.

The crushing of Solidarity by military force on 13 December 1981 even reinforced the already dominant conviction that "Yalta is the first fact of life in contemporary

Poland". The USA and West European states reacted with protest and sanctions; if any leaders of Solidarity expected them to behave in a hawkish way, they were soon to be disappointed. Yalta stood; the place of Poland in the Second World War prescribed the limits of Western reactions.

On the other hand, neither a Polish Pope nor Solidarity was foreseen at the Crimean conference table. To explain this in a few words: millions of Poles attended John Paul II's first visit to Poland in 1979; allegedly about 10 million joined Solidarność in 1980-81. When Mikołajczyk had returned to Poland in summer 1945, he put all his hopes in the free elections promised in Yalta. The vote, he repeatedly stressed, would "enable us to count ourselves", that is to say, to prove that most of his countrymen were for democracy and against communism. In 1946-47 the communists prevented the Poles from "counting themselves" and only the events of 1979-81 delivered the proof that state socialism was the option of a minority. This knowledge provided the point of departure for the last chapter of the Polish People's Republic in the late 1980s, when the authorities decided to enter into negotiations with the remnants of Solidarity. Again Yalta played a role: at first there were enormous reservations within leading circles of Solidarity that the communists were cheating again, that they aimed at repeating their scheme of 1945-47. Secondly and even more important was the conviction that Yalta still determined the framework of Polish-Polish negotiations. The recent experience of society proves, said Bronisław Geremek in early 1989, that Poland has to limit her aspirations to "reasonable borders", which meant that the desired transformation from the Polish People's Republic into normality would proceed gradually and in an evolutionary way, always taking into account Moscow's special role based on the Crimean decisions and their interpretation.

From the press cuttings of this time one can learn about another, "practical" dimension of the Yalta syndrome. In the argument preceding the unification of Germany, an old communist diplomat denounced the new foreign policy – the opening towards the West of the Solidarność government in 1989 – under the headline "Yalta is still valid", meaning that Warsaw is still part of the Soviet sphere of influence and should follow the Master's voice. One of his opponents countered that "Yalta is not eternal": it was the partition of Germany that petrified the division of Europe. The Polish revolution undermined first the division of Germany, then the Iron Curtain and eventually the whole structure of the world created in Yalta (Ludwig, pp. 37/63, 27/40; Senat 23 X 91); luckily the latter was right.

Did the "revolution" of 1989 thrust Yalta aside? In practical terms one can have little doubt about that. Still, the key notions that have formed the political imagination of two generations remain present as undercurrents or points of reference, even after they have moved into the archive of political ideas; that's why we can find the notion of "a new Yalta" in the current debates on terrorism, the Middle East or Chechnya. In debates over contemporary Polish foreign policy, they are difficult to trace. Here we witness the surfacing of another aspect of our topic – the borders. The Polish-Russian border was designed by Hitler and Stalin, then by and large confirmed by Churchill and Roosevelt. The Polish-German border was Stalin's idea, also approved by the

USA and the UK with certain reservations. The two solutions – and this was what made Anglo-American approval definite – formed a package to implement the idea of "unmixing peoples": by the forced migrations of many millions of Germans, a few million Poles, hundreds of thousands of Ukrainians and less substantial numbers of Belorussians and Lithuanians.

The result is a central and eastern Europe where, for the first time in eighty years, border issues and minority questions do not dominate inter-state relations. The success or failure of the transformation cannot be attributed to the presence of "others" – it remains basically our own merit or failure. But this is certainly one of the results of Yalta that no one among the perpetrators, participants or victims had ever foreseen.

## Bibliography

Ash, T.G., *The Polish revolution: Solidarity, 1980-1982*, London, 1983.

Dülffer, J., *Jalta. 4. Februar 1945: Der Zweite Weltkrieg und die Entstehung der bipolaren Welt*, Munich, 1998.

Gaddis, J.L., *We now know*, Oxford University Press, Oxford, 1997.

Kersten, K., *Jałta w polskiej perspektywie*, London and Warszawa, 1989.

Nicieja, S. (ed.), *Jałta z perspektywy półwiecza*, Opole, 1995.

Zubok, V., and Pleshakov, K., *Inside the Kremlin's Cold War: from Stalin to Khrushchev*, Harvard University Press, Cambridge, MA, 1996.

# Chapter 26
# Yalta, Potsdam and the emergence of the Cold War: an overview from Germany in the light of the latest research

*Wolfgang Benz*

## Germany and the Yalta Conference

More than any other wartime conference held by the anti-Hitler coalition, the meeting of the Big Three – Roosevelt, Churchill and Stalin – at Yalta from 4 to 11 February 1945 has become legendary (Smyser, 1999; Graml, 1985; Dülffer, 1998). In Germany, the conference in the Livadia Palace was almost immediately stylised into a conspiracy against Europe and an agreement to divide the world, in doing so surrendering eastern Europe to Soviet rule (see, for example, Stöver, 2003; Mastny and Schmidt, 2003; Ressing, 1970; Laloy, 1990).

Historical research has brought to light that, at Yalta, Stalin was mainly concerned with maintaining recognition of eastern and south-eastern Europe as a sphere of Soviet interest or, because Churchill so strongly put a brake on these efforts, with at least establishing a clear formulation of Poland's borders and the Soviet role in the Balkan states. Furthermore, Stalin was interested in determining the reparation sum to be imposed on Germany and the share the USSR was to receive. Stalin proposed $20 billion as a total sum, demanding 10 billion for the Soviet Union, and this demand was still theoretically to be discussed at Yalta. Half a year later at Potsdam, the stereotype of the 10-billion postulate contributed decisively to the deterioration of relations between the Soviet Union and the Western powers. And the reparation problem then divided Germany for decades after Potsdam, because it was decided that each occupation power should gain reparations in their own zone of occupation.

The concerns of President Roosevelt at Yalta were mainly focused on gaining Stalin's commitment to enter the war against Japan (after the defeat of Germany) and, secondly, on securing the co-operation of the Soviet Union in establishing the United Nations. The foundation of a permanent peace organisation was, after all, the most important Allied war aim since its ceremonious declaration at the signing of the Atlantic Charter in 1941. Thirdly, like Churchill, Roosevelt wanted to avoid the expansionist push of the Soviet Union into eastern and south-eastern Europe from spiralling out of control, trying to harness it through a kind of friendly mistrust.

The negotiations at Yalta were chaotic because the Western Allies were suspicious of the Eastern partner, because great changes had to be initiated on the basis of an uncertain future, and because the interests of the participants and their various clients were so different. The consequences of some agreements only became evident much later, for instance the fateful consequence for hundreds of thousands of Soviet citizens who had left their homeland in the wake of the retreating German army – whether voluntarily or because they were forced. After 8 May 1945, they were sent back by the Repatriation Commission to the Soviet Union, whether they wanted to or not, where most of them faced a dismal fate.

Relevant for Germany, or more precisely what was to remain of Germany, was the decision of the Big Three to ensure its complete disarmament and demilitarisation, and to impose large reparations on the defeated opponent. Also of great importance was the agreement to invite France (that is the provisional government under Charles de Gaulle, which was first recognised by the Western powers in the autumn of 1944 and somewhat later by the Kremlin) to participate in Allied control over Germany as a fourth power and to grant the French their own zone of occupation. The French zone of occupation was to be in south-western Germany, taken from the American and British occupied area, while the Soviet zone remained unchanged.

The four main aims that de Gaulle had propagated since the summer of 1944 were: the German Reich was to be federalised, that is broken down into autonomous components; the Rhineland was to be separated completely from Germany for the sake of French security interests; the Ruhr area was to be placed under international control; and the Saar area with its coal mines was to be affiliated with or incorporated into France. There were certain points of contact between French and Soviet interests. When de Gaulle accepted the Oder-Neisse line as the future eastern border of Germany during his visit to Moscow in December 1944, he did so hoping that in response Stalin would recognise the Rhine border in the west; and international control of the Ruhr (with Soviet participation) was for the Kremlin an extremely desirable goal (Wolfrum, 1999, pp. 60-72).

The far-reaching French plans then proved illusionary to a great extent, precisely because France was viewed as a junior partner at best in the consortium of the great powers. As was the case at the Yalta Summit in February, de Gaulle was also not invited to attend the Potsdam Conference in July 1945. Paris suffered immensely from the realisation that it was being viewed and dealt with as a second-rank power. This had considerable consequences for French policy towards Germany in the coming years.

The plans and considerations on dividing and carving up Germany rapidly became antiquated in the final phase of the war. Already in the autumn of 1944 British military planning staff had reached the conclusion that a political dismemberment of Germany would exert such a grave impact on its economic capacity that serious problems could be expected, namely the dependency of the newly created states on other countries, a fall in the standard of living, which would endanger the independence of these new states, and the reduction of the German capacity to pay reparations. One of the most important arguments made by the British experts was the consideration that dissection would lead to an impoverishment of Germany, would slow down the recovery of the entire world from the damages caused by the war and thus, in the long term, would also damage British economic interests.

The British Chancellor of the Exchequer, Anderson, had opposed the plan to divide up Germany at the beginning of March 1945 (expressly stating his scepticism about the results of the Yalta Conference). He, too, gave economic reasons: as he wrote in a memorandum, in his view Great Britain could pursue either a reparations or a carve-up policy, but certainly not both at the same time (Jacobsen, 1977).

The intention to carve up Germany, as propagated at the Teheran summit of the anti-Hitler coalition in November 1943 and apparently reinforced and institutionalised by the establishment of a corresponding commission at Yalta, was in fact already buried by February 1945, before the capitulation of the Third Reich, and stylised into a mere threat. If Stalin did not want to slaughter the German cow that was to be milked, then the politicians in Washington and London, thinking in economic terms, certainly did not want to turn the knife on themselves: accompanied by disarmament and demilitarisation, control over German industry would both guarantee security and accord with British economic interests. The British Foreign Minister, Eden, attempted to convince the revanchist politicians of this: a handful of small German states would become both an economic burden for the war victors and a political mistake, and taken together both factors would form an insurmountable handicap on the path to the new order Europe was hoping for (Benz, 1994, p. 45).

## German reactions

Public opinion in Germany on the Crimea conference was still under the control of Goebbels and was manipulated accordingly. In the German press – in the *Völkischer Beobachter (VB)* – the slogans were spread that shaped the image Germans had of the conference – and in part still have to the present day. If in the lead-up to the conference it was said that, following British proposals, millions of Germans were to be sent to Siberia as slaves (Benz, ibid.), it was now the carving up of the German *Reich* and "the extensive destruction of the German people" that were to be elevated to the official war aims of the anti-Hitler coalition (*VB*, 3 February 1945) – that was the tenor of its report in the face of the communiqué dispatched upon the conclusion of the Crimea conference. The *VB* claimed that Stalin had taken the Western powers to the cleaners, Roosevelt and Churchill had "received commands from Stalin for eight days" and been forced to make Stalin's "extermination and hate slogans" their own (*VB*, 14 February 1945). Allegedly, Stalin had allowed his partners to play mere minor roles at Yalta, a claim expressed in lines such as "Roosevelt and Churchill towed along by Bolshevist world revolutionaries" (*VB*, 15 February 1945), and that the "death sentence" had been passed on Europe. Now, Germany would be the only power able to counter Moscow:

"while the English and American press are attempting to erase the impression of Roosevelt and Churchill's absolute capitulation in Yalta, the prevailing view amongst neutral observers is that the Soviets have gained a complete victory and have decisively advanced the Bolshevist world revolution. With the extermination plans against Germany, the seed of new wars has been planted; the tyrannical decrees on the fate of Poland and Yugoslavia are being evaluated as a finale for all smaller nations. The certainty is growing that Germany has been named, but Europe is meant, that after the eradication of the German people the continent is to lose its stable middle and become subjugated to the limitless tyranny of the Bolshevists." (*VB*, 16 February 1945)

And so it continued: it was said that while Yalta was the "product of brains dangerous to the public", the general population in the enemy countries was beginning "to suspect that at Yalta a crime was planned, the consequences of which will be terrible for the whole of mankind" (*VB*, 17 February 1945). This was just as much dreamt up by Nazi propaganda as was the declaration, offered elsewhere in the National Socialist press, that the Bolshevist plan to rule Europe was a part of an old Jewish programme to gain world domination (*NS-Kurier Stuttgart*, 11 March 1945). All means possible were used to exploit Yalta for the purposes of German propaganda and its rallying calls.

In the most reputable Nazi paper, *Das Reich*, there was also talk of "Stalin's new order" and "Anglo-Saxon submission" – and, astonishingly, the metaphor of the "iron curtain" was already used here, the coining of which was to be ascribed to Churchill in his 1946 speech in Fulton, Missouri: "The iron curtain of a Bolshevist *fait accompli* has, despite Churchill's trip of entreaty to Moscow before the Roosevelt election, fallen across the whole of South-East Europe" (Noelle and Neumann, 1956, p. 140).

The slogans of Nazi propaganda continued to influence the imagination of the Germans long after the collapse of the Nazi state, because they were also exploited during the Cold War in the West. The anti-communist slogans were particularly effective and lasting, also serving as a source of consolation in the ruins of defeat. These slogans also made it easier to submit to the Western victors, because they soon enabled a perception of them as the protectors against the Stalinist Soviet Union. Further, the open display of anti-communism nurtured a lie that many Germans have held onto till today, namely the illusion that, in an alliance with the Western powers, Germans could and should have immediately continued to fight in 1945 against the Bolshevist enemy in the east.

This idea, promoted naturally by Goebbels, was that the Western powers had failed at Yalta and Potsdam in the confrontation with the Soviet Union. That both conferences were not confrontations but meetings between allied partners was not recognised by German propaganda and all its followers.

In any case, an opinion poll conducted in the Federal Republic of Germany in September 1951 posed the question as to what was the greatest mistake the occupation powers had made. Of those citizens surveyed, 15% responded with the answer: "wrong conduct towards the Russians (Yalta, Potsdam)". This was the second most frequently given response (after the "dismantling and destruction of industry" with 21%) and far exceeded the reproach "expulsion of the Germans from the Eastern territories" (given by 3% of those surveyed).

This relation in the assignment of blame is also interesting, for the Germans were rather well informed about the expulsions from the Eastern territories, while the average citizen knew little about the other issues negotiated at Yalta and Potsdam. This emerges from another survey conducted in November 1951. Asked about the most important points of the "Potsdam Agreements", 20% named the "ceding of the Eastern territories, the injustice inflicted on the expellees" and 19% nominated the "division of Germany". The next answer, given by 12% of respondents, stated "the enslavement of Germany, the end of German autonomy". Then followed, with 11%, "demilitarisation, de-Nazification, the war crime trials" and, with 8%, the dismantling of industry. Just 10% of respondents had no specific answer and more than the half of those surveyed, namely 55%, had no idea what the Potsdam Agreements meant at all (*Mannheimer Morgen*, 29 May 1953).

## German re-unification and the legacy of Yalta and Potsdam

With ever greater distance from the event itself, detailed knowledge about what was discussed and decided at Yalta and Potsdam gradually faded and the Cold War turned "Potsdam" or the breaching of the Potsdam Agreements into a formula that could be politically exploited and held against the respective opposing side.

One of the basic elements in the understanding of the Western allies was the emphasis on the temporary function of the Potsdam resolutions on reparations and the de-Nazification, demilitarisation and democratisation of Germany; another aspect of this understanding in the initial post-war years was that Potsdam would be the first step on the way to the establishment of a peace that, prepared by the institutionalised council of the foreign ministers, would culminate in a peace treaty with Germany. This was the process the Germans pinned their hopes on, and to this belonged at the beginning the idea of the unification of the four occupation zones into a new German state and the notion that at least part of the lost eastern territories could be regained. After the failed London Foreign Ministers Conference in December 1947, the fourth meeting of its kind, where the Great Powers could not reach agreement on a joint German policy, hopes for a solution to the "German question" in the near future were given up by most.

To the degree that Germans in the Federal Republic came to terms with the status quo and accepted it – expressed mainly in the joyfully completed Western integration, in following the line of the protecting power, the USA, and in turning to the idea of a united Europe – thus, as the reality of the division of Germany and the separation caused by the Cold War became more and more a matter of fact, so the details of the Potsdam agreements became increasingly forgotten.

One of the largest regional newspapers in the Federal Republic articulated this in the spring of 1953 under the headline "What actually was 'Potsdam'?" After describing the occasion for the conference and the results, it said of the Potsdam Agreements:

"in the meantime history has passed over them. The protocols live on *de facto* for the Soviets alone, but only in so far as they believe that these could serve their own political purposes." (*Frankfurter Allgemeine Zeitung*; Neues Deutschland, 15 February 1955)

In the German Democratic Republic the official SED organ and mouthpiece of Party and Government *(Neues Deutschland)* spread in contrast the Eastern version, according to which the Western powers had propagated the carving up of Germany at Yalta and subsequently realised this policy at and after Potsdam:

"The repeated rejection of Soviet proposals for forming central administrative organs, the separate currency reform, [and] the creation of a separate Western German state are all links in a chain designed to split Germany, which is now to be completed with the help of the Parisian war pacts, founding a west German NATO mercenary army ... In contrast, during the past ten years, the Soviet policy towards Germany was guided by the principles established at Yalta and anchored in the Potsdam Agreements. These principles, as is proven by the entire development of the post-war era, are identical with the interests held by the German people. While the policy of the Western powers has sought to tear apart Germany forever and to drive the German people into a suicidal fratricidal and nuclear war on German soil, the government of the USSR has again and again set out proposals for bringing about a peaceful reunification of Germany." (See also relics of this discourse in, for instance, *Frankfurter Allgemeine Zeitung*, 23 November 1995 and 30 November 1995)

The agreements made at Yalta and Potsdam held little interest for the average citizen in the Federal Republic, and the same was undoubtedly the case in the German Democratic Republic (GDR) during the Cold War and the years of political confrontation. Attention was devoted to everyday life, first with rebuilding and then with securing a livelihood. In the GDR, the spirit of Potsdam was called upon at anniversaries and similar occasions, and it was recalled that a return to one of the Potsdam agreements would overcome the division of Germany (joint administration of the whole of Germany). In the West, the other side of the reckoning was always presented, listing when and how the Soviet Union had violated other agreements laid down at Potsdam and that it was solely to blame for the status quo.

To the Western reception in the 1950s and 1960s belonged the question, posed again and again and discussed in the media, whether the alleged secret agreements made at Yalta were valid; another issue was discussion about the annexation of German territory on the basis of the geographical ignorance and uninterest of the Americans and British. The key points here were Stettin, which became Polish even though it lies to the west of the Oder, whether the whole of Silesia should have been ceded or rather only the eastern part, and the question whether the Gorlitz Neisse was planned as the river forming the border from the very beginning, or whether it was not the Eastern Neisse. These were, though, academic and theoretical discussions on whether Germany still existed in terms of the 1937 borders under international law; that is, about whether the territories east of the Oder and Neisse were in fact irretrievably lost for Germany. The persistence with which the marking of the 1937 borders was propagated and defended in schoolbooks, a practice continued into the 1970s, and the narrow-minded earnestness that made an issue of the weather map on West German television (the issue being whether the territories east of the Oder were to be marked as part of Germany) could not distract from the fact that Germans were simply not greatly interested in such Cold War practices.

The territorial decisions made at Potsdam and their consequences remained present in the collective memory of the Germans in another way, even if they were not associated with the Potsdam conference. And they remained more present than the economic and social principles (demilitarisation and democratisation) because they directly affected many people existentially (Timmermann, 1997).

At the Potsdam conference in the summer of 1945, the three Great Powers had established what had been decided long before: the expulsion of the German minorities from Poland, Czechoslovakia and Hungary. Stalin asserted at Potsdam that the German eastern territories to be ceded to Poland, and those the Red Army had already placed under the administrative control of the provisional Polish government, were deserted: all the Germans had fled. With this claim Stalin reassured the conference partners, if they were truly worried at all, about the fate of those German civilians who were faced with "orderly and proper transportation" out of Poland, Czechoslovakia and Hungary. The expulsion was to proceed in a humane manner. In December 1944, in a speech given to the House of Commons Churchill had described this expulsion as the "most satisfactory and long-lasting way" to establish peace:

> "There will be no mixing of populations through which endless troubles arise, as for example in Alsace-Lorraine. Things will be sorted out." (Churchill, 1974, pp. 7213-14)

The term "ethnic cleansing" did not yet exist; it was in practice, though, what was meant.

At the end of the war and afterwards, a huge stream of people poured into the smaller, devastated Germany divided into four zones of occupation. By the end of October 1946, over 9.6 million expelled had been counted. By the time of the census in September 1950, the number had risen by two million; the final total was over 16 million people who, having been forced to flee and been handed the fate of expellees, had now attained new rights of domicile in the Federal Republic and the GDR. At first, they were regarded as strangers, as a disruptive disturbance of the peace, as undesirable poor people with unusual customs and habits. The locals let the expellees know that they were strangers. But the integration of refugees and expellees became reality within a couple of years. Maybe this was the real wonder in Germany after Hitler.

An indication of how quickly and completely the expellees became integrated into their new homeland is the loss of significance suffered by the lobby groups and the refugee party, the Bloc for Expellees and Those Deprived of Rights. This party, in the first half of the 1950s a popular coalition partner that achieved notable electoral successes on both federal and state levels, disappeared completely from the political scene at the beginning of the 1970s; as it was always a party representing the interests of a narrowly defined group, its demise was a sign that the group identity of the voters no longer existed: the expellees had now settled into their new homeland.

This was not yet foreseeable in August 1950 as the speakers of the *Landsmannschaft* (a welfare and cultural association) and the leaders of expellee associations, "aware of their responsibility before God and man", formulated the Charter of Ethnic German Refugees. At the Stuttgart rally, where the charter was announced under the celebrated renunciation of revenge and retribution, was postulated the "right to a homeland as one of the basic rights of mankind gifted to us by God". Above all in Poland and Czechoslovakia, this formulation was understood as an expression of a need for revenge, and the West German expellee politicians ensured that misunderstandings took root, most obviously in their vehement resistance to the social-liberal *Ostpolitik* at the beginning of the 1970s and at a meeting of expellees from Silesia in 1985, whose fatal motto was "Silesia remains ours!" In the GDR, these unfortunate turns of phrase in the West were always gratefully received; after all, the annual meetings held by the *Landsmannschaft* at Whitsun, defamed as "revanchist meetings", also stabilised the official self-understanding of the better Germany that had learnt its anti-Fascist lessons, while the Federal Republic was seen as merely waiting for the day of revenge.

The integration achievements of the GDR were equal in every way to the efforts made and the results achieved in the Federal Republic. Certainly, there part of the solution resided in placing the problem under a taboo, for, fundamentally and exclusively, mention was made of mere "re-settlers" and expellee meetings were not even permitted.

## Conclusions

In summary, we can see that the Germans accepted the territorial and ethnic status laid down at Potsdam in 1945. That was certainly not all Germans, but the minority situated on the extreme right of German society, who dreamed of Germany's 1937 borders, exerted no influence and had no political weight. The occasional din from the expellee associations and its politicians, such as that set off by the motto "Silesia remains ours!" in 1985, was not a sign of widely held hopes and desires for a territorial revision of the Potsdam agreements.

On the 50th anniversary of the Potsdam Conference, a leading article was published in the newspaper enjoying the highest circulation amongst Germany's serious press. The article carried the heading, "History of a beneficial humiliation. Fifty years ago the Allies decided the fate of the Germans at Potsdam". In conclusion I would like to quote the final sentences of this article because they contain a clear pointer to the mood prevailing amongst the majority of Germans, and this in the fifth year after the unification of the GDR and the Federal Republic, a unification which so many had feared:

> "Apart from the material results of the Potsdam Conference, which were various and in part did not last long, what remains worth noting is that never in modern history had defeated powers of such stature been so humiliated as Germany and Japan were here in 1945. But

precisely this appears to have benefited both countries. That is the inescapable impression half a century later." (*Süddeutsche Zeitung*, 29 July 1995 and 30 July 1995)

# Bibliography

Benz, W., *Potsdam 1945: Besatzungsherrschaft und Neuaufbau im Vier-Zonen-Deutschland*, Munich, 1994.

Churchill, W.S., *His complete speeches, 1897-1963*, New York, 1974, Vol. VII, pp. 7213-14.

Dülffer, J., *Jalta. 4. Februar 1945: Der Zweite Weltkrieg und die Entstehung der bipolaren Welt*, Munich, 1998.

Graml, H., *Die Alliierten und die Teilung Deutschlands: Konflikte und Entscheidungen, 1941-1948*, Frankfurt, 1985.

Jacobsen, H.-A., *Der Weg zur Teilung der Welt: Politik und Strategie*, Koblenz and Bonn, 1977.

Laloy, J., *Wie Stalin Europa spaltete: Die Wahrheit über Jalta*, Vienna and Darmstadt, 1990.

Mastny, V., and Schmidt, G., *Konfrontationsmuster des Kalten Krieges, 1946-1956*, Munich, 2003.

Noelle, E., and Neumann, E.P., (eds.), *Jahrbuch der öffentlichen Meinung, 1947-1955*, Allensbach, 1956.

Ressing, G., *Versagte der Westen in Jalta und Potsdam? Ein dokumentierter Wegweiser durch die alliierten Kriegskonferenzen*, Frankfurt, 1970.

Smyser, W.R., *From Yalta to Berlin: The Cold War struggle over Germany*, Basingstoke, 1999.

Stöver, B., *Der Kalte Krieg*, Munich, 2003.

Timmermann, H. (ed.), *Potsdam 1945: Konzept, Taktik, Irrtum?*, Berlin, 1997.

Wolfrum, E., "Französische Besatzungspolitik" in Wolfgang Benz (ed.), *Deutschland unter alliierter Besatzung, 1945-1949/55*, Berlin, 1999, pp. 60-72.

# Chapter 27
# Note: a perspective from Ukraine

*Mikhailo Kyrsenko*

The Yalta Conference failed to establish a reliable peace and security system because of deep mutual mistrust between the West and the Soviets. The Cold War, with its armaments race and ideological witch-hunts, put an end to noble principles and promises. Nevertheless, Yalta deserves attention and deserves to be analysed in the modern context. So let us look at its most important global, regional, national, local, foreign and domestic aspects.

From the point of view of the bipolar world confrontation and military power balance, it was a vague attempt to divide Europe into imperialist spheres of influence. Let us just recollect an ill-fated Churchill-Stalin exchange of opinions concerning their comparative percentage of impacts in Albania, Bulgaria, Greece, Hungary, Romania and Yugoslavia. A gentlemen's agreement with a criminal could never be relied upon.

The agrarian, liberal, social-democratic and other moderate parties seemingly were represented in the central European and Balkan governments. Just the conservative and clerical right wing were excluded. The Communists took part in the post-war cabinets of Italy, France and other Western countries. Yet they lost elections and carried on as a legal opposition within these democracies. This differed from the situation in the East.

The short-lived peoples' democracies ended in brutal communist usurpation of power. Armed resistance in Ukraine and the Baltic countries had been suppressed, as well as spontaneous revolts in Germany, Poland, Hungary and Czechoslovakia. All dissident dreams of "socialism with a human face" proved an illusion. The people could not be happy in a divided Europe with the Berlin Wall as its visible symbol.

Policy-making is an art of possibilities. Yet the price paid by the West for its uncertain prosperity seems high. The relative thaw in the Soviet Union and its puppet clients was replaced with late-totalitarian stagnation. Helpless public opinion faced the selfish indifference of the Great Powers. The Spirit of Yalta made it possible. Whether it saved peace still remains doubtful, though history does not know conditional terms.

National independence is just a good slogan in our mutually interdependent world. The point is to possess real sovereignty, an opportunity to consciously and freely define one's optimal priorities, and the forms, measure and duration of voluntary dependence at any moment. It is difficult to talk seriously of statehood in the east/central European socialist republics, whether within or outside the rigidly centralised Soviet Union.

Ukraine did not exist at that time as a sovereign subject of international law. Under totalitarian rule the country lost at least one-third of its population as a result of persecutions and man-made famine. No one had illusions about the Soviet Ukraine's membership at the United Nations. She did not even have the formal attributes of identity such as a state emblem, flag and anthem. National colours were forbidden as being "bourgeois nationalist".

Polish nationalists keep perhaps the most painful memory of Yalta. For them it was a "fourth partition" of their motherland. The number is wrong since it does not take into account all the repartitions of the early nineteenth century. But it certainly was an act of violence to the legacy of the Polish-Lithuanian Commonwealth, 1569-1795, and of the Second Republic, 1918-39. The Ukrainian context here was crucially important.

For a Pole, the eastern frontier drawn at Yalta looked quite artificial, cutting off Vilnius, Grodna and Lvov (in Polish: Wilno, Grodno, Lwów). Patriotic fervour urged that they be re-claimed. However, there was no wish to give up the Oder-Neisse frontier with Germany, as established in Yalta. Any revision could endanger newly acquired Gdańsk, Szczecin and Wrocław.

For a Ukrainian, the arbitrary borderline with Poland was likewise unbearable since it deprived Ukraine of Peremyshl and Kholm, as well as Lemko and other areas. So-called exchanges of population on both sides proved to be forcible deportations. Mutual accusations of mass murder in Volhynia and elsewhere aggravated inter-ethnic tension provoked by Moscow between Kiev and Warsaw.

It made it easier for the Communist State Security forces to strangle the guerilla warfare of the Polish Home Army *(Armija Krajowa)* and the Ukrainian Rebel Army (UPA). Under totalitarianism the AK men were persecuted in Poland like bandits, yet now they have been recognised as combatants. Their Ukrainian counterparts still have to prove that their fighting against the Nazis and Soviets was a national liberation struggle.

Sometimes even now one can witness provocations by marginal groups funded from abroad. However, on the official and the intellectual level, Ukraine has no territorial disputes with Poland or any other neighbouring country. All the central European and Baltic states have achieved membership of the North Atlantic Alliance and are close to admittance to the European Union. Ukraine repeatedly declares this to be her final strategic goal.

The Yalta Conference certainly was a great step forward in consolidating Allied forces for the victory over their common enemy, the Nazis. There is controversy whether Yalta did play a positive role in the future of Europe. It has been reflected in the terminology. The communist hardliners used to glorify the "Great Patriotic War". It is true from the perspective of the Soviet Union since it was the only defensive war in its history. The Russian Empire also had just one patriotic war, against Napoleon. The rest of its military campaigns were aggressive, slightly covered with messianic demagogy. The world regards the German-Soviet conflict as one chapter of the Second World War. Moreover, unlike the West, the Ukrainians and the rest of east/central Europe liberated from the Nazis were subjugated to another totalitarianism, with millions of victims.

The West did not pay attention to the symbolic totalitarian surrealism of holding the Yalta Conference in a desert. The Crimea was empty after the recent forcible deportation of the Tartars and other native peoples. The administrative border separated the peninsula from its natural homeland, Ukraine. It looked and was a virtual *tabula rasa*, even more than the rest of post-war Europe. Another coincidence is that we are commemorating a Yalta anniversary at a place that just about ten years ago could have – yet fortunately did not – become a starting point for bloody conflict in the post-Soviet area. On the eve of the Soviet collapse, the hardliners did their best to postpone or even reverse the final disintegration. To hinder the Union republics' gradual drift to sovereignty, Moscow backed local separatism within them. One could observe a lot of examples in the Caucasus, Baltic lands, Moldova and Ukraine. The old functionaries restored the Crimea's autonomy, keeping native peoples as far as possible from its affairs.

Sometimes we still face attempts to provoke inter-ethnic tension or conflicts around the Russian Black Sea Fleet based in Sebastopol, close to the Ukrainian navy. Some local authorities deny to the Ukrainian and Crimean Tartars an identity infrastructure in their own homeland.

All creations on a country's soil are its legal memory. Ancient Greek city-states and neighbouring tribes, medieval Italian, Armenian and Jewish communities, and the Tartar Khanate are chapters of Ukraine's history. Kiev never conquered them. The predominantly Russian-speaking Crimea is an inalienable constituent part of Ukraine while the neighbouring Ukrainian-speaking region of Kuban belongs to Russia.

Modern nations are defined by *Landpatriotismus* and *Volkspatriotismus*. North American English-speakers do not identify themselves with British subjects. Political loyalty does not always coincide with native tongue. A Ukrainian, like other Europeans, is supposed to speak at least his or her national language, a minority ethnic or local dialect (for example, Russian) and English as a means of international communication.

When the Big Three were discussing and deciding the future of east/central Europe in Yalta, the region's nations had different experiences behind them. The Poles, Czechs, Estonians, Latvians and Lithuanians kept in memory fruitful though not cloudless inter-war evolution. In contrast, Ukrainian rebirth was interrupted; its intellectual elite and human potential were drastically exhausted during the Great Terror and after. No wonder, then, that the recovery of this country is so terribly slow. Ukraine's policy often lacks a predictable consistency in fighting corruption and reforming society. On the other hand, there is no alternative to the nation's repatriation to the European family, except suicide.

Yalta offered two options. One of them led to deadlock. A sad joke said that Communism is the longest way from Capitalism to Capitalism. The other option resulted in European integration based on such generally recognised principles as civic equality, political pluralism, private property, elective governments, democratic freedoms and human rights. The balance of power has been replaced with a consensus of interests.

Nineteenth-century diplomacy invented a European Concert of the Great Six: Austria-Hungary, France and Italy, as well as the British, German and Russian empires. Neither the League of Nations nor the United Nations has been able to prevent destructive wars and preserve peace unless based on clear, real and realistic rules of game. The age of empires has gone forever. We still have a Europe of nation-states. None of them is eager to cede its sovereignty. All of them are ready to give up some prerogatives to common co-ordinative bodies in order to strengthen their own security. Yalta and Potsdam symbolised Europe divided into militant camps by invisible frontiers of ideological and political confrontation. Maastricht and Schengen now symbolise a Europe integrated by common tradition, prosperity and stability.

Ukrainian lands were components of the Byzantine civilisation, feudal Slavic principalities, the Grand Duchy of Lithuania, the Hungarian and Polish kingdoms, the Ottoman and Russian empires, and Austria-Hungary and her successor states, such as Czechoslovakia and Romania. Orthodox, but also Catholic and Protestant, Ukraine shared all intellectual values as Renaissance, Baroque, Classicism, Romanticism and other phenomena.

Republicans and royalists many times replaced one another in Europe. But its history has no precedent of a multinational empire being restored. The problem is just to persuade Russia not to support dangerous trends. The Chinese wall and Roman *limes* proved unable to check barbarian invasions. It would not be the best solution for Europe to construct a new Iron Curtain, this time between Poland and Ukraine.

An eventual pacification or involvement of Russia can be achieved only with the quite necessary precondition that Ukraine keeps outside it as a part of Europe. Kiev is faced now with the choice between mortal poverty and responsible, hard-working freedom. The West also has to decide whether to admit Ukraine in future or to abandon her definitely in a Yalta-like treason with very dangerous and unpredictable consequences.

Europe is now gradually moving from archaic Empires through nations to a network of autonomous regions. This consolidation opportunities completed by cultural diversity-bringing is thinkable just in such a Western-orientated unified economic area. As a country with access to the Mediterranean and the largest east/central

European nation, despite her losses Ukraine has the potential to greatly contribute to this constellation for common benefit and progress. It is neither Russia's twin-sister nor a bridge between Asia and Europe. The backwardness is transitory, while the geo-political situation and strategic interests are permanent. Nothing can be achieved by a miracle, yet to push Ukraine away would be a criminal mistake.

# PART FIVE

# 1989 in European history

# Introduction to 1989

At the beginning of 1989 few expert commentators would have predicted the momentous changes that were to take place that year in the Soviet Union and central and eastern Europe. In the autumn of 1987 there had been mass demonstrations in the Baltic States. A year later, Estonia declared itself a sovereign autonomous republic. In Poland in the summer of 1988 the leadership of the Polish Communist Party granted legal status to opposition groups including Solidarność, the independent trade union. Elections were held and the Communist Party did badly. Having failed to form a coalition government, General Jaruzelski asked the editor of the *Solidarność* newspaper, Tadeusz Mazowiecki, to form the first government in central and eastern Europe since the late 1940s which was not communist-controlled.

In September, Hungary opened its borders with Austria to draw international attention to the plight of the Hungarian minority in Romania. Thousands of East Germans used this as an opportunity to escape to the West. Whilst many East German "tourists" were heading to West Germany via Austria, others were besieging West German embassies in Warsaw and Prague demanding exit visas to the West. There were also riots and demonstrations in Dresden and Leipzig. When, on 9 November, Egon Krenz, General Secretary of the German Democratic Republic's (GDR) Communist Party, appeared to have ordered that crossing points in the Berlin Wall should be opened, crowds of East Germans began to cross to West Berlin. In the following days people started pulling down the Wall, without any attempt by the border guards to stop them.

The events in Berlin triggered changes elsewhere in eastern Europe. In Bulgaria, the Communist regime resigned the day after the Berlin Wall was breached. In Czechoslovakia, the Communist government tried to introduce reforms and a government containing some non-Communists was set up in December 1989, but the opposition did not accept it and a new, non-Communist government emerged in its place. There was surprisingly little violence. There was some police brutality in Czechoslovakia and the GDR, but it was only in Romania that there was any prolonged fighting in the streets. The bloody events that led to the disintegration of the former Yugoslavia were still to come.

What could not have been predicted at the beginning of 1989 was the kind of domino effect that took place after the Iron Curtain had been breached for the first time. The fall of each regime seemed to undermine the legitimacy, credibility and stability of all the others. Furthermore, people could see the demonstrations on their televisions every day and could also see that in most cases the state was not responding with extreme violence. Equally important, it was also clear that the Soviet leader, Mikhail Gorbachev, had removed the threat of military intervention by the Soviet Union. Ironically this decision had been taken so that Moscow could concentrate on the survival of communism in the Soviet Union. Yet less than two years later Gorbachev was unable to prevent the fragmentation of the Soviet Union itself.

# Chapter 28
# 1989: The year of miracles in retrospect

*Jussi Hanhimäki*

The year 1989 has been called the Year of Miracles, a year when an old order was swept away and the makings of a new international – or at least European – system was erected. A year when, against all expectations, one totalitarian government after another collapsed, defying the predictions of knowledgeable observers, whether they were journalists, politicians, historians or others. A year when Poland, Hungary and other countries of the so-called Soviet bloc, suddenly became "free" and the final dissolution of the Soviet Union became, at least in retrospect, all but inevitable.

To be sure, 1989 was also a year of some foreboding. For, after four decades of the Cold War, it seemed all but impossible that one of the defining elements of the international system – the Soviet Union and its domination of east/central Europe – could disappear without a fight. Throughout the dramatic sequence of events – the introduction of a multi-party system in Hungary, the legalisation of Poland's Solidarity movement, the fall of the Berlin Wall, the execution of Romania's dictator Nicolae Ceauşescu – there was a concern that this simply could not happen, that there would at some point be a backlash. In fact, there were several apparently knowledgeable commentators warning that the "tanks would soon roll in" to squash the demonstrations in east/central Europe (in Romania, there was a period of fierce fighting in late 1989 that resulted in several thousand casualties); and there was the example of a brutal suppression of a democracy movement in the summer of 1989 in China. Indeed, some of this foreboding would remain until the final dissolution of the Soviet Union in late 1991.

And yet, as we now know, in 1989 the seemingly impossible happened: a large group of countries in east/central Europe became "free" from their decades of domination by an external hegemonic power and moved to establish (albeit with varying speed) democratic rule within their own borders. The question that this essay will explore is simple. Why? Why did communist rule collapse in east/central Europe in 1989?

A word of caution may be appropriate. As a historian, one is in the happy position of trying to make sense of something that has already taken place; one is rarely called upon to make judgments about what the "next big thing" will be or theorise about what the world will look like a decade from now. This is of course a luxury, but also an easy trap to fall into: for history is hardly an unstoppable locomotive that runs on a fixed track to an already known destination. Its course depends on accident and, more specifically, on the actions of individuals. With regard to the revolutions of 1989, one basic point must therefore be underlined at the outset: the dramatic changes were not inevitable.

And yet, in making sense of the past – the basic job of a historian – the task of trying to create some structure within the context of this unpredictable narrative cannot be avoided. For there were broad changes that created the conditions in which people made the choices they did in 1989.

Therefore, after a brief overview of the highlights of 1989, this chapter will focus on two central and general developments. First, in the 1980s, the Cold War changed beyond recognition; in large part because the Soviet Union changed, but also because there were other developments throughout the world that made the Cold War far less the dominant structure of international relations. Second, as the global setting changed, Europe as a whole began to change in ways that made the division of Europe less palatable if not completely impossible.

The chapter will close by bringing out the human dimension of 1989. For, ultimately, while trends and structures may provide a context for action, individuals always face a choice, or an array of choices. Perhaps the most remarkable fact of 1989 is that so many individuals, in so many walks of life and in so many countries, chose paths that dramatically altered the course of contemporary European history.

## Revolutions of 1989

The revolutions started in two countries that had, already in previous decades, exhibited independence: Hungary and Poland.

In Poland, the Solidarność movement headed by Lech Wałęsa, which had been declared illegal with the imposition of martial law almost a decade earlier, began talks with Polish government officials in early February 1989. On 7 April, Solidarity was re-legalised. Soon thereafter, the Roman Catholic Church received full legal status whereas, in contrast, the traditional May Day parade was cancelled in Warsaw. In elections in June, Solidarity won an astonishing 99% of freely elected seats – 35% of those in the lower house *(Sejm)* and all in the upper house. Although General Wojciech Jaruzelski remained president (for another year), the new government that took over in August was headed by Solidarity activist and journalist Tadeusz Mazowiecki. Poland boasted the first non-communist government in eastern Europe since the 1948 coup d'état in Czechoslovakia. By the end of the year, the Polish Parliament had voted for a new constitution that effectively ended Poland's history as a socialist state.

Much as in Poland, the dismantling of the socialist state proceeded rapidly and relatively smoothly in Hungary. Although popular protest played an important role, the Hungarian Communist Party helped matters by legislating itself into extinction. In late 1988 and early 1989, new laws permitting the rights of association and assembly had been passed by the Hungarian parliament. In January 1989, the party announced that a commission of inquiry into the suppression of the 1956 uprising – previously described merely as a heinous counter-revolutionary act – was to be formed. Thus, the party de-legitimised its own past. In February, the multi-party system was formally reintroduced. In subsequent months came denunciations of Janos Kadar's long rule, the dissolution of the communist youth organisation and talks with the opposition. On 16 June, 300 000 Hungarians watched as the now-rehabilitated Imre Nagy and four other victims of Kadar's rule were reburied as national heroes. One English observer noted, however, that the event, far from being the funeral of Nagy was, in fact, "the funeral of Janos Kadar". Symbolically, three weeks later (on 6 July 1989), Kadar died. On 23 October – thirty-three years after students in Budapest had started a historic march to Stalin's statue that had ended in bloody repression – the Hungarian People's Republic became, simply, the Republic of Hungary.

The Hungarians had also done their part to push the broader dissolution of the Soviet bloc ahead. On 3 August, the Hungarian government had announced that it would offer asylum to citizens of East Germany. Thousands came. On 10 September, the government in Budapest decided to open its border with Austria and the next day (11 September of all days) started dismantling the barbed-wire fences. During that first day that the Iron Curtain was being physically torn down, approximately 125 000 East Germans went to Austria.

As defections mounted, the days of the German Democratic Republic (GDR) were quickly numbered. In early October, the 40th anniversary of the GDR's founding was noticeable for the chants of "Gorbi, Gorbi" that were heard when party leader Erich Honecker, standing next to the Soviet leader Mikhail Gorbachev, tried to address a crowd in Berlin. Within 10 days, Honecker was gone; within a month – in November 1989 – the Berlin Wall, the most potent and notorious symbol of the Cold War division of Germany and Europe – was opened and, eventually, torn down. A year later, on 3 October 1990, the previously unthinkable would take place: Germany was not only unified, but it would remain a member of NATO.

In Czechoslovakia, 1989 had begun ominously with the arrest of 14 leading Charter 77 activists. By May, however, the relaxation of suppression was evident as the activists, Vaclav Havel among them, were released. In August, the police hardly intervened in demonstrations commemorating the Warsaw Pact invasion of 1968. In November, talks between the Jakes regime and opposition groups (the Czech Civic Forum and its Slovak counterpart Public Against Violence) started. After several shifts in government over the next month, Czechoslovakia's Velvet Revolution finally culminated in late December when Vaclav Havel was elected president. Alexander Dubček, the leader of the reformist socialists who had been crushed in 1968, became the speaker of the Federal Assembly. Major constitutional reforms followed in early 1990, as Czechoslovakia became the Czech and Slovak Federated Republic (and eventually two states).

A few days before the election of Havel, Romania had seen the culmination of its own, far more violent, revolution of 1989. On Christmas Day, Nicolae Ceaușescu and his wife Elena were executed after a brief mock trial. The long-time dictator had tried to hold on to power and suppress the growing opposition, but to no avail. In fact, suppression had only sparked off fighting between Ceaușescu's *Securitate* forces and the supporters of the so-called National Salvation Front. There were hundreds of victims and, for some time to come, questions about the nature of the coup against Ceaușescu. But the broad reality was that, as elsewhere, a communist dictatorship was gone and Romania's traditional political parties began to re-emerge.

The same was true of Bulgaria, where the Communist party had forced the long-term leader Todor Zhivkov to resign on 10 November, the day after the Berlin Wall came down. Although there was no outright revolution in 1989 (but rather a palace coup), Bulgaria held its first free election in 1990 with the now socialist party receiving 47% of the vote. As in Romania, change was in the air, but the pace slower. Fortunately, Bulgaria did not see similar violence or executions as Romania.

The revolutions in east/central Europe also affected developments in the Balkans. In Yugoslavia, the discrediting of communism probably played an important role in the rise of nationalism, ethnic tension and brutal violence, although the changes that led to the disintegration of Tito's former federation had already begun before the Berlin Wall came down. In Albania, isolated from much of the rest of the world, the public demonstrations – and eventual change – came a bit later. But even there, by the spring of 1992, a non-communist government was in power.

On top of all this – the collapse of communism in eastern Europe, the unification of Germany, and the subsequent dissolution of the Warsaw Pact – the Soviet Union itself disintegrated. Long-suppressed nationalism burst into various declarations of independence from the Baltic States to Georgia, Armenia and Azerbaijan. In fact, already in 1988, popular protest against Soviet domination had been widespread in Estonia, Lithuania and Latvia. And, in the end, by 1991, there was not only no Soviet bloc; there was no Soviet Union.

The year 1989 – and the process unleashed that year – was therefore nothing but a massive revolution that transcended national boundaries and destroyed the old order, ultimately throughout a huge span of the Eurasian land mass. Within one year, the basis was destroyed of what had been, for more than four decades, the central paradigm of the international system, that is the Cold War. In this, 1989 represented an earthquake, a seismic shift in recent international history.

But why? Why did all this happen in 1989? Why did the collapse of communism occur so rapidly and without much resistance from those who held power?

## The Cold War: the big picture

One answer to the question is seemingly straightforward: the big picture had changed; the Cold War became less central as a structure of international relations in the 1980s.

The dividing lines – between East and West, between capitalism and communism – were no longer such dominant features of the international system as they had been in earlier decades.

In order to understand that argument, one needs to look beyond the superpower conflict itself. For there were many broad changes that were making it increasingly unlikely that the Cold War could remain as the main dividing line in international politics. Some of the more fundamental changes were economic, such as the increase in international trade, the economic rise of East Asia (most particularly Japan and the South-East Asian "tiger" economies) and the decline in prices for raw materials, perhaps most importantly that of oil in the 1980s. The common denominator for such changes was that they all stimulated the economies of the capitalist countries while holding back those of the Soviet bloc and its Third World allies. Another such change included dramatic innovations in technology, such as communications and computers, almost all of which were developed in the West and hardly developed in the Soviet Union.

At the time, however, the political effects of the economic and technological changes were difficult to predict. Ironically, in the early 1980s at least, many observers thought that the challenges to the West were probably bigger than those facing the Soviet bloc. In terms of productivity and economic management, many Americans viewed Japan as rapidly surpassing the United States and feared the long-term economic consequences of a less dominant US role in the global economy. The election of a right-wing Republican, Ronald Reagan, as President in 1980, reflected therefore not only what were seen as political challenges internationally – the breakdown of *détente*, the Soviet invasion of Afghanistan and the Iranian Revolution – but also a general perception that America's position in the world was in decline and a stronger US response was needed. Reagan's policies came to reflect that mindset, with its rhetorical excesses (the evil empire), its willingness to intervene against revolutionary regimes and its massive build-up of American military power.

In contrast, the Soviet leadership came into the 1980s hopeful that there would be a continuing global trend favouring socialism. After all, socialism had triumphed in South-East Asia and parts of Africa in the mid-1970s. But, by the time Leonid Brezhnev died in 1982 (if not earlier), the notion that history was on the side of the Soviet Union and socialism was evaporating. The Soviet economy seemed unable to keep up with the West, and the increased military spending in the late 1970s and early 1980s created severe shortages in the consumer industry. The war in Afghanistan was going badly for the Soviets and the costs of assisting their Third World allies were mounting as Reagan's anti-revolutionary offensive (focused on Central America, Afghanistan and Angola among other places) took hold. For the ailing general secretaries who succeeded Brezhnev, Yuri Andropov (1982-84) and Konstantin Chernenko (1984-85), the world situation seemed increasingly bleak.

But the broader point about the 1980s was not that one side in the Cold War was "up" and the other "down". To many, the Cold War – and the Soviet-American confrontation – appeared largely irrelevant. In this context, it is important to note that a major signal – that the Cold War dichotomy was receding as the main global ideological division line – was the growth, from the late 1970s onwards, of political Islam or Islamism. Reading political doctrines – including a critique of both liberal democracy and Communism (the two Satans as they were called) – into the Holy Koran, the Islamist groups began to organise against regimes that they saw as stooges of Western (and, to them, this meant both US and Soviet) influence. The Iranian Revolution in 1978-9, where Islamist groups played a central role in toppling the US-supported dictatorship of the shah, provided inspiration for young Muslims to join such movements elsewhere, even though both their political and religious messages would differ from that of Ayatollah Khomeini. The Soviet war in Afghanistan proved a fertile ground for radical Islamist groups, who organised the refugees and who – in spite of their anti-Western message – received strong support from the United States and the conservative Arab regimes because of their effectiveness in fighting the Soviets (of course, it was in Afghanistan that the Saudi-born Osama bin-Laden first made his mark as a fierce anti-Soviet fighter).

Mikhail Gorbachev was elected General Secretary of the Soviet Communist Party in 1985, at a time when the Soviet bloc was in dire economic straits, the United States was engaged in a reinvigorated effort to brand the USSR as an evil empire and fight Moscow's real or imagined stooges around the globe, and the ideological foundations of the Cold War were receding despite Reagan's hard-line rhetoric.

Gorbachev understood the problems. But he had no ready plan to implement. Instead, he attempted to reduce tension with the United States and western Europe in order to buy time for a reorganisation of the Soviet economy. Gorbachev's initiatives led to a series of agreements in which the nuclear arms race was constrained, even beyond the limitations envisaged during *détente*.

To the Reagan administration, this suggested that Soviet Communism was in retreat internationally. Ronald Reagan, therefore, had no hesitation in reducing the danger of nuclear war since history, after all, was on the side of the United States. This did little to help Gorbachev. By 1986-87, the nuclear accident at Chernobyl and the resistance he had met within his own party forced Gorbachev to adopt more radical policies in his search for perestroika ('restructuring') – including some form of freedom of speech (glasnost, 'openness'). Towards the end of the decade, both the Soviet Union and the Cold War seemed to be in rapid change.

The revolutions of 1989, in short, occurred at a time when the basic structure of international relations, in place since the late 1940s and early 1950s, was fading. The new challenges that both superpowers – but particularly the Soviet Union – faced in the 1980s pointed in the direction of fundamental changes in international relations. But that alone hardly explains the drama of 1989 or why the events transpired in east/central Europe.

# A changing continent: Europe in the 1980s

In the 1980s, within the context of the broad challenges to the Cold War international system, an aura of change was evident on the European continent. Briefly put: the division of Europe was looking increasingly unnatural to Europeans, and the dependency and submission to external control increasingly unpalatable. A general discrediting of totalitarianism – in all its forms – swept through much of the European continent in the 1970s and 1980s. And there was a search for economic solutions to the many ills plaguing the "stagnant" continent in the early 1980s.

In the 1980s, though, such changes and challenges meant different things on the two sides of what was still the Iron Curtain.

# Western Europe and the European project in the 1980s

In western Europe, European integration began to pick up speed in the mid-1980s. It can be argued that this was the result, in large part, of two broad developments.

For one, western Europe had seen its own democratic revolutions in the 1970s. What I mean is that Spain, Portugal and Greece moved away from authoritarianism. The death of Franco in 1975, the collapse of the Portuguese dictatorship a year earlier, and the demise of the colonels' junta in Greece, also in 1974, had paved the way for the European Economic Community's (EEC) southern enlargement. Greece joined in 1981, Spain and Portugal in 1986. The nine became 12. Few noticed that Greenland left the EEC in the midst of all this.

The southern enlargement was symptomatic of the second major development in western Europe: the re-invigoration of the European project in the mid-1980s. Most significantly, there was the negotiation of the Single European Act (SEA) that came into effect in 1987 and foresaw the move towards a fully integrated single European market by 1992. As the text of the SEA reads, the goal of the signatories was to create an area "in which persons, goods and capital shall move freely under conditions identical to those obtaining within a member state". But it went beyond that. The SEA included measures to boost political co-operation and shift power away from member states towards central European institutions. In short, the SEA was a precursor of the 1992 Maastricht Treaty, a progenitor of the EU.

The SEA signalled a rather dramatic change in western Europe in the late 1980s. If, in the early 1980s, people had invented the term "eurosclerosis" to describe the West European economy that experienced double-digit unemployment numbers and a politically patchy network of nation-states, the second half of the 1980s saw an improving economic situation and increased political co-operation. Whether these were necessarily closely connected developments or not hardly mattered. The point is that, by 1989, "europhoria" had, if only for the time being, replaced "eurosclerosis" and "euroscepticism".

# Eastern Europe I: economic stagnation

Western Europe's re-invigorated integration and economic upswing stood in stark contrast to the state of the Soviet bloc economies. Indeed, the true "eurosclerosis" was to be found in the countries that participated in the 1989 revolutions. By the 1980s, eastern Europe and the Soviet Union were in chronic economic stagnation.

Some numbers may help to illustrate this point. First, take economic growth rates. The figures are naturally unreliable for the Soviet bloc pre-1989, but the general trend was as follows. In the 1950s and 1960s, east European countries saw economic growth rates (that is GDP per capita growth) that averaged somewhere between 5.5 and 7.6% per year. Such rates were in most cases higher than those in the West and seemed to indicate that the planned economic system was delivering what it promised: better living conditions for all. This began to change in the 1970s, with most countries seeing less than 3% GDP per capita growth. The slowdown accelerated in the 1980s, with most countries either growing less than 1% or in some cases experiencing negative growth. By 1989, Hungary's growth rate was negative 1% and Romania's a staggering negative 11%.

In addition, it should be noted in this context that these percentages do not take into account the role of the black market, often the only source for basic goods for many citizens. The black market, in the 1980s, saw high rates of inflation translating into a steep rise in the cost of living. According to estimates, real wages declined in Poland by 17% in the first half of the 1980s; in Yugoslavia by as much as 25%, and in Romania even more.

## Why did this happen?

In broad terms, the figures are illustrative of an artificial economic growth that had run out of steam: a model of economic development that, after the initial transformation to a state-run system, was rigid in its inability to reinvent itself. In other words, after the Second World War, eastern European countries replicated a Soviet model of development that created some form of economic growth as Stalin's idea of socialism in one country was replaced with the idea of socialism in one bloc. Forced industrialisation and a new emphasis on creating heavy industry, which had not been a central part of the economies of east/central Europe, employed many in new jobs – thus it was no wonder that overall growth rates were relatively high. There was no significant growth, however, in consumer industries.

That alone was a recipe for stagnation and discontent. But, in the 1960s and 1970s, the problems of forced industrialisation could be held at bay by various safety valves. There was tinkering at the edges and some short-term success with limited economic decentralisation. Secondly, Soviet subsidies kept east European economies going, allowing them to import energy and raw materials at low cost while exporting otherwise non-competitive industrial goods to the USSR. Thirdly, trade with the West began to open up slightly and was often helped by Western credits in the 1970s.

But these three pillars broke down in the 1980s. For one thing, decentralisation was viewed as a serious challenge to the political system and, therefore, any serious overhaul of the system was over-ruled by political authorities.

Perhaps more importantly, the Soviet Union's subsidies to East European economies were reversed as a result of the oil crises of the 1970s. The Soviets initially cashed in on the higher prices by selling more oil to the West and getting hard currency for these sales. As long as prices were high, this still worked; Soviets were making profits and could subsidise eastern Europe. But, in 1983-84, oil prices suddenly fell and Soviet hard currency reserves were depleted. As a result, the system began to break down when the Soviets demanded that East Europeans also pay the market price – or something close to the market price – for their oil. Subsidies were gone.

In practice, this meant that, within the context of the barter system that was the foundation of Soviet bloc economic system, East Europeans had to send more goods for the same amount of oil. One example will illustrate the point: in 1974, Hungary could exchange a million tons of Soviet oil for 800 Ikarus buses; in 1981, it had to pay 2 300 buses, in 1988, 4 000. Call it "barterflation".

It is worth noting that the impact of the oil price decreases was exactly the opposite in the West: energy costs became lower, providing a boost to industries and economies. Indeed, it is hard to think of a better case-study to illustrate the fact that, in the 1980s, eastern and western Europe operated very much in two different economic systems.

In addition, as hard currency reserves were depleted in the Soviet bloc, western Europeans – who had assumed that the USSR would effectively underwrite eastern Europe's debt with its hard currency oil revenue – stopped offering credits to East Europeans. As a result, East-West trade began to contract. East European countries' hard currency debt soared in the 1970s and 1980s – from a low of about US$8.7 billion for the region in 1970 to roughly ten times that figure by the mid-1980s. At the time of the revolutions of 1989, there were several countries – Hungary, Poland and Bulgaria among them, whose total foreign debt was more than the annual value of their exports. In the case of Poland, foreign debt was three times the size of its annual exports.

The morale of the story is that the Soviet bloc economic system suffered a meltdown in the 1980s and that meltdown was devastating to the political systems in the region. After all, socialism had promised plenty for all; it was manifestly failing to deliver. As one historian put it:

> "The rising living standards which had once been so prominent a feature of communist propaganda now caused embarrassment, with experience flatly contradicting ideology to such a degree that Marx's theory of pauperisation of the workers seemed a far more fitting description of socialism than of capitalism."

307

So, the broad point within the European context is as follows: while in western Europe we see a re-invigoration of the process of integration and a move from stagnation to a dynamism of sorts, in Eastern Europe the situation was the opposite. Until the 1970s, there had been some rise in living standards, but the 1980s saw a stagnation, a blossoming of a heavily inflationary black market and a decline in living standards.

## Eastern Europe II: end of isolation and the demand for change

In addition to the economic and political changes throughout Europe that challenged the legitimacy of the communist systems, one additional aspect of the changing European setting needs to be noted. In the late 1970s and throughout the 1980s, the political legitimacy of one-party rule was under severe strain.

Two points will illustrate why this was so. First, there was the CSCE (Conference on Security and Co-operation in Europe). The Helsinki Accords of 1975 had introduced a new set of international norms that, even if not respected by all 35 governments that had participated in the process, did provide a manifesto that could be used by opponents of totalitarian rule to lobby for free speech, freedom of assembly and other freedoms. Perhaps most importantly, the so-called Basket III meant that it was now possible to point out to, say, the Soviet Government or the Polish Government, or the Czech Government, that they had signed a pact to respect certain basic human freedoms. Thus, in the years following the Helsinki Accords, the banner of human rights was picked up by Charter 77 in Czechoslovakia, the Solidarity movement in Poland and various Helsinki Watch groups in East Germany, the Soviet Union and elsewhere. It was hardly a co-ordinated movement. But they clearly exposed the moral deprivation of communist rule at a time when economic stagnation was setting in. Indeed, as the journalist Martin Walker puts it, the Helsinki Accords became "the West's secret weapon, a time bomb planted in the heart of the Soviet Empire".

Second, the spread of, and access to, information increased. For an agreement on paper – such as the Helsinki Accords – is one thing; the ability to spread the word is something else. And, in the 1980s, the word was indeed being spread: the dissemination of information was much improved. As Gorbachev himself put it in a speech to the UN General Assembly in 1989: "Nowadays, it is virtually impossible for any society to be 'closed'."

In practice, this meant that, for example, in most of eastern Europe, the jamming of Western radio ceased in the 1980s. As a result the BBC, Deutsche Welle, Voice of America and Radio Vatican gained an ever growing audience. Television – either directly or via videocassettes – was even more important. East Germans, Czechs and Slovaks could watch West German television, Estonians could follow Finnish television, Albanians could watch Italian television, and many Bulgarians could get reception from Turkey.

This meant several things. It meant that people in eastern Europe had an alternative source of news. Of course, no radio or television broadcast is free of bias, but it seems that the Western broadcasts at least offered a conflicting source of probably more reliable information. In 1989, moreover, television and radio played a crucially important role in spreading the information about events in other east/central European countries, and news of uprisings in Poland and Hungary undoubtedly encouraged people in other countries to follow their example.

Equally, if perhaps not more, importantly, east Europeans were now exposed to what one might call the "glitter effect". Western television shows portrayed a different way of life, societies filled with consumer goods that were available in eastern Europe only – if at all – at high prices on the black market. In short, the West had an appeal that was felt increasingly by those in the East – this was why, for example, East Germans so badly wanted to go to West Germany.

A related point is the easing of travel restrictions after the Helsinki Accords. By 1988, for example, there were very few travel restrictions – other than financial ones – for the citizens of Bulgaria, Hungary and Poland. Of course, all depended on your country: Albanians could not go anywhere, and Romanians still faced serious travel restrictions. But the point is that, in a number of east European countries, knowledge of the West did not come merely from television and radio, but increasingly from actual life experience.

So what did all this mean when put together? Did it mean that 1989 was inevitable because of the economic decline and stagnation, because of the many other structural challenges that were delegitimising the socialist system; because people could see and hear that there were other economic and political systems that were delivering the goods? Not really. I would say that all these were probably necessary causes, but even in combination they were not sufficient causes for the 1989 revolutions to take place. In the end it took something else.

## 1989: the human element

Indeed, while general trends do condition and set the parameters of change, it is people's actions that bring it about. My last general point about what made 1989 "happen" is the human element. There are many examples.

First, Mikhail Gorbachev did not have to abandon eastern Europe to its own devices. Whatever his motives, it was the right thing to do. Undoubtedly, it was not the only possible course of action. Gorbachev may go down in history as a "super loser" of sorts; but, in the end, his acknowledgement that eastern Europe had the right to go its own way – that the Brezhnev Doctrine was dead, and there was no point in supporting such leaders as Honecker – was instrumental in bringing about the revolutions. As the Chinese students, among others, learned in the summer of 1989, there was another possible response.

Second, reformers within the communist parties of several east/central European countries did not need to accept the inevitability of change. Not all did of course, as the example of Ceaușescu in Romania and Honecker in the GDR showed. But many – such as the Grosz government in Hungary – did accept it, and they helped to bring about the end of a system that, if they looked at it in a narrow selfish sense, was geared towards giving them certain rewards. Instead, they chose the unpredictability of reform, even if it was managed reform that, ultimately, got out of their control.

Third, the leading critics of communist rule – Wałęsa, Havel and others – did not have to continue risking their lives. In fact, everything in their experience – their personal history, their countries' past – cautioned against such protest. But they chose to challenge the existing power structure in a struggle that, in 1989, still appeared as one against formidable odds.

Fourth, the thousands of people demonstrating against one-party rule, calling for a true accounting of past injustices, calling for democracy, did not have to risk their lives and place themselves in danger. The risk was real and, in fact, many did lose their lives in the process. It had always to be borne in mind that, even in 1989, all pro-democracy movements did not inevitably succeed; something the student demonstrators at Beijing's Tiananmen Square found out in June.

Indeed, ultimately, the revolutions of 1989 were a consequence of the rebellion of those many in east/central Europe who were tired of economic want and political oppression, and who gradually came to believe that the Soviet Union under Gorbachev would not act, as it had done before, to defeat their political demands. In other words, while broad systemic changes and structural shifts may have created the conditions for change, it was the people who ultimately brought about change.

## Conclusion: 1989 in retrospect

In 1992, only a few years after the revolutions of 1989 and a year after the dissolution of the Soviet Union, historian Walter Laquer made two comments about the post-war era in (east/central) Europe. He wrote, first, that "the history of post-war Europe reads almost like a Hollywood movie of the old-fashioned kind, with all kinds of tensions and conflict but a strikingly happy ending". Then he inserted a degree of scepticism about what would happen after the – at the time very recent – "happy ending".

> "With regard to the Soviet Union and eastern Europe, it is easy to see what political, social and economic systems have failed. It is impossible as yet to say what will succeed them."

Indeed, unlike a Hollywood movie, history did not end in 1989.

Do we know better now? Fifteen years after the revolutions? Do we know what has succeeded the totalitarianism of the cold war? And where the region, that was for so long dominated by an ideology, political system and military pressure imposed from abroad, is heading?

Yes and no. For one, we know that, by precipitating the end of the Cold War and the collapse of the Soviet Union, the revolutions of 1989 played an important role in shaping today's globalised world and made the return to the bipolar dichotomies of the Cold War virtually impossible. But we do not know any better than Laquer in 1992 where that world is heading and what sudden dramatic event – such as 11 September 2001 – may move history to a new, yet unknown, direction.

We also know now that, regionally, the events of 1989 were far-reaching in their impact. We know, for example, that 1989 made possible 2004 (the admission of former Soviet bloc countries to the EEC) and may perhaps have even made possible 1995 – the first enlargement (the neutral countries Austria, Finland and Sweden). The widening of European integration was indeed one of the major outcomes of 1989. But whether this will allow for an ever deeper union – that is another question. Perhaps, we will have an answer to that in 15 years from now.

In addition, we do know that people's lives in the countries that experienced 1989 have been dramatically transformed. And the changes have been, it is fairly safe to say, mostly for the better. Whatever today's problems, however serious they may be, they probably pale into insignificance when thinking back to the time before 1989: totalitarian dictatorship, secret police, economic mismanagement and decline. Ultimately, 1989 stands out as a seismic historical turning point; an unpredictable earthquake of massive consequences, conditioned by structural forces, but prompted by the actions of individuals.

Did everything turn out well? Of course not. Two generations of experience with communist rule, preceded by disastrous wars, could not simply be erased. Historical memories could easily result in – and sometimes have resulted in – entirely justified demands for retribution. Nor could one expect a change from one economic model to another to take place without some pain. Indeed, in the years immediately after 1989, former Soviet bloc economies crashed. Only in 1994, for example, did Hungary experience positive economic growth. And yet, by 1 May 2004, many of the countries of the former Soviet bloc – Hungary, Poland, the Czech Republic, the Slovak Republic – and even three nations that used to be part of the Soviet Union itself – Estonia, Latvia and Lithuania – became members of the European Union. If one had floated that idea in front of any knowledgeable observer in 1989, they would most likely have responded with scorn or amusement.

What happened in 1989 was, in short, a surprise and a shock, a regional series of events that changed the course of European and, ultimately, world history. But it is worth underlining that 1989 was far more than that. That no one foresaw the revolutions of 1989 is, in fact, an insignificant question when compared to what these revolutions tell us about the intangibles of history, about the role of humans as actors, rather than of mere observers, concerning the unfolding of events. Ultimately, the revolutions of 1989 are far more significant as a reminder of the fact that, as no less a man than George Kennan, perhaps the principal architect of the American foreign policy doctrine that called for the containment of Soviet Union and communism in the 1940s, once wrote:

> "There is nothing in a man's plight that his vision, if he cared to cultivate it, could not alleviate. The challenge is to see what could be done, and then to have the heart and the resolution to attempt it."

In 1989, there were many who rose to that challenge. If anything, that fact is worth repeating.

# Chapter 29
# 1989: The end of the Cold War and the ensuing break-up of the Soviet Union

*Alexei Filitov*

Pondering over the break-up of the Soviet Union, I came to the conclusion that its scope should be broadened to give a balanced view of both internal and external dimensions of the processes culminating in the event, which has been treated in many different ways by different groups in my country (and abroad as well). So we agreed on the revised title of my presentation. The following questions should be covered in it:

- the interconnection between the end of the Cold War and the collapse of the Soviet regime/state;
- the interplay of objective and subjective factors behind both phenomena;
- the possible alternatives and the "missed chances".

I will begin by quoting from a review article by a well-known German historian:

> "Ten years after the end of the Cold War, there is an ever greater need to re-examine the global conflict that began with the rise of the superpowers after the Second World War and ended with the collapse of the Soviet Union." (Loth, 2003, p. 157)

The formulation of the problem raises no objections, but the wording of this introductory phrase of a reviewer may lead to one confusion. It seems to imply that, either the Cold War continued for two years after the fall of the Berlin Wall and the Malta summit (these two events of November and December 1989 are most frequently cited to mark its end), or the Soviet Union ended its existence two years before the Red Flag over the Kremlin tower was replaced with the Russian tricolour. Many people (this author included) would tend to disagree with both conclusions. The same may be said of the implied cause–effect interpretation: it is more reasonable to suppose (at least, it is my thesis) that the process of "fading away" of the Cold War led to the break-up of the Soviet-type systems in Europe, and eventually of the Soviet Union itself, and not vice versa.

Much of the confusion may be explained by semantics. Too often such notions as "global conflict", "East-West competition" and "Cold War" are used interchangeably, even though they stand for different realities. The global antagonism of two socio-political systems "East" versus "West" ("socialism" v. "capitalism", "totalitarianism" v. "free world" and so on: the tags may be applied at will) dated at least from 1917 – some writers go even further into the past, even to the time of the French Revolution

– and it was a real "zero sum" game: one side should prevail, the other fail. The "convergence" thesis, formulated first in 1944 by the Russian emigré social philosopher, Pitirim Sorokin, arose more out of wishful thinking generated by the spirit of the anti-Hitler coalition than on the basis of a thorough analysis of the world situation.

Quite different, in both time-span and manner, is the phenomenon of the Cold War. It was arguably a specific form of East West conflict (even though the relationship between, say, the USSR and Yugoslavia in 1948-53, or between the USSR and China in the late 1960s and 1970s, or between China and Vietnam in the late 1970s might also easily be put under this heading). If the specifics of the Cold War are seen in the bipolarity engendered by the two superpowers, the period of the Cold War may be seen to extend from 1945 (conferences of Yalta and Potsdam) to the mid-1960s (when de Gaulle in the West and Mao in the East challenged the "leaders" in either camp). If one defines it as being an unrestricted arms race, especially in the high-tech field of the ABC-weapons (nuclear bombs, missiles, chemical and bacteriological warfare), its beginning could be traced to somewhere around the year 1948. Until then demobilisation on both sides went on apace, with war budgets sinking, manpower reduced and the stockpile of atomic bombs in the USA, which had a monopoly of this "winning weapon", stagnating; and the final act(s) in the Cold War could be dated to the years 1963 (Test Ban Treaty), 1968 (Non-Proliferation Treaty) or 1972, 1979 (SALT 1 and 2) or 1987 (INF Treaty). All the accords on the limitation of the arms race were the result of a careful give-and-take and none of them prompted the conclusion that either of the superpowers could claim a "victory".

On the other side, the list of candidates for the laurels of "winners" is long enough: France and China, and all the former satellites in both blocs, but above all the states of Finland and Yugoslavia, which managed to disengage from the confrontation at the beginning. It may be guessed, however, whether their success depended more on the existence of the Cold War than on its termination. The Yugoslavian case indicates rather the former. At any rate, as far as the confronting adversaries were concerned, the historical events of 1989 could best be characterised as their mutual withdrawal from the battlefield – some sort of "Peace without Victory" as put forward by President Wilson in his speech to the Senate of 22 January 1917 (Jonas, 1984, p. 121).

However, back to our agenda. If the Soviet Union could not be considered as the defeated side in the Cold War (at least not a bigger loser than the United States), how can their different destinies in the post-Cold-War world be explained? After all, the Soviet Union broke up, and the international status of its successor state – the Russian Federation – was reduced (to say the least), while the former adversary, the United States, retained and – it may be argued – confirmed its status of "superpower". This outcome was not a foregone conclusion in the year when the Cold War ended, that is, in 1989. Some Soviet people had thought that the "peace dividend" would boost the Soviet economy, which, once freed from the unproductive military spending of the senseless arms race, was bound to demonstrate its inherent advantages over the rotten capitalist system. I said "thought", but a more fitting word would be "hoped". As with the convergence idea, it was more a case of wishful thinking. It was admittedly also my own perception at the time, even though, having had (unlike most of my co-citizens) opportunities to visit Western countries, I should have been less prone to such naive dreams.

By way of self-consolation, it should be noted that some illusions about the prospects of reforming the Soviet-type system were shared by very perceptive thinkers in the West as well. I may quote here from the address of Arthur Schlesinger Jr delivered at the Soviet-American seminar on the origins of the Cold War, of 27 June 1990:

> "Communism in the form practised in the Soviet Union and imposed on Eastern Europe – an absolutist polity based on the dictatorship of infallible creed, an infallible party and infallible leader – is simply and palpably an economic, political and moral disaster. Democracy has won the political argument between East and West. The market has won the economic argument. Difficulties lie ahead, but the fundamental debate is over.
>
> And why the triumph of democracy? – because of the superior flexibility of a free political and economic system, its superior capacity to adapt to the transformations wrought by the unending revolutions of science and technology. Communism, shielded from debate, dissent and irony, frozen in a rigid, static and righteous ideology, failed to adapt to change, failure provoking resentment, resistance and finally revolt.
>
> The rest of the world wishes communism all success in escaping from its own straitjacket. And, if all nations absorb the lessons of the Cold War, we may perhaps look forward to an unprecedented time of harmony, at least in Europe."

Even today, the style and the overall interpretation characteristic of this masterpiece are impressive. The emphasis on the ideological shortcomings of the Soviet regime, with only passing reference to geopolitical and economic phenomena, betrays, however, the same optimistic outlook: the idea of infallibility was out, "debate, dissent and irony" in, and "communism" will succeed in "escaping its own straitjacket". In an article published after the total disintegration of the Soviet system and of the Soviet Union itself, in a special issue of *Diplomatic History* on the end of the Cold War, the American scholar omitted, of course, his good wishes to "communism", as well as the prediction of the "time of harmony" (Schlesinger, 1992, pp. 49, 53).

In contrast, my own contribution to the same issue of *Diplomatic History* still reflected the spirit of great expectations. As the editor of the collections of essays formerly published in *Diplomatic History* aptly noted:

> "To Filitov, the struggle actually slowed a historic trend toward political democracy and market economies, both in the Soviet Union and elsewhere. It is fair to say that Filitov, and to some extent LaFeber, see the end of the Cold War marking a return to history, not its end. With that great struggle in the background, it is possible for the Russians and others to resume the march toward political and economic liberties that the Cold War interrupted." (Hogan, 1992, p. 4)

In fact, I did not hesitate to use pathetic phrases in my article at that time. Without the Cold War, so runs my argument, "the triumph of 'market and democracy' would have come much sooner and would have cost much less" (Filitov, 1992, p. 56). Now I would certainly think twice before choosing the word "triumph" for the description of the situation in the post-Cold War world, especially as far as my country was concerned – even though the mere mentioning of "costs" for the reforms was not very fashionable in 1991, when the article was written. My practical recommendation – for the Soviet republics (still existing at that time) to make use of the NATO experience in creating their new defence structure – sounded hollow and utopian even then. What I would leave unchanged even today in my balance sheet of the Cold War is the much lower priority that I attached – unlike Schlesinger – to the factor of misperceptions in explaining the causes and the course.

Where Schlesinger's and my opinions converged was in emphasising the institutional underpinnings and aftermath of the Cold War. Again, I cannot resist the temptation to quote at length from his article:

> "In Washington by the 1950s, the State Department, the Defence Department, the Central Intelligence Agency, the Federal Bureau of Investigation, and the National Security Council developed vested bureaucratic interests in the theory of a military expansionist Soviet Union. The Cold War conferred power, money, prestige, and public influence on these agencies and on the people who ran them. By the natural law of bureaucracies, their stake in the conflict steadily grew. Outside of government, arms manufacturers, politicians, professors, publicists, pontificators, and demagogues invested careers and fortunes in the Cold War.
>
> In time, the adversary Cold War agencies evolved a sort of tacit collusion across the Iron Curtain. Probably the greatest racket in the Cold War was the charade periodically enacted by generals and admirals announcing the superiority of the other side in order to get bigger budgets for themselves. As President John F. Kennedy marked to Norman Cousins, the editor of the *Saturday Review*, in the spring of 1963, 'the hard-liners in the Soviet Union and the United States feed on one another'.
>
> Institutions, alas, do not fold their tents and silently steal away. Ideas crystallised in bureaucracies resist change. With the Cold War at last an end, each side faces the problem of deconstructing entrenched Cold War agencies spawned and fortified by nearly half a century of mutually profitable competition. One has only to reflect on the forces behind the anti-Gorbachev conspiracy of August 1991." (Schlesinger, op. cit., p. 49)

My own remarks, polemically directed against the interpretations of the Cold War as a war against Stalinism, were less sweeping (not to say in their linguistic terseness), but, on the whole, in the same vein:

> "[The] Cold War only served to strengthen Stalinist structures in the Soviet camp and, also, in the long run, began to undermine the 'market and democracy' foundations of American society ... One can argue that Western Cold Warriors were not so much concerned with 'victory' or 'superiority' as they were with maintaining a continuing 'enemy' that served their particular goals. [The] Cold War tended for both sides to undermine democracy as well as common sense and rationality in politics generally." (Filitov, 1992, pp. 56, 57)

Some critics may blame both authors – American and Russian (then Soviet) – for this sort of "equidistant" approach to the main adversaries in the Cold War. True, I had tried to highlight some distinctions in order to explain "Western success and Eastern failure", among them the fact that the Europeans in their path to integration displayed "a genuine Marxist approach" – unlike "professed 'Marxists' of the Eastern camp" (ibid., p. 58). From today's perspective, I would venture a broader generalisation prompted by the witty answer once given to the question whether the Soviet Union had its own military-industrial complex (MIC): "The verb 'to have' does not apply:

the Soviet Union *is* a military-industrial complex." It might be a bit of an exaggerated view, but it explains a lot.

It explains, firstly, why and how the Soviet Union, despite the disparity in starting conditions and relative paucity of resources, could achieve and maintain strategic parity with the USA and thus save the world from World War Three, which in the absence of mutual deterrence could easily be unleashed under the guise of "humanitarian intervention" (to use the modern term).

It explains, secondly, the inherently defensive, reactive character of Soviet armament and foreign policies: the Soviet MIC did not need a victory over the capitalist "enemy"; it just needed this enemy to be in place – to justify and legitimise its own existence.

It explains, thirdly, the enormous difficulties encountered by the states of the former Soviet Union in the transition from the "mobilisation" model of society to a "normal" one. It was not the question of reallocation of resources, of the "conversion" in the sense usually attributed to this term. I recollect the comment in, if I am not mistaken, the French media in connection with the Chernobyl disaster: "The Soviets are producing energy just as they wage war – without taking into account the costs and risks". The problem is that the Soviet people did not know any alternative way, not only of production, but of life in general. More than that, they felt the "mobilisation model" as justified and legitimised by historical experience, and in fact not without reason. I refrain here from citing the well-known facts: intervention after the October Revolution, Hitler's invasion, US "atomic diplomacy".

Seeing the Soviet Union as an MIC explains those things. What my generalisation does not explain is why the Soviet leaders agreed to wind up the Cold War and arguably even took the initiative in this process. Were they blind enough to ignore the obvious consequences – that the disappearance of the "enemy image" would delegitimise the existence of the MIC, the regime it was based on, and ultimately their own positions of power? Different reasons have been given to explain this phenomenon: geopolitical, military, economic, social and, naturally, personal. I will briefly comment on some of them.

Among the geopolitical reasons, the "China factor" was traditionally highlighted: confronted with the threat from the East, the Soviets would inevitably gravitate to the West. It was from just this perspective that Chancellor Konrad Adenauer had derived his faith in Soviet concessions on the German question and eventual reunification. One may only guess what led him to this belief, but it can hardly be judged as well-founded. The exacerbation of the conflict on the Sino-Soviet border in 1968-9 should not be discounted in describing the *détente* policy, but it did not alter the fundamental features of Soviet foreign policy, and even less of the internal Soviet regime. And when this change came, the relations with China were actually improving. Still, even taking for granted the basic hostility between these two Communist giants, one can imagine the horror scenario of a protracted "tripolar" Cold (or even sometimes "Hot") War, such as that described in George Orwell's *1984*, with the aptly pictured prospect in a Soviet joke of the early 1960s: the optimists learn English, the pessimists learn Russian, and the realists – Chinese.

The idea of the Soviets "throwing in the towel" because of the American military build-up under Reagan is too spurious to be taken seriously. The defence industry in the Soviet Union operated quite well in general and could compete on equal terms with those of Western countries. The relative gap in high-tech innovations may be diagnosed, but the resulting shortcomings were not fatal, and they were both quickly remedied and partly offset by the mass production of more traditional weapons, on the one side, and by successful intelligence activities, on the other.

More relevant is the reference to the relative backwardness of the consumer sector in the Soviet economy. The resulting strains and difficulties experienced by ordinary people did not, however, really bother the ruling body, since they did not lead to mass protests. The competent expert enumerated four reasons for such an attitude:

> "Those who were part of this low-information mass were wont to be satisfied that:
> (1) their jobs were secure;
> (2) their rent was low;
> (3) they could afford basic goods (even if, somehow, the goods seemed increasingly hard to find);
> (4) they were living at a time when, despite many difficulties, living standards were 'not all that bad' compared to earlier decades." (Connor, 2003, p. 69)

This explanation is a bit inconsistent. If the basic goods were "increasingly" hard to find, how could a positive comparison with "earlier decades" be maintained? My personal memory may be imperfect and my experience, as an inhabitant of a metropolitan city, can be judged as not representative, but both suggest that living standards were still rising, albeit perhaps at a lesser rate, and the real crisis came with *perestroika*.

The same expert reaffirms this assessment as he states:

> "It is notable that, until late in Gorbachev's era, strikes were not launched to demand actual improvements in living standards; instead they were intended to protest at the deterioration of the "normal" – rather grim – conditions that existed under the old, poorly implemented contract." (ibid., pp. 61-2)

The fundamental change, he asserts, did not come from the "low-information mass" nor even from the "well-educated 'doubters'", but from the "privileged elites who served the regime [and] were able to learn about the reality of life outside the USSR through their access to foreign media, to the restricted ('coloured') version of TASS news agency reports, and to books and periodicals that were normally off-limits" (ibid., pp. 67-9). The decisive factors were "the advent of Gorbachev and his policy of glasnost (greater openness in the media)":

> "A flood of information about the Soviet past and present and about the world outside engulfed Soviet society, serving as a mirror in which the 'Soviet way of life' was reflected as poor and oppressed. Soviet citizens suddenly realised that, from the standpoint of the world outside, daily life in the USSR was unremittingly grim and 'uncivilized'. It hard-

ly helped matters that the leading Soviet officials themselves voiced a desire to have the Soviet Union join the ranks of 'civilized countries' – implying, of course, that it was not yet in those ranks." (ibid., p. 69)

The picture is basically true, but it does little to explain why the privileged elites decided to give up their privileges (at least, as far as the monopoly on information is concerned) and to voice a desire that amounted to a rejection of the preceding seventy years of Soviet "civilisation". In order to understand what prompted those "privileged elites" (or, at least, a substantial part of them) to join ranks with the "doubters" (or the "dissidents", both real and potential) and to dismantle the iron curtain with fatal consequences for the old regime, we should return to the concept of the Soviet MIC and its specific features.

Unlike their counterparts in the West, the members of the Soviet MIC (as well as the ruling elite in general – what was usually dubbed the *nomenklatura*) were severely restricted in using their privileges. One Russian writer (incidentally with a conservative, pro-Stalinist outlook) aptly compared his position in Soviet society with that of Ostap Bender, a hero of the satirical novel by Ilya Il'f and Evgeniy Petrov, who in the corrupt conditions of the NEP managed to amass a million – only to find that he was unable to spend it in the conditions of an emerging "socialism" (Mukhin, 2003, p. 709). So, this "great crook" converted his profits into gold and jewels, and made his way across the border, but was robbed by Romanians and pushed back over the border. He eventually decided to start a career in *upravdom* (head of housing infrastructure, a job usually linked to illicit, if petty, business in a state-run economy). The parallel is striking, even though Ostap Bender's successors made their fortunes legally and could convert their money into dollars and travel abroad when they wished. They could only do it, however, on a very limited scale, subject to the whims and caprices of their superiors in the party-state hierarchy; and the rights of the "secret-bearers" (that is, most MIC people) were limited even more. This bred discontent and frustration.

Just let me give you one personal example to illustrate my point. In autumn 1983, a delegation from Brezhnevski district council, Moscow, to which I was assigned as interpreter, was invited to pay a visit to the sister Tower Hamlets district of London. Two members were banned from the mission: an engineer in charge of the cable network and the chairman of the council's executive committee, who should have been the head of delegation. The former was considered a security risk, and the latter was punished by the First Secretary of Moscow City Party Committee, Viktor Grishin, for the bad conditions in the district's depot responsible for storing vegetables and fruit. Both were not in any way dissidents, but they had probably become enthusiastic supporters of Gorbachev, whose programme was quite simple: to transform the Soviet Union from a "besieged fortress" into something more "normal".

Is, "normality", however, the right definition for the society that emerged after the fall of the Soviet regime and the break-up of the Soviet Union? Certainly, it is not. Bearing in mind who initiated the process of perestroika, this outcome should not come as a surprise. The lack of economic rationality and of social consciousness, of transparency and accountability, to say nothing of other vices, were the birthmarks of the MIC/*nomenklatura* environment, and they made their natural imprint on post-Communist reality. On the other hand, the relative limitations which were imposed on the MIC and the ruling elite in the liberal-democratic countries of the West may explain their less painful transition into the post-confrontation era – and the continuation of the superpower status of the USA. In this context, it is understandable why the transition from "socialism" to "capitalism" went relatively smoothly in the "people's democracies". There were no MICs in those countries compared to the one that existed in the former USSR.

The question arises whether decommunisation or liberalisation could have been enacted in a more "normal", that is, less painful way? I venture to offer my personal view, which many would call unduly conservative. In short, it is based on the theory that sufficient democratic potential was concentrated in the institution of the Communist Party of the Soviet Union (CPSU), and this potential could be (but was not) used in reforming the state and society. In other words, I mean that the democratised party should have played the role of locomotive to launch the train of society and ensure that it did not derail.

On what premises do I base my thesis? The members of CPSU were usually described as a bunch of careerists and pliant servants of the regime. This is basically true, but it is not the whole truth. The party cells, at least in some academic institutions (of which I have a better knowledge) were permeated – and sometimes headed – by so-called "intrasystemic dissidents" whose views differed sharply from those in the *nomenklatura*, and sometimes succeeded in influencing them. It is hard to say whether the democratic impulse from "below" could succeed in reforming the overall party structure so as to dismantle the power of the *apparatchiki*. Some trends in this direction can be discerned, anyway. My institute colleague, Dr Pyotr Cherkassov, has just completed a monograph on the history of IMEMO – a Moscow-based academic "think-tank", where the sensational story of the life-and-death struggle between this institution's Party organisation and the *apparatchiki* from the Central Committee and state organs is presented. Under Brezhnev and Andropov, the latter prevailed, but their triumph (never complete) was short-lived. The advent of perestroika brought about fundamental changes. For instance, the candidates for Party Secretaries "recommended" by the *raikoms* (district committees) were progressively voted down, and the Party cells obtained the right to gather half the members' dues collected for their own needs. If money means authority, this innovation potentially led to the "diffusion of power" and to what may be called a democratisation of the party.

Could this process lead to the democratisation of society? It is a moot question. The representatives of the "non-system dissidents" answered with a categorical "no": they drew a parallel with apartheid in South Africa, where democratic rules were secured for a fraction of the population, with the majority excluded from political life. The comparison was false, of course. Nobody could change their skin colour, while the party was in principle free for those wishing to join, provided they displayed a measure of social responsibility. In this sense, the CPSU could really have become the nucleus of an emerging civil society in the USSR, which is still a far cry from reality in today's Russia. At any rate, as a hypothesis, this view merits, in my opinion, some consideration.

It was more than fifty years ago that the great Marxist (and anti-Communist) thinker Fritz Sternberg made his perceptive analysis of the Soviet regime – by defining it as a terrorist dictatorship with an immense potential for internal transformation into socialist democracy. He predicted that it would be mistaken to think that this transition/ revolution could take the form of free elections and an emerging parliament where the different parties could be represented; the decisive impulse, he thought, would come from the trade unions and rural "collectives" (Sternberg, 1950, pp. 214-16). He turned out to be wrong. The revolution, as was the rule in Russian history, came from "above" and it was largely stymied by the unholy alliance between the MIC/*nomenklatura* and the ultra-liberal "non-system dissidents" through the instrument of formally free elections. If, however, one takes these words by Fritz Sternberg as a warning against the premature and artificial introduction of liberal-parliamentary norms, it may be said that he was certainly quite right.

The first example of this pseudo-democratisation in the former USSR bore him out. The elections of 26 March 1989 were free in the sense that practically anyone could declare him/herself a candidate and place on the wall his/her photo and programme to impress the voters. But, in a strange situation, where no positive programmes to replace the CPSU's largely defunct functions were on the agenda and where the personal appeal of a candidate counted more than his views or qualifications, it was no small wonder that the elected body, the Congress of People's Deputies (first session: 25 May-12 June; second session: 12-24 December 1989) played no constructive role and actually contributed to total political and economic chaos.

If counter-questions – such as whether the CPSU could be democratised? and, if so, could this democratised party succeed in reforming the Soviet Union in such a way as to save it from disintegration? – cannot be answered with any certainty, there is every reason to think that the failure of the party on both counts inevitably meant a death sentence for the USSR. Some writers attribute the break-up of the united multi-national Soviet state to an upsurge of so-called localism (Akhieser, 1997, pp. 653-63). I would rather use another term: nationalism.

Arnold Toynbee in his *Experiences* (a sort of memoir, which he published in 1967) called nationalism the strongest and most dangerous ideology of the twentieth century (comprising, in his opinion, 90% of two others – "capitalism" and "communism"). The only remedy to cure its debilitating effects he found in the propaganda of mixed marriages. Strangely enough, the great British historian neglected the more real and effective way to combat the evils of nationalist excesses – the principle and practice of supranationality, rooted in the idea and the reality of European integration. (Perhaps he neglected it just because he was British – bearing in mind that even in the late 1960s many in Great Britain were not sure of the prospects of the Common Market?) More to the point, it is worth mentioning that supranationality of a sort was practised in the former Soviet Union as well. The notion of the "Soviet people as the new international community" was, so to speak, not an empty phrase.

It has been argued that this formula was a sham, behind which was the reality of the dominance of the Russian nation, if not a complete Russianisation of all other "Soviet" nations. I do think that this kind of reasoning is as convincing as that of Eurosceptics who feared that the United Europe would be a German Europe. Certainly, the safeguards against the *diktat* by one nation (or a group of them) in the EU were and are quite different compared with those in the former Soviet Union, but it does not mean that there were none of them in the latter. Basically, they were represented by the implicit and sometimes explicit, even institutionalised, practice of self-denial on the point of the Russians – in such matters as living standards, cultural interactions (Russian culture was tuned more to absorb the specific features of other national cultures than to expand and "project" its own) and, not the least, the Party structure. The mere fact that there were Communist Parties in Ukraine, Belarus and the rest, and none in Russia, served to counter the claim that the rule of the CPSU was tantamount to reign by the Russians. It contributed to the ideology of internationalism or, in other words, of "supranationality".

Conversely, any step to articulate Russianness – even under the fine-sounding slogan "Russians should be equal to other Soviet nations" – served to foster centrifugal tendencies in the former Soviet Union. Absolutely fatal in this respect was the decision to create the Russian Communist Party (RCP). The formation of the United Front of the Working People by the group of orthodox Leningrad communists (today St Petersburg) as a predecessor of the RCP (its constituent Congress took place in June 1990) in June 1989 may be described as a starting point in the disintegration of the USSR (and not only of the CPSU).

Admittedly, the formation of the RCP was legitimised by a sort of party referendum. Even in my Moscow district, where there were many doubters, two-thirds of the voters turned out to be in favour of a new party. Was it an expression of democratic practices? Rather the opposite is true: taking into account the lack of any in-depth discussion and the abundance of cheap demagoguery, it could be said that the vote was manipulated. Anyway, the fact that the communists in Russia fell easy prey to the nationalist trick did not do them credit. And it certainly raises doubts as to whether the more normal and less painful way to the "market and democracy" could be found.

Much depended, of course, on the personality of the leader. De Gaulle, after all, managed to save France in a situation that many saw as catastrophic. Gorbachev did not. Many reasons can be cited for his failure. I would specify a single one: unlike de Gaulle, he did not possess a disciplined and efficient team of advisers. I came to this conclusion in the course of my research into Soviet policies on German reunification (the German question after the Second World War is my specialisation as a historian).

As a summary, the following points may be offered:

1. The Soviet Union did not lose the Cold War; it lost much more – the contest of socio-economic systems, and, consequently, much of its legitimacy.
2. The victory of the West was achieved not by military or subversive activities directed against the adversary in the Cold War (both rather delayed it), but by the mere fact of its existence, through the fascination projected by its image into the mentality of the Soviet ruling elites, and of the public at large.
3. The break-up of the Soviet Union as a multi-ethnic and largely "supranational" entity was not caused primarily by the processes of democratisation and "marketisation" per se; it was the loss of control over these processes by society, with the concomitant rise of nationalism (Russian nationalism in the first place), that made the demise of the USSR all but inevitable.

## Bibliography

Akhieser, A., *Russia: The critique of the historical experience*, Vol. 1, Novosibirsk, 1997. [in Russian]

Connor, W.D., "Soviet society, public attitudes, and the perils of Gorbachev's reforms", *Journal of Cold War Studies*, 2003, Vol. 5, No. 4.

Filitov, A., "Victory in the postwar era: despite the Cold War or because of it?", *Diplomatic History*, 1992, Vol. 16, No. 1.

Hogan, M.J., "Introduction", *The end of the Cold War: its meaning and implications*, Cambridge, MA, 1992.

Jonas, M., *The United States and Germany: a diplomatic history*, Ithaca, NY, 1984.

Loth, W., "General views on the Cold War", *Cold War History*, 2003, Vol. 3, No. 2.

Mukhin, Y., *The murder of Stalin and Beria*, Moscow, 2003.

Schlesinger, A., "Some lessons from the Cold War", *Diplomatic History*, 1992, Vol. 16, No. 1.

Sternberg, F., *Marx und die Gegenwart*, Cologne, 1950.

# Chapter 30
# Heroes, "pasts", participants, people – Hungary, 1989

*Janos Rainer*

All of fifteen years – or perhaps only fifteen years – have gone by since 1989. The year has almost passed into history, but 1989 and the transformation process are still an unfinished story. There have been many analyses of 1989, but most of society (having experienced it) is still full of personal recollections. A generation has grown up since, which only studies those events, but even for them the story is a personal one. Although they did not see it as a historical event at the time and have only a child's memories, they are close to parents, grandparents, relations and friends with memories of another kind.

So I cannot approach 1989 simply as an analyst. It is a personal story for me as well, too personal to allow me to talk of broad processes. I cannot even give the full story of some of the actors in it. Let me instead focus on a single event that took place over a few hours on a single day. It is possible to create a bird's eye view or a panorama of the event, but I hope some shots can be enlarged to show details that take it back in time and bring it closer to the present. They have a different meaning, just as the detail of the picture in the film *Blow up* by Michelangelo Antonioni (and in the short story by Julio Cortazár, on which the film is based) gained a distinct meaning, telling a story of its own.

The event I am going to discuss took place on 16 June 1989 in Budapest's *Hősök tere* ('Heroes' Square'). It was a valediction to a dead man, Imre Nagy, the former prime minister of Hungary. He was hanged exactly thirty-one years before, in 1958, in the yard of a prison on the edge of Budapest, and he lay for thirty-one years in an unmarked grave in the cemetery opposite the prison. On that June day, he was reburied in the same place.

Budapest has two large, imposing squares capable of holding large crowds of people, both of them created about the turn of the nineteenth and twentieth centuries. One bears the name of Lajos Kossuth, leader of the 1848 Revolution and war of independence, and is dominated by the parliament building. The first, second and third Hungarian republics were declared there in 1918, 1946 and 1989, and there the people of Budapest gathered on 23 October 1956 to protest against the Stalinist system. That crowd was addressed by a communist politician, Imre Nagy, who became Prime Minister next morning. His government recognised the demands of the revolution and declared a multi-party system, and Hungary's neutrality and withdrawal from the Warsaw Pact. That revolution was crushed by Soviet forces on 4 November 1956, but Imre Nagy did not resign or join the communist counter-government of János Kádár. He was, therefore, charged with high treason and with overturning the communist system of state. That is why he was executed.

*Hősök tere* is a grand memorial to the official historical memory of Hungarian statehood. While Parliament in *Kossuth tér* is the most important institution of Hungarian statehood, *Hősök tere* depicts the thousand-year history of that state as perceived at the beginning of the twentieth century. In the centre of the monument are equestrian statues of the Hungarian chieftains who conquered the Carpathian Basin, headed by Árpád. The statues in the colonnade on each side depict the kings seen as greatest at the beginning of the twentieth century. The row begins with St Stephen, founder of the western European-type christian kingdom, and it used to end with members of the Austrian house of Habsburg, who seized the Hungarian throne in the sixteenth century. The last figure was Franz Joseph I, who had crushed the 1848 struggle for independence, but reached a compromise with the Hungarian ruling elite two decades later. The memorial represented the foundation of the Hungarian state, the alliance between the nobility descended from the chieftains and the kings (after the sixteenth century, the Habsburgs), and thereby the Hungarian noble constitution.

When the dual Austro-Hungarian Monarchy broke up in 1918, the last group of statues was removed. On 1 May 1919, during the short-lived Hungarian Bolshevik dictatorship, the whole memorial was draped in red cloth. Under the authoritarian regime of Miklós Horthy, who overturned the revolutions, the statues of the Habsburg kings were returned. Placed before the chieftain group in 1929 was the memorial stone to the Hungarian war heroes, inscribed "1914-1918. For the thousand-year frontiers", an allusion to the 1920 Treaty of Trianon. For the end of the Great War meant more than the end of the dual monarchy for Hungary: it meant loss of two-thirds of its territory and half its population. The memorial expressed the Horthy regime's aim of recovering the historical territory of Hungary.

A quarter of a century later, after 1945, the Habsburg kings were removed from the monument again and replaced by Hungarian leaders and statesmen (including Kossuth) who had struggled against the Habsburgs. The inscription on the memorial to the Hungarian heroes was removed and, in 1956, replaced by a new text stating that they had laid down their lives "for the freedom and independence of the Hungarian people". The historical recollection of the Hungarian noble state was altered in line with the agenda of the communist authorities that took over after 1945, but the conflict lay, not in certain figures, but between the monument and the authorities altering it. The communist system was imposed by the Soviet troops that occupied Hungary in 1945, against the will of the majority of Hungarian society.

However, not even the communist system wanted to abandon all historical archetypes. On 1 May 1957, just a few months after the defeat of the 1956 Revolution, János Kádár made a speech in *Hősök tere* before a quarter of a million people. Partly identifying and partly distancing himself, the spokesman stood before the historical tableau, but with his back to the statues, which were neither removed nor changed.

Not long after May Day 1957, János Kádár told a national conference of the communist party:

> "A high proportion of the working masses are interested primarily not in general questions of politics, but in correct solutions to economic and cultural questions that affect their daily lives. Nor do they develop their opinions of the party and the system on the grounds of political issues."

That none-too-democratic truism became the foundation of "Kádárite consolidation". The essence of it is an unspoken bargain. So long as their living standards keep rising, slowly but evenly and predictably, the "working masses" will acknowledge the realities of international politics and the Soviet occupation, not question the legitimacy of the communist authority, and accept that certain political questions, including the political structures of the national past, are taboo. It is clear from the case of *Hősök tere* that Hungary has rich traditions of developing representative epic stories of the national past.

The Kádár system had long been trying flexibly to meet its side of the bargain. Reforms introduced in the late 1960s included elements of a market economy, but the reform process was stalled at the beginning of the 1970s at the behest of the Soviet Union, with enthusiastic agreement from the Hungarian party apparatus. This led the Hungarian economy to lose its ability to adapt to processes taking place in the world economy, at a time when the reforms had made the Hungarian economy more dependent on the world economy. By the end of the 1970s, living standards began to stagnate and, in the mid-1980s, to decline. Leadership of the Soviet party was taken over in 1985 by an unpredictable Mikhail Gorbachev, who was committed to change. This naturally led to unease among the political elite in Hungary and elsewhere in Eastern Europe.

Other crisis factors were specific to Hungary. The Hungarians could compare their living standards, for instance, to those of their predecessors – many of whom had lost everything in the successive catastrophes of the first half of the twentieth century – or to those of their neighbours in the East and the West. Almost a quarter of a million people had fled to the West in 1956, most of them young men. Hundreds of thousands were allowed to travel abroad again in the early 1960s and the émigrés could visit home. As long as living standards in Hungary lay somewhere between East and West, the Kádárite bargain worked. When its reliability began to erode and there was a threat (even remote) of falling to the level of the Poles or the Czechoslovaks, discontent appeared in society. This was expressed initially by opposition groups and then by young technocrats in the party and state apparatus.

Those technocrats were able to speak quite sensibly about the diseases from which the communist system was suffering and what reforms were needed to remedy them. It was in their interest to have freer speech and relax the communication monopoly of the ruling elite. But the causes of the diseases lay in a past for which they and the whole system shared a moral deficit. The biggest barrier was János Kádár himself. He personified the defeat of the 1956 Revolution, whereas the great successes of his regime in the 1960s and 1970s were only memories ten years later. Only the democratic opposition could express that clearly.

Kádár was removed as party leader with Gorbachev's assistance in the summer of 1988. His successors were keen to start dialogue with the politically active minority and showed a willingness to make concessions: economic reforms, partial freedom of speech and assembly, and some kind of reappraisal as well. The biggest burden was 1956 and the symbolic figure of the executed Imre Nagy, who had no marked grave. That was felt acutely by the Hungarian opposition as well, whose radicals were seeking to break up the communist system completely:

> "The leaders of the Hungarian Socialist Workers' Party themselves are talking of some separation between party and state, some kind of socialist pluralism. Whatever these utterances may mean, everyone has to realise that no real political opening or conciliation is possible while unburied corpses still block the path of compromise."

That was the philosopher János Kis, leading figure of the democratic opposition, speaking at a demonstration in 16 June 1988. That same summer, a voluntary committee of those formerly convicted of political crimes, the Historical Justice Committee, successfully applied pressure on the communist party to search for the remains of Imre Nagy and associates, and allow their families to bury them. The genie was out of the bottle. In February 1989, General Jaruzelski in Poland sat down with Solidarność. In the spring, parties were formed in Hungary too and sought to negotiate with the Hungarian Socialist Workers' Party. There was more and more coverage in the press and on television about the past, the dead, the repression and 1956. The authorities retreated step by step. The funeral of Imre Nagy could not be confined to a family burying its kin. That is how the venue became *Hősök tere*, the Hungarian national place of memorial.

So the actors in the Hungarian democratic transition gathered in the square on the morning of 16 June 1989. Not everyone was there. The bones of Imre Nagy reposed in a coffin that had been found in the furthest corner of Budapest's biggest cemetery, after several months' investigation. It was not the real spirit of Imre Nagy that filled the Heroes' square. Nagy had belonged to the first generation of Hungarian communist politicians. He had joined the Bolshevik party in 1918, while he was a prisoner-of-war in Russia. There was still uncertainty in 1989 about several periods in his life, including his time in Russian exile in the 1930s. He is known to have debated frequently with his party's leaders, advocating some kind of communism with a human face. He had been one of the party's first reformers, but his ideas had been defeated during his first term as prime minister in 1953-54. Nor was he a revolutionary in 1956, though he had remained a believer in Hungary's independence and was more inclined to heed the strongly expressed will of Hungarian society than the policies of Moscow. He was a communist – a national, democratic communist, if that is not too strong a contradiction. But the paradox was resolved by his trial and execution. On 16 June 1989, the communist Imre Nagy seemed to the public to be a 1956 martyr, a victim of the communists. Those buried with him were also communist party members.

The other main actor was not there either: 77-year-old János Kádár lay in his villa on the opposite bank of the Danube, mortally ill and his faculties dimmed. He, like Nagy, had helped to build a Soviet-type system in Hungary, but unlike Nagy he had never doubted that he was doing right. He joined as a member of Nagy's revolutionary government in 1956, but then accepted the role of a Quisling. He was to blame for the execution of Nagy and numerous revolutionaries, as the Soviet leadership had not, to our present knowledge, insisted on bloody reprisals. Later, he was seen as the most successful Eastern European reformer and gained acceptance from the majority of the Hungarian people. But latterly, he had been terrified of change and, in 1989, of being held to account for his deeds. Kádár was present in the square as a murderer of the Hungarian revolution and of the freedom of Hungary, though nobody chose to say so.

*Hősök tere* had been decorated for the occasion. Scenery designed by Gábor Bachmann and László Rajk shifted the focus from the representation of Hungary's state history to a catafalque erected on the south side, outside the Műcsarnok art gallery. Rajk was born in 1949, but his father, a communist politician, had been arrested a few weeks later and executed after the first great Hungarian show trial. The son became a leading activist in the Hungarian democratic opposition in the 1970s. Rajk's vision of the square underlined the left-wing, plebeian aspect of the 1956 Revolution and a timeless spirit of mourning. There were simple black and white drapes. The symbol of the Hungarian revolution (a national flag with a hole where the Soviet-style coat-of-arms badge had been cut out) hung on a battered, leaning structure of rusty pieces of iron resembling a crane. Some saw it as a gallows and some as the mast of a sinking ship.

That day, 16 June 1989, was a weekday, but some 200 000 people attended the event. It was shown live on state television all day, without permission either from the party or government. The speakers delivering the funeral orations were former colleagues of Nagy, chosen by the Historical Justice Committee, who had been convicted after the revolution. The one-party Hungarian government and Parliament requested the new Historical Justice Committee to place their wreath on the catafalque. The communist party sent no representative. The Political Committee had debated for hours about whether to fly flags on the party building and, if so, which ones. It was eventually decided to show a black flag and a national tricolour, and omit the red flag of socialism. Three days before the 16 June event, the party sat down to negotiate with a coalition of opposition parties on a new constitution, legislation for the transitional period and free elections. The transition that Rudolf Tőkés called Hungary's "negotiated revolution" had begun.

The speakers in the square spoke of the dead and the revolution. What they envisaged was not a continuation or revival of 1956, but a peaceful transition intended to attain the goals of 1956. The atmosphere was celebratory, solemn and a little tense. Only a few days before, the bloody incident with the students demonstrating for democracy in Beijing's Tiananmen Square had occurred. The Hungarian political police (still commanded by old-style communist officers) drew up a plan of action to ensure that the funeral went peacefully. But there were only a few policemen visible at the ceremony – it was stewarded by activists of the opposition parties. There was little applause or cheering and the crowd went home quietly after ceremonies lasting several hours, and watched on television as the coffins were buried. There were no incidents.

The burial of Nagy on 16 June 1989 was a psychological turning point in Hungary's change of system. It buried an era. As Péter Kende, a political scientist, wrote a couple of months later:

> "One of the most important factors of the collapse of the *ancien régime* was that of the moral. This ceremony of mourning was like the elevation of the Host and the Evil One fleeing from it with a whimper."

It seemed the country's communist elite would certainly never regain the initiative. Actually, its moral disintegration helped greatly to promote a peaceful course for Hungary's change of system. The overall crisis in the Soviet system, the Gorbachev factor and other factors obviously helped as well, but let us stay with the specific features of the Hungarian case.

And now a few words about how much that June day presaged what happened in Hungary during and after the transition. Among those present in *Hősök tere* were three of Hungary's five prime ministers since 1990: József Antall, Viktor Orbán and Péter Medgyessy. They belong to three generations and have three far-from-typical histories, but in many respects they typify the Hungarian transition and its strange relationship with the past.

József Antall was born in 1932. His father was a high-ranking Interior Ministry official, before and during the Second World War, who had taken charge in 1939 of lodging and providing for Polish refugees. After the war, Antall Senior had become a Smallholders' Party Member of Parliament and a minister in the coalition government, which he remained after the communist takeover, right up to 1953. He wanted his son to be a politician and sent him to the best church secondary school in Budapest. József Antall entered university in 1950 and qualified as a history teacher, but was dismissed from teaching under political-police pressure in 1959. He was not arrested, however, and remained in an intellectual occupation. He became deputy curator of a museum in the late 1960s and curator in the 1980s.

Although he was under police surveillance for decades – his closest friend and schoolmate was an informer reporting on him for thirty years – he took part in no direct opposition activity. Nonetheless, close acquaintances saw him as a politician. Conversant and purposeful in history and law, Antall in the summer and autumn of 1989 led the delegation of the heterogeneous, populist Hungarian Democratic Forum to the "three-sided" negotiations with the communist party. He took over as head of the movement in the autumn and became prime minister when it emerged as the biggest party in the 1990 elections. He sought to mould the Forum into a conservative party of a western European type, but did not succeed in doing so. He died of cancer in 1993.

Viktor Orbán was born in 1963 to a rural family in Transdanubia. His parents were no longer in agriculture. His father was a middle manager in a mining company that had been privatised at the time of the change of system, so that he became a rich quarry owner. His son studied law in Budapest in the 1980s. The grassroots collegiate organisation that he helped to establish was named after István Bibó, a political philosopher who had served in the 1956 government of Imre Nagy. The specialist college heard regular lectures from leading figures in the democratic opposition, not just the university faculty. In 1988, Viktor Orbán became a founder member of FIDESZ, a radical liberal youth party. He was the only speaker at the Nagy funeral who had not, and could not have had, a 1956 past. He was asked by the organisers to speak on behalf of Hungarian youth and responded with the boldest and saddest words of any, calling for the withdrawal of Soviet troops and stating that the coffins contained also the life of the generation growing up in the 1980s, in an allusion to the difficulties and price to be paid for the change of system. Orbán in the 1990s took a different turn and organised a Hungarian conservative party, a curiously eclectic mix of Western-style christian democrats, extreme right-wingers harking back to the authoritarianism of the inter-war years, and pragmatic young people of a generation even younger than his.

Péter Medgyessy was born into a Transylvanian family in 1941. His father was a Hungarian diplomat in the communist period, while he in the 1960s attended the Budapest university of economics, which was the bastion of reform socialism at the time. Medgyessy then entered the state apparatus and the communist party. He was quickly promoted within the Ministry of Finance, while working for some years also as a secret counter-intelligence officer. Towards the end of the 1980s, he became finance minister and deputy prime minister, and a member of the Central Committee of the Hungarian Socialist Workers' Party. He worked alongside Prime Minister Miklós Németh on creating a market economy and stood beside him as he laid a wreath on Imre Nagy's catafalque. In 1989, he did not join the new socialist party. He became head of the Hungarian subsidiary of a big French bank and a wealthy financier. In 2002, he was chosen from outside the socialist party to be its Prime Minister.

The Soviet-type system in Hungary fell in 1989. Free elections were held the following year, and two years after the funeral the Soviet occupation forces left the country. The economy was reorganised on a market basis within a few years and began to grow again in the mid-1990s, after a severe recession. Decisive steps to transform the economy were taken in 1995 by Finance Minister Lajos Bokros, who had written analyses for opposition *samizdat* publications in the 1980s, under the pseudonym David Ricardo. The head of the 1994-8 government, Gyula Horn, had taken arms against the revolution in 1956, but earned great merit in 1989 as foreign minister for precipitating the events that contributed to the fall of the Berlin Wall. Seen from a distance, the Hungarian change of system was a peaceful, orderly transition from one quality to another; from a mild, flexible version of the post-Stalinist Soviet system to a liberal democracy. However, generations and a multiplicity of strategies were built into its close, personal histories: the values and bad genies of the inter-war period,

331

the moral heritage of 1956, the successes of the Kádár period, and the criticisms and recognitions of the crisis periods.

This applies to the real protagonists too. For on 16 June 1989 the real protagonists were the crowd, the 200 000 in the square and the millions watching on television. No doubt they were thinking a thousand thoughts as they watched the ceremony. Even a few years before 1989, the majority of Hungarian society had not been wholly opposed to the regime built on the crushed revolution. The catharsis of 16 June awakened memories no one had recalled for a long time: the year of introducing the Soviet system, 1956, and the reprisals that followed it. For a moment, there appeared in bright colours what almost everyone felt: they wanted to live better – like the Austrians, say. If the past was now implying that this could not be accomplished without freedom and democracy, they would believe it. It did not matter that they had lived well after 1956 (albeit not so well as the Austrians) and they were not bothered about memories, crimes or criminals. All that mattered was that day of mourning, which incorporated everything. Thereafter, the past would disappear with the bodies into the grave and they would not have to deal with it.

All those conclusions have turned out in the last fifteen years to be partly true and partly false. On one hand, different concepts and different narratives of the past still have great importance in the political divisions in Hungary; different memories are still in the front line in public discourse. On the other hand, the practical, pragmatic character of the majority of Hungarian society has not changed. Twelve years after 1989, my daughter received an assignment at secondary school to write the history of her family in the twentieth century. She had this to say of the period since the change of system:

> "This period has brought change mainly in my father's life. Since 1989, he has been able to deal legally with what interests him: the 1956 revolution."

This I felt in its simplicity to be true. The story of 1989 has not ended. By telling our personal tales of 1989, great and small, and asking and thinking about matters, we are helping to ensure that the real message of that day fifteen years ago – namely, the importance of dealing with the past, the importance of one's relationship to freedom, the importance of people's destinies in history – will remain and reach those for whom this is ever less of a personal memory.

# Chapter 31
# The history of the fall of Communism: an area of inquiry for the social and human sciences

*Lavinia Betea*

## The research plan –
## Case study: the 1989 Romanian revolution

As we know, 1989 saw the collapse of the communist regimes in Central and eastern Europe and the beginning of a complex process of individual and collective transformations. It scarcely needs to be said that the Romanian context was different, and that the transfer of power there occurred in a different manner to the "velvet revolutions" in the other European countries. Hence, in the process of the collapse of the communist regimes in Europe, the transfer of power in Romania followed a classic revolutionary pattern (according to Karnoouh, 2000).

In his analysis comparing the Romanian revolution to the changes which took place in the other European communist countries, Gabanyi (1999) points to the following distinctive features of the transfer of power:

1. Only in Romania was there a bloody overthrow of the regime, claiming 1 104 lives and leaving 3 352 wounded.
2. Violence was used not just prior to the fleeing of Ceauşescu and his wife from Bucharest, but especially in the aftermath (22-25 December 1989). The aim of these actions was to confer an appearance of legitimacy on the seizure of power by the new leaders, and to secure that power by changing the institutions and the top-ranking elite.
3. Only in Romania was the party leader, Nicolae Ceauşescu, and his wife, Elena Ceauşescu, executed following a trial that harked back to Stalinist methods.
4. A short time after the overthrow of this nationalist-communist dictatorship, reformist communists came to power.

The controversy surrounding the popular and revolutionary nature of the uprising, including the manipulation of information by the mass media between 22 and 25 December 1989, the legitimacy of the new elite which seized power, the trial of Ceauşescu, his wife and their close associates, and the role of the army and the former *Securitate* (secret service) in the overthrow – and particularly in the terrorist attacks which were used subsequently to justify the use of violence – represented (simultaneously and successively) a set of disparate and often contradictory meanings and reinterpretations of Romanians' social memory.

Despite the plethora of writings on the collapse of the communist regime and, by implication, "the bloody revolution in Romania", no study so far has applied the theories and methodologies of the social and human sciences.

Our research will be conducted on two main fronts:
1. researching the formation and transformation of meanings and reinterpretations arising, over a fifteen-year period, out of a historical event of considerable scale and importance;
2. studying the relationship between the social representations of certain phenomena, institutions and characters (for example, "the anti-Ceauşescu revolt", the "communist secret services", the *Securitate*, "the terrorists and heroes of the revolution") and the factors (propaganda, commemoration, etc.) which contributed to transforming the content of a certain socially significant memory.

The basic methodology of the case study will be as follows:
1. content analysis of speeches (official speeches, but also newspaper interviews) and conversations with "involved spectators";
2. creative interviews with participants in the events of December 1989;
3. the biographical method, studying documents and autobiographical accounts.
This will involve the use of analytical methods from the social and human sciences, drawing in particular on the main social psychology theories and analyses.

First of all, we will focus our attention on the phenomenon of collective representations as a form of social knowledge. Analysing the formation and transformation of social representations relating to the events of December 1989 in Romania will enable us to highlight some aspects of the relationship between the inner circle and those around them, and the role of context and ideology in the formation of social memory.

With the help of these social representations, we will compare individual and social memories. The social memory of the events of 1989, taken to mean a form of conversion and expression of social thought, will be approached as an outcome of the socio-political context. As regards the formation and changing of meanings attached to memory, particular attention will be given to the role of public events, commemorations, statues and the emergence of certain traditions aimed at creating harmony between the sense and/or new meanings attached to certain memories.

In our proposed study, we will draw a particular cognitive approach to collective memory, which involves analysing the "flashbulb" memories (M. Conway, 1994) that "involved spectators" retain, either of the demonstrations and protests that eventually culminated in the collapse of the Romanian communist regime, or of certain tense moments around that time ("the fleeing of Ceauşescu", "the terrorist attacks" and the like).

We also believe that, from the perspective of social psychology theory and methodology, analysing the content of certain episodes in recent history – in this instance, the 1989 Romanian revolution, one of the most widely covered global events in the mass media – may help shed light on a hotly disputed historical topic.

## Practical application: *groupthink* in the Romanian revolution

It must be added that in communist Romania, the Ceauşescu regime (1965-89) excelled at preventing and quelling any form of resistance, by means of the control it exercised over citizens by the secret police and the censoring of information to which the public had access. This phenomenon can be explained by the fact that the communist leader held power and controlled the media and the special police over a long period.

In 1965, under the pretext of "developing democracy", Ceauşescu replaced the former Political Bureau with the Political Executive Committee (Polexco), a body with an extended structure (79 members) and with what were in reality formal powers. In 1967, two years after coming to power, Ceauşescu abandoned the principle of separation of powers between party and state, and became the President of the State Council. In 1974, the leader of the single party proclaimed himself President of Romania. He was commander-in-chief of the armed forces as well as leader of the collective organisations and mass movements. At the height of his power, he ran a "clan dictatorship", with the most important posts being held by Ceauşescu, his wife, other family members and a small number of loyal associates.

During the latter stages of the regime, the machinery of power operated in such a way that there was no alternative to the government. Thus, for instance, the principle of "rotation of senior officials", which meant that high-ranking activists moved frequently from one portfolio to another, prevented the establishment of close relationships which might have crystallised into a form of opposition.

Following his famous condemnation of the invasion of Czechoslovakia in 1968, which earned Ceauşescu considerable plaudits abroad, it was decided, under the pretext of preventing a change of leader by the Soviets, that the President should be elected by party members. Later, before the last sessions of the party congress, meetings of all party organisations featured an agenda item on "approving the candidacy" of Comrade Ceauşescu for the office of Secretary General of the Romanian Communist Party. As a result, the delegates to the congress became mere messengers for the mandate delivered by four million party members who had unanimously approved the re-election of Ceauşescu as supreme leader. Thus, it became impossible to oust him as leader of the party and the country, and his hold on power appeared to be unassailable.

On 25 December 1989, during the Christmas festivities, Ceauşescu and his wife were shot following a sham trial. This fact testifies to the failure of Ceauşescu's policies, but also marked a poor start for Romanian society in transition. From the point of view of political scientists and journalists, the analysis of the recent past ends here.

In social psychological terms, however, the causes of the situation outlined above could be found in the characteristics of the decision-making group, the Permanent Bureau of the Political Executive Committee elected by the Communist Party Central Committee. The supreme decision-making structure and the oligarchic style of leadership instituted by Ceauşescu explain the political reality behind the events of December 1989.

# The *groupthink* model, adapted from I. Janis and L. Mann (1977)

If we compare the situation in Romania with movements for reform in neighbouring countries, and examine the official powers of the Polexco, the first conclusion we come to is that of a failure within the decision-making group. This phenomenon could be explained by reference to I. Janis's *groupthink* theory (1977). According to this theory, formulated following a study into relations within a decision-making group and the effectiveness of the decisions adopted, all the political decisions leading to the failure of American policy in the wake of the Second World War were characterised by *groupthink*, an effect found in groups which typically develops as follows:

**The antecedents**
1. strong cohesion within the decision-making group;
2. isolation of the group from external influences;
3. a powerful, authoritarian leader;
4. absence of norms/procedures for examining the pros and cons of alternative courses of action;
5. high levels of stress engendered by external threats and low expectancy of finding a better solution than that advocated by the group leader.

*Strong desire for consensus (complete agreement)*

**Symptoms of *groupthink***
1. illusion of invulnerability;
2. belief in the inherent morality of the group;
3. collective rationalisation;
4. stereotyped views of out-groups (incarnation of evil);
5. self-censorship of doubts or opposing (different) opinions;
6. illusion of unanimity;
7. direct pressure on dissenters;
8. tacit appointment of ideological "mindguards".

**Consequences**
1. incomplete survey of alternatives;
2. incomplete survey of group objectives;

3. failure to assess risks of preferred choice;
4. failure to reappraise alternatives;
5. poor information search (by experts);
6. selective bias in processing information;
7. failure to work out contingency plans.

*Low probability of a successful outcome*

In applying this model in the Romanian context, we shall use information from transcripts of the trials of 24 members of the Political Executive Committee Permanent Bureau (1991) and the historical accounts written by "involved spectators" (such as D. Popescu and P. Niculescu-Mizil, members of the Polexco; S. Curticeanu, former chief of the Central Committee chancellery office; and C. Mitea, former head of the press section of the Central Committee). According to these sources, the antecedents to the *groupthink* effect lay in the responsibilities of the decision-making group and the working relationships established by Ceauşescu and his wife, who monopolised the decision-making process, as well as in the principle of rotation of senior officials, which meant that the dictator and his wife moved officials to different posts at very short intervals.

The characteristics of the decision-making process within the Polexco were echoed throughout the lower levels of decision-making (the party's departmental committees, which liaised with Ceauşescu through weekly teleconferences, and the local and municipal committees and grassroots organisations). The principle of unanimity imposed on Romanian political life following the establishment of the personality cult, the procedures governing the selection and promotion of party activists and the election of the leader by the delegates to the party congress on a mandate from local political organisations confirming him in the post, all represent a strong desire for consensus, to the point where, in Romania, individual dissenters were unable to unite around a common rallying-point. This situation was, in some ways, analogous to that in Bulgaria (although there were attempts at reform in the latter), where the Church remained completely subservient to the ruling party. Romanians expressed their discontent by means of what became known as "kitchen-sink confidences" (Iakovlev and Marcou, 1999).

The account given by the former chief of the Central Committee's chancellery office gave details of relations within the inner circle of power (Curticeanu, 2000). Thus, the members of the Polexco were appointed directly by Ceauşescu and his wife. The list of Polexco members, which was not read out until the eve of the party congress (for approval by the participants), was a surprise even to those appointed. The reports and materials, the discussion and approval of which formed the basis for the members' appointment, were made available to them inside the conference hall. After a speech outlining the topics, endorsed by Ceauşescu, the leader concluded with phrases of the kind: "I have no doubt that you will join me in approving …". The report was then presented to the party congress and approved by the members of the Polexco, who had no prior knowledge of its contents ("You would be far more bored if you had heard it before entering the hall" reasoned Ceauşescu).

The omnipotence of the ideology embodied in the leader made it impossible for information or influences from outside the country to reach the other members of the group. The "technical control" exercised by the secret police over those involved in decision-making meant that, as the events of December 1989 unfolded, the members of the Polexco were wholly reliant on Ceauşescu for their information. Meetings of the decision-making group, according to all the testimonies, were extraordinarily tense affairs. Excessive reliance on the ideological dictates of the group leader – an essential prerequisite for consensus within the decision-making group – produced the situation recorded in the transcript of the Polexco meeting of 17 December 1989.

Following the distorted version of the events in Timişoara delivered by Ceauşescu (the actions, he claimed, had been planned jointly by East and West in a bid to destroy socialism), he and his wife addressed those in positions of responsibility within the security forces, effectively issuing them with orders, military-style. Finally, the group leader decided:

> "We will fight on to the last man; we must approve this move, because independence and sovereignty are won and upheld through fighting, and because if we had not acted as we did in 1968, they would have invaded us as they did Czechoslovakia when the Russians and Bulgarians were at the border."

The tumultuous events that followed Ceauşescu's speech on the balcony (delivered in a state of confusion as to the sequence and cause of the events unfolding, the spread of the uprising, the collapse of the regime after Ceauşescu and his wife had fled) represent the failure caused by *groupthink*, which resulted in there being no alternative government. The situation had a variety of causes, among them the "Romanian Tele-revolution" and the "terrorist affair".

The subsequent appraisal of the alternatives by the former members of the Polexco bore out the distorted manner in which the initial difficulties were assessed, after the correct decision had become clear. Some of those involved in the decision blamed themselves afterwards for having overlooked essential and patently obvious facts. These guilt feelings, moreover, produced neuroses in the form of depression or compensating behaviour. Hence, following the trial of former members of the Polexco, some died or committed suicide (N. Giosan, I. Totu); others wrote their memoirs, chiefly in an attempt to justify the decisions taken by the group of which they were members (D. Popescu, P. Niculescu-Mizil, S. Curticeanu).

## Conclusions

The above considerations represent an overview of a larger project currently in progress. We have confined ourselves here to setting out the motives for adopting a multi-disciplinary approach to this episode in contemporary history, presenting the methodology and summarising one chapter, thus proving the value of employing social psychology theories in areas that cannot be analysed solely by recourse to conventional historiography. Without doubt, extending the analysis to encompass the changes that have occurred in social memory and the persistence of representations, stereotypes and clichés stemming from half a century of communist rule, is a long-term and labour-intensive project; it should prove valuable to researchers and, by extension, to historians concerned with the recent past and its effects on both the present and the future of the former communist countries of Europe.

## Bibliography

Bardin, L., *L'Analyse de contenu*, PUF, Paris, 1993.

Betea, L., *Psihologie politică: Individ, lider, mulțime în regimul comunist*, Polirom, Iași, 2001.

Curticeanu, S., *Mărturia unei istorii trăite*, Edit. Albatros, Bucharest, 2000.

Dahrendorf, R., *Reflecții asupra revoluției din Europa*, Edit. Humanitas, Bucharest, 1990, 1993.

De Montbrial, T., *Memoria timpului prezent*, Polirom, Iași, 1995, 1996.

Furet, F., *La Révolution en débat*, Gallimard, Paris, 1999.

Furet, F., *Atelierul istorie*, Corint, Bucharest, 1982, 2002.

Gabanyi, A.U., *Revoluția neterminată,* Edit. Fundației Culturale Române, Bucharest, 1999.

Halbwachs, M., *La Mémoire collective*, PUF, Paris, 1950.

Henry, P., and Moscovici, S., "Problèmes de l'analyse de contenu" in *Langage*, 1968.

Iakovlev, A., and Marcou, L., *Ce que nous voulons faire de l'Union soviétique*, Editions du Seuil, Paris, 1999.

Ilut, P., *Bordarea calitativă a socio-umanului,* Polirom, Iași, 1997.

Janis, I., and Mann, L., *Decision making: A psychological analysis of conflict, choice and commitment*, Free Press, New York, 1977.

Karnoouh, C., *Comunism, postcomunism și modernitate târzie*, Polirom, Iași, 2000.

Markova, I., *Dialogistica și reprezentările sociale*, Polirom, Iași, 2004.

Mitea, C., "Jurnalul unui fost", in *Revista Totuși Iubirea*, 1991, No. 25 (June).

Moscovici, S., *La Psychanalyse, son image et son public*, PUF, Paris, 1976.

Mucchielli, A., *Dicționar al metodelor calitative în științele umane și sociale*, Polirom, Iași, 1996, 2002.

Neculau, A., and Constantin, T., "Memoria socială", in *Manual de psihologie socială*, Polirom, Iași, 2003.

Niculescu-Mizil, P., *O istorie trăită*, Edit. Enciclopedică, Bucharest, 1997.

Popescu, D., *Am fost și cioplitor de himere*, Edit. Expres, Bucharest, 1994.

Soulet, J.F., *Istoria imediată*, Corint, Bucharest, 1994, 2000.

Yin, R.K., *Case study research*, Sage Publications, Thousand Oaks, CA, 1989.

Stenographic transcript of the meeting of the Political Executive Committee of the PCR Central Committee held on 17 December 1989, in M. Bunea, *Praf în ochi, Procesul celor 24-1-2*, Edit. Scripta, Bucharest, 1991.

# Chapter 32
# The response of the United States to the events of 1989

*Wolfgang Krieger*

Any reflection on this subject must begin with at least a brief sketch of America's global power structure which, in theory, gives Washington a great number of possible ways of responding to international crises. In practice, however, America's global reach makes things infinitely complicated. Each step must be considered, first, in the light of potential counter measures on the part of actual or potential opponents, second, with an eye to how each move might be interpreted by America's friends, and third, with reference to the escalation potential of each action.

It is all too easy to set in motion a series of responses that can be exploited by the opponent, misunderstood by friends and hard to reverse or even control. In that sense, America's global power structure is both an asset and a liability when it comes to finding an appropriate response to an international crisis, particularly if that crisis – such as the one which afflicted the Soviet sphere of influence in 1989 – cannot be confined geographically and in which great powers have a big stake. (In addition to the Soviet Union, the hard-to-gauge People's Republic of China was continually on the minds of Washington's decision makers.)

Since the Second World War, the United States has maintained not only a number of critical military alliances, above all NATO and the alliance with Japan, but also a vast network of military bases. They encompass not only port facilities, airfields, ammunition depots, depots for fuel and other supplies, command posts, military housing and medical facilities – to name only the most obvious types – but also a multitude of technical facilities for communications and technical intelligence. Many of them date back to wartime use before 1945. Later on, the development of military and communications technologies added a host of new types of installations. Satellite relay stations are the most obvious example of those post-war technologies which, since the 1980s, have been referred to as RMA (revolution in military affairs). To move and to guide America's aircraft carrier groups and submarines, her espionage vessels, air forces and armies around the globe, this vast network of facilities is crucial. In other words, even if another power, say the European Union, had its own aircraft carriers, submarines, bomber fleets, mobile missile platforms, special forces and so on, those assets could not be deployed around the globe and would not be ready for action without a comparable infra-structure.

In Europe, between the early 1950s and 1990s, the United States maintained forces totalling about 320 000 men (later men and women) in uniform, with about 6 000 nuclear weapons in storage – to name only those two average figures (which, of course, varied somewhat from year to year). Incidentally, there would have been no way to maintain those forces stationed overseas, most in the middle of the national territories of allied nations (some 240 000 in western Germany alone), without the existence of a political, economic and cultural network which paralleled this military structure.

All around Western Europe, those forces were stationed in arrangements which the Norwegian historian, Geir Lundestad, has termed "empire by invitation". What he means by this term is that the host nations (by and large) accepted those US force deployments because they believed them to be in the interest of their national security. At the same time, however, there was a constant need to re-invent those friendships. The ups and downs of Soviet-American relations, the threat of nuclear war, the some-times "imperial" behaviour shown by the United States in Europe and the rest of the world produced uncounted NATO crises, anti-American impulses, and "Yankee go home" street demonstrations.

To explain why this "empire by invitation" lasted so long, why it outlasted so many crises, is beyond the scope of this paper. It must suffice to point out that military policy alone, even the brutal threat posed by Soviet foreign policy, was not enough to keep NATO from disintegrating. There was a web of parallel relationships which kept things stable. Beyond the credits and goods that flowed to Western Europe through the Marshall plan, secret funds went to a long list of labour unions, political parties, civic organisations and individual anti-communist leaders to support their political struggles. The CIA covert support for the April 1948 Italian elections was only one of the more prominent examples at the time, with many lesser-known interventions running in parallel elsewhere. Support for Poland's Solidarność during the 1980s was perhaps the last major example of such secret, non-violent aid. American weapons shipments to the Mujahedin, who fought the Soviet occupation of Afghanistan, were organised by the CIA at about the same time. Outside Europe, particularly in South America, the USA sometimes even gave secret aid to support the activities of private US companies in those markets.

Based on a wide network of US investment and business relations established well before the war, the Americans greatly intensified their foreign business activities soon after 1945. During the 1960s, so much US private investment went to Europe that a prominent French liberal journalist published a book called *Le défi américain* (The American challenge). It became an instant best-seller. Obviously, it struck a chord in western European publics. Was US business becoming a danger to the sovereignty of smaller and even middle-sized industrial countries?

Different from its main rivals, the USA sent a powerful cultural message around the globe. The "American way of life" (whatever its exact meaning) became a catchphrase. Millions of people around Europe wished to hear American jazz and pop music. They wore denim trousers, watched cowboy movies and admired American wealth and lifestyle, or perhaps what they thought they knew about it. By contrast, few people wished to adopt a Soviet way of life or listened to Russian folk music – few people other than Russians. There were no Soviet consumer products to kindle people's fantasies. By the 1970s at the latest, Soviet-style "socialism" had become thoroughly discredited. Economic stagnation became ever more visible, while the electronic media carried Western lifestyles into more and more homes in Eastern Europe and even in the Soviet Union.

It is a matter of debate whether the global role played by the United States can properly be called "imperial" or "hegemonic". There can be no doubt that Washington assumed global leadership, essentially in what was understood to be a global struggle between freedom and totalitarian dictatorship, or between liberal democracy and Soviet-style communism. All local and regional conflicts were understood to belong in this context as soon as communist or, at any rate, Moscow-friendly groups were involved in them. When the Sino-Soviet break-up occurred in the late 1950s, China was taken to be a second challenge essentially of a similar nature.

At the same time, however, successive American administrations made it clear that they would pursue a policy of peaceful coexistence with the Soviets, and later with the Chinese. In determining America's grand strategy vis-à-vis Soviet communism, US presidents Truman and Eisenhower categorically ruled out any thought of a pre-emptive attack. Such ideas were discussed by a minority of military experts at a time when the Soviets had begun their nuclear weapons programme but had not yet reached a capability that would allow them to launch a direct nuclear attack on US territory. The two concepts that largely characterised US policy were "containment" and "nuclear deterrence". The former was in essence a tacit guarantee that the Soviets could maintain their territorial gains and their vastly extended zone of influence gained by the end of the Second World War. (In a sense, it could be called a variation on the concept of appeasement carried over from the 1930s.) The latter was shaped into a US hegemonic concept because, in the Western camp, the US alone had the resources to build up a truly global system of nuclear deterrence (backed up by massive conventional deterrence and intervention forces). From 1961 onwards, Washington and Moscow (supported by Britain, but opposed by France and China) arrived at a concept of nuclear non-proliferation, which would make sure that the "great game" of nuclear deterrence was to have only two major players, namely those two superpowers (as they were henceforth called).

To be sure, this global arrangement did not work smoothly. It generated a huge amount of wasteful spending on armaments. It could never completely ensure that war would not happen either as a result of misjudgment or misunderstanding, or due to reckless leadership on the part of the two superpowers. Both in Washington and in Moscow, there was a deep-seated fear that their respective allies or even their distant satellites and clients would trick the superpowers into a direct confrontation. Thus, there developed a certain shared sensitivity, which led each side to concentrate the essential decision-making functions in the two metropolitan centres. At the same time, there was in each of the two centres a keen readiness to take advantage of any weaknesses shown by the other side and to improve one's own position either quietly or overtly. The many crises in the Far East, in the Middle East and in Africa, were believed by both sides to offer such opportunities.

## US-Soviet relations from Reagan to Bush

On the eve of the international revolutions of 1989, the United States and the Soviet Union were locked into a number of conflicts, which largely determined the political atmosphere at the time. After the end of the American war in Vietnam, in 1973-75, the collapse of the Portuguese empire in 1974 afforded the Soviets a number of opportunities to expand their influence in southern Africa. From the former Portuguese colonies of Angola and Mozambique, the Kremlin sought to build an African empire of its own from which pressure could be exerted on South Africa and on the oil-rich Arab world. By gaining control of Africa's mineral wealth, Moscow would gain enormous economic leverage to be directed against western Europe and Japan, which crucially depended on Middle Eastern oil shipments. Even the United States would have sorely felt the consequences of such a newly-gained Soviet influence on key world commodities.

In Central America, Nicaragua and El Salvador were two key targets of Soviet subversion. In collaboration with Fidel Castro's Cuba, the Soviets sought to gain a foothold on the American continent. Cuban and East German military forces were deployed in the civil wars in southern Africa. The Soviet leader, Leonid Brezhnev, seemed to have found an indirect strategy which might undermine America's global strength while avoiding war between the superpowers. Another part of his strategy was to cultivate left-wing sympathies around western Europe and beyond, both for his policy of "anti-colonialism" in the third world and for Moscow's "responsible" approach to nuclear deterrence in contrast with America's ideological and techno-logical "recklessness". President Jimmy Carter's human rights policy met with little sympathy among Western neo-Marxists, who had largely hegemonised intellectual discourses since the 1968 student revolts. The political struggle over the deployment of medium-range nuclear missiles in Europe (the INF crisis) dealt a heavy blow to NATO even though, in plain military terms, it was largely a storm in a teacup.

But then the Soviets went a step too far when, in December 1979, they sent massive forces into Afghanistan. It was the first such invasion on the part of the Red Army since 1945. Around the same time, the slowly escalating political struggle between the Warsaw regime and the independent Solidarność labour union forced Moscow into an agonising reappraisal of its policy in Eastern Europe. How should the Kremlin respond to such an unarmed but clearly anti-communist movement? Should it risk civil war and a major Soviet military operation, possibly much bloodier than the events in Hungary in the autumn of 1956? Or should it try to preserve the advantages the Soviet bloc had gained from the 1975 Helsinki agreement, which had done so much to convince Western publics of the inherently peaceful and benign qualities of Soviet power?

By postponing a definitive answer to the Polish issue, the Kremlin inadvertently encouraged dissident forces all across the Soviet empire. While none of their activists believed that Soviet power was inherently benign, they saw more and more evidence that Soviet policy had become locked into a policy dilemma. At a time when Brezhnev had become senile, and then was followed by two other senile leaders (Andropov and Chernenko), no bold decisions could be expected, even though the military adventure in Afghanistan had turned into a disaster and also despite the growing challenge posed by the "Helsinki groups" which had sprung up everywhere, claiming to have certain civil rights which had been publicly declared and signed by their governments in the Finnish capital.

While the Kremlin was virtually without an effective leadership during the early 1980s, two fiercely anti-communist leaders came into office in London and Washington. One was the British Prime Minister, Margaret Thatcher, who was determined to impose a thorough programme of economic and political reforms to save Britain from economic stagnation. The other was the US President, Ronald Reagan, essentially a moderate Republican in his political convictions but a radical in the sense that he was prepared to challenge the basic assumptions from which the United States had conducted its domestic and foreign policies since it had lost the war in Vietnam. Both leaders were prepared to provide massive weapons shipments to local forces opposing Soviet-sponsored movements around the third world. In Afghanistan, they even supplied advanced weapons, most famously those man-held Stinger anti-aircraft missiles which were used not only against Moscow's proxies but directly against Soviet soldiers and Soviet aircraft. They spoke out openly in support of the dissident forces active within the Soviet camp. (Most certainly, they provided direct funding and other support to those groups.) In March 1983, President Reagan even went so far as to call into question the wisdom of "mutually assured destruction", the strategic arrangement dating back to 1972 (ABC Treaty) by which the two superpowers foreswore the construction of missile defence systems, believing that mutual vulnerability was the key to deterrence and hence to world peace. Now Reagan proposed a massive research programme from which it was hoped that a space-based missile defence system would emerge. Remarkably, Reagan even offered to share the know-how of such a system with the Soviets once it was deployed by the Americans.

The Afghanistan quagmire and the new message of political confrontation from London and Washington shook the Kremlin leadership to its foundations. The Soviet economy was performing poorly. Soviet technology was hopelessly behind in those computer technologies which were crucial to the new developments in armament and global communications. A consensus began to form that a bold new leadership with fresh ideas was needed if Soviet power was to survive. In April 1985, such a new leadership was formed under Mikhail Gorbachev, who designed new policies labelled glasnost and perestroika. In order to gain the support of the Soviet people, Gorbachev called for more open debate on the shortcomings of the Soviet economy and the Soviet state apparatus which, in his view, was in need of a thorough overhaul. However, such reforms could only be financed if Soviet military expenditure was reduced from its excessive levels, around 20% (or more?) of GNP. Quite obviously, such a reorientation required a new strategic bargain with the West. The new Kremlin leadership hoped that a new relationship would provide better access to Western capital markets and technologies.

To the surprise of many in the West, Gorbachev got on remarkably well with Thatcher and Reagan. Other Western governments had to scramble for a place at the new negotiating table, where discussions on arms limitations took a radically new direction. Most dramatically, in the 1987 Washington Treaty, the Soviet Union agreed to destroy all its most advanced medium-range SS-20 missiles and allowed, for the first time, the implementation of the treaty being controlled by on-site inspection.

No doubt, East-West relations promised to undergo fundamental changes. But in what direction? What were Gorbachev's long-range goals? Was he essentially a younger Brezhnev with a more daring agenda or was he about to dismantle the repressive Soviet system? If the latter was his intention, what would the Soviet Union look like after a few years of reform? What would be the implications for the satellite states? And in what direction would Soviet foreign policy eventually develop?

It seems that the majority of professional diplomats and policy-makers believed in the "younger Brezhnev" hypothesis. They counselled the Western powers to adopt a friendly but business-like approach of "wait and see". President George H.W. Bush, who took office in January 1989, was surrounded by advisers who were sceptical of the "Gorbachev factor", some of them more so than others. Significantly, Bush himself was quite willing to take an optimistic approach but he wished to be careful. No doubt, he was also intimidated by the right wing of his Republican Party, which considered Bush a closet-liberal.

As it happened, Bush had less time to construct a programme than he wished. This was due to Gorbachev's fast-growing popularity among Western publics and, even more significantly, among those in Eastern Europe who hoped to break free from the old Soviet system. While the Soviet leader was well on his way to becoming a political folk hero, the Bush team stuck to traditional ideas on arms reductions. Bush himself hoped to present what he termed a "bold" set of proposals. But he did not feel comfortable with the enthusiasm created by Gorbachev. He did not quite see how sweeping reforms could be brought about without risking another failure along the lines of the 1968 Prague Spring, which had ended in ever more repression. If a similar reform movement were to be launched and were then to collapse – this time not in a small satellite country but in the Soviet motherland! – the result would be much more destabilising than in 1968. Inevitably, the West would watch helplessly. The Helsinki groups, who undoubtedly expected Western support, would have had to be abandoned because such help could not possibly be granted.

After weeks of deliberations, the Bush concept took shape. Its focal point was to test the true value of Gorbachev's intentions on two key issues: arms control and Soviet policy in Eastern Europe, particularly towards Poland and Hungary. In those two countries, the democratic movements had struggled hard and with some success. In December 1988, the Hungarian Government had announced a plan to legalise non-communist parties and to introduce reform policies. In Poland, the communist government had begun to negotiate with the Solidarność leadership.

Bush defined two principal goals. The first was a reduction of conventional forces. This would lessen the pressure the Soviets could exert on their European satellites. The second goal was to reward those communist states that were introducing truly democratic reforms. This was a significant change from previous Western practice, which had favoured states which dissented somewhat from Moscow's foreign policy line while maintaining repressive regimes towards their own populations. Nicolae Ceaușescu's Romanian regime was a particularly bad example of that older approach.

Bush outlined his strategy in a series of four speeches in April and May 1989. He praised Poland's readiness to hold at least semi-democratic elections, and he promised US loans as well as some trade liberalisation. "Moving beyond containment" was one of his catch phrases; challenging the Soviets to "earn" their way to a new relationship with the United States was another. To bring about dramatic changes in East-West security relations, the Soviet Union would have to abandon its offensive military strategy and make the Warsaw Pact into a defensive alliance such as NATO.

The response among America's NATO allies was rather mixed. Many opinion leaders considered the Bush proposals to be founded on "old thinking". His call for modernising NATO's military forces, particularly its arsenal of nuclear-tipped short-range missiles (Lance modernisation), met with strong resistance on the part of the conservative-liberal government in Bonn where the foreign minister, Hans-Dietrich Genscher, refused outright to go along with it. Differing from many other decision-makers, Genscher had come to the conclusion that Gorbachev's intentions were honest and should be given a chance. Quite obviously, Genscher was keenly aware of Gorbachev's popularity. Even Chancellor Helmut Kohl, who had shown great courage in the political battle for INF deployments in the early 1980s, did not have the stomach to fight for more modern missile systems. By contrast, Margaret Thatcher insisted on modernisation, quite obviously in an effort to make life difficult for Germany, where old dreams of a special relationship with Moscow, even the rebirth of a unified Germany, were becoming increasingly popular, both among conservatives and among left wing socialists. (The latter were hoping that Moscow would demand Germany's withdrawal from NATO in exchange. This would free the Germans from the "yoke of Capitalist America".)

At the NATO summit in late May 1989, Bush got himself into a difficult position. Many in the alliance preferred Gorbachev's proposals to those coming from Washington. Bush decided to go to "the lion's den" – West Germany – in order to show people that he was not a narrow-minded, defence-orientated cold warrior. In various speeches during his journey, he called for an end to the division of Germany, "a Europe whole and free". He offered Germany a special position as a "partner in leadership" (with the United States), and he indicated his support for German unity provided international stability could be maintained.

A few days later, on 3-4 June, China saw the "massacre of Tiananmen". Armed forces were ordered to move against a large crowd of students and others who had assembled on Beijing's largest square to demand reforms and an end to corruption within the communist regime. For two reasons, this was an event with truly global ramifications: the first concerned the future of China's own reform movement. The second was about the impact such a repressive step would have on the fragile reform agendas in other communist states.

Earlier in the 1980s, China had embarked on its own particular path to reform. The concept of Deng Xiaoping, the leading spirit behind all this, demanded a gradual transition to a market economy, but did not provide for democratisation at the political level. The powers of the Chinese communist party would not be reduced, though some of its corrupt leaders were removed from office or even put on trial. Reformist zealots within the party would be dealt with quite brutally.

It was against this stubborn refusal to consider political reforms that students and others began to protest in April 1989. A protest movement quickly developed, which attracted widespread sympathies among younger party officials. Their demands were even echoed within the military. The government's initial response was cautious. Negotiations took place between officials and protest leaders in order to find a peaceful solution. During a visit by Gorbachev in mid-May, some of his public appearances were disturbed. Some events even had to be cancelled. Now, the party leadership felt a need to assert its authority. A number of loyal military units were called to Beijing to put down this growing peaceful revolt. It was a bloody affair, which met with outrage around the world. But the Chinese communist leadership offered no apologies. Quite obviously, this step was taken with the explicit consent of Deng Xiaoping.

How was the Bush administration to react to this step? President Bush, who had once been US ambassador to Beijing, was strongly committed to the further development of US-Chinese relations. He had paid a short visit in February, following the funeral of Emperor Hirohito of Japan. China was thought to be on the way to becoming a great power, both in economic and military terms. It was seen as a vast and rapidly developing market, which offered a wealth of opportunities to America. And it was considered as something like an insurance policy in case of a massive reversal in the Soviet Union. Although Bush had to concede to the mood in Congress and punish China for its barbarous act, he tried to keep communications open. Indeed, he sent his national security adviser, Brent Scowcroft, on a secret mission to Beijing in order to show his deep interest in smoothing things out quickly. The Chinese leaders, who met Scowcroft, told him in no uncertain terms that they were deeply sceptical of Gorbachev's reform policies and that they would stick to their own agenda. Economic reforms would have to come first, with political reforms to follow at a much later stage.

Were the events of Tiananmen a model for dealing with the democratic movement? This question was hotly debated around the world. Significantly, Gorbachev gave the Chinese leadership his support, even publicly. His hardline colleagues in eastern Europe did the same. In East Germany, the use of the military against the protesters was greeted particularly warmly. The head of state, Erich Honecker, and his intelligence chief, Erich Mielke, both highly critical of Gorbachev's reform policies, were particularly satisfied. They had even begun to ban official publications from Moscow in which Gorbachev's reforms were praised. East Berlin's official party line was that reforms were unnecessary in their country. Socialism was doing very well, thank you.

The East German Government had come under strong pressure as a result of Soviet reform policies. Various reform groups were demanding not only an end to the power monopoly of the communist party but a return to the German nation-state, unification with the West German state. Thousands applied for emigration visas. Their numbers increased dramatically when, on 2 May, the barbed wire fence between Austria and Hungary was dismantled in a televised ceremony led by the two foreign ministers.

For a long time, the vast majority of East Germans had made it a habit to watch West German television where they could see the glaring differences in levels of consumer spending and lifestyles. Now, there was something unique to watch on television: the top Soviet leader, with the popular appeal of a star, who was on tour in West Germany, France and before the Council of Europe during June and July. Everywhere, he and his reform programme were met with increasing enthusiasm. The old accolade "learning from the Soviet Union is learning to be victorious" took on an entirely new meaning.

On 10 July, President Bush visited Poland, had dinner with Solidarność leader, Lech Wałęsa, in his modest Gdańsk home, spoke in the national parliament *(Sejm)* and privately worked to persuade the communist leader, General Jaruzelski, to put his name forward in the Polish presidential elections. The next day, Bush arrived in Hungary, where he spoke at Budapest's Karl Marx University. Just three weeks before, on 16 June, a crowd of 250 000 had attended the re-burial of Imre Nagy, the tragic reform leader of 1956. In both countries, hopes were flying sky-high that, this time, the communist shackles would come off for good.

To make sure that Gorbachev did not have all the attention in this "springtime of nations" – as the British historian, Michael Howard, termed it – Bush attended the celebrations in Paris of the 200th anniversary of the French Revolution on Bastille Day (14 July). His strategy was to meet Gorbachev only after Washington had a coherent policy in place, a policy supported by his key allies. Planning was under way for a summit meeting, possibly to be held in Malta, in late November. For some obscure reason, the summit planning anticipated that the meeting would be held off the coast of Malta on the two warships used by the two leaders for the trip. This turned out to be a disaster, both because poor weather made it difficult to get from one vessel to the other and because the unusual meeting place seemed to signal that there was something particularly awkward about this meeting. But in fact, Bush and Gorbachev had already met and were eager to arrive at a positive summit outcome.

What neither of them could anticipate was the extent to which the situation in eastern Europe would become even more dramatic just before the scheduled meeting of the two leaders.

On 7 October, the Soviet leader visited East Berlin to help celebrate the 40th anniversary of the second German state. The organised festivities turned into a big embarrassment for the East German leadership as the crowds shouted "Gorby, Gorby" in an obvious effort to show their enthusiasm for Gorbachev's reform agenda. By the same token, they expressed their deep dissatisfaction with their own leaders, who still refused to adopt any part of the perestroika programme. But how could the rulers of a communist satellite prevent their people from cheering the chief representative of the Soviet Union? Conceived by Erich Honecker as a great triumph in his political life, the celebrations quickly turned into deep embarrassment. No display of triumphalism could make people forget that, all through the spring and summer of 1989, thousands of East German citizens had packed their bags and left their home country. Some were finally granted exit visas by the authorities. Others pretended to go on holiday in one of the neighbouring "socialist" countries, where they sought refuge in West German embassies. All this was happening under the close scrutiny of Western television cameras and televised every night on the main television channels in West Germany, which could be watched in most East German homes.

Was there a way out for the East German regime? Would the Soviet Union provide support for police and military measures to be brought against the dissident movement? This was not certain, but the East German leadership certainly tried to find a way. On 18 October, Honecker was forced to step down. A younger set of leaders was ready to take over and introduce some new policies, including a less restrictive emigration regime. They hoped to win the support of Moscow, perhaps even some backing in other Western capitals. After all, many around Europe more or less secretly favoured a continued division of Germany.

While President Bush openly preferred German unification, he was told in no uncertain terms by Prime Minister Margaret Thatcher that she did not like what she considered a dramatic change in European politics. President Mitterrand of France was undecided. He did not wish to put Franco-German friendship at risk, but neither was he keen to see a much larger Germany.

Had East Germany been the only Soviet bloc country in crisis, the old ways of dealing with the German question might have prevailed. More Western money might have been pumped into the East German economy in return for more political concessions, while the four powers might have preserved their leverage on the Bonn republic. But the 1989 revolution was transnational in character and directed against Soviet-style socialism in all forms. It was indeed a return of central and eastern Europe's national identities. German unity could, therefore, not be kept off the agenda of that revolution, particularly if the East Germans demanded it and if the Soviets tolerated it. Both conditions were clearly met when, in the autumn of 1989, East Germans began to take to the streets to conduct their own "peaceful revolution" with the Monday demonstrations in Leipzig taking the lead, and when the Kremlin gave orders that no armed counter-measures could be taken on the part of the East German Government. In November 1989, with the "velvet revolution" in Czechoslovakia, East Germany became completely surrounded by non-communist governments.

## Conclusion

By the end of the year, it was still far from clear how these anti-bolshevik revolutions would end. President Bush and his administration had still not achieved a completely trusting relationship with Gorbachev's Kremlin, and Central America was still a divisive issue between the two. The Malta Summit had been successful in terms of "atmosphere" but had not produced any tangible results. Bush was eager to preserve his good relations with the Chinese leadership in Beijing. Indeed, he secretly briefed them about all aspects of the Malta Summit. But none of this amounted to a satisfactory answer to the European revolutions. It was still far from clear how the international institutions, above all NATO, the Warsaw Pact, the European Community (later the European Union) and Comecon were to be transformed to accommodate the new post-communist governments in Europe. The anticipated withdrawal of Soviet and American military forces was to be considered in the light of a newly emerging European security architecture.

In other words, most of the national and international issues were unresolved at the end of 1989. For the Bush administration, the most difficult question was to find out if President Gorbachev had a plan of how to guide the Soviet Union through all those revolutionary changes. What were "his real intentions"? How could Washington find out about them?

The year 1989 had opened up unprecedented questions about the political future of Europe and, more widely, about international relations at the global level. But there were few agreed and workable answers to those questions. The people of central and eastern Europe had made it quite clear what sort of public life they rejected and what their demands were with respect to the future. Some answers had been given at the national level or were at least in the process of being worked out. But the overall shape of Europe's political and economic future remained painfully uncertain.

# Chapter 33
# The reunification of Germany

*Manfred Görtemaker*

More than 15 years have elapsed since the dramatic scenes of 1989, when history was daily overtaken by events. Much research has been done to clear the picture and come up with explanations. We have gained access to archives. We have been able to interview policy makers and eyewitnesses in large numbers. We have read their personal accounts. And we have founded research institutes like the *Zentrum für Zeithistorische Forschung* in Potsdam, which deals almost exclusively with the history of the recent past, sometimes with surprising results. For instance, it was maintained quite seriously that the GDR was not a dictatorship, but merely a *durchherrschte Gesellschaft*, a "thoroughly-governed society", and that in the GDR it was Stalinism that failed, not Socialism.

It is fair to say, however, that before 1989 no one, particularly in the West, was prepared for the collapse of the GDR, and many in the West as well as in the East were unhappy to see it come. This was particularly true in France, where there was often paranoia about a reunified Germany. But uneasiness was widespread – not least in Britain where Prime Minister Margaret Thatcher would have preferred not to see German reunification at all, but, if she had to see it, she wanted to bring the process under some form of international control.

Even in Germany, most of the experts had it wrong. Only months before the collapse of the German Democratic Republic, they insisted that the question of Germany could no longer be one of reunification, but rather it had to be one of two states coming to terms with each other in the framework of East-West stability and European security. The editor of the weekly German newspaper *Die Zeit*, Theo Sommer, for instance, noted as late as in September 1989:

> "We are not an inch closer to reunification than a year ago, or five or ten years ago. [...] The issue of German unity is not hotter than ever. On the contrary: It stays on one of the rear cook-tops of world politics, and there is no fire under the pot." (*Die Zeit*, 29 September 1989)

It seems that only the Americans had genuinely come to accept the Federal Republic of Germany unreservedly as a responsible pillar of the democratic West and thus they welcomed German reunification as a fulfilment of post-war policies and a victory for the West in the Cold War with the Soviet Union. However, a senior French official noted in March 1990 that the American position was only due to the fact that "the

Americans are so bad at history and are so naive to believe a people like the Germans can change" (quoted from J.E. Mroz in Görtemaker, 1994, p. viii).

Thus important questions remain: Why did the collapse of the GDR come as a surprise to almost everyone? What made it happen so quickly? And what made it happen at all?

In this chapter, I will try to explain why the sudden reunification of Germany was not the result of carefully crafted policies in Bonn, but rather a side-effect of the collapse of Soviet-dominated communism in eastern Europe followed by a genuine uprising by the people of East Germany. I will argue that the revolution was made possible by the restrained policies of Mikhail Gorbachev and the actions of neighbouring Warsaw Pact states, particularly Poland and Hungary, and that the fast-breaking East German events of 1989 were not "Germanic" in nature but similar to those being expressed in other East European countries under Soviet domination at the time. And I will make the case, finally, that, if East Germany was steamrollered at all by the weight and power of Federal Chancellor Helmut Kohl, this happened after, not before, the liberation from communist rule.

## 1. East Germany, Eastern Europe, and the Soviet Union

The GDR came into being only within the framework of the Soviet empire in eastern Europe created after the Second World War. Without Soviet support, the GDR would not have been founded. Without Soviet backing, the GDR could not have survived. Throughout its 40 years of existence, the SED (Socialist Unity Party) regime never managed to gain legitimacy among most of its citizens. Even Markus Wolf admits in his memoirs that the regime had never been fully accepted by more than one-third of its people – and usually by much fewer than that (Wolf, 1991). And Wolf should know: he was the long-time head of the *Hauptverwaltung Aufklärung*, the espionage organisation of the GDR within Erich Mielke's Ministry for State Security. Until the Berlin Wall was built in 1961, a total of 2.7 million citizens had fled the country and were registered in West German refugee camps – about 14% of the GDR's population in 1949.

This is also the reason why the GDR was different from other East European countries and could not afford liberty or freedom from repression. Poland would remain Poland, and Hungary would remain Hungary, even without the communist regime. But, without Soviet-guaranteed communism in East Germany, the GDR was almost certain to merge with the prosperous dominant West and would cease to exist as a state. During the Cold War, Soviet backing was never put in question. When tensions relaxed and Willy Brandt embarked upon his "new *Ostpolitik*" at the end of the 1960s, however, the GDR faced the dilemma of weighing desirable international recognition and co-operation against the danger of allowing the West to undermine its internal cohesion by the so-called "exchange of people, information and ideas" (Nawrocki,

1985). Thus the policy of *détente*, not the Cold War, posed the first serious threat to the existence of the GDR.

From a Western point of view, the East German attempts to contain the unwanted side-effects of *détente* through a policy of demarcation and the strengthening of state security constituted a violation of the spirit of co-operation, as for the West the increase in personal contacts and the special nature of intra-German relations were major assets, not flaws, of the *détente* process. Willy Brandt in particular had made great efforts to defend his policy as a means of bridging, rather than widening or deepening, the gap between East and West (Brandt, 1969). His policy was designed to open new possibilities for "change through rapprochement," as Egon Bahr had stated in July 1963 at the Evangelical Academy in Tutzing, underlining the policy's dynamic, rather than static, aspects (Bahr, 1988, pp. 325-30). The same view had been expressed by another architect of the new *Ostpolitik*, Peter Bender, who called for "offensive *détente*" in the title of a book published in 1964 (Bender, 1964).

The question now was whether the dynamic forces of the policy would prevail, leading even to a democratic revolution in the GDR and some form of reunification, or whether the East German leadership would be able to contain the unwelcome destabilising effects of *détente* and transform it into a vehicle for international recognition with domestic prosperity and acceptance. The development of *Ostpolitik*, *détente* and intra-German relations, during the 1970s and into the 1980s, would provide an answer to these questions.

In the early 1970s, the GDR leadership seemed confident that the potentially dangerous implications of accepting the terms of West German *Ostpolitik* could be kept under control. The Soviet government under General Secretary Leonid Brezhnev provided unwavering support, and the benefits of international recognition and economic co-operation with the West were too important to be missed. Yet there were early signs of increasing social instability towards the end of the decade and in the early 1980s, which found expression in several forms: the expulsion of GDR citizens, notably intellectuals and artists; the formation of grassroots opposition, beginning with the peace movement *Schwerter zu Pflugscharen* and environmental groups, later focusing around the East German Protestant Church; and the growing number of people asking for exit visas or entering Western embassies to obtain permission to leave the country. The most prominent example was Ingrid Berg, a niece of GDR Minister President Willi Stoph; on 24 February 1984, she fled to the West German Embassy in Prague, where 14 other East Germans had already asked for asylum. In October of the same year, the embassy even had to be temporarily closed when more than 100 GDR citizens sought refuge there. Similar incidents were reported from Bucharest, Budapest and Warsaw (Martin, 1986, pp. 55-7).

One of the reasons why so many East Germans were desperately trying to leave the GDR was because they had lost all hope of reform in the foreseeable future. According to a survey by the Munich-based communications research institute Infratest and the University of Wuppertal among 2 000 emigrants *(Aussiedler)* from the GDR, the reasons for which they had decided to leave East Germany were "a lack of freedom of opinion", "political repression" or "limited possibilities for travelling". Economic motives had apparently played only a minor role in their decision to emigrate, though the motivation was generally a mix of several factors (Martin, ibid., p. 98).

The frustration of the East German population about the absence of reform in the GDR was multiplied by examples of change in Poland, Hungary and even the Soviet Union itself. The failure of the SED leadership to implement similar reforms contributed significantly to the loss of hope among GDR citizens that finally provided the basis for the East German revolution of 1989. Developments in Poland in particular had a destabilising effect on the GDR as early as summer 1980, when worker unrest escalated in the shipyards of Gdańsk and Gdynia, and the Solidarity movement presented a dangerous challenge to established communist party rule (Fils, 1988, pp. 43-54). The disturbances in neighbouring Poland shattered the confidence of the GDR leadership and caused many SED civil servants to wonder whether the sense of internal calm that had been imposed on the country during the 1970s could be maintained. Nationwide protest strikes and the organisation of independent labour unions by East German workers seemed unlikely but not impossible. On 30 October 1980, the SED Politburo decided to end visa-free traffic between the GDR and Poland, and to impose strict conditions on travel between the two states. Demarcation to the West was now complemented by delimitation to the East. Within the GDR, Minister of State Security Erich Mielke publicly vowed to increase the activity of security agencies throughout the country. This was necessary, he argued, to combat the "inhuman and anti-socialist plans and machinations" of the forces of counter-revolution (*Neues Deutschland*, 17 October 1980).

But unrest nevertheless spread, and the spill-over of reforms from Poland into other countries of eastern Europe became evident when a heated debate began in Hungary about János Kádár's "Goulash communism" and the fundamental goals of the country's economic and political future (Tökés, 1984, pp. 6-8) and when similar discussions started in Czechoslovakia – site of the "Prague Spring" of 1968 – as well. The real problems for the GDR began, however, and the situation changed drastically when Mikhail Gorbachev became the new general secretary of the Communist Party of the Soviet Union on 10 March 1985. Despite various changes in tactics and political emphasis under Stalin, Khrushchev, Brezhnev, Andropov and Chernenko, the USSR had been a bastion of Leninist orthodoxy. For the communist leadership of the GDR, the continuity in the nature of Soviet government had meant above all stability. The conservative Kremlin, afraid of revolutionary change and democratic upheaval, had ensured, through the sheer presence of Soviet troops as well as through the application of psychological pressure and physical force, the power of the SED as the ruling force in East Germany. The role of the 380 000 Soviet troops stationed in East Germany had been as much directed at keeping the SED in power as it had been at providing external security for the Warsaw Pact. As long as Soviet behaviour did not put in doubt the disciplinary function of the Red Army presence – which constantly implied the readiness to use force in order to crack down on opposition, as had been the case in 1953 in the GDR, 1956 in Hungary, and 1968 in Czechoslovakia – neither the stability of the GDR nor the existence of the Soviet empire in eastern Europe was seriously at stake.

All of this changed when Gorbachev assumed power, though not overnight. The new Soviet leader did not possess a master plan for reform beyond the catchwords of glasnost and perestroika. His approach was gradually to develop, as an ongoing process dependent on challenges that called for improvised action, a concept for the transformation of Soviet policy, economy and society. This was also true of Soviet-East European relations. Whereas Gorbachev seemed to have a general idea – that is, a vision – about urgently needed economic modernisation and political reform in the Soviet Union, as well as a general readiness for a return to *détente* and arms control with the West, his early policies toward the countries of eastern Europe remained contradictory. Professions of diversity alternated with demands for unity. Yet Gorbachev did little to discourage open debates about political and economic changes. In fact, by refraining from the application of traditional Soviet pressure, he actually encouraged such debates (see Gorbachev, 1987, pp. 73-8; Palmer, 1990, pp. 6-13).

In the GDR, Erich Honecker embraced Gorbachev's efforts for a renewal of East-West *détente*, but said there was no need for greater openness or economic reform in the GDR (McAdams, 1988, p. 51). Honecker later admitted that Gorbachev's new policy came as a great surprise to the East German communists. Unlike their East European counterparts, Honecker and the SED leadership reaffirmed their own "correct course", past and present, and apparently felt no need for reform at all. Honecker insisted that the GDR should not be forced to adopt the Soviet model, but should be allowed to develop socialism "in the colours of the GDR". SED Politburo member Kurt Hager, the party's chief ideologist, even stated in an interview with the West German magazine *Der Stern* that "a policy of imposing the Soviet system on Germany would be false; such a policy does not correspond to the current conditions in Germany". And, referring to Gorbachev's vision of a Common European Home, Hager added somewhat sarcastically: "If your neighbour chooses to re-wallpaper the walls of his house, would you feel obliged to do the same?" (*Der Stern*, 9 April 1987).

Thus the GDR's self-isolation progressed. After the demarcation against the West in the 1970s and the delimitation against Poland in 1980, the SED now even isolated itself from the Soviet Union. Yet the growing autism of the leadership contrasted sharply with the political development of the GDR population, especially the young people, for whom Gorbachev was not a threat but a symbol of hope. The SED's loss of contact with its own domestic sphere as well as with the surrounding world – including the Soviet Union –was soon to become a major factor in its demise, as an increasing number of East Germans began to ask what was left to hope for.

The impact of the "reformist encirclement" of the GDR by the ever-increasing moves toward greater democracy and pluralism in Eastern Europe can hardly be overstated. Encouraged by Gorbachev's own attempts at internal reform, these countries were free to move in entirely new directions when, during his visit to Prague in April 1987,

Gorbachev's repudiation of the Brezhnev Doctrine liberated them from the fear of Soviet intervention. Unlike Leonid Brezhnev in 1968, who had crushed the Prague uprising by military force, Gorbachev accepted the idea of diversity and declared:

> "We are far from calling on anyone to copy us. Every socialist country has its specific features, and the fraternal parties determine their political line with a view to the national conditions. [...] No one has the right to claim a special status in the socialist world. The independence of every party, its responsibility to its people, and its right to resolve problems of the country's development in a sovereign way – these are indisputable principles for us."
> (*Pravda*, 11 April 1987)

Renewed confrontation in April and May 1988 between striking steel mill and shipyard workers and the regime of General Jaruzelski in Poland, as well as the ousting of János Kádár in Hungary on 9 May 1988, soon indicated that Gorbachev's friendly words had been well received. By the end of 1988, it remained to be seen just how long the GDR would be able to remain an island of tranquil orthodoxy in a turbulent sea of shifting political, economic and ideological structures.

## 2. The implosion of the GDR

By early 1989, the nervousness of the GDR leadership about Gorbachev's policies of glasnost and perestroika, and about the reform attempts in Eastern Europe, was compounded by the problem of growing unrest in East Germany itself. When the situation exploded, or rather imploded, in 1989, however, the sudden outburst of dissatisfaction demonstrated with a vengeance that the former stability had been no more than superficial, and that the substance of GDR society had long been undergoing dramatic changes, which had been overlooked by Western experts and Eastern politicians alike.

Apart from the rather spectacular and highly visible protests and demonstrations of the peace movement, environmental groups and articulate intellectuals, there were at least two other manifestations of dissent within the GDR society which, in 1989, dealt a fatal blow to the SED regime: the question of *Übersiedler*, or re-settlers, and the increasing flow of refugees, as well as the intensifying mass demonstrations in a growing number of East German cities.

The refugee problem had been an issue for some time already. But when the new Hungarian government decided on 2 May 1989 to open its border with Austria, events got out of control. When the SED Politburo gathered two days later, on 4 May, for a regular meeting and Defence Minister Heinz Kessler passed on the "solid information" he had received from his military attaché in Budapest, that the Hungarian Government was reducing installations but that border checks would continue, the Politburo members felt relieved and went on with their session and a scheduled discussion about the outlook for the potash industry in the GDR (Cordt Schnibben, *Der Spiegel*, 16 April 1990, p. 73). Günter Schabowski, a member of both the SED Central Committee and the Politburo, who was present at the meeting on 4 May, later recalled that he had immediately had a hunch about the "explosive force" which the Hungarian dismantling of the Iron Curtain might have for the GDR, but that he, like the other members of the Politburo, had preferred to ignore his foreboding, since General Kessler's spirited explanation had provided a comfortable "alibi" (Schabowski, 1991, p. 221).

Yet 120 000 East Germans had already filed exit applications by the spring of 1989, and the opening of the Iron Curtain by Hungary on 2 May immediately encouraged others to do the same or, even worse in the view of the GDR Government, take a direct route via Hungary and Austria to the Federal Republic. On 19 August, some 660 GDR citizens used a "picnic" of the Pan-European Union near Sopron, on the border between Hungary and Austria, for their spectacular escape to the West, while the Hungarian border guards looked carefully the other way and did not intervene. In the SED Politburo, Günter Mittag accused the Hungarians of "treachery to socialism". A GDR deputy foreign minister, sent to Budapest as an SED representative "to slow things down", returned empty-handed. The Hungarians were no longer in control and, moreover, apparently no longer had any intention of regaining it. The démarche in Budapest only confirmed the worst. The emissary reported that the Hungarian foreign minister, Gyüla Horn, was the "driving force behind the development", while the military continued to be "loyal to the expectations of the GDR", but was no longer united (see Schabowski, 1991, p. 222; Schnibben, ibid., pp. 87-90).

Honecker, therefore, ordered his foreign minister, Oskar Fischer, to sound out Moscow about whether a Warsaw Pact meeting could be arranged to discipline the Hungarians. But Gorbachev declined. The time when a departure from the general line could be corrected by majority pressure was past. The GDR was alone. Within one month, the number of East Germans who had crossed from Hungary to Austria on their way to the Federal Republic climbed to more than 25 000. On 10 October, the Ministry for Intra-German Relations in Bonn reported that, during the first nine months of 1989, a total of 110 000 East Germans had resettled in the Federal Republic, with or without the consent of the GDR authorities. Some 32 500 GDR residents had registered in West German reception centres in September alone (*The Week in Germany*, Press Bulletin, 6 October 1989, p. 1).

Yet the exodus of GDR citizens to the West was just one catalyst of change. Public demonstrations against the regime were at least as powerful as the refugee movement in signalling ever-growing opposition to the SED regime. Demonstrations had been held regularly on the seventh day of every month since June, drawing attention to the manipulation of the local elections on 7 May. In addition, weekly Monday demonstrations began in Leipzig on Monday 4 September, after some 1 200 people gathered for peace prayers in the Nikolai Church and attempted to march to the Market Square in the city centre, chanting demands for freedom of travel and the right of assembly. By early October, the Monday demonstrations had become an established tradition and the focus of the opposition in the GDR. The number of participants had grown to about 5 000 on 25 September and as many as 20 000 on 2 October.

Encouraged by the success of the demonstrations and the lack of government response, a number of political organisations were formed: on 26 August, the SPD in the GDR; on 10 September, New Forum; on 12 September Democracy Now; and on 14 September Democratic Awakening (*Neue Chronik*, DDR, Vol. 1, pp. 18-40). The SED leadership now faced both a refugee problem and an increasingly powerful internal opposition fuelled by mass demonstrations and organised political groupings. The celebration of the 40th anniversary of the GDR on 7 October only underlined the need for substantial change when Gorbachev, who had been invited to attend the festivities, used the opportunity to declare at a meeting with the SED Politburo at Niederschönhausen Castle that time was running out and that "We have only one choice: to go forward resolutely". According to the verbatim protocol, Gorbachev stated:

> "I think it to be very important not to miss the right time and not to waste an opportunity. [...] If we stay behind, life will punish us. [...] This is a time of important decisions. They must be far-reaching decisions, they must be well thought through in order to bear rich fruit. Our experiences and the experiences of Poland and Hungary have convinced us: If the [communist] party does not respond to life, she will be condemned. We have only one choice: to go forward resolutely; otherwise we shall be beaten by life itself." (Berlin-Niederschönhausen, 7 October 1989, p. 9)

For the GDR, it was in fact already too late. The resignation of Erich Honecker as General Secretary of the SED on 16 October, and his replacement by Egon Krenz, did little to ease the tension. The refugee movement and the mass demonstrations continued. On 6 November, 500 000 people gathered in Leipzig, 60 000 in Halle, 50 000 in Karl-Marx-Stadt (Dresden), 10 000 in Cottbus and 25 000 in Schwerin. The following day, the entire government of the GDR stepped down and, on 8 November, the Politburo also resigned as a group. It was replaced by a new leadership that consisted basically of the anti-Honecker elements of the former regime, among them Egon Krenz, Hans Modrow and Günter Schabowski. Modrow was eventually appointed as the GDR's new prime minister.

Within this framework, the opening of the Berlin Wall on 9 November, however dramatic and symbolic, constituted no more than one of many steps in the decline and eventual collapse of the GDR (Krenz, 1990). But German reunification, which had so far been a distant prospect since the fundamental changes in eastern Europe and the Soviet Union had begun, now became a strong possibility, when joy and exuberance were expressed on top of the wall in front of the Brandenburg Gate. Now the entire world realised that a revolution was in the making and that a new national awareness of the German people was about to come into play, even if unification had not been the main demand of the millions whose demonstrations had forced the SED to its knees.

The former US Secretary of State, Henry Kissinger, pointed to an already visible future, when, in a *Newsweek* article on 4 December, he cited the nineteenth-century Austrian Foreign Minister, Count Metternich, who once had written:

> "Policy is like a play in many acts which unfolds inexorably once the curtain is raised. To declare then that the performance will not go on is an absurdity. The play will be completed either by the actors or by the spectators who mount the stage." (Kissinger, 1989, p. 51)

And Kissinger was right: after the structures of the Cold War had been weakened by *détente* and were finally abandoned by the leaders of eastern Europe and the Soviet

Union, the GDR had little chance of survival. The new Prime Minister, Hans Modrow, was among the first to realise how bad the situation was, particularly in economic terms. In January 1990, he moved forward the date for general elections from May to March, arguing that the GDR might no longer exist in May. On 1 February, he presented a plan for a German-German confederation, entitled "For Germany, United Fatherland" (Modrow, 1991, pp. 184-5). A few days later, on 6 February, he urged the federal government in Bonn to come up with a quick solution for a currency union between the two German states, knowing that, if the German mark did not come to the East Germans, the East Germans would go for the German mark.

The astonishing proposals of the East German head of government, put forward within a matter of two weeks, made it clear beyond any doubt that the GDR was unable to continue any longer. The SED regime had been able to survive only under the laboratory conditions of the Soviet empire. Now, encircled by reformist states all over eastern Europe, suffering from open borders that allowed East Germans to travel freely, and confronted with Mikhail Gorbachev in the Kremlin, the communist regime in the GDR no longer had a future. It simply could not cope with the realities of freedom. It could only surrender and allow its people to unite with the Federal Republic, as most East Germans had wished since 1945.

## 3. The role of the Federal Republic

Until late November 1989, the West German government had been extremely cautious not to exploit or escalate the delicate situation that had developed in the East and which could easily explode in an uncontrolled manner. In his annual State of the Nation Address on 8 November, one day before the Wall was opened, Chancellor Kohl still declared that the Federal Republic was prepared to support reforms implemented by the new GDR leadership. He called on the GDR's ruling communist regime to abandon its monopoly on power, permit independent parties and give assurances of free elections. Bonn would be willing, Kohl said, to discuss "a new dimension of economic assistance" to the GDR, if there was a fundamental reform of the economic system, the removal of bureaucratic economic planning and the development of a free market system (Kohl, 1989a, pp. 1058-9).

Even after the opening of the Wall, in another speech before the *Bundestag* on 16 November, Kohl remained reluctant. Instead of indulging in euphoria about the possibilities of German reunification, he only stated the facts of recent inner-German developments in a sober and concise analysis, and confirmed that the Federal Republic would "of course respect any decision that the people in the GDR come to in free self-determination" (Kohl, 1989b, p. 1108). All members of the parliament, including the Greens, applauded. A few hours later, however, officials in Bonn were told by US ambassador Vernon A. Walters: "I believe in reunification. Whoever speaks out against it will be swept away politically" (Teltschik, 1991, pp. 32-3). The following day, the government in Bonn received the text of a speech Gorbachev had made before students in Moscow on 15 November, which also referred to "reunification". Finally, on 21 November, Nikolai Portugalov, a Soviet specialist on Germany, appeared in the chancellery in Bonn and presented a handwritten note, hastily translated into German, in which the Soviet Government raised specific questions about co-operation between the two German states, particularly about reunification, the GDR's accession to the European Community, membership in alliances and the possibility of a peace treaty. In a conversation with Horst Teltschik, the foreign policy adviser of the chancellor, Portugalov added "As you can see, we are pondering over everything in the German question, even ... the unthinkable" (ibid., pp. 43-4).

Teltschik, naturally, was electrified. So was the West German Government. Apparently the considerations within the Soviet leadership on German reunification had proceeded much further than had hitherto been assumed in Bonn – even further than the Federal government had allowed itself to think. So Teltschik's responses to the Soviet questions had to be kept evasive and circumspect. But, of course, he immediately informed the chancellor and arranged for a meeting, which took place in the chancellery on 23 November. Here Kohl and his advisers decided to develop a concept for the unification process, the famous Ten-Point Plan, which was incorporated in a speech that Kohl would deliver to the *Bundestag* on 28 November – not in a dramatic new State of the Nation address, but within the scheduled debate on the budget.

Kohl's proposal for a German confederation amounted to a major earthquake. This was, after all, the first time since the 1960s that a German chancellor had spoken in public about the possibility of reunification, saying "Reunification, the re-attainment of German state unity" remained "the political goal of the Federal government" (Kohl, 1989c, pp. D732-3). With respect to the external aspects of his programme, Kohl added:

> "The future of Germany must fit into the future architecture of Europe as a whole. The West has to provide peace-making aid here with its concept for a permanent and just European order of peace. [...] The European Community is now required to approach the reform-orientated states in central, eastern and southern Europe with openness and flexibility. [...] This of course includes the GDR. The Federal government therefore approves the quick conclusion of a trade and co-operation agreement with the GDR. This would expand and secure the GDR's entry within the common market, including the perspectives of 1992." (ibid., p. D733)

Not surprisingly, the chancellor continued to be cautious, trying to avoid anything that could further unsettle the already shaky political balance in the centre of Europe. His concept envisaged only long-term changes and was aimed at creating a European framework for any steps taken towards German unification. But when he visited the GDR three weeks later and stepped before the crowds at the ruin of the *Frauenkirche* in Dresden on 19 December, he quickly realised that East Germans did not want long-term, but immediate change, that time was running out quickly and that nothing short of German reunification would satisfy the demands of East German people. In fact, demonstrators at the regular Monday demonstrations had already changed their slogans from "We are the people" to "We are one nation" in early December. Kohl himself, who was also affected by the emotions in Dresden, concluded his speech by proclaiming: "God bless our German fatherland" (Kohl, 1989d, p. 1262).

Subsequently, Prime Minister Modrow's proposal "For Germany, United Fatherland" and his plea for a currency union were welcomed by the Bonn government as steps in the right direction. Yet Chancellor Kohl was no longer prepared to respect a government that had not been elected freely by the East German people and decided to wait for the outcome of the parliamentary elections on 18 March 1990 before continuing to do business with the GDR. And he was certainly pleased when the East German CDU under Lothar de Maizière, with 48.1% of the votes, scored a landslide victory over the SPD, which received only 21.8%, and the citizens' movements with a disappointing 2.9%.

In reality, of course, it was a victory for Kohl, who had given the East Germans the impression that his government and his party, unlike many of the opposition Social Democrats, were inclined to live up to their decades-long promises of solidarity with their fellow countrymen in the East. In contrast, Saarland Prime Minister Oskar Lafontaine, who was named on 19 March by the SPD executive committee as the party's candidate for chancellor in the *Bundestag* elections scheduled for 2 December 1990, had repeatedly appealed for a "cautious transition" to a currency union with the GDR, which required "careful preparation" and thus indicated that he was opposed to a rush toward unification (*Frankfurter Rundschau*, 20 March 1990).

Yet it was Kohl's, not Lafontaine's, strategy that was going to prevail. The chancellor's last-minute announcement, only five days before the election, of a 1:1 conversion of savings accounts turned out to be crucial in upsetting the predicted outcome of the vote. Kohl brought his authority, and the financial power of the Federal Republic, into play to help his party win the election. The outcome was a resounding call for quick unification and a market economy, as well as an indication of the persuasive promises by Kohl and his CDU and CSU colleagues, who had told the East Germans that only the Christian conservatives could provide the money needed to revive the country's suffering economy and to establish a unified Germany without undue delay. In fact, the large vote for the CDU or, more precisely, for the parties backed by the government in Bonn and Chancellor Kohl, was "in effect a death sentence for the German Democratic Republic and an endorsement of absorption, as quickly as possible, into big, rich West Germany", Serge Schmemann noted (*New York Times*, 19 March 1990, p. A1).

To cut a long argument short: Kohl stepped in at a very late moment, only after the GDR was finished politically as well as economically, but when he did, he did so quite effectively. It would be unfair to say that the Federal Republic pushed the development towards German reunification either too early or too offensively, before the East German people had made up their minds. But after the decision had been taken – by the Modrow government as well as by the electorate on 18 March – Chancellor Kohl did not hesitate to take the lead and steer the unification process in the direction he wanted it to go.

## 4. Consequences of German unity

The history of the Reich since 1871 seemed to prove that a united Germany was simply too big and dynamic for any stable European state system and that the German tendency towards political aggressiveness was not simply an expression of the legitimate pursuit of German national interests, but also a reprehensible sign of the internal character of the German nation. Recalling seventy-four years of German unity, two world wars, Nazism and 65 million people killed either by warfare or in concentration camps, it was said that Germany's political, economic and military power inevitably threatened the independence and well-being of its neighbours and that the German character had made Germany not only aggressive abroad but also susceptible to totalitarianism at home.

After the Second World War, the partition of Germany and the Soviet-American hegemony over Europe seemed to have resolved the so-called German problem. By dividing and containing German power and ambition, thus keeping the German menace at bay and the German people safe from themselves, Europe and the world were thought to be safe from the Germans once and for all. Memories of the historical Reich faded, and the idea of German reunification was overshadowed by the continued integration of the two former constituent German entities in their respective alliances and by the developing relations between the two states. Willy Brandt's new *Ostpolitik* finally led to the "normal, good-neighbourly relations" spoken of in the Basic Treaty between the Federal Republic and the German Democratic Republic of 1972. Germany and the Germans no longer seemed to pose a threat to the international order, and the world got accustomed to the reality of German partition.

Now, after 1989, Germany is united again. Even if history does not tend to repeat itself, the question arises as to what the consequences might be.

In view of the dramatic changes that have occurred since 1989, the entire political, economic, social and military setting of Europe has come under review. While the eastern part of the continent has eventually restored its ties with the West, Europe as a whole is in the process of trying to find a new identity, reinstate its past, define its borders and develop new strategies and instruments for a better future. In other words, the end of the Cold War is not, as an article by Francis Fukuyama once suggested, "The end of history". The opposite is true: the unification of Germany, the liberation of eastern Europe from Soviet-dominated communism and the collapse of the Soviet Union have opened a new chapter in books of European history.

Germany's role within this process of restructuring Europe is still very much in question. Long before the unification of Germany had become a reality, at a meeting of the Human Rights Forum of the Conference on Security and Co-operation in Europe (CSCE) on 5 June 1990 in Copenhagen, the West German Foreign Minister, Hans-Dietrich Genscher, declared that the federal government wished "to make the destiny of Germany part of the destiny of Europe". Genscher also cited Thomas Mann's statement that "We want a European Germany and not a German Europe". On the day of unification, 3 October 1990, Chancellor Kohl confirmed in his "Message to all governments of the world" that Germany with its newly achieved national unity wanted to "serve peace in the world and promote the integration of Europe". And President Richard von Weizsäcker asserted during the Day of Unity state ceremony in the Philharmonic Hall in Berlin that German unification was "part of a pan-European historical process aimed at the freedom of all people and a new peace order on our continent".

The perception of a post-unification Germany firmly anchored within the stable framework of "pan-Europeanism" was certainly the most favoured scenario among Germans and non-Germans alike. The question was, however, if a scenario of reduced tensions between national interests, increased European integration and flourishing freedom and democracy was also realistic.

On the other hand, the second perception of Germany after unification, envisaging a return to nationalistic eruptions at home and a Bismarckian foreign policy abroad, had its flaws as well: Would Germany really dislodge its anchor with the West, as it rediscovered the old ties with Russia and the East? Would it earnestly try to play the old game of becoming a middle-man between East and West again, or to play the East against the West for its own advantage? And could it possibly have forgotten the tragic lessons of German and European history in the nineteenth and twentieth centuries? Could it repeat the mistakes of the past?

United Germany is in the centre of Europe and cannot escape the effects of the transformation of the European order after 1989-90. It will have to participate in making possible the transition of eastern and South-Eastern Europe from repressive dictatorships and state-planned economies to pluralistic democracies and free-market management. Therefore, Germany will no longer be able to sail in the lee of world politics, as was the case for four decades of US-Soviet predominance. It is now asked to search for, and find, a new role for itself in almost every respect.

By now, it seems apparent that Germany's future will hardly be characterised by a return to patterns of the past. The political balancing act that the German Reich performed during the Wilhelminian period, under Chancellor Bismarck and his successors between 1871 and 1918, as well as during the Weimar Republic – let alone the nationalist-racist course under Hitler – was neither sensible nor feasible in the international environment on the threshold of the twenty-first century. Whereas the unification of the Reich in 1871 had led to isolation throughout the late nineteenth and early twentieth centuries with disastrous results, the unification of Germany in 1990 was achieved on the basis of firm and continuous institutional ties to the West and with the acceptance of its neighbours all around. While the former Reich had been established by war and had lived – and/or to some extent may have been forced to live – in opposition to the existing order with disputes over borders and clashes over diverging national interests, the united Germany of 1990 not only relinquished any historical or legal claims to former German territories, but had been created via negotiations in the two-plus-four process and thus from the outset constituted an integral part of the international community.

Maintaining Germany's ties with multilateral institutions was not just a matter of belief, however, but a concern of national interest. Both a see-saw *Schaukelpolitik* between East and West and the attempt to establish a position of hegemony had proved to be fatal mistakes. The Federal Republic's close association with the West after the Second World War, on the other hand, had brought about economic prosperity as well as political stability. A change of course and the return to a nationalistic policy outside well-tried institutions was thus highly unlikely – indeed, out of the question.

The idea of rejuvenating the *Reichsgedanke* by turning the Federal Republic into a fourth Reich after unification remained the dream of only a few. The rise of nationalism in Germany – as well as in most other countries of Europe at the beginning of the 1990s, especially in the East – was actually less the result of an attractive new ideology or the expression of an inner wish of a major portion of the people than an upshot of the collapse of communism and an effect of social and economic turmoil in the aftermath of the revolution of 1989.

In fact, the "Europeanisation" of the German question prevailed. It not only helped to make the unification of Germany more palatable to its neighbours. It also eased the difficulties in coming to terms with the past, both Nazi and Stasi, as the debate over how unique the Nazi terror had been, compared for instance with the crimes of Stalinism, was now followed by painful revelations and a heated internal discussion about the mechanisms and practices of the East German secret police.

The European dimension of German unification was stressed by the foreign minister, Hans-Dietrich Genscher, as early as at the first two-plus-four conference in Bonn on 5 May 1990, when he maintained that, rather than creating new problems for Europe, the unification of Germany would "play a part in ensuring a new and lasting stability". Moreover, Genscher added, the German government considered

> "the transformation of this insight of European history into a policy for Germany and for a gradually uniting Europe to be Germany's European mission as we approach the end of this century".

That mission has not changed and was adequately expressed in the enlargement of the European Union that happened on 1 May 2004.

# Bibliography

Andert, R., and Herzberg, W., *Der Sturz: Erich Honecker im Kreuzverhör*, Berlin, 1990.

Bahr, E., "Wandel durch Annäherung. Ein Diskussionsbeitrag in Tutzing, 15. Juli 1963" in K. Schröder and E. Bahr, *Mit einem Beitrag von Günter Grass*, Rastatt, 1988.

Bender, P., *Offensive Entspannung: Möglichkeit für Deutschland*, Cologne, 1964.

Berlin-Niederschönhausen, Stenographische Niederschrift des Treffens der Genossen des Politbüros des Zentralkomitees der SED mit dem Generalsekretär des ZK der

KPdSU und Vorsitzenden des Obersten Sowjets der UdSSR, Genossen Michail Sergejewitsch Gorbatschow, am Sonnabend, dem 7. Oktober 1989 (Verbatim Protocol), 7 October 1989.

Brandt, W., *A peace policy for Europe*, New York, 1969.

Fils, A., "Crisis and political ritual in post-war Poland", *Problems of Communism*, 1988, Vol. 37.

Gorbachev, M., *Perestroika: Die zweite russische Revolution. Eine neue Politik für Europa und die Welt*. Munich, 1987.

Görtemaker, M., *Unifying Germany, 1989-1990*, London, 1994.

Holzer, J., *Solidarität. Die Geschichte einer freien Gewerkschaft in Polen*, Munich, 1985.

Kissinger, H., "Living with the inevitable", *Newsweek*, 4 December 1989.

Kohl, H. (1989a), "Policy declaration on the state of the nation in a divided Germany", *Bulletin*, 8 November 1989, No. 123, pp. 1058-9.

Kohl, H. (1989b), "Erklärung der Bundesregierung zum offiziellen Besuch des Bundeskanzlers in Polen und zur Lage in der DDR", Statement by Chancellor Kohl before the Bundestag, *Bulletin*, 16 November 1989, No. 129.

Kohl, H. (1989c), Zehn-Punkte-Programm zur Überwindung der Teilung Deutschlands und Europas, vorgelegt von Bundeskanzler Helmut Kohl in der Haushaltsdebatte des Deutschen Bundestages, *Europa-Archiv*, 28 November 1989, Vol. 44, pp. D732-3.

Kohl, H. (1989d), Speech at the Frauenkirche in Dresden, *Bulletin*, 19 December 1989, No. 150.

Krenz, E., König, H. and Rettner, G., *Wenn Mauern fallen: Die Friedliche Revolution-Vorgeschichte, Ablauf, Auswirkungen*, Vienna, 1990.

McAdams, A.J., "The new logic in Soviet-GDR relations", *Problems of Communism*, 1988, Vol. 37.

Martin, E., *Zwischenbilanz: Deutschlandpolitik der 80er Jahre*, Stuttgart, 1986.

Modrow, H., *Aufbruch und Ende*, Hamburg, 1991.

Nawrocki, J., *Relations between the two states in Germany: trends, prospects and limitations*, Stuttgart, 1985.

367

Palmer, T.G., "Why socialism collapsed in Eastern Europe", *Cato Policy Report*, 1990, Vol. 12, No. 5.

Schabowski, G., *Der Absturz*, Berlin, 1991.

Teltschik, H., *329 Tage: Innenansichten der Einigung*. Berlin, 1991.

Tökés, R.L., "Hungarian reform imperatives", *Problems of Communism*, 1984, Vol. 33.

Wolf, M., *In eigenem Auftrag: Bekenntnisse und Einsichten*, Munich, 1991.

# Chapter 39
# The emergence of national differences, 1989-92: the break-up of Czechoslovakia

*Jan Rychlík*

## Historical background to the Slovak question

Czechoslovakia came into being on 28 October 1918 as a result of the First World War. The union of the Czechs and Slovaks was based on the proximity of their languages. Czech and Slovak are so closely related that they are mutually comprehensible. This had already led in the nineteenth century (mainly on the Czech side) to the conclusion that Czechs and Slovaks were just two branches of one "Czechoslovak" nation. The Czechoslovak state was welcomed by both Czechs and Slovaks, but they did not understand it in the same way. For the Czechs, the new state was just a revival of the medieval Bohemian kingdom, but extended to the east. For most Slovaks, however, the new state was rather the union of two nation-states connected by a roof structure in some form of loose federation. What was more important was that the Slovaks had their own national consciousness and never considered themselves either Czechs, or Czechoslovaks.

In the years 1918-38, Slovakia was only an administrative unit within Czechoslovakia, with no special autonomous status. Autonomous movements were strong, however, and were finally successful on 6 October 1938 as a result of the weakening of the state after the Munich *diktat*. Six months later, Czechoslovakia ceased to exist for the first time when the rest of Bohemia and Moravia were annexed to the German *Reich*, and Slovakia was proclaimed formally independent under the protection of Germany. In 1945, Czechoslovakia was restored. Slovakia again became an autonomous unit, but this autonomy was gradually reduced, first in 1946 and then again after the communist coup of 1948. The new "socialist" constitution of 1960 reduced the autonomy of Slovakia to almost zero (Rychlik, 1995, pp. 180-200).

Slovak demands for federation were formally accepted as a part of the "Prague Spring", the 1968 reform movement in Czechoslovakia. Constitutional Law No. 143/1968 of 27 October 1968 (the Czechoslovak Federation Act) established, on the territory of the former unitary Czechoslovak Socialist Republic (*Československá socialistická republika* – ČSSR), two "new" nation-states: the Czech Socialist Republic (ČSR) and the Slovak Socialist Republic (SSR). Both republics had their own legislative and executive bodies: there was the Czech parliament (called the Czech National Council: *Česká národní rada* – ČNR) and the Slovak parliament (the Slovak National Council:

*Slovenská národná rada* – SNR). There was also a Czech Government and a Slovak Government (these parliaments and governments were called national bodies, whilst the authorities ruling the whole federation were known as federal bodies).

According to the preamble of the Czechoslovak Federation Act, both Czech and Slovak Republics were, in theory, two completely sovereign states who voluntarily delegated part of their sovereignty to federal organs – the Federal Assembly and the federal government. The latter could make decisions only in a narrowly delimited realm. The Federal Assembly *(Federální shromáždění)* had two houses: the House of People *(Sněmovna lidu)* and the House of Nations *(Sněmovna národů)*. The House of People was elected on the basis of proportional representation throughout the country, so the Czech Republic had a larger number of deputies. The House of Nations had equal representation whereby each republic elected 75 deputies.

The passage of laws required majority approval in both houses, whilst the passage of constitutional laws required a three-fifths majority in both houses. There was a specific and unique provision in the constitutional system, the so-called minority veto *(zákaz majorizace)*. The Czech and Slovak deputies in the House of Nations voted separately. All constitutional laws and many other motions required a majority (qualified majority for constitutional laws) from both Czech and Slovak parts of the house. The majority (or qualified majority) of both parts of the house was always calculated on the basis of 75 deputies, not only those who were actually present at the moment of voting. The minority veto meant that the Czech deputies could not over-ride the votes of their Slovak counterparts. On the other hand, it also meant that 31 deputies elected to the House of Nations in the same republic could block any constitutional law or any legislation where a three-fifths majority was required (for example, the election of the president). In other words: the Czechoslovak federation was based on the principle of consensus of Czech and Slovak representations. But, if such consensus was not reached, there was no constitutional solution and no way out of the deadlock.

The passage of the constitutional law on federation took place after the August 1968 Soviet occupation of Czechoslovakia (21 August 1968). It became effective on 1 January 1969 in the conditions of so-called normalisation, that is, the gradual undoing of the democratic reforms of spring 1968 and the restoration of the communist dictatorship. On 17 April 1969, Gustáv Husák, the Slovak communist, the "father of federation" and the protégé of Moscow, replaced Alexander Dubček (who was also a Slovak). He soon liquidated what remained of the 1968 reform movement. Federation itself was not abolished. In reality, however, in the years 1969-89 the federal framework had minimal significance. A series of laws from December 1970 seriously limited the prerogatives of the republics in favour of the federation (see Constitutional Law No. 125/1970). The parliaments, federal, Czech and Slovak, had no significance, nor did the elections in which voters were given the "choice" of only one candidate. Just like the parliaments, the governments (federal and republican) were mere transmission belts for the Communist Party of Czechoslovakia. The Communist Party was not federalised and this meant that the political decisions were still made in Prague.

For all these reasons, the federation had, in its own way, a strange impact on Czech-Slovak relations. The Czechs saw the federation only as an endless procession of Slovak officials at the federal ministries and as a transfer of resources from the federal budget to Slovakia. The Slovaks were just as dissatisfied as the Czechs with the federation, because it did not fulfil their expectations. The Slovaks wanted Slovak matters to be decided in Bratislava, not in Prague. They also expected that the federation would give Slovakia increased visibility on the world stage. Neither of these aims was realised. The outside world continued to view Czechoslovakia as a Czech state, so that the adjectives Czechoslovak and Czech were frequently interchangeable in foreign languages.

## The Velvet Revolution and the Slovak question

The fall of the communist regime in Czechoslovakia (17 November to 4 December 1989) reopened the question of Czech-Slovak relations, a problem with which Czechoslovakia had wrestled since its inception in 1918. In November 1989, two different organisations were founded: the Public Against Violence (*Verejnosť proti násiliu* – VPN) in Slovakia and Civic Forum (*Občanské fórum* – OF) in the Czech lands. There were also attempts to found a Civic Forum in those Slovak areas where the citizens traditionally felt strongly pro-Czechoslovak, especially in Košice (administrative centre of eastern Slovakia), but these did not survive and were subsequently transformed into the VPN.

OF and VPN made an agreement that each movement would be responsible for the democratic changes in the "domestic" republic, and that they would only co-ordinate their policy. For this reason, OF focused on changes in the federal government, while VPN concentrated on Slovak national government. It is significant that the Czech national government was not of the first concern for OF at this stage.

After November 1989, Slovakia's proper status was a plank on the platform of every political party in Slovakia; the differences among them turned only on the degree of Slovak autonomy they favoured. In this regard, VPN and the Democratic Party were moderate parties, which supported the modification of the existing Czechoslovak federation, while the Christian Democratic Party (*Kresťansko-demokratické hnutie* – KDH), led by former Catholic dissident Ján Čarnogurský, was more radical in its proposals. Most radical in this respect was the Slovak National Party (*Slovenská národná strana* – SNS) of Víťazoslav Moric and Jozef Prokeš, which demanded only a very loose Czech-Slovak connection. In both the KDH and SNS, there were many proponents of an independent Slovak state, but, in the first half of 1990, even the SNS had not yet formally introduced this demand. Whilst Czech and Slovak communists gradually parted ways, and an independent Slovak Communist Party was born (*Komunistická strana Slovenska* – KSS; later the Party of the Democratic Left – *Strana demokratickej ľavice*, SDĽ), the latter's embrace of the Slovak national programme meant the Slovak communists were well placed in the new political scene.

# The Hyphen War and the new power-sharing

At the beginning of 1990, the first open Czech-Slovak conflict took place in the federal parliament. Following the political and socio-economic changes that had occurred since November 1989, President Václav Havel proposed on 23 January 1990 that the officially used title, the Czechoslovak Socialist Republic, should be amended to the Czechoslovak Republic, its official name up to 1960. Alexander Dubček, the new chairman (Speaker) of the Federal Assembly, accepted the proposal as a presidential initiative and sent it to the committees of the Federal Assembly and both national councils for their comments, according to the procedure laid down in the constitution and the Federation Act of 1968.

The Slovak National Council fundamentally opposed the proposed change, demanding instead that the new state be called the Federation of Czecho-Slovakia. In this way, the world would be put on notice that Czechoslovakia did not comprise one state, but instead consisted of two. This proposal was supported by a clear majority of the Slovak public, but it was rejected in the Czech lands. For the Czechs, the name Czechoslovakia evoked bitter memories of the post-Munich (or Second) Republic, when it was officially used. Most Czechs did not understand why the hyphen was so important for Slovaks. On 29 March 1990, after long discussions, the Federal Assembly approved constitutional law 81/1990. The new name, considered to be a compromise, established the official name in two forms: the Czechoslovak Federal Republic *(Československá federativní republika)* in Czech and the Czecho-slovak Federal Republic *(Česko-slovenská federatívna republika)* in Slovak.

But this compromise did not satisfy Slovaks, because it did not show to the outside world the separate existence of the Slovaks (it was clear that the Slovak version would be used only in Slovakia). Demonstrations against the new name immediately erupted in Slovakia, and, for the first time, slogans demanding an independent Slovakia appeared. VPN had accepted the new name during the Federal Assembly deliberations, so Slovak critics now accused the party of the betrayal of Slovak national interests. Czech deputies in the Federal Assembly backed down in the end. On 20 April 1990, another constitutional law (101/1990) proclaimed the official name to be the Czech and Slovak Federative Republic (*Česká a Slovenská Federativní republika* in Czech, or *Česká a Slovenská Federatívna republika* in Slovak – ČSFR in both languages). The unofficial name, Czechoslovakia, and the adjective, Czechoslovak, would thereafter be written in Czech as one word, but in Slovak with a hyphen (as Czecho-slovakia). The so-called Hyphen War indicated that subsequent discussions were not going to be easy and that the Slovak side would propose a maximal loosening of the federation.

The first free elections took place on 8 and 9 June 1990. The elections were based on the principle of proportional representation, but parties that did not receive at least 5% of the vote (3% in the elections to the Slovak parliament) received no seats in parliament. In Slovakia, VPN won with 29.3%, followed by KDH's 19.2%, SNS's

13.9%, KSS-SDL's 13.3%, and the Hungarian coalition with 8.7%. The Democratic Party and the Green Ecological Party (*Strana zelených* – SZ) entered not only the Slovak National Council, but the Federal Assembly. In the Czech Republic, the Civic Forum was victorious, as was the Czechoslovak People's Party (*Českoslov-enská strana lidová* – ČSL, in fact the Catholic Party), which joined the coalition with the small Christian Democratic Party (*Křesťansko-demokratická strana* – KDS). In addition, the Communist Party, the Movement for Self-Governing Democracy and the Society for Moravia and Silesia (*Hnutí za samosprávnou demokracii-Společnost pro Moravu a Slezsko* – HSD-SMS), which proposed a three-way federation of Bohemia, Moravia and Slovakia, also had seats in parliament.

The new federal government was made up essentially of a coalition between VPN and Civic Forum, with the support of the Czech and Slovak centre-right parties (the coalition of ČSL-KDS and KDH), and it was headed by Marian Čalfa of VPN, who had already been prime minister in the previous federal government. The Czech Government was again headed by Petr Pithart, but the Slovak Government's leadership changed: Milan Čič was replaced by the former Slovak Minister of the Interior, Vladimír Mečiar (VPN). Negotiations between the Czech and Slovak governments were not affected by this and they continued. There were also negotiations between the chairman of the Slovak National Council, František Mikloško (VPN, after 1992 KDH), and his counterpart in the Czech republic, Dagmar Burešová (OF), and their vice-chairs.

Official negotiations between the Czech and Slovak Governments took place on 8-9 August 1990 in Trenčianské Teplice. They continued on 10-11 September in Piešt'any, on 27 September in Kroměříž and on 28 October in Slavkov, where President Havel also participated. On 5 November 1990, the Czech-Slovak relationship was the subject of negotiations between the prime ministers of all three governments. Four days later, in Luhačovice, Pithart and Mečiar met again.

Because fundamental agreement proved impossible, the representatives of the governing parties, along with President Havel and representatives of all three governments, issued a declaration on 28 October 1990, which emphasised their will to maintain the ČSFR. The Czech and Slovak sides also simultaneously agreed that the division of powers would be rearranged and a definitive solution would be subsequently worked out. The final shaping of the division of powers took place in the presence of President Havel and all three premiers at Prague Castle on 12 November 1990. The proposal was then evaluated by the national councils and passed on to the Federal Assembly.

In the version of the power-sharing law presented to the Federal Assembly, the Czech National Council and the Czech government proposed several changes (to the 12 November 1990 proposal). In this context, the enlarged presidium of the Slovak Government, headed by Mečiar, suddenly came to Prague on 6 December 1990. Mečiar presented Pithart with an ultimatum: if the power-sharing law was not adopted in its original form – that is, if the Czech National Council or the Federal Assembly amended the draft version of the law – the Slovak National Council would declare the supremacy of Slovak laws over the laws of the federation. This would mean de facto paralysis and dissolution of the Czechoslovak Federative Republic. The Slovak side also further emphasised that the Federal Assembly had no business interfering in Czech-Slovak negotiations. The Czech Government parties, especially Civic Forum, instructed their deputies to vote for the original version of the power-sharing law, which was adopted on 12 December 1990 as constitutional amendment 556/1990.

The new power-sharing law significantly reduced the power of the central (federal) organs. In contrast to the 1968 constitutional amendment that created the federation, this law eliminated the exclusive prerogative of the federation in foreign policy and defence, which opened up the future possibility of separate international treaties and even the creation of republic-level armed forces. The power-sharing law, however, did not remove the crux of the problem and therefore represented only a temporary compromise. While the Czechs viewed the amendment as their maximum concession, for the Slovaks it was only the first step toward their final goal: the attainment of a loose Czech-Slovak commonwealth or confederation in which Slovakia could reap the benefits of its own statehood while retaining all the advantages of a common state.

## Czech-Slovak negotiations in 1991-92

In 1991, the changing political landscape in the Czech and Slovak Republics transformed the negotiating atmosphere. On 24 February 1991, Civic Forum splintered into Václav Klaus's right-of-centre Civic Democratic Party (*Občanská demokratická strana* – ODS) and Jiři Dienstbier's centre-left Civic Movement (*Občanské hnutí* – OH). Immediately after the elections of June 1990, the Slovak National Party declared full Slovak independence to be its ultimate goal. At the same time, several smaller parties and movements emerged, which openly evoked the traditions of the totalitarian Slovak state (1939-45) and the inter-war autonomous Slovak People's Party. On 3 March 1991, the conflict between Vladimír Mečiar and VPN's leadership, above all with Fedor Gál, the representative of its liberal wing, caused an acute crisis to erupt within the VPN. Under the auspices of VPN, Mečiar founded his own platform, For a Democratic Slovakia (*Za demokratické Slovensko*). A month later, he completely separated from VPN, creating an independent Movement for a Democratic Slovakia (*Hnutie za demokratické Slovensko* – HZDS).

On 23 April 1991, the presidium of the Slovak National Council recalled Mečiar from his position as Prime Minister of the Slovak Government, as well as all those of his supporters who refused to respect the decisions of the VPN leadership. As a result, the government was reconstructed, with Ján Čarnogurský, the chairman of KDH, becoming the new prime minister. Čarnogurský was in favour of Slovak independence, but for the time being he did not regard it as the republic's most pressing issue. In his view, Slovakia would become independent only after Czechoslovakia had joined the European Community. In contrast to the representatives of VPN, who favoured an enduring state bond with the Czechs, Čarnogurský viewed Czechoslovakia as a temporary formation, and he made no secret of this. When negotiating with

Petr Pithart, a former fellow dissident, Čarnogurský demanded that the foundation of Czech and Slovak cohabitation should rest on a legally binding treaty between the two republics, whose acceptance should precede the adoption of any new constitution.

During 1991, Czech-Slovak negotiations continued. At first, Dagmar Burešová, the chairwoman of the Czech National Council, rejected the Čarnogurský notion of a treaty between the two republics. Eventually, the Czech side accepted it as a political initiative. In contrast, the Slovak side demanded that the treaty should have a binding character, which meant, in effect, that it should assume the form of an international treaty, creating an association of two states. Such a solution was unacceptable to the Czech side, because it presupposed the transitory nature of the Czechoslovak state or commonwealth. The Czech side rightly feared that Slovakia would take advantage of the existence of the common state only to fortify its own position and then declare its independence anyway.

In May and June 1991, negotiations continued in a series of meetings of the representatives of Czech and Slovak politicians and political parties: on 12 May 1991 in Lány (the president's official residence, a castle outside Prague), then at the end of May in Budmerice and, on 19 June 1991, in Kroměříž. President Havel took part in all these negotiations and meetings, and asked the representatives of particular political parties to answer some questions connected with their vision of the common state. It became clear that the Slovak political parties (with the exception of the SNS, which openly advocated full independence) understood "common state" to mean, not "one state" as the Czechs understood it, but rather the union of two states. As one Austrian journalist rightly stated, the Slovaks wanted a *Staatenbund*, or confederation, while the Czechs required a *Bundesstaat*, or federation. The negotiations ended without result, and the political parties agreed that the only legal way to divide the state should be through a referendum.

On 3 November 1991, Havel invited the representatives of all three governments and parliaments to his private weekend house at Hrádeček (near Trutnov). Here, he presented the participants with a proposed Czech-Slovak treaty, which would be incorporated into the federal constitution and subsequently ratified by both national councils. The proposal was taken as the basis for further negotiation. With the exception of the deputy chairman of the Czech National Council, Jan Kalvoda (Civic Democratic Alliance: *Občanská demokratická aliance* – ODA), all those present reached an agreement early in the morning of 4 November on a binding Czech-Slovak treaty, even though the legal procedure for the incorporation of the treaty into the national and federal constitutions remained undefined. Despite that, Czech and Slovak representatives did not reach an agreement on the character of the treaty. The Slovaks considered it the more or less standard treaty between two states, while the Czechs saw it only as political agreement. The Czech representatives had the impression that the Slovak negotiators were bent on squaring a circle, aspiring to have a Slovak state while at the same time resisting it. From the Slovak perspective, however, it seemed that the Czechs did not want to accept legitimate Slovak demands.

375

A turning point in the balance of political power came when Mečiar's HZDS adopted an anti-federation stance, by its support for the notion of Slovak *zvrchovanost* or sovereignty. The notion of Slovak *zvrchovanost*, put forward in the spring of 1991 by the Slovak National Party and other nationalists, demanded the immediate transfer of all competencies to Slovak authorities, and only thereafter would an agreement with the Czech Republic be possible. Mečiar, who had been a federalist up until that point, engaged in demagoguery by announcing that *zvrchovanost* meant neither state sovereignty nor the destruction of Czechoslovakia. HZDS explicitly demanded international recognition of Slovakia, while claiming (and the Slovak public had largely come to believe this claim) that even this demand was compatible with the continued existence of the common state.

In this situation, Ján Čarnogurský was forced to seek a compromise with the Czechs. In the autumn of 1991, it seemed that a compromise between Pithart and Čarnogurský – that is, between the Civic Movement on the one hand, and KDH and VPN on the other – would be possible. The Pithart government was willing to accept the treaty between the Czech and Slovak republics based on Havel's proposal from Hrádeček, even though the matter was complicated by the formal legal conflict (in reality, groundless) over whether the republics could even enter into such a treaty while the federation still existed. The treaty was supposed to precede the federal constitution, which would then be bound by it.

On 10 January 1992, representatives of the Czech and Slovak national councils agreed in Prague that the treaty would be signed by the Czech and Slovak republics, represented by their respective national councils. On 23 January 1992, a commission representing both national councils was created in Bratislava and entrusted with the responsibility of preparing the final version.

During the period of 3 to 8 February 1992, in Milovy near Žd'ár nad Sázavou, there was a final round of negotiations between the expert commissions of the Czech and Slovak national councils and the governments of both republics as well as the federation. The result was a draft treaty between the two republic parliaments. KDH gave up its original demand that the treaty be signed by the republics (which would render it an international treaty between two independent states). On the other hand, the treaty stipulated the framework of the future federal constitution and, in this respect, accommodated Slovak demands. The agreement was to be ratified by both national councils, which represented a concession from the Czech side.

On 12 February 1992, the presidium of the Slovak National Council considered the draft. Normally, the presidium consisted of 21 members, but one seat was vacant at that time. Ten members voted for the proposal, and 10 voted against. Therefore, the proposal was defeated and could not be submitted to the Slovak National Council as a whole. There was no voting over the draft in the presidium of the Czech National Council. On 5 March 1992, the presidium declared that further negotiation with the Slovak side would be pointless. Furthermore, on 7 March, the draft treaty from Milovy caused the fragmentation of the KDH. The nationalist wing formally separated and created the Slovak Christian Democratic Movement (*Slovenské kresťansko-demokratické hnutie* – SKDH). As a result, the government coalition, made up of KDH-VPN-DS-MOS (*Maďarská občanská strana* – Hungarian Civic Party), became a minority government. On 11 March, the chairs of the Czech and Slovak national councils, Dagmar Burešová and František Mikloško, agreed that further negotiation should be left to the winners of the next elections.

## The break-up of Czechoslovakia

New elections to the Federal Assembly and both national councils took place on 5-6 June 1992. In the Czech Republic, Václav Klaus's ODS (in coalition with the tiny Christian Democratic Party, or KDS) won. The ODS-KDS coalition had entered the election campaign with a programme of continuing radical economic reform and of completing the transition to a democratic and capitalist society. On the matter of the constitutional framework, it had adopted the slogan, "Either a functioning federation or the division of Czechoslovakia into two states" while clearly preferring the former to the latter. In Slovakia, Vladimír Mečiar's HZDS won, with a programme of social compromises that endorsed various populist demands. As far as the constitutional framework was concerned, it was a vague platform, which combined (in reality) mutually exclusive demands for sovereignty, international recognition for Slovakia and the maintenance of a common state with the Czechs.

Mečiar succeeded in persuading a substantial part of the wider Slovak public that demand for international recognition was fully compatible with the continued existence of Czechoslovakia. At the same time, he claimed that he had five variants for the constitutional arrangements (including a confederation, which in reality was not a common state) for Czech-Slovak relations, whose ultimate fate was to be decided by a referendum. The HZDS leadership chose to ignore the objections that any of these variants would require the agreement of the Czech side, which had made it clear that it would insist on dividing the state if the Slovaks rejected the federation. In this way, HZDS won a substantial number of votes from supporters of the common state, especially voters with less education. The supporters of an independent Slovakia gave most of their votes to the Slovak National Party.

The ODS-KDS obtained 33.9% of the vote and 48 seats in the House of People, and 33.4% and 37 seats in the House of Nations. The necessary majority in the House of People was 76 deputies, and 38 deputies in the Czech part of the House of Nations. This meant that ODS-KDS was just one vote short of a majority in the Czech part of the House of Nations.

As a result, the ODS-KDS was forced to look for allies, not only on the Czech but also on the Slovak political scene. Since another potential ally, the rightist Civic Democratic Alliance (ODA), had entered the Czech National Council but not the Federal Assembly, only the centrist Catholic Christian Democratic Union-Czechoslovak People's Party *(Křesťansko-demokratická unie)* or KDÚ-ČSL was a candidate for this role on the Czech political scene. It won seven seats in the House of People and six in the House of Nations, and the ODS-KDS was preparing to create a coalition with it in the Czech Government. In Slovakia, Čarnogurský's KDH was another potential ally, but it won only six seats in the Chamber of the People and eight seats in the Chamber of the Nations. Therefore, the ODS-KDS-KDU-ČSL-KDH combination could not garner a majority in the House of People.

The situation in the House of Nations was even more tragic, because the ODS-KDS needed allies in the Slovak part of the house to pass any law where the minority veto applied, such as the government programme, votes of confidence and the election of the president. Apart from HZDS, however, there were no parties on the Slovak side that could be effective legislative partners. A conglomeration of smaller Slovak parties, that had emerged in the Federal Assembly after the elections, could not be relied upon, for they spanned incompatible ideologies and could never have agreed on a common programme.

As early as Sunday 7 June 1992, Václav Havel had asked Václav Klaus to begin negotiations to form a new federal government and designated him as its next prime minister. The first negotiations between ODS and HZDS took place in Brno on 8 June 1992. Both parties assumed that these negotiations would be difficult but not impossible.

According to the testimony of one of the participants, Miroslav Macek, the negotiations began with a private meeting between Klaus and Mečiar. According to Macek, Mečiar was attempting, as usual, to use vague formulations to blur the irreconcilable conflict over international recognition. While the Klaus-Mečiar conversations were taking place, Macek spoke with Michal Kováč, who described to him a Slovak proposal for an economic and defence union, apparently without previous consultation with Mečiar. Macek – who subsequently dubbed this proposal a "Slovak state with Czech insurance" – immediately realised that this project could not, and must not, be accepted by the Czech side, because it signified an evolutionary approach to Slovak state building, funded by Czech taxpayers. That is why, after Klaus and Mečiar had joined the larger meeting, Macek declared that the matter had become quite clear: the only solution was the dissolution of Czechoslovakia.

Even after the Brno talks, Klaus apparently had not given up all hope that Mečiar would back away from some of his demands and that the dissolution of the state could be averted. That is why that subject was on the agenda at subsequent meetings in Prague on 11 and 17 June 1992. At these negotiations, the ODS put pressure on the HZDS to give a clear response: either a functioning federation or two separate states. After six hours of futile negotiations, during which the HZDS again blurred the distinction between the two alternatives, relying on such contradictory formulations as "a common state in the form of a confederation" or "defence and economic union", Klaus's patience ran out. He asked the HZDS leaders whether they wanted to build a Slovak state with Czech money and whether or not the Slovaks were a proud nation. Mečiar replied that each republic would be responsible for its own finances. With this response, Mečiar sought to return to the question of confederation, but the Czech side interpreted his declaration as yet another step toward Slovak independence. In the end, they agreed on the composition of a reduced federal cabinet, which, in addition to the Prime Minister, would have only ten ministers. Apart from the premiership, which went to the ODS, there was equal representation in the cabinet for each party, but the HZDS demanded the ministry of foreign affairs and the ministry of defence.

Václav Klaus apparently had changed his mind as early as 17 June 1992, but the ODS only made its position clear after the fourth round of negotiations with the HZDS, which took place in Bratislava on 19 June 1992. The negotiations lasted a full twelve hours and confirmed that the only thing on which the parties could agree was the division of the country. On 20 June 1992 at 1.30 a.m., both parties issued a declaration, which stated in part:

> "the ODS does not regard a confederation, in which both republics are subjects of international law [which was the HZDS proposal] as a common state, but instead as a union of two separate states. Rather than a confederation, the ODS prefers two completely independent states, i.e. a constitutional dissolution of the federation."

On 24 June 1992, a new Slovak Government, headed by Vladimir Mečiar, was formed. On 2 July, Václav Havel appointed the last federal cabinet of Jan Strásky. On the same day, a Czech Government was formed by the coalition ODS-KDS-ČSL-ODA, under the leadership of Václav Klaus.

Both the opposition and the government repeatedly considered the question of a referendum. Surveys of public opinion showed that, when asked "Are you for a common state?", most voters in both the Czech and Slovak republics responded positively. To rule out erroneous conclusions stemming from conceptual confusion promoted by the HZDS, the opposition (ČSSD) maintained that the question should be worded to make it clear that, in a common state, Slovakia would not have international recognition. But the problem of the referendum had several layers: even if it had clear popular support for the maintenance of the common state, the opposing political forces would have remained in power, making a compromise impossible. At the same time, surveys of voters' preferences indicated that new elections would not have brought about any change. Irrespective of the outcome of the referendum and thanks to a political system with a powerful minority veto, the stage was clearly set for government paralysis and the gradual dissolution of the state. Legal means could not overcome the political stalemate.

With the end of Havel's presidential term and new presidential elections in the Federal Assembly, the unfolding dissolution became apparent. Havel's term ended on 5 July 1992 and the election was to take place within the next three months. During this period, Havel was to remain in office. The HZDS not only refused to support the candidacy of Václav Havel for the next term, but it also declined to propose and back its own alternative candidate. But the ODS refused to appoint any other Czech candidate except Havel, stating that the president should be "either Havel or nobody". It was clear, however, that, owing to the minority veto system, Havel could not be re-elected without the votes of the HZDS and SNS. The election took place on 3 July 1992. Havel did not obtain the required qualified majority in the Slovak part of the House of Nations and his candidacy failed. On 17 July 1992, the Slovak National Council, with the support of the HZDS, SNS and, surprisingly, SDL', passed the declaration of Slovak sovereignty, which declared Slovakia to be the state of the Slovak nation. The declaration passed over the dissenting votes of KDH and the Hungarian parties. On the same day, Václav Havel resigned from office; no new president was chosen for the remainder of Czechoslovakia's existence.

Klaus presented Mečiar with a draft law on the end of federation, which the Federal Assembly was to approve by 20 September. The draft assumed four formal possibilities: (1) declaration by the Federal Assembly; (2) agreement of the national councils; (3) a referendum; and (4) a unilateral departure from the federation by one of the republics. Instead of a union, Klaus proposed a series of bilateral agreements. The final agreement was reached in Brno on 26 August, when a timetable was established and the date was set for Czechoslovakia's expiration on 31 December 1992, the end of the budget year. On 1 September 1992, the Slovak Republic adopted a new constitution, which had been conceived to function as a constitution for an independent state (Constitutional Law No. 490/1992). It did not take into account the existence of Czechoslovakia, except for the validity of some articles which were to come into effect as of 1 January 1993.

Nevertheless, as it turned out, the division of Czechoslovakia was not an easy matter. On 11 September, the opposition forced a special session of the Federal Assembly, which again demanded that a referendum should be held. The federal government refused this demand, arguing that, if the referendum were to endorse the continued maintenance of the common state, which surveys of public opinion indicated was virtually certain, it would be in no position to act on such a result, for the disintegration of the state had already gone too far. On 1 October 1992, the Federal Assembly had voted on the constitutional amendment concerning the end of the federation. The opposition defeated the proposal. Miloš Zeman, then deputy chair of the ČSSD, took advantage of the situation and proposed a constitutional commission that would be entrusted with the transformation of the federation into a Czechoslovak union. The proposal, which enjoyed the support of the opposition as well as many of the HZDS deputies, was actually approved. The ČSSD's proposal presupposed the existence of two states with common organs for foreign policy, defence and finance. Decisions were to be made on the basis of parity, and the question of international recognition was left open.

The vote in favour of such a commission was a great victory for the opposition and the HZDS. Nevertheless, the ODS had already decided to divide the state come what may, and, if no other way was open, it would proceed without the help of the HZDS. The Czech governing coalition refused to send any representatives to the new commission. Instead, on 6 October 1992, the ODS and HZDS delegations met in Jihlava. Klaus insisted that the HZDS explicitly reject union and confederation, and commit itself to the division of Czechoslovakia into two fully independent states. In the end, Mečiar agreed. As a result, the union project was shelved.

On 18 November 1992, the Federal Assembly met to vote on a new version of the constitutional amendment concerning the end of the federation. The various modes of how the federation might end were no longer an issue. According to the new draft, the federation would simply end at midnight on 31 December 1992.

By the time the assembly voted on this law, Czechoslovakia had already de facto been partitioned. The law, however, was accepted only in the House of People, and another vote had to be held a week later on 24 November. Because the day was foggy and the special aircraft with Slovak deputies could not land in Prague, voting was postponed until the next day. By lobbying the opposition deputies, the government coalition in the end persuaded some right-wing Republicans, and some Czech and Slovak Social Democrats, and succeeded in obtaining the votes needed. By a narrow majority in both houses and both parts of the House of Nations, the constitutional amendment finally passed on 25 November 1992 at 12.22 p.m. (Constitutional Law No. 542/1992). On 16 December 1992, the Czech National Council adopted the constitution of the Czech Republic (Constitutional Law No. 1/1993). On 31 December 1992, the Czech and Slovak Federative Republic ceased to exist.

## Conclusion

The answer to the question of why the break-up of Czechoslovakia was so easy and peaceful is straightforward: there was no dispute over the borders and no Czech minority in Slovakia or Slovak minority in the Czech Republic. Slovaks in the Czech Republic, and vice versa, lived in diaspora and had no special claims. Equally important was the fact that the Czechs had lost interest in Slovakia.

## Bibliography

Rychlík, J., "From autonomy to federation" in J. Musil (ed.), *The end of Czechoslovakia*, Central European University Press, Budapest, London and New York, 1995.

# Chapter 35
# Media, parties and political transition: contrasting approaches of sister-disciplines

*Zsolt Enyedi*

We are all accustomed today to the pre-eminent role of the mass media in politics. The success of political parties is typically presumed to depend on how often they adapt to the logic of news media. Political events, particularly party congresses, are carefully pre-staged, and the real leaders of the parties are the unelected media specialists, the so-called spin-doctors.

In 1989 in eastern Europe, the mass media were, of course, different from today. They were much more amateurish and disorganised. The personal sympathies of particular journalists were often more responsible for what was aired on television or written about in the papers than the central directives issued by the directors of these media.

This relative immaturity of media organisations did not stop them from playing a crucial historical role in the collapse of Communism and the development of liberal democracy. There are some important structural reasons that privileged the media at that time, more than ever before or after. In 1989, there was a fundamental lack of consensus over norms in eastern European societies. The socialising agents who normally inculcated values, norms and attitudes in citizens were all in deep crisis. Churches, schools, families, trade unions and other influences were too deeply embedded in the socialist system to provide guidance. Journalists had a past as well, but they had information about Western norms and, working in the most modern sector of the society, had the credibility to spread these norms. And they had the opportunity to develop a non-partisan image, to play the role of *vox populi* in 1989.

Whilst the political parties had to face a strong anti-party popular mood, journalists were indeed relatively highly regarded. The prestige of television typically surpassed that of parliament. This is particularly significant, given that east Europeans spent more time in front of television than west Europeans, while membership in voluntary organisations was well below western levels.

Political actors did not forget, even in the most difficult moments, the relevance of the media. In Romania, the revolution and the military clashes happened in front of the cameras and, according to many analysts, for the cameras. In Hungary, one of the most important questions, for both the old and the new elite, was who could stand next to the coffins at the reburial of Prime Minister Imre Nagy in Heroes' Square. Political actors knew that their behaviour in these well-televised moments could determine their political career. .

One could argue that politicians in 1989 were in general particularly conscious of the fact that they were making history, that they would end up in history books. The concern within the communist elite about how they would be remembered was one of the reasons for the large-scale destruction of files. At the same time, the fact that such a considerable amount of evidence was destroyed, or in some cases falsified, should warn us against taking the remaining documents at face value.

Next to these conscious efforts at manipulation, the media themselves modified the image of reality in many ways. By nature, the mass media personalise problems that are structural and disregard social processes. Even if those in the mass media have the best intentions, they cannot have access to certain kinds of information (such as secret negotiations) and cannot provide equal access to all relevant players. For all these reasons, historians and history teachers must treat the material produced by the 1989 mass media with caution.

At the same time, the mass media should not be perceived just as manipulators. The years that followed 1989 proved that political forces that were treated with disdain by the media elite still managed to win elections. Popularity among journalists did not guarantee political survival. But undoubtedly, the media played and continue to play an important role in setting the political agenda, raising the relevance of certain issues and sidelining others.

The sister-disciplines of political science and history can help each other in uncovering the true nature of the events of 1989. Before pointing out what historians could learn from political scientists, let me mention something they should not learn. One of the biases of political science that historians should not copy is their emphasis on elites. This bias comes from the fact that political scientists are obsessed with the question "Why?" And, indeed, the final cause of the political transition in Europe in 1989 lay in Moscow: it was related to the lost arms race and it was originally manifested by Gorbachev's glasnost. But the question "How?" is equally important, and historians are better able than political scientists to answer this question. The answer must take into account the masses, represented by demonstrations and by public opinion. The fast pace of events that year was largely due to pressure from below on the decision makers.

Political science should be praised, however, for treating 1989 in a comparative way, embedding it in the international context. It noticed – and highlighted – that the events in various countries of the region formed a chain and that each new transition was characterised by a decreasing level of uncertainty.

The comparative perspective has various advantages even when the analysis goes beyond the borders of the region. By comparing eastern Europe to southern Europe in the 1970s and 1980s, one can demonstrate how profound and comprehensive the post-communist transformation was. A new economic system, a new political system, a new constitutional regime and, sometimes, a new state were all to be built at the same time. If revolution is defined by radical changes, 1989 presents us with some particularly clear cases of revolution.

The inter-regional comparison helps us to see something that is otherwise not visible: namely the lack of certain actors. In 1989, with the exception of Romania, the military played a secondary, almost non-existent role. The role of the churches was almost negligible. Elite groups, the mass media and civic initiatives that turned into political parties, these were the protagonists.

Parties faced different challenges in this period than in any other period since western and southern Europe became democratised. In western Europe, competitive oligarchic systems became democratised in the nineteenth century, while in southern Europe both mobilisation and contestation were at low levels during the periods of authoritarian regimes. In contrast, when democratisation reached eastern Europe, its citizens were already mobilised and politicised. Endowed with the skills of "cognitive mobilisation", they could rely on their own education-based knowledge and on the information provided by the mass media. Therefore, political parties in eastern Europe had a weaker role in shaping society than in shaping power.

As a result of the specificities of the post-communist transition, parties had to face the legacy of weak or non-existent democratic experiences, and a complete concentration of power under communism. Developing party politics became characterised by a particularly intense competition due to the high stakes (new constitutions, privatisation and much else).

Scholarship has recently moved away from emphasising the underlying commonalities, towards accentuating the sub-regional specificities within the world of post-communism. But heterogeneity makes post-communist party politics even more popular as a target for research. A similar recent past and diverging outcomes in respective countries promise researchers the unique possibility of tracing the effects of various institutional and cultural factors.

The more thoroughly one researches the respective countries, the more one realises that the starting points were in fact different. Communism meant something different in different countries. Accordingly, the post-communist political oppositions also varied. Even the *ancien régime* forces were structured differently in the various countries: they basically evaporated from some Baltic countries, they remained unreformed but marginalised in Czechoslovakia (and then in the Czech Republic), they stayed equally unreformed and yet still played a principal role in Ukraine and Russia, they slowly transformed themselves and stayed dominant in Romania, they turned nationalist in Serbia, and they turned social democratic in Poland and Hungary.

The staggering variance on these and other issues calls for explanations. The explanation is likely to lie in history. At this point, it is the political scientists who must realise that they cannot make progress without the help of the historians.

# Sales agents for publications of the Council of Europe

**BELGIUM/BELGIQUE**
La Librairie Européenne -
The European Bookshop
Rue de l'Orme, 1
B-1040 BRUXELLES
Tel.: +32 (0)2 231 04 35
Fax: +32 (0)2 735 08 60
E-mail: order@libeurop.be
http://www.libeurop.be

Jean De Lannoy
Avenue du Roi 202 Koningslaan
B-1190 BRUXELLES
Tel.: +32 (0)2 538 43 08
Fax: +32 (0)2 538 08 41
E-mail: jean.de.lannoy@dl-servi.com
http://www.jean-de-lannoy.be

**CANADA and UNITED STATES/
CANADA et ÉTATS-UNIS**
Renouf Publishing Co. Ltd.
1-5369 Canotek Road
OTTAWA, Ontario K1J 9J3, Canada
Tel.: +1 613 745 2665
Fax: +1 613 745 7660
Toll-Free Tel.: (866) 767-6766
E-mail: orders@renoufbooks.com
http://www.renoufbooks.com

**CZECH REPUBLIC/
RÉPUBLIQUE TCHÈQUE**
Suweco CZ, s.r.o.
Klecakova 347
CZ-180 21 PRAHA 9
Tel.: +420 2 424 59 204
Fax: +420 2 848 21 646
E-mail: import@suweco.cz
http://www.suweco.cz

**DENMARK/DANEMARK**
GAD
Vimmelskaftet 32
DK-1161 KØBENHAVN K
Tel.: +45 77 66 60 00
Fax: +45 77 66 60 01
E-mail: gad@gad.dk
http://www.gad.dk

**FINLAND/FINLANDE**
Akateeminen Kirjakauppa
PO Box 128
Keskuskatu 1
FIN-00100 HELSINKI
Tel.: +358 (0)9 121 4430
Fax: +358 (0)9 121 4242
E-mail: akatilaus@akateeminen.com
http://www.akateeminen.com

**FRANCE**
La Documentation française
(diffusion/distribution France entière)
124, rue Henri Barbusse
F-93308 AUBERVILLIERS CEDEX
Tél.: +33 (0)1 40 15 70 00
Fax: +33 (0)1 40 15 68 00
E-mail: prof@ladocumentationfrancaise.fr
http://www.ladocumentationfrancaise.fr

Librairie Kléber
1 rue des Francs Bourgeois
F-67000 STRASBOURG
Tel.: +33 (0)3 88 15 78 88
Fax: +33 (0)3 88 15 78 80
E-mail: francois.wolfermann@librairie-kleber.fr
http://www.librairie-kleber.com

**GERMANY/ALLEMAGNE
AUSTRIA/AUTRICHE**
UNO Verlag GmbH
August-Bebel-Allee 6
D-53175 BONN
Tel.: +49 (0)228 94 90 20
Fax: +49 (0)228 94 90 222
E-mail: bestellung@uno-verlag.de
http://www.uno-verlag.de

**GREECE/GRÈCE**
Librairie Kauffmann s.a.
Stadiou 28
GR-105 64 ATHINAI
Tel.: +30 210 32 55 321
Fax: +30 210 32 30 320
E-mail: ord@otenet.gr
http://www.kauffmann.gr

**HUNGARY/HONGRIE**
Euro Info Service kft.
1137 Bp. Szent István krt. 12.
H-1137 BUDAPEST
Tel.: +36 (06)1 329 2170
Fax: +36 (06)1 349 2053
E-mail: euroinfo@euroinfo.hu
http://www.euroinfo.hu

**ITALY/ITALIE**
Licosa SpA
Via Duca di Calabria, 1/1
I-50125 FIRENZE
Tel.: +39 0556 483215
Fax: +39 0556 41257
E-mail: licosa@licosa.com
http://www.licosa.com

**MEXICO/MEXIQUE**
Mundi-Prensa México, S.A. De C.V.
Río Pánuco, 141 Delegacíon Cuauhtémoc
06500 MÉXICO, D.F.
Tel.: +52 (01)55 55 33 56 58
Fax: +52 (01)55 55 14 67 99
E-mail: mundiprensa@mundiprensa.com.mx
http://www.mundiprensa.com.mx

**NETHERLANDS/PAYS-BAS**
De Lindeboom Internationale Publicaties b.v.
M.A. de Ruyterstraat 20 A
NL-7482 BZ HAAKSBERGEN
Tel.: +31 (0)53 5740004
Fax: +31 (0)53 5729296
E-mail: books@delindeboom.com
http://www.delindeboom.com

**NORWAY/NORVÈGE**
Akademika
Postboks 84 Blindern
N-0314 OSLO
Tel.: +47 2 218 8100
Fax: +47 2 218 8103
E-mail: support@akademika.no
http://akademika.no

**POLAND/POLOGNE**
Ars Polona JSC
25 Obroncow Street
PL-03-933 WARSZAWA
Tel.: +48 (0)22 509 86 00
Fax: +48 (0)22 509 86 10
E-mail: arspolona@arspolona.com.pl
http://www.arspolona.com.pl

**PORTUGAL**
Livraria Portugal
(Dias & Andrade, Lda.)
Rua do Carmo, 70
P-1200-094 LISBOA
Tel.: +351 21 347 42 82 / 85
Fax: +351 21 347 02 64
E-mail: info@livrariaportugal.pt
http://www.livrariaportugal.pt

**RUSSIAN FEDERATION/
FÉDÉRATION DE RUSSIE**
Ves Mir
9a, Kolpacnhyi per.
RU-101000 MOSCOW
Tel.: +7 (8)495 623 6839
Fax: +7 (8)495 625 4269
E-mail: zimarin@vesmirbooks.ru
http://www.vesmirbooks.ru

**SPAIN/ESPAGNE**
Mundi-Prensa Libros, s.a.
Castelló, 37
E-28001 MADRID
Tel.: +34 914 36 37 00
Fax: +34 915 75 39 98
E-mail: liberia@mundiprensa.es
http://www.mundiprensa.com

**SWITZERLAND/SUISSE**
Van Diermen Editions – ADECO
Chemin du Lacuez 41
CH-1807 BLONAY
Tel.: +41 (0)21 943 26 73
Fax: +41 (0)21 943 36 05
E-mail: info@adeco.org
http://www.adeco.org

**UNITED KINGDOM/ROYAUME-UNI**
The Stationery Office Ltd
PO Box 29
GB-NORWICH NR3 1GN
Tel.: +44 (0)870 600 5522
Fax: +44 (0)870 600 5533
E-mail: book.enquiries@tso.co.uk
http://www.tsoshop.co.uk

**UNITED STATES and CANADA/
ÉTATS-UNIS et CANADA**
Manhattan Publishing Company
468 Albany Post Road
CROTTON-ON-HUDSON, NY 10520, USA
Tel.: +1 914 271 5194
Fax: +1 914 271 5856
E-mail: Info@manhattanpublishing.com
http://www.manhattanpublishing.com

**Council of Europe Publishing**
F-67075 Strasbourg Cedex
Tel.: +33 (0)3 88 41 25 81 – Fax: +33 (0)3 88 41 39 10 – E-mail: publishing@coe.int – Website: http://book.coe.int